TEACHING TEXAS

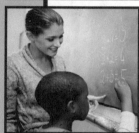

A Complete and Practical Approach to Understanding and Applying the Pedagogy and Professional Responsibilities (PPR) TExES

Fifth Edition

TERI BINGHAM, Ed.D.
West Texas A&M University

Kendall Hunt
publishing company

Contents

DOMAIN 1 Designing Instruction and Assessment to Promote Student Learning

Competency 1 Human Development 1
Teri Bingham

Competency 2 Multiculturalism and Education: Opportunities for All Students 35
Teri Bingham and Angela Spaulding

Competency 3 Designing Effective Planning 61
Teri Bingham

Competency 4 How Learning Occurs 87
Teri Bingham

DOMAIN 2 Creating a Positive, Productive Classroom Environment

Competency 5 The Importance of a Positive Classroom Environment to Enhance
Academic Achievement and to Promote Effective Social Interactions 107
Teri Bingham and Angela Spaulding

Competency 6 Managing Student Behavior 119
Teri Bingham and Sheryn Johnston

DOMAIN 3 Implementing Effective, Responsive Instruction and Assessment

Competency 7 Principles and Strategies for Effective Communication 141
Teri Bingham and Amy Andersen

Competency 8 Student Motivation and Engagement 153
Teri Bingham and Judy Lopez-Kutcher

Competency 9 Using Technology as an Effective Instructional Tool 171
Jim Rutledge

Competency 10 Assessment 185
George Mann, Teri Bingham and E.W. Henderson

DOMAIN 4 Fulfilling Professional Roles and Responsibilities

Competency 11 Increasing Parental Involvement:
A Key Component of School Improvement and Reform 203
Angela Spaulding and Teri Bingham

Competency 12 Reflective Practice and Professional Responsibilities 219
Teri Bingham and Angela Spaulding

Competency 13 Legal and Ethical Requirements for Educators 233
E.W. Henderson

Designing Instruction and Assessment to Promote Student Learning

Competency 1 _

Human Development

Teri Bingham, EdD
West Texas A&M University

> **Competency 1:** The teacher understands human development processes and applies this knowledge to plan instruction and ongoing assessment that motivate students and are responsive to their developmental characteristics and needs.

The beginning teacher:

A. Knows the typical stages of cognitive, social, physical, and emotional development of students in early childhood through grade 12.

B. Recognizes the wide range of individual developmental differences that characterizes students in early childhood through grade 12 and the implications of this developmental variation for instructional planning.

C. Analyzes ways in which developmental characteristics of students in early childhood through grade 12 impact learning and performance and applies knowledge of students' developmental characteristics and needs to plan effective learning experiences and assessments.

D. Demonstrates an understanding of physical changes that occur in early childhood through adolescence, factors that affect students' physical growth and health (e.g., nutrition, sleep, prenatal exposure to drugs, abuse), and ways in which physical development impacts development in other domains (i.e., cognitive, social, emotional).

E. Recognizes factors affecting the social and emotional development of students in early childhood through adolescence (e.g., lack of affection and attention, parental divorce, homelessness) and knows that students' social and emotional development impacts their development in other domains (i.e., cognitive, physical).

F. Uses knowledge of cognitive changes in students in early childhood through adolescence (e.g., from an emphasis on concrete thinking to the emergence and refinement of abstract thinking and reasoning, increased ability to engage in reflective thinking, increased focus on the world beyond the school setting) to plan developmentally appropriate instruction and assessment that promote learning and development.

G. Understands that development in any one domain (i.e., cognitive, social, physical, emotional) impacts development in other domains.

H. Recognizes signs of developmental delays or impairments in students in early childhood through grade 4.

I. Knows the stages of play development (i.e., from solitary to cooperative) and the important role of play in young children's learning and development.

J. Uses knowledge of the developmental characteristics and needs of students in early childhood through grade 4 to plan meaningful, integrated, and active learning and play experiences that promote the development of the whole child.

K. Recognizes that positive and productive learning environments involve creating a culture of high academic expectations, equity throughout the learning community, and developmental responsiveness.

L. Recognizes the importance of helping students in early childhood through grade 12 learn and apply life skills (e.g., decision-making skills, organizational skills, goal-setting skills, self-direction, workplace skills).

M. Knows the rationale for appropriate middle-level education and how middle-level schools are structured to address the characteristics and needs of young adolescents.

N. Recognizes typical challenges for students during later childhood, adolescence, and young adulthood (e.g., self-image, physical appearance, eating disorders, feelings of rebelliousness, identity formation, educational and career decisions) and effective ways to help students address these challenges.

O. Understands ways in which student involvement in risky behaviors (e.g., drug and alcohol use, gang involvement) impacts development and learning.

P. Demonstrates knowledge of the importance of peers, peer acceptance, and conformity to peer group norms and expectations for adolescents and understands the significance of peer-related issues for teaching and learning.

KEY TERMS

Abraham Maslow
assisted learning
autonomy vs. shame and doubt stage
Carol Gilligan
classification
cognitive development
concrete-operational stage
conservation
conventional morality
diffusion
disequilibrium
ego integrity vs. despair stage
egocentric
equilibrium
Erik H. Erikson
Erikson's stages of psychosocial development
formal operational stage

generativity vs. stagnation stage
Gilligan's stages of ethical care
goodness as self-sacrifice
identity achievement
identity foreclosure
identity moratorium
identity vs. role confusion stage
industry vs. inferiority stage
initiative vs. guilt stage
intimacy vs. isolation stage
James Marcia
James Marcia's identity states
Jean Piaget
Kohlberg's stages of moral development
Lawrence Kohlberg
Lev Vygotsky
Maslow's hierarchy of needs

moral development
morality of nonviolence
object permanence
orientation to individual survival
postconventional morality
preconventional morality
preoperational stage
private speech
psychosocial development
reversibility
scaffolding
schema
self-actualization
self-esteem
sensorimotor development
seriation
trust vs. mistrust stage
zone of proximal development

This competency deals with two distinct topics: environmental influences and human development. Environmental influences relate to aspects of a student's family life and community that impact their quality of life and affect their ability to learn. Although the student may or may not participate in distracting behaviors, he may be influenced by the choices of those around him. For example, a child may not have control over his parents divorcing each other, but he is affected by the results of their decisions. Students are subjected to factors outside of their control, such as gangs, illicit drugs, a parent's incarceration, prostitution, alcoholism, death, long-term illness, malnutrition, abuse, neglect, crime, alternative lifestyles, peer pressure, and so on.

Although teachers may not be able to control or change these environmental influences, they can provide a classroom climate that feels safe and promotes student learning and self-esteem. The classroom community needs to be responsive and supportive to student needs. A responsive teacher shows consideration for learners' unique needs and characteristics. A supportive classroom community is one in which learners are encouraging and helpful, with low levels of threat. Students' self-esteem is based on their perception of their own worth and potential. Their perception is affected by factors both in and outside of school. A student's self-esteem is impacted by classroom grouping practices, teacher expectations, and prior school experiences. It behooves teachers to use a variety of small-group configurations and not just group by ability. Groups should be fluid and deliberately designed for both academic and social benefits. Students make assumptions about themselves and others based on which group they are assigned. A student will determine the degree of confidence a teacher has in the student's skill and knowledge based on which group the teacher places him. This can impact the student's self-esteem and self-image.

Students need to feel safe, accepted, competent, and productive in the classroom. It should be every teacher's goal to plan instruction to enhance all students' self-esteem and create a positive learning climate. It is the teacher's responsibility to engineer the classroom environment where students feel safe—both safe physically and emotionally. Students need to feel confident that in the classroom they will not be embarrassed, humiliated, intimidated, threatened, or caused to lose their dignity. Teachers set the standards and model respectful behavior.

Students need to believe they will not be judged based on stereotypes. The classroom climate should be one where students feel accepted regardless of their race, religion, socioeconomic status (SES), family background, culture, native language, gender, needs, and so on. Effective teachers are those that see the potential in students and view differences as assets rather than deficits.

When students feel capable they are more likely to engage in academic tasks. It is the responsibility of the teacher to design educational endeavors whereby students are competent. Most individuals have experienced an educational setting where they realized that the teacher controls how hard or easy he or she wants the new material to be perceived. By using best teaching practices teachers can create experiences for students to begin to feel proficient or to strengthen students' self-efficacy.

Students feel productive when they perceive the classwork as meaningful, relevant, interesting, and valuable. Teachers are responsible for conscientiously selecting learning activities that are perceived as productive. By deliberately choosing activities that engage students in the learning process, student productivity is increased.

Although teachers cannot control outside environmental influences that affect the lives of students, we can identify when our students are feeling stressed and provide them a safe and supportive climate. Clearly there are different ways individuals cope with stress, but the two most common visible signs of stress in students is increased aggression and a sudden drop in grades. An increase in aggression could be manifested in their behavior or mood; a student may appear irritable, moody, hostile, belligerent, antagonistic, insistent, or ill-tempered in a way that is not typical of the student. A student's grade may be lower as a result of not turning in homework, not studying for tests, not coming to class prepared, and not taking notes or listening. All of these behaviors should be red flags to a teacher indicating that a student may be experiencing an inordinate amount of stress and not coping well. Although we cannot remove the stressors in a child's life, we can provide a caring attitude and a listening ear, or make sure the student's parent is aware of services that are available in the community to take care of his or her needs. For example, if the gas has been shut off because the parent cannot pay the gas bill and the student's house is cold during the winter, the teacher can discretely provide information regarding community services designed to help in such situations.

Teacher expectation is as important as student background and ability. Regardless of the home environment, environmental setbacks, and capabilities of a student, a teacher can make a difference. Teachers that have high, yet reasonable expectations of children tacitly communicate belief and confidence in them. What a teacher believes about a child has great impact on how the child views him- or herself. Teacher expectations affect student self-esteem. It is common for students to live up to a teacher's expectations, whether those expectations are high or low; positive or negative. Teachers tacitly communicate their expectations to students based on grouping practices, assignments, projects, wait time, and the level of cognition required to answer a specific question. Again, it is imperative that teachers hold high, yet reasonable expectations for all students. This may require extra time with a child, more scaffolding during the lesson, the use of differentiated instruction to reach all learners, or alternative assessment to truly gauge the students' level of mastery.

When discussing teacher expectations of students, we need to be aware that this does not mean we should treat all students the same. On the contrary, we need to remember how "fairness" needs to be applied in the classroom. Fair implies that we treat each student the same. However, let's look at a medical model to see how this idea isn't what we are really looking for. Suppose you went to your family practitioner with symptoms of a sore throat and a high fever. The doctor determines you have strep throat and gives you a prescription for birth control pills. We would suspect the doctor has lost his or her mind. The doctor explains to you that the patient he saw just before you needed birth control pills and he wants to be fair to his patients, so he gives you the same prescription. Obviously, this is ludicrous, but it is how we often approach students in our class. We want to be "fair" so we treat all students the same, when in fact we need to exercise equality rather than fairness. Equality is where we give each student what he or she needs for success.

The other area of focus of Competency 1 is human development, which comprises four areas: cognitive, psychosocial, moral, and physical. Teachers who understand human development processes are prepared to nurture student growth through developmentally appropriate instruction.

Many theorists studied human development and contributed to the body of knowledge that led to Competency 1. Those whose work has exerted the most obvious influence are Abraham Maslow, Jean Piaget, Lev Vygotsky, Erik Erikson, James Marcia, Lawrence Kohlberg, and Carol Gilligan. Competency 1 directs teachers to be attentive to changes in students as they grow *physically*, *emotionally*, *cognitively*, and *socially*.

Teachers must be responsive to students' environment, personality, emotional needs, and reasoning skills and adjust the classroom, playground, and extracurricular activities accordingly. When teachers are planning their instruction and student assessment, they need to consider how to best motivate students and be responsive to developmental stages.

The Texas state certification test for professional and pedagogical responsibilities provides scenario-based questions based on the work of the theorists previously mentioned. The body of work of these researchers provides insight about expected physical, cognitive, psychosocial, and moral development. When taking the Texas state certification test for professional and pedagogical responsibilities, preservice teachers must analyze situations and make professional decisions. When teachers apply this insight in the classroom, they are positioned to provide appropriate opportunities for learning.

WHERE DOES OUR KNOWLEDGE BASE FOR COMPETENCY 1 ORIGINATE?	
The Internal Environment	Abraham Maslow (1906–1970)
Cognitive Development	Jean Piaget (1896–1980) Lev Vygotsky (1896–1934)
Psychosocial Development	Eric Erikson (1902–1994) James Marcia (1902–)
Moral/Ethical Development	Lawrence Kohlberg (1927–1987) Carol Gilligan (1936–)

THE INTERNAL ENVIRONMENT

Abraham Maslow

Abraham Maslow (1906–1970) was a humanistic psychologist who suggested that what people need determines the level at which they function. Unlike behaviorists, who focus on stimuli and reinforcement, and unlike psychoanalysts, who focus on unconscious instinctual impulses, humanists focus on human potential. They believe people seek to reach higher and higher levels of capability and wisdom.

Maslow acknowledged that people respond to their basic instincts, but emphasized that they also have "a higher nature that includes needs for meaningful work, for responsibility, for creativeness, for being fair and just, for doing what is worthwhile and for preferring to do it well." (Maslow, 1968, p. 222). He devised a theory of a hierarchy of needs. He proposed that when a need is met, the need goes away. Unmet needs remain. As needs are met, people move to higher levels of consciousness.

According to Maslow, as they begin life, people have deficiency needs. Deficiency needs include the need for:

1. Physical survival: Shelter, food, clothing, warmth
2. Safety: Freedom from physical or emotional threat
3. Belonging and love: Love and acceptance from family and peers
4. Self-esteem: Recognition and approval

We are all social human beings, and our needs in these areas precede intellectual needs. If our students believe that we genuinely care about them, and are truly committed to them as individuals, their motivation increases. If not, it can decrease. Maslow would advise teachers, "No one cares how much you know until they know how much you care." He would also say that teacher expectations are as important as student background and ability.

Maslow believed that if physiological needs are unmet, people have difficulty learning. If a student does not feel physically or emotionally safe, he may struggle in school. It is difficult for children to learn when they have basic needs that are unmet. The child who struggles with physical survival is too distracted to learn new vocabulary words. The child who feels threatened has trouble focusing when expected to read. The child who feels unloved, rejected, or alone may not care about doing his homework. And the child with low self-esteem knows just passing the test won't necessarily make him feel worthy. If the need for esteem is unmet, people feel incompetent, out of control, inferior, and helpless. If they experience difficulty gratifying deficiency needs, it will likely hinder their learning, and unmet needs remain. *Deficiency needs energize or move people to meet them when these needs are unfulfilled.*

If deficiency needs are met, people are able to address growth needs. *Growth needs expand and increase as people have positive experiences with them.* Growth needs include:

1. Intellectual achievement: Knowing and understanding
2. Aesthetic appreciation: Order, truth, beauty
3. Self-actualization

If people experience intellectual achievement, then they want to know and understand more. If they experience aesthetic appreciation, they desire more experience with the arts. Ultimately, if all other needs have been satisfied, the need for self-actualization can be realized, and the human personality is free to become all it can be.

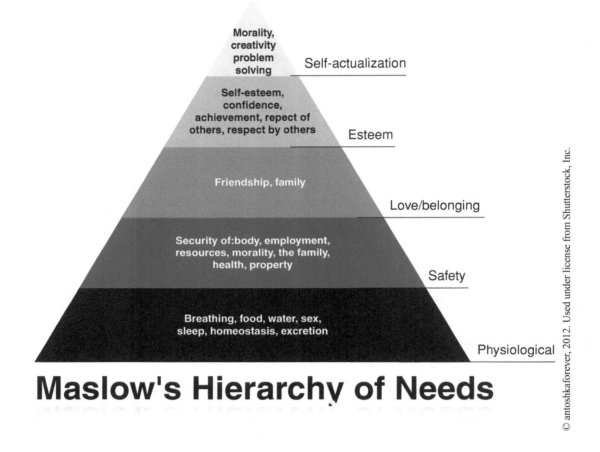

Maslow's Hierarchy of Needs

© antoshkaforever, 2012. Used under license from Shutterstock, Inc.

Maslow's Hierarchy of Needs

A positive classroom climate is established by the creation of a physically appealing work environment for students as well as by teacher caring, high expectations for learning, effective instructional practices, and the development of positive social skills. Incorporating all of these components into one's daily duties of teaching is complex. Maslow's (1970) hierarchy of needs is a valuable construct to help teachers evaluate their classroom climate through the needs of their students. It has five levels, and as one's needs are met at one level, theoretically one is more able to progress to the next higher level.

The lowest level of Maslow's hierarchy concerns physiological needs, which are basic physical needs such as food, clothing, and shelter. There often is a wide range of differences concerning how well the physical needs of students are met in their homes. For example, some students just do not have the resources for food, clothing, and shelter whereas other students live in affluent environments. Physiological needs are important considerations for teachers because students will not learn to their potential if they are hungry or cold or have other unmet physical needs.

Maslow's second level, safety needs, is important in a similar way. Students need to feel safe in order to learn to their full potential. Students who worry about potential violence at school, home, or in their neighborhoods will have a more difficult time concentrating on their academic work than will those students who do not have these worries. A safe environment for students in the classroom context also includes a physically safe environment for activities such as science laboratories and an emotionally safe environment. An emotionally safe environment is established through teacher caring, the development of positive social skills for students. In addition, the employment of effective instructional strategies to enhance students' academic achievement and decrease unnecessary frustration caused by ineffective teacher explanations or poorly designed assignments creates the conditions of a safe environment.

The third need on Maslow's hierarchy, belonging and love needs, is especially important in the classroom context. Everyone has the need for acceptance and encouragement. Students who do not have these needs fulfilled at home often act out in the classroom to get attention, even if it is negative attention. Other students may withdraw and avoid classroom activities and people. Nevertheless, teachers can develop a positive classroom climate in which all students are accepted, and this encourages students to do their best academic work. Establishing a classroom in which all students—regardless of race/ethnicity, gender, income level, or ability groups—is essential for maximizing learning and the cooperation of students.

The fourth level on Maslow's hierarchy concerns esteem needs. Students must develop a healthy sense of self and a strong self-esteem if they are to learn to their potential. Self-esteem is an important aspect of achievement in any endeavor in life, and this includes academic achievement as well. When teachers use effective culturally responsive methods to teach lessons, students are more apt to succeed academically and to raise their self-efficacy. Equally important, when students believe they belong, they usually increase their sense of self-esteem.

The last and highest level on Maslow's need hierarchy is self-actualization, which concerns the need for a person to strive to reach his or her potential. Maslow believed that most people do not reach this stage. However, teachers may help students to find and develop gifts and talents that may enable them to reach this stage later in life. Meeting student needs, regardless of which level of Maslow's hierarchy, helps create a classroom climate that is productive and conducive to learning. Indifference to students with special needs creates negativity because all students, as emphasized by Maslow, need to know that they belong and that their learning and roles in the classroom are important.

APPLICATION OF MASLOW IN THE CLASSROOM

When children are hungry and tired they are not able to learn. When adults in their lives have not provided for their safety, children are suspicious of adults, and they hesitate to trust their teachers. If the teacher is absent, the student may feel betrayed and angry. The student who has been denied love and a sense of belonging demands a great deal of the teacher's time. Students without self-esteem may lack confidence and initiative to do their school work. Students who suffer from a combination of unmet deficiency needs may be quite burdened and have difficulty functioning in the classroom. Teachers act in response to Maslow's research when they do what they can to meet the need. These teachers are empathetic and support students' interests. They are fair and patient, and provide positive feedback. They realize that the intervention of teachers may enable children to overcome the damaging effects of inadequate home environments. Maslow emphasized that students need to feel valued and cared about. Students' basic needs must be met in order to learn to their potential.

Maslow's work not only has implications for teaching and learning in the classroom, his work suggests that schools must match their objectives to the needs of students if society is to benefit from the maximum contribution each individual has to offer.

COGNITIVE DEVELOPMENT

The Work of Jean Piaget

Jean Piaget (1896–1980) was a pioneer in the field of educational psychology. His work formed a basis for the present body of research about the behavior of children and how they learn. Piaget conducted detailed studies of intelligence, learning, and memory.

From his precise and extensive studies, Piaget noticed that cognitive development (how knowledge develops) undergoes transitions at about age 2, age 7, and age 11. To Piaget, these transitions defined stages of cognitive development in children. According to Piaget, everyone progresses through the same sequence of cognitive development at approximately the same age. He has identified four distinct stages and the approximate age range of expected cognitive development, described in the table below. According to Piaget, moving from stage to stage requires reorganizing one's view of the world. Cognitive disequilibrium is when a child holds two conflicting views of a situation. For example, knowing that wood can float but ships sink causes disequilibrium in a child's thought process. Inspired teachers use this concept to get students curious and engaged in the lesson. As a child strives for intellectual equilibrium he must assimilate or accommodate new knowledge. *Assimilation* is where new knowledge is integrated with existing knowledge. *Accommodation* is where the learner must adjust his schema to fit new information and experiences. *Schema* is a mental representation or actions that help organize knowledge.

The contribution of Jean Piaget to the field of education cannot be overstated. In addition to conceiving his stage theory, he went on to conclude that that although the order of succession through the stages is constant for individuals, progressing from stage to stage depends on previous experience, maturation, and the social situation (Gruber & Voneche, 1977, p. 815), a perspective that until this day influences research.

Paiget's visionary comment at the conclusion of *The Origins of Intelligence in Children*, " . . . intelligence is the construction of relationships . . ." (Piaget, 1952, p. 418), sets the stage for the constructivist movement, to which our current concepts of education as activity and inquiry can be traced.

APPLICATION OF PIAGET IN THE CLASSROOM

Keep in mind that cognition is developmental. If we saw someone who was physically incapable of climbing stairs we would not expect him to use the stairs but rather point him to the elevator. However, because cognition is invisible, unlike physical attributes, sometimes teachers forget that a child may be at a lower stage of cognition and not be able to understand or perform certain new skills or tasks. Yes, he will eventually get there, but he needs instruction to be at his developmental level.

When we consider Piaget's ideas we see them reflected as teachers employ play, exploration, and debate and as they show more concern that children are making sense of concepts rather than memorizing facts. Whenever students are active in inquiry, exploration, and discovery, rather than sitting as vessels to receive direct instruction, the foundation Piaget built is supporting education.

PIAGET'S STAGES OF COGNITIVE DEVELOPMENT	
Stage	**Characteristics of the Stage**
Sensorimotor (Birth to 2 years of age)	Child learns through the senses and through motor development. Listening and language development begin at birth, and speech emerges in the latter part of the first year. *Milestones:* **Object Permanence:** That an object still exists even when it is out of sight. Prior to this there is no stable sense of object permanence. **Goal-Directed Actions:** Motor movements have intention and purpose (e.g., reaching for a toy, grabbing a spoon, rolling over, crawling, pointing, reaching to be held). **Reversal of Actions:** When a baby can do actions in reverse operation.
Preoperational (2–7 years of age)	After experiencing the tangible, the learner can *think* operations through in one direction. Child is imaginative, likes to pretend, and language develops very rapidly. The teacher needs to use examples that are familiar to the children and connect with their prior knowledge. *Milestones:* **Semiotic Function:** ability to use symbols, language, pictures, signs, and play pretend. **Egocentric:** Believes others experience and inteprets the world the way he or she does. **Collective monologue:** Children in a group talk but do not interact.
Concrete Operations (7–11 years of age)	Child can think two directions *after* experiencing hands-on activities with concrete (tangible) items. Students in middle school and below especially desire and need physical hands-on activities, not just observational learning a child at this stage. Is unable to engage in thought that is strictly formal (abstract) and solves problems logically through use of concrete objects or life experience. As a child's cognitive development approaches formal operations, he or she can learn through observations. This age group needs peer interaction. *Milestones:* **Conservation:** Knows the quantity remains constant even if the shape is changed. **Reversibility:** Mentally reverses a series of steps. **Classification:** Groups objects according to a characteristic. **Seriation:** Arranges from large to small or small to large. This stage is predominate for most adolescents.
Formal Operations (11-adulthood)	There is variation among persons in this age group, and they show some characteristics only some of the time. Whether all people achieve complete formal operational thinking is a major question. Most persons test ideas, engage in abstract reasoning, and consider hypothetical situations (situations do not have to be experienced to be imagined). *Examples:* form a hypothesis, consider variables, interpret metaphors, solve complex riddles, recognize inconsistencies in logic, make generalizations, reflect. By high school some students are beginning to move into abstract thought and become interested in adult/world ideas. Develop concern for ethics and identity. *Milestones:* **Abstract thought:** Can perform mental tasks without having previously experienced them. **Adolescent egocentrism:** Understanding that others have different perspectives and beliefs, but assuming that everyone shares his or her thoughts, feelings, and concerns. Yet believes he or she is unique and no one could possibly understand how he or she feels. Can lead to an imaginary audience ("Everyone is watching me").

Stage	Application of Piaget in the Classroom
Sensorimotor (Birth to Age 2)	Allow child to explore. Provide opportunities to experience new materials and toys. Stimulate senses and encourage motor development.
Preoperational (Age 2–7)	After experiencing the tangible, the learner can think operations through in one direction (pre-kindergarten through first or second grade). Use concrete props, pictures, and other visual aids such as art supplies and simple musical instruments. Let children manipulate physical objects. For example, let them use cutout letters to build words. Explain rules in brief. Act out expected behaviors. Explain the effects of their choices and decisions. Show finished work as examples to illustrate expectations. Take time to extend conversations to explain meanings, assist with experimentation and explorations. Support interactions. Encourage new experiences. Invite guest speakers and storytellers. Take field trips to gardens, farms, zoos, theaters, concerts, and museums. Avoid lessons that are removed from children's life experience. Be aware that children may invent words. Ask them to explain the meaning of their invented words. Words may have different meanings to different children.
Concrete Operations (Age 7–11)	Provide hands-on experiences. Encourage pursuit of areas of interest. Provide opportunity for success. Use props, visual aids, timelines, diagrams, pictures, and models. Engage students in problem-solving and inquiry activities. Allow them to manipulate and test objects. Present new information in steps. Assign reading in short chapters, moving to longer reading assignments when a student is ready. Compare their life experience to what is presented in class.
Formal Operations (Age 11–adult)	For most adolescents the concrete operations stage is still dominant, and they experience conflict as they enter formal operations. Provide hypothetical situations and opportunities for reflection. Encourage use of logic. Allow for individual differences. Encourage and support their endeavors. Encourage social interaction. Recognize the effects of adolescent egocentrism. They do not realize that others of their age group share the same feelings, are extremely self-conscious because they think everyone is watching them (imaginary audience), and may believe they are invincible ("I will never get an STD or I can use illegal drugs recreationally and not get addicted"). They may see themselves as heroic figures ("I have a magic destiny"). They may play out fantasy scenarios ("I wonder how they would they react if I . . . ").

Guidelines for Teaching the Preoperational Child

1. Use concrete props and visual aids.

2. Make instructions short and specific. Using actions and demonstrations as you explain a procedure.

3. Provide opportunities for children to practice hands-on with a new skill to serve as a building blocks for more complex skills.

4. To broaden children's foundation for conceptual understanding and language, provide a wide range of diverse experiences. Children need an assortment of rich and varied experiences to draw upon in the school setting.

Guidelines for Teaching the Concrete-Operational Child

1. Use concrete props and visual aids to help students learn, understand, and retain new skills and knowledge.
2. Give students opportunities to manipulate materials and explores objects.
3. Teacher presentations should be brief and well organized.
4. Student readings should be developmentally appropriate and of interest to children.
5. Use familiar examples to explain more complex ideas.
6. Provide opportunities to classify and group objects and ideas on increasingly complex levels.
7. Present problems that require logical and analytical thinking so students can manipulate materials to arrive at the answer.

Lev Vygotsky

Lev Vygotsky (1896–1934), a Russian scholar, identified private speech (speech as thinking out loud) and emphasized the importance of social interaction to cognitive development. As a researcher, he observed people interact and learn in the context of socially organized labor and wondered how children learn. From Vygotsky we have learned it is more than just that thought influences the words we use. Words and the social context in which we have learned them affect the way we think. From this perspective, learning occurs in a social context and private speech is indicative of thinking.

Collaboration among a learning community was key to Vygotsky's perception of how learning occurs. "Every function in the child's cultural development appears twice: first, on the social level, and later, on the individual level; first, between people (interpsychological) and then inside the child (intrapsychological). This applies equally to voluntary attention, to logical memory, and to the formation of concepts. All the higher functions originate as actual relationships between individuals" (Vygotsky, 1978, p. 57). Children learn best when they are interacting with others.

Vygotsky identified the zone of proximal development (ZPD) as a place of learning where a child can master a task if given appropriate help and support. The ZPD is a transition between being able to accomplish a task with help and being able to accomplish a task independently. The ZPD is also referred to as the magic middle: the space between what the child already knows and what the student isn't ready to learn, the place where a learner can understand with guidance from the teacher.

The language children use influences the way they understand their environment. Language is central to cognitive development. Given his perception of learning in a social context, it is easy to understand why Vygotsky placed great importance on the role of play in the learning of young children.

FIVE CONTRIBUTIONS OF VYGOTSKY TO UNDERSTANDING OF COGNITIVE DEVELOPMENT	
Social Interaction	We learn through interaction with others.
Private Speech	Thought and language are interrelated.
Scaffolding	Support for learning allows students to complete tasks they are not able to complete independently. Teachers give the right amount at the right time.
Assisted Learning	Strategic help in the initial stages of learning gradually diminishes as students gain independence.
Zone of Proximal Development	Learning occurs in a zone where students' development is advanced enough for them to learn but they require help to get there.

THEORIES OF EGOCENTRIC OR PRIVATE SPEECH COMPARED		
	Piaget	**Vygotsky**
Significance to Development	Negative. Shows inability to understand another person's perspective and engage in conversation.	Positive. Shows self-communication and self-guidance.
Span of Development	Declines with age.	Increases in young children, then becomes inaudible and resides as internal verbal thought.
Relationship to Social Speech	Negative. Socially mature children use less private speech.	Positive. Private speech is an outcome of interaction with others.

APPLICATION OF VYGOTSKY IN THE CLASSROOM

In the classroom, the work of Vygotsky is applied as students and teachers work collaboratively to ensure that those who are less able have help (assisted learning). Students work in teams or with partners, and the teacher enables advanced peers to structure or arrange tasks so novices can be successful (scaffolding tasks) for their less able peers. Teachers realize that most testing does not measure the zone of proximity and does not give a complete account of what is known, so they use a variety of assessments to determine a zone of proximity for each student. Teachers use mediation of some form to help each child to advance the zone of proximity. Vygotsky's concept of scaffolding encourages teachers to:

1. Break a problem down into steps.
2. Provide an example or modeling.
3. Think out loud.
4. Ask leading questions.
5. Provide cues and prompts.
6. Give gentle reminders.
7. Adapt instructional materials.
8. Shower students with praise and encouragement.
9. Provide outlines, diagrams, visual aids, graphic organizers and figures that provide an image on which to hang ideas.
10. Regulate the difficulty of the task, then escalate after the learner understands it.
11. Anticipate difficult areas and provide support.
12. Model for students by thinking out loud about the process you are doing.
13. Provide frequent, appropriate practice in *varied* context spaced over time.
14. Foster growth and independence of the learner.

Thanks to Vygotsky, teachers make certain to provide play that allows children to imitate the cultural patterns of adults, and opportunities for children to reenact real-life situations.

PSYCHOSOCIAL DEVELOPMENT

Erik Erikson

Erik Erikson (1902–1994) was born in Germany to Danish parents. His research interests were varied: art, psychoanalysis, combat crisis, childrearing practices of native Americans, the play of disturbed and normal children, adolescent identity crises, juvenile delinquency, social behavior in India, social change in the United States, the generation gap, racial tensions, changing sexual roles, and the danger of nuclear war.

Regarding human psychosocial development, Erikson concluded that all people develop their personalities throughout their lives as they move through eight stages of development: trust versus mistrust, autonomy versus shame and doubt, initiative versus guilt, industry versus inferiority, identity versus role confusion, intimacy versus isolation, generativity versus stagnation, and integrity versus despair. The quality of a person's life influences success at each stage of life. Everyone young and old faces crises. Erikson identified developmental crisis as a specific conflict (issue) whose resolution prepares the way for the next stage. If an issue is not resolved positively or remains unresolved, a person faces that issue over and over. The issue is carried into subsequent psychosocial stages and complicates each stage of life afterward. A positive resolution of each crisis leads to greater personal and social competence and a stronger foundation for solving crises in the future.

STAGE 1: TRUST VERSUS MISTRUST (INFANTS)

In *Dialogue with Erik Erikson*, by Richard Evans, Erikson says, "Now, the basic psychosocial attitude to be learned at this state is that you can trust the world in the form of your mother. . ." (1976, p. 15). Trust means that others are consistently dependable and reliable. The major developmental task of infants is to learn whether or not people can be trusted to satisfy basic needs. When caregivers can be depended on to feed a baby, change a soiled diaper, provide affection and intellectual stimulation, and meet the needs of the infant, an infant learns trust.

Mistrust means the world is an undependable, unpredictable, and possibly dangerous place. If infants, on a regular basis, do not get what they need—diapering, nurturing, sleep, food—or experience inconsistent care, neglect, or abuse, they learn that people cannot be trusted, and it may take years for them to move past this issue. The child trusts adults and develops a positive sense of his or her own trustworthiness only if, as an infant, he or she has learned that people can be trusted. Erikson noted that ". . . [trust] has to be developed firmly, and then be confirmed and reaffirmed throughout life" (Evans, 1976, p. 18).

STAGE 2: AUTONOMY VERSUS SHAME AND DOUBT

For children age 1–3 years, they are developing physical skills: walking, feeding themselves, dressing, washing, and potty training. The adults in their lives are keys to confidence, self-control, and independence. Parents who show pride in accomplishments, rather than criticism for mistakes, help children to successfully negotiate this stage. Children develop a sense of autonomy—a sense that they can handle problems on their own—when parents encourage self-sufficient behavior of the toddler.

When caregivers demand too much too soon, refuse to let children perform tasks of which they are capable, or ridicule early awkward attempts, children may develop shame and doubt about their ability to handle situations in their environments. Children feel shame and doubt when parents are too controlling and overprotective, too. Lacking basic trust, or dominated by a parent who breaks his or her will, a child will feel shame and doubt about self-control and independence. Erikson says, "If in some respects you have relatively more shame than autonomy, then you feel or act inferior all your life—or consistently counteract that feeling" (Evans, 1976, p. 20). When parents encourage self-sufficient behavior, children develop a sense of autonomy, a sense that they can handle problems on their own.

STAGE 3: INITIATIVE VERSUS GUILT

Children age 3–7 are becoming more assertive, want to make their own choices, and want to initiate activities they want to pursue. Sometimes children initiate activities that they can readily accomplish. At other times they may try to undertake projects that are beyond their limited capabilities or that interfere with the plans and activities of others. When caregivers encourage and support children in their efforts to plan and carry out their own activities, while gently helping children recognize that those activities must be realistic and not conflict with the needs of others, children develop initiative. The development during this stage is critically important and must be handled carefully in play settings where children want to exert their initiative on other children. By supporting children in these actions they develop a sense of responsibility. If adults dismiss children as silly or bothersome or criticize them harshly for irresponsibility, children feel anxious and guilty. Primary caregivers must be careful not to engender excess guilt for small misdeeds; realize the child is still learning. For example, a child may want to dress herself, but her clothes do not match. If a parent chastises her, the child will feel incompetent and after repeated humiliation no longer want to try. Parents who are too attached, do too much for the child, or are too controlling leave the child feeling guilty for wanting to try or incompetent because he or she cannot do anything right.

STAGE 4: INDUSTRY VERSUS INFERIORITY

If children age six to puberty live up to the academic expectations of our culture (to read and write), if they have successful learning experiences at home, at school, with friends, and in the larger society, they will feel competent and industrious. Children perceive themselves as industrious when they are praised for their effort and not just perfection. For children to be successful they must be shown and encouraged in the new skill or knowledge. If they do not receive praise, encouragement, or recognition they will feel inadequate and inferior. A child feels industrious when he or she receives recognition for producing things: drawing a picture, writing his or her name, solving a math problem, and reading. A child who does not master these skills may feel inferior. When students are discouraged or even punished for their shortfalls, they feel inadequate, even if they have not been taught the necessary skills to be successful.

When children this age do not excel in academic areas the school deems important, they risk dropping out of school later.

STAGE 5: IDENTITY VERSUS ROLE CONFUSION

It was Erikson who is remembered for describing an "identity crisis." According to Erikson, adolescence is the stage in which a person seeks the true self. At this stage, young people try to gain their own identity and what career to strive for. Many teenagers know what their parents believe and have taught them, but at some point a teenager has to work out for himself what he believes and what is of value to him. Adolescents are struggling with their beliefs about their future occupation, gender roles, sexuality, politics, adulthood, values, morals, and religion. Almost simultaneously they are undergoing several major changes in their bodies, cognition, mobility, independence, and level of responsibility. As they transition between childhood to adulthood they wrestle with questions of who they are and how they fit into an adult world, striving to gain a sense of identity—who they are, what they really believe, and what is meaningful. During this struggle, they frequently turn to their peers for emotional support. What a teenager's peers believe and value can become of more importance than what his parents have tried to instill in him. As a result, teenagers may become more susceptible to peer pressure, reject authority figures, and become more loyal to groups outside the family.

Adolescents frequently switch friends and try new ones on for size. They change loyalties often as well as they shift from parents to peer groups for approval. They try out new attitudes as often as they try new hairstyles and music. They may align themselves with a particular peer group, rejecting former friends, or may adhere rigidly to a specific brand of clothing, shoes, or hairstyle. They experiment with all aspects of their lives, including sexuality. They think they are invincible. They may believe they can drink and drive, experiment with drugs, and have unprotected sex without risk of accidents, drug dependency, STDs, or pregnancy.

STAGE 6: INTIMACY VERSUS ISOLATION (YOUNG ADULTHOOD)

According to Erikson, if a reasonably well-integrated personality emerges from stages 1–6, the young adult is capable of emotional intimacy. When a person is capable of emotional intimacy he is ready to expose himself in a relationship. He feels safe revealing his inner thoughts, ideas, dreams, fears, experiences, and who he really is—warts and all. When a person is not capable of true emotional intimacy he will experience isolation. Even in a crowd of friends he will feel lonely and separate.

STAGE 7: GENERATIVITY VERSUS STAGNATION (MIDDLE ADULTHOOD)

At this stage people must develop and lead useful lives. They need to feel they are making a contribution to their children, work, church, social organizations, or extended family or they will feel that they have done nothing to help the generation that follows and they will experience feelings of stagnation. Individuals in this stage must believe they are making a contribution to the next generation and/or making a difference in society to feel they are of value. If they are not helping others or improving the world, they will question their value and feel idle, lackluster, or lifeless.

STAGE 8: EGO INTEGRITY VERSUS DESPAIR LATE ADULTHOOD

This is the stage in which people look back to evaluate their lives. If they believe they have led a good life, left the world a better place, been of service, and made a contribution to their sphere of influence, they will experience integrity; if not, they will experience despair. In late adulthood a person will feel a sense of despair as he reflects back on his life and realizes he is unfulfilled as a result of being self-centered, ungrateful, and unforgiving, and possibly sacrificed relationships out of selfishness. And, generally, it is too late to change it. This is the stuff some movies are made of—when a person gets to go back and relive their life to do better.

ERIKSON'S EIGHT STAGES OF PSYCHOSOCIAL DEVELOPMENT

Age	Conflict	Important Event	Significant Relations	Description
1. Infant to Toddler	Trust vs. Mistrust	Feeding	Mother	Forms a loving, trusting relationship with caregiver or develops a sense of mistrust.
2. Toddler to Age 3	Autonomy vs. Shame and Doubt	Toilet Training	Parents	Learns to control physical movement (e.g., walking, grasping, and controlling the rectal sphincter). May develop shame and doubt if not properly parented.
3. Preschool	Initiative vs. Guilt	Independence	Family	Child takes more initiative, becomes more assertive, but may be too forceful and become ruthless, leading to guilt feelings.
4. Age 6–12	Industry vs. Inferiority	School	Neighborhood and school	Learns new skills or risks a sense of inferiority, failure, and incompetence.
5. Adolescence	Ego- Identity vs. Role Confusion	Peer relationships	Peer groups, role models	Struggles to achieve identity in occupation, gender role, politics, and religion.
6. Young Adult	Intimacy vs. Isolation	Love relationships	Partners, friends	Develops intimate relationships or suffers feelings of isolation.
7. Middle Adult	Generativity vs. Self-Absorption	Parenting	Household, workmates	Finds some way to contribute to the next generation.
8. Late Adult	Integrity vs. Despair	Reflection and respect of one's life	Mankind or "my kind"	Has a sense of self- acceptance and fulfillment.

APPLICATION OF ERIKSON IN THE CLASSROOM

Erikson is remembered for shedding light on psychosocial development, which describes the relationship between the emotional needs of the individual to the social environment. Erikson's theory of psychosocial development helps teachers anticipate and understand expected behaviors at various ages.

If children's needs have been met as infants and toddlers, they come to school trusting. Children whose needs have not been met do not inherently trust their teachers. If, for example, the teacher is absent, they are angry with the teacher. From their perspective, the teacher has broken their trust. If the home environment continues to neglect basic needs, these issues continue to interfere with a child's learning. When teachers demonstrate that they are reliable and can be trusted, teachers help young children overcome mistrust of adults. In early childhood the teacher's role is to foster initiative and to mold the child's attempts at independence. Teachers enable children to feel a sense of accomplishment, and this helps compensate for guilt. Accidents provide an opportunity for teachers to convey confidence and empathy by telling students, "We all make mistakes." Wise teachers show children that teachers are reliable and dependable. They support the efforts of very young children to plan and carry out activities. They also understand the importance of providing much praise and support. Be aware that some students may at first be mistrustful of others or doubtful about their ability to handle problems. Students may lack confidence in their ability to solve problems and take care of themselves. Place reasonable expectations on their behavior and encourage self-sufficiency so children can develop self-confidence about newly discovered independence.

During the preschool years, children begin to get their own ideas about the things they want to do and the activities they want to pursue. Development during this stage is critical in play settings. Sometimes children initiate activities they can readily accomplish. At other times they may try to undertake projects that are beyond their limited capabilities or that interfere with the plans and activities of others. Children in this stage need opportunities to make and act on their own choices. When teachers encourage and support children in their efforts to plan and carry out their own activities, while *gently* helping children recognize that their activities must be realistic and not conflict with those of other children, they are helping children develop initiative. Initiative is independence in planning and undertaking activities.

To encourage initiative in the preschool child, teachers need to make sure that each child has a chance to experience success. This may involve designing and explaining activities to help a child achieve success. Be tolerant of accidents and mistakes, especially when a child is attempting to do something on his or her own. Create an environment that will increase the likelihood of success (i.e., use cups and pitchers that are easy to pour and hard to spill). Also, encourage the children to experience a wide variety of roles when playing make-believe.

When parents are too attached and controlling, a child may feel guilty or incompetent. When adults discourage children from pursuing activities that interest them or dismiss children's ideas as being silly or bothersome, then children may develop guilt about their desires to pursue such activities independently. It is important that teachers not make children feel guilty for small misdeeds, but use the misdeed as a positive learning opportunity. Teachers should encourage children to be assertive and to initiate activities of their choice. They should support children in their efforts to plan and carry out activities.

Between the ages of 6–12, youngsters are learning the skills of their culture. At this age they are expected to master many new academic skills and the social skills necessary to interact appropriately with others their age. Children learn to achieve recognition by producing things (industry), for example, drawing pictures, solving math problems, writing sentences, and reading books. Teachers should teach the skills that are necessary for success. When students succeed at tasks and are praised for it, children begin to perceive themselves as industrious. When students are punished or discouraged for their efforts, they feel inferior and inadequate. When the child is not successful in the academic skills our culture values, the child risks dropping out of school later. Teachers should praise effort, not demand perfection. Students may lack confidence in social settings. Teachers should teach students the skills for cooperative learning and allow students to work in pairs or in groups. They should encourage students to make and do things. They should praise them for their accomplishments. A few guidelines for teachers to follow to encourage industry in students are:

1. Make sure that students have opportunities to set and work realistic goals.
2. Allow students to show their independence and responsibility.
3. Provide support and encouragement to students who seem discouraged.

Teachers of adolescents understand that teenagers seek identity in areas such as occupation, gender roles, politics, and religion. Adolescents undergo several major changes almost simultaneously in their bodies, cognition, mobility, independence, responsibilities, and jobs. As they make the transition between childhood to adulthood, they wrestle with questions of who they are and how they fit into the adult world. They strive to establish a sense of identity. Teachers can assist students by providing a variety of appropriate role models in literature and history, and by inviting guest speakers. Frequently they turn to their peers for emotional support during this search for identity. Peer pressure increases greatly during this time. They may align themselves with a particular peer group, or they may adhere rigidly to a certain brand of clothing or hairstyle. Adolescents are likely to participate in faddish behavior. As a teacher, be tolerant of teenage fads as long as they do not offend others or interfere with learning.

Adolescents begin to have loyalty to groups outside their family. Adolescents benefit from rules even though at this age they may say they hate rules. Help students find resources for working out personal problems by talking with the school counselor or seeking community services.

Students in this age group appreciate a teacher who does not attempt to be a friend but acts as a guide and serves as a sounding board. They are glad for someone who shares rational, realistic feedback and a healthy sense of humor.

Tips for Working with Adolescents

1. The teacher needs to become more of a facilitator in helping students solve their own problems, not just offer answers. Teachers are in a position to help teens become decision-makers and problem-solvers.
2. In general, adolescents think they are invincible and do not think about the consequences of their actions.
3. When adolescents are making college or career choices they should consider their strengths, weaknesses, and interests.
4. When a teacher has concerns to discuss with a student, privately state objective facts.

Tips to Enhance the Learning Environment as it Relates to Psychosocial Development

1. Teachers may need to provide support for students in social settings where they may lack confidence.
2. Teachers need to encourage students to respect others' perspectives, experiences, and views. Students need to learn to be open-minded, slow to judge, and adjust their own views and opinions as they learn new information. Cooperative learning fosters this type of development.
3. When having students work in groups give them a time limit and an expected product or outcome so they stay focused and know what they should be doing.
4. Students need to manage their time and their progress.
5. The various developmental areas are independent of one another, but can influence each other.

James Marcia

James Marcia expanded on Erikson's characterization of identity crisis, dividing it into four states and characterizing the states by describing the ways in which an individual establishes and maintains a sense of identity. He described these states as conditions adolescents may experience, with all adolescents experiencing at least one of these states, at least temporarily. Consideration of these states informs us about how young people make critical choices, such as in careers and relationships.

JAMES MARCIA'S IDENTITY STATES

Identity Foreclosure—In this state adolescents have accepted without question the identity and values that were conferred in childhood. They accept parental life choices without consideration of options.

Identity Moratorium—The individual in this state has begun to develop an identity but has difficulty resolving moral and ethical issues. He suspends his decisions because of the struggle.

Diffusion—The adolescent in this state may have tried to explore identity, but is no longer motivated to do so.

Identity Achievement—In this state the crisis in identity has been resolved, and the person has defined basic values and goals after free consideration of alternatives. Typically, these decision-making skills lead to a strong sense of commitment to life choices.

JAMES MARCIA'S IDENTITY STATES	
State	**Characteristics Associated with the State**
Identity Foreclosure	A state of dependence. Loving and respectful to parents. Operates by parental values, beliefs, and expectations. Sees complex issues as black and white, no gray. Bases opinions and decisions on expectations of others and society. Exhibits strong ethnic identity and high level of prejudice. Represses anxiety and has low self-esteem. Has experienced no life-altering conflict or identity crisis, and is preconventional in moral development. Stereotypical rather than intimate relations with others. Identity is closed until individual explores on his or her own what is to be valued.
Identify Moratorium	Self-directed. Ambivalent relations with parents. Has given self a moratorium but is conflicted by family expectations, demands of society, and evolving perception of own aspirations and abilities. Moderate ethnic identity, prejudice, and anxiety. High self-esteem and high anxiety. Begins to develop an identity but has difficulty resolving moral and ethical issues. Occupational goals unclear. Does not seek opinions of others nor refer to social norms. Relations with others are intimate. A state in flux.
Diffusion	Dependent, detached, floating, drifting. Relationship with parents is stereotypical or isolated and withdrawn. Sees simple issues as complicated and delays decision making. Moderate in ethnic identity and prejudice. Moderate anxiety. Seeks advice from others regarding personal and ethical issues. Preconventional or conventional in moral development. Isolates self from others or has unstable relationships. Lacks initiative and does not accept responsibility. May have tried to explore identity, but is no longer motivated to do so.
Identity Achievement	Self-directed with high self-esteem. Balanced opinion of strengths and weaknesses. Loving and caring toward parents. Strong ethnic identity. Low prejudice. Seeks new knowledge and insight and considers opinions of others. Post-conventional moral development. Intimate relationships. Identity crisis has been resolved. Basic values and goals are defined. Assumes responsibility for actions and for self.

APPLICATION OF MARCIA IN THE CLASSROOM

Teachers who consider Marcia's identity states are better able to help adolescent students succeed. They acknowledge problems common during adolescence associated with identity states. They understand that their students are required to shoulder burdens of their families from which they were sheltered at an earlier age. Compassionate teachers take teens seriously. They listen with respect to fears and concerns. They understand that the stress of identity issues is compounded by adolescent sexual behavior, shrinking family incomes, overcrowded classrooms, disintegrating neighborhoods, exposure to alcohol and drugs, and confusion in the broader culture. They realize that students who are experiencing a diffused identity state lack confidence and self-direction, whereas others in the same classroom are taking risks and testing their limits as they explore their evolving identities. Capable teachers help students develop coping strategies and help them set and enforce boundaries for appropriate behavior. They are alert to warning signs of depression and intervene when students become despondent, self-destructive, or socially isolated. They encourage participation in school programs and volunteer activities. They provide opportunities for students to explore career options.

MORAL/ETHICAL DEVELOPMENT

Lawrence Kohlberg

Lawrence Kohlberg (1927–1987) was born to wealthy parents in New York. Although he attended the finest prep schools, he chose to become a merchant marine. As a sailor, he helped sneak Jews through a British blockade of Palestine. This experience inspired him to explore moral reasoning.

Kohlberg became a professor at Harvard University. He maintained that Piaget's stages are necessary but not sufficient to describe the stages of moral reasoning. Kohlberg concluded there are three levels of moral development, each having two stages, based on what he learned from a study of the reasoning of men and boys in response to moral dilemmas he presented to them.

LAWRENCE KOHLBERG'S SIX STAGES OF MORAL JUDGMENT

Level One: Preconventional Morality

One's judgment is based solely on a person's needs and perceptions.

> Stage One: Punishment-Obedience Orientation. The individual follows the rules of authority, acts to avoid punishment, does not consider the interests of others. The risk factor of getting caught determines whether it is considered good or bad by the individual.

> Stage Two: Individualism and Exchange. The individual recognizes that people act in their own interests and follows rules when it is in his or her immediate best interest.

Level Two: Conventional Morality

The expectations of society and laws are taken into account.

> Stage Three: Good Boy-Nice Girl Orientation. The individual lives up to expectations of the family to maintain trust and respect. The right action is one that will be approved by others.

> Stage Four: Law and Order Orientation. To maintain social order, set rules must be obeyed. The individual obeys laws to maintain the system in society.

Level Three: Postconventional Morality

Judgments are based on abstract, more personal principles and values of an individual that are not necessarily defined by society's laws.

> Stage Five: Social Contract and Individual Rights. The individual abides by laws for the good of everyone, but finds it difficult to always integrate moral and legal points of view.

> Stage Six: Universal Principles. The individual is committed to justice, equality, and respect for the dignity of all persons. Laws, rules, and regulations need to be obeyed but sometimes the unique circumstances of an individual must be taken into consideration. These uncommon situations should influence the ultimate decision.

LAWRENCE KOHLBERG'S STAGES OF MORAL DEVELOPMENT	
Stage	**Characteristics Associated with the Stage**
Preconventional	
Stage 1 Punishment and Obedience	Immediate consequences of an act determine if it is good or bad. Usually age 1–5, but adults as well as children operate within this stage whenever they act out of fear of punishment. Might makes right. To be good, you obey. If I can get away with it, it's okay. If I get caught, it's not okay.
Stage 2 Marketplace Exchange	Usually age 5–10. You scratch my back; I'll scratch yours. Do to others what they do to you. An eye for an eye, a tooth for a tooth. What can you do for me? I'm looking out for #1.
Conventional	
Stage 3 Nice Boy/Nice Girl	I want to be nice. I act to please others. I conform to expectations. I want approval. I am respectable. I would rather forgive than take revenge. I shouldn't be punished if others are getting away with it. I didn't mean to hurt anyone, so it's not my fault.
Stage 4 Law and Order	I do my duty to maintain order in my society. I respect my leaders. Anyone who breaks the law deserves have to pay a debt to society. Laws are there to maintain social order.
Postconventional	
Stage 5 Social Contract	I believe in universal abstract moral principles. Society protects the rights of the individual. The freedom of the individual prevails unless the actions of the individual limit the freedom of another person.
Between stages 5 and 6 there is a transitional stage. Young adults may reject conventional morality in favor of "doing their own thing"—but not act from commitment to universal principles.	
Stage 6 Universal Ethical Principles	I act out of respect for the equality, dignity, and worth of every person.

APPLICATION OF KOHLBERG IN THE CLASSROOM

The conclusion of the book *Lawrence Kohlberg's Approach to Moral Education*, coauthored by F. Clark Power and Ann Higgens and published after his death, may be interpreted as a warning about the lack of civics education in the United States. Kohlberg and his coauthors describe "the values of the community, democracy, fairness, and order" to call attention to implications for civics education. They conclude that, "If the school is a transitional society between the family and the larger *polis*, then it is crucial that students develop there an understanding of these political values" (1989, p. 296).

To encourage students to increasingly think and act at higher moral stages, teachers engage them in questions that require moral reasoning indicative of higher stages. When addressing inappropriate moral behavior, teachers encourage students to "move up" one step on the moral ladder. For example, consider that a child operating on Level One, Stage Two picks up a quarter from the floor and claims it as his, even though the girl at the desk beside the quarter says she dropped it and that it is part of her lunch money. The teacher encourages the boy to consider, "What would your mom want you to do right now?"

Or, for the student who has violated the rules, the question might be, "What would happen if everyone acted this way?"

Following Kohlberg's method, teachers also formally educate students to become more ethical by presenting moral dilemmas for discussion. Discussions, according to Kohlberg, elevate students to higher levels of moral reasoning. When teachers do not inject their own opinions into discussions of ethics and allow students to engage in respectful debate about issues of justice, for example, students can adjust their moral reasoning upward, enlightened by the ethical reasoning of their peers.

Carol Gilligan

Carol Gilligan was Lawrence Kohlberg's student. She was concerned that personality psychology had focused studies on men and had left out half of the people on the planet. She questioned the methods and instruments that had resulted in lower scores for women on Kohlberg's stages of moral development. She hypothesized that Kohlberg's theory was flawed because it did not consider an orientation of caring for others. Gilligan interviewed women and observed that they based moral decisions more on consideration of others than on rules. Her research suggested that existing stage theories were too simplistic to explain all variations in scores over time. Her work implies that their male perspective conditioned the great male theorists. For example, Erikson's theories suggested growth had to do with gradual separation and independence. This suggested that women who stayed home to care for aging family members were deficient because they did not become independent. Gilligan asserted that women were not inferior; their perspective was different. Women focused on connections rather than separations and were more concerned about care for others than justice for all. She pointed out that Kohlberg interviewed only males, and his approach did not describe moral development of women. Gilligan proposed a stage theory of moral development for women that suggested they advance morally from individual survival to realizing that responsibility to others is good, to realizing that self sacrifice is good, to recognizing that personhood was good, to recognizing that nonviolence to self and others is good.

Gilligan's work points out that there is more than just the justice dimension to moral reasoning. Some of the greatest men in history were dedicated to nonviolence. Gilligan challenges educators to wonder had Kohlberg considered caring as evidence of moral reasoning, would males also show progression to self-sacrifice and nonviolence.

GILLIGAN'S STAGES OF THE ETHIC OF CARE	
Stage	**Goal**
Preconventional	Survival of the individual
Transition from feelings of selfishness to a sense of responsibility to others.	
Conventional	Self-Sacrifice = Goodness
Transition from valuing self-sacrifice as goodness to valuing oneself as a person.	
Postconventional	Nonviolence: Do not hurt self or others

APPLICATION OF GILLIGAN IN THE CLASSROOM

In the classroom Gilligan's perspective plays out as teachers see boys more inclined to engage in a hierarchy of power, a pecking order, and girls more inclined to care more about connecting to others. Often, when boys argue during play, they resolve it. When girls have arguments, they often quit playing rather than risk damaging their relationships. To help girls and young women move away from an attitude of subservience and self-sacrifice, teachers help girls to assert themselves and to assume roles of leadership in small groups. They encourage boys as well as girls to be caring.

PHYSICAL DEVELOPMENT

It is important for teachers to know age-level characteristics of children. Teachers need to know at what age he can expect a child to perform a certain behavior. For example, if a teacher plans on having the students cut out pictures to make a collage representing healthy foods, he needs to know if the children in his class, in general, have the physical dexterity to use scissors.

Age-Level Characteristics

Children are continually growing and maturing. Although each child grows and develops at his or her own rate, some characteristics are common to specific ages. Teachers who are familiar with regular developmental progress better understand children and have reasonable expectations. As professionals, teachers are expected to know and understand progressive child development and recognize possible developmental delays. The characteristics listed below of each age group are general observations. The author acknowledges that every child is an individual who grows and develops at his or her own rate, personality, and temperament. There is a wide range of differences among children of the same age.

© Andresr, 2014, Used under license of Shutterstock, Inc.

BIRTH TO THREE YEARS OLD

- Sits, crawls, walks, begins to run.
- Picks up, grasps, stacks, and releases objects.

THREE-YEAR-OLDS

- Likes dramatizing characters in a story (e.g., dog, horse, duck, etc.).
- Short attention span and likes changes of activity about every 6 minutes.
- Likes stories, but they should be short and simple.
- Likes to talk, but needs to learn that others like to talk also.
- Curious about people and animals and asks simple questions about them.

FOUR-YEAR-OLDS

- Fond of saying "I have seen that," "I did that before."
- Can carry on a conversation.
- Likes to talk about "my mother," "my father," "my baby."
- Lives completely in now, yesterday means nothing and tomorrow is a vague promise but shows great excitement for upcoming events.
- Likes to listen to stories and nursery rhymes and wants to hear favorites over and over again.
- Likes to dramatize characters after a story.
- Can run, jump, and climb easier.

FIVE-YEAR-OLDS

- Can now cut and paste pictures and color predrawn pictures.
- Serious when asks "What is that for?" or "How does this work?"
- Extremely active.
- Self dependent in eating, dressing, toileting, and sleeping.
- Starts losing baby teeth.
- Far-sighted, requiring large objects and close contact.
- Interested in other children, yet individualistic.
- Loves the teacher and thinks it a privilege to sit by the teacher.
- Loves to hear and tell stories, and asks about same story over and over again (repetition).
- Can tell a story almost verbatim.
- Good reasoning power.
- Can make judgments with adult guidance.
- Can plan and carry out plans (sometimes needs guidance with realistic plans).
- Likes to try new words.
- Naturally curious.
- Can skip, jump, turn somersaults, and hop.

SIX-YEAR-OLDS

- Attention span has increased to 15–20 minutes, though he gets restless.
- Enjoys whole body movements, climbing trees, etc.
- Likes games and competition.
- Can be impulsive.
- May be a dawdler, getting off task for a different interest.
- May not be interested in his or her clothes or hair.
- Desires to be a winner.
- Boastful to establish superiority.
- Teacher's opinion is very important, likes to sit by and help.
- Likes to hear stories and dramatize them, likes to wear grown-up clothes.
- Can skip, gallop, climb, run, wrestle, and hop.

SEVEN-YEAR-OLDS

- Can print easily.
- Full of energy but tires easily.
- Often restless and fidgety.
- Likes to collect things and talk about them.
- Attention span is 20–25 minutes.
- Becoming more independent in his or her thinking.
- Aware of right and wrong.
- Desirous for freedom and may grow away from adults.

- Aggressive and sympathetic by turns.
- Emotional—may be afraid of imaginary or improbably danger.
- Sensitive to ridicule, failure, or embarrassment.
- Plays with boys and girls as equals.

EIGHT-YEAR-OLDS

- Wants to feel independent.
- Developing hand–eye coordination.
- More interested in interacting with same gender.
- Interested in clubs, teams, and gangs.
- Does not want to depend on teacher and the teacher becomes less an ideal; is still accepted if business-like and good sport.
- Increase interest in people of long ago as time has greater meaning.
- Likes to listen to stories, present and past; wants to distinguish between real and imaginary.
- Sensitive to criticism, feelings are very tender.
- Works well with large groups.

NINE-YEAR-OLDS

- Energetic and daring.
- Interested in clubs, teams, and gangs.
- Scornful of the opposite sex.
- Self-centered.
- Untidy.
- Unwise in spending money.
- Interested in factual material.

TEN-YEAR-OLDS

- Increasingly aware of and interested in others' ideas and beliefs.
- Increased loyalty to clubs, teams, and gangs.
- Able to concentrate for longer periods of time.
- Getting better at time management.
- Fully capable of personal hygiene.
- Slow and steady in growth.

ELEVEN-YEAR-OLDS

- Interested in organized games.
- Growing rapidly; girls, in general, outgrow boys.
- Wanting group approval.
- Becoming more independent.

- Increased appetite.
- Sensitive to hurting other's feelings.
- Self-conscious about physical activities unless skilled.
- Becoming more analytical.
- Starting to really notice the opposite gender.

12- TO 14-YEAR-OLDS

- Entering adolescence and puberty.
- Rapid physical development.
- Has strong peer attachments.
- Concerned about physical appearance.
- Beginning to have social relationships with opposite sex.
- Wants to belong and be accepted.
- Becomes more responsible.
- Becoming more aware of others.
- More independent and autonomous.
- Want to be like peers in dress, opinions, hairstyles; differences are not accepted.
- Becoming curious about sex.
- Aware of their physical changes and may be overly sensitive.
- Imaginary audience.
- Does not believe adults can understand them.
- Increased self-efficacy awareness—the degree to which one believes he or she is capable or prepared to handle a particular task. If a student has a strong self-efficacy he or she is more likely to try than a student with a low self-efficacy. Self-efficacy becomes a strong influence on academic, athletic, and social behavior.

© baldyrgan, 2014, Used under license of Shutterstock, Inc.

TIPS FOR COMPETENCY 1: HUMAN DEVELOPMENT

1. A teacher needs to use examples that are familiar to the students and connect to their prior knowledge.
2. Maslow emphasizes that students need to feel valued and cared about. Students' basic needs must be met in order to learn to their potential.
3. Middle-schoolers need:
   a. Peer interaction
   b. Integration of hands-on experience with observational learning
4. Teachers need to be aware of the influence of grouping practices on students' self-image.
5. Students in middle school and below especially desire and need physical hands-on activities (concrete operational), not just observational learning.
6. By high school some students are beginning to move into abstract thinking (formal operations) and become interested in adult/world ideas.

© YanLev, 2014, Used under license of Shutterstock, Inc.

THE IMPACT OF EARLY AND LATE MATURATION		
	Characteristics as Adolescents	**Characteristics as Adults**
Early-Maturing Boys	Self-confident, high in self-esteem, likely to be chosen as leaders (but leadership tendencies more likely in low-SES boys than in middle-class boys)	Self-confident, cooperative, sociable but also rigid, moralistic, humorless, and conforming.
Late-Maturing Boys	Energetic, bouncy, given to attention-getting behavior, not popular, lower aspirations for educational achievement.	Impulsive and assertive but also insightful, perceptive, creatively playful, able to cope with new situations.
Early-Maturing Girls	Not popular or likely to be leaders, indifferent in social situations, lacking in poise (but middle-class girls more confident than those from low-SES groups) more likely to date, smoke, and drink earlier	Self-possessed, self-directed, able to cope, likely to score high in ratings of psychological health.
Late-Maturing Girls	Confident, outgoing, assured, popular, likely to be chosen as leaders.	Likely to experience difficulty adapting to stress, likely to score low in ratings of overall psychological health.

Prework

1. Instructions: Using the Internet find statistics regarding environmental influences

1. What percentage of children and at what ages live in poverty?
2. What percentage of children and at what ages have parents that are divorced?
3. What percentage of children and at what ages are homeless or live in a shelter?
4. What percentage of children and at what ages suffer from malnutrition?
5. What percentage of children and at what ages begin *experimenting* with illegal drugs and alcohol?
6. What percentage of children and at what ages are *addicted* to illegal drugs?
7. What percentage of children and at what ages are engaging in promiscuous behavior?
8. What percentage of children and at what ages are sexually active?

9. What percentage of children and at what ages have a parent that is incarcerated?

10. What percentage of children and at what ages are involved in gang activities?

11. What percentage of children and at what ages suffer from abuse and/or neglect?

2. Cognitive Development: Jean Piaget

Using any resources you want, explain in writing each stage below and the approximate age it occurs. Give an example of each stage. Explain each vocabulary term and be ready to explain and give an example of each. You will participate in a class activity using the information below. You may use any notes you have.

1. **Sensorimotor stage**

    a. Object permanence

    b. Goal-directed actions

    c. Reversal of actions

2. **Pre-operational stage**

    a. Semiotic function

    b. Egocentric

    c. Collective monologue

3. **Concrete operational stage**

    a. Conservation

    b. Reversibility

    c. Classification

    d. Seriation

4. **Formal operational stage**

    a. Abstract thought

    b. Adolescent egocentrism

    c. Imaginary audience

5. **In general:**

    a. Assimilation

    b. Accommodation

    c. Schema

LEV VYGOTSKY AND COGNITIVE DEVELOPMENT

Vygotsky made several significant contributions to our understanding of cognitive development and learning.

Explain the Following Ideas and Terms

1. Explain the role social interaction and culture plays in a child's cognitive development.

2. Explain what Vygotsky means by "private speech."

3. What is "scaffolding" and list five ways a teacher can scaffold.

4. Explain "assisted learning"

5. How are *scaffolding* and *assisted learning* alike and different?

6. Explain the "zone of proximal development."

7. What is the "magic middle"?

ERIK ERIKSON

Erik Erikson describes the physical, emotional, and psychological stages of development and relates specific issues, or developmental work or *tasks*, to each stage. The outcome a person has affects his working through the next issue. For example, if a person has a positive resolution to the issue he is better prepared to face the next issue; if the person has a negative resolution to an issue he carries that negative resolution into the next issue he encounters.

Directions: Be ready to explain what psychosocial development means in general, as well as each stage listed below with examples and age ranges. Identify a stage you have struggled with, the outcome, and how it has impacted your life. What stage are you in now in your life?

Erikson's Eight Stages of Psychosocial Development

Trust versus Mistrust

Autonomy versus Shame and Doubt

Initiative versus Guilt

Industry versus Inferiority

Identity versus Role Confusion

Intimacy versus Isolation

Generativity versus Stagnation

Integrity versus Despair

CLASSROOM ACTIVITIES

Piaget Application Activities

Read each situation below and discuss how it could be improved knowing Piaget's work with cognitive development. Identify each stage and "term" portrayed.

1. Mrs. Dawson teaches seventh-grade prealgebra and wants the students to understand that in the function $2x + t$, the coefficient represents the cost of a hamburger, with x being a hamburger and t being the tax. The children clearly do not understand what she is talking about. What does Mrs. Dawson need to know about cognitive developmental stages and what are some ideas to help her teach this concept to the children at their level?

2. Dane's young baby is very cooperative and never cries when he leaves the baby with Mika, the sitter. However, yesterday when Dane put his baby into Mika's arms, the baby howled. Both Dane and Mika are startled and do not understand what is going on. Mika thinks the baby doesn't like her and Dane wonders what is happening during the day that makes the baby uncomfortable going to Mika. What would you explain to Dane and Mika so they understand what is really happening?

3. Lacey and Bailey are asked by their teacher where they each live. Lacy answers Canyon and Bailey says, "No we don't, we live in Texas." They start arguing. Why are they confused and what does the teacher need to understand why they do not agree?

4. As Tyler, a junior in high school, is getting ready for school his mom notices that he is spending a lot of extra time on his appearance. Tyler's dad teasingly says, "Tyler, you still look as ugly as you were before you went into the bathroom." Tyler is visibly upset. What is going on?

5. Lee, Rob, and Mark are outside in the sandbox playing with their trucks at Rob's house. As the mothers listen to the boys talking they are concerned that they do not listen to each other and are almost unaware the others exist. The mothers begin to wonder what is wrong. What would you explain to them?

6. Jodi and Adelle are each working on 25-piece jigsaw puzzles. When Adelle finishes her puzzle, Jodi still has 13 pieces left and complains that Adelle's puzzle is bigger. What doesn't Jodi understand?

7. During recess Faith falls down and skins her knee. She begins to cry so Kevin brings his "blankey" over to her and hands it to her. Faith throws his blanket on the ground and gives him a dirty look. Kevin hits her. The caregiver comes over and thinks Faith is crying because Kevin hit her. You saw the entire incident. Explain what is really going on.

8. April is having a sleepover for several of her high school friends. She tells them how to get to her house, but the next morning the girls are arguing how to get back out to the main road. Brittney says you make a right at the yellow house and Miranda says you should make a left. Catherine pipes up that you clearly make a left, because you made a left when you came. April's dad comes in and says what to the girls so they understand what is going on?

9. It is Marla's first day teaching preschoolers. She holds up a picture of a horse and says, "This is a horse." Trent quickly responds, "That is *not* a horse, I have a horse, you can't ride that, it is a piece of paper." Jacob says, "That looks like a dog to me because he has four legs." Marla is confused because each child is dealing with a different issue. You are the supervisor, explain to Marla what is going on.

10. Jennifer and Jarrod are so excited because their toddler, Cassandra, has learned to put her toys back in the plastic bin for the first time ever. But then Cassandra just ruins it by dumping them out again. Their friends, Trent and Chancie, are visiting and begin to laugh when Jennifer and Jarrod are disappointed because they went through the same thing with their child. What do Trent and Chancie understand about reversal of actions that Jennifer and Jarrod do not?

11. Sarah calls Gari Sue first thing in the morning and is very upset because she has a blemish on her forehead. Gari Sue appears not to care. Sarah runs into her mom's bedroom crying. Her mom thinks

Sarah's sister Jordan must have done something to Sarah and starts to yell, "Jordan, get your hiney in here!" Meghan, the eldest, comes running to explain to her mother that it is just Sarah thinking she is the center of the universe. Now the mother is really confused and Jordan feels blamed for everything. Explain the problem.

12. Kristina is teaching high school students about the different customs in the Middle East. Michelle asks, "Why can't those guys just get along over there?" Jarad replies, "Yeah, just agree to disagree." Lisa, Natasha, Lacy, and Kody nod their head in agreement. Kristina explains it is not that simple and realizes which stage of cognitive development in which they are operating. Knowing this, how does she help the students understand?

Erik Erikson's Psychosocial Stages Application Activity

Instructions: Each of the situations below represents a *negative outcome* of one of Erik Erikson's psychosocial stages. Determine which psychosocial stage resulted in each set of behaviors described below; speculate as to what circumstances may have resulted in the negative outcome; and describe what behaviors would be indicative of a positive outcome of that same stage.

1. Jason is a 14-year-old seventh grader who moved to Saint Cloud this summer from another state. He has recently been referred to the school psychologist because of concerns about both his academic performance and school behavior. A review of his school records shows that Jason repeated kindergarten and third grade. His elementary school grades were primarily S's ("Satisfactory") and N's ("Needs Improvement"). His current teachers state that they are unsure of Jason's academic skills because he typically does not turn in assignments and appears to "clown around" and not take exams and assignments seriously.

2. Brenda is a fifth-year undergraduate student at the College of Saint Benedict. She began her post-secondary education at CSB as a nursing major, but decided she wanted to pursue a career in special education, so she transferred to Saint Cloud State University. After a year at SCSU, she discovered that special education was not for her, so she transferred back to CSB where she registered for courses in the social science–secondary education sequence. She is now a Liberal Studies major, and will graduate in May. Brenda has thought about applying to law schools, but recently decided she really didn't want a career in law. At this point she has no firm career plans. Rather, she has decided to work as a waitress for at least a year, and after that, who knows?

3. Carrie is a 36-year-old woman who is currently being seen for counseling at a community mental health center. Her second marriage recently ended in divorce, and she has sought counseling so that she might "find" herself and get her life "back on track." Carrie married for the first time at age 18, but she and her husband grew increasingly apart and found they had little in common other than their two children. She remarried shortly after her first divorce as she felt lonely and thought both she and her children needed a man in the house, but that marriage also proved unsuccessful. She is now thinking of attending college, and is trying to figure out what to do "with the rest of her life."

4. Eric's kindergarten teacher is very concerned about him. He is hesitant to get involved in group activities, and though he seems bright verbally, he tells his teacher he "can't" do the work and will not start assignments unless the teacher is there to help and reassure him. Additionally, he always waits for the teacher to help him put on his coat and boots, even though she has encouraged him to do so himself.

5. Anna is currently enrolled in a special needs program for children with severe and profound developmental delays. She is 4 years old and has been diagnosed as suffering from a pervasive developmental disorder. Her behavior is often "autistic-like" as she avoids eye contact, makes repetitive and bizarre hand movements, and her speech is often echolalic. A review of her developmental history shows that her development was apparently "normal" for the first 6 months of her life. It was at that time Anna's mother developed severe depression and spent a year in a mental institution. During that year, Anna was left in the care of an aunt, who reportedly abused her both physically and psychologically. It was after her mother was released from the hospital that Anna was first seen at the mental health center and diagnosed as developmentally delayed.

6. Joe is a college junior with a mediocre academic record. Though he is very intelligent, his teachers often describe him as lacking in initiative and creativity. He does well in lecture classes, but is hesitant to participate in group discussions and has difficulty coming up with ideas for independent learning projects. He is hesitant to take chances and try new things.

7. Karl is a 78-year-old widower who lives in a senior-citizens apartment complex. Though he is reasonably healthy, both physically and mentally, Karl rarely gets out and typically does not take part in activities offered through the local senior citizens center. Rather, he mostly sits at home and broods. He rarely interacts with his neighbors in the apartment complex, and even his children and grandchildren avoid visiting him because all he does is complain about how bad his life has been.

8. John is a 36-year-old divorced man whose ex-wife has custody of their three children. Though John has visitation rights, he rarely exercises them. Even when the family lived together, he was only minimally involved with his children as he was always "too busy." His job often required long hours and extended travel, but even when he was not working, John found little time for his kids. However, he always seemed to find the time for golf outings, poker night, and hunting and fishing trips with his buddies.

Sample Test Questions

1. A seventh-grade teacher has taught a new math skill to her class and finds that some students have caught on quickly. Others are having difficulty applying the skill. Based on Vygotsky's principles of assisted learning and zone of proximal development, the teacher should:

   a. Give students who are experiencing difficulty more practice problems.

   b. Group students for more practice, paring those who have mastered the skill with those who have not.

    c. Reteach the skill using a different approach and math manipulatives.

    d. Move on to the next skill and place students in cooperative learning groups.

2. A first-grade teacher notices that several children are frequently coming to school hungry, tired, and dressed in dirty clothing. According to Abraham Maslow, these children will be unable to pay attention because the following need has not been met:

    a. Self-esteem

    b. Safety and security

    c. Love and belonging

    d. Physiological

3. Tom, age 13, a foster child in a low-income family, is bussed to a school in a wealthy suburb. Although Tom's daydreaming, late assignments, and poor work habits challenge his teachers, they should recall Erikson's theory of psychosocial development and remember that Tom is probably in the stage of identity versus role confusion. From Tom's perspective, what seems most important to him at this stage in his life?

    a. Acceptance of his place in life

    b. Independence from others

    c. Love relationships

    d. Peer relationships

Answers

1. A is not correct. The students who are experiencing difficulty do not need more problems, they need assistance with the problems they already have.

   B is the correct answer. The focus of the question is the impact of Vygotsky in education. Students who have learned a skill can assist others to expand the zone of proximal development.

   C is not correct. Although the use of math manipulatives is a very good idea, it relates to Piaget's work and not Vygotsky's. Furthermore, when reteaching a skill it is best to teach the way it was originally taught and not change strategies.

   D is not correct. The students should never be left confused.

2. A is not correct. The unmet needs address physical ones. Although this may influence their self-esteem, it is a byproduct of physiological needs not being addressed.

   B is not correct. Again, the need described is about physical deprivation.

   C is not correct. The description in the vignette relates to physiological needs, not love and belonging.

   D is the correct answer. The conditions describe physiological needs.

3. A is not correct. Tom is most likely still struggling with his place in life.

   B is not the correct answer. Teenagers are dependent on approval of their peers and increase their loyalty to them.

   C is not correct. Thirteen-year-olds are usually not addressing the issue of love relations yet. Their crisis focuses on peer relationships.

   D is the correct answer. From an adolescent's point of view, peer relationships are most important.

REFERENCES

Evans, I. E. (1976). *Dialogue with Erik Erikson*. New York: Harper & Row.

Gruber, H., & Voneche, J. (1977). *The essential Piaget*. New York: Basic Books.

Kohlberg, L. (1984). *Essays on moral development*: Vol. 2. *The psychology of moral development*. San Francisco: Harper & Row.

Maslow, A. (1968). *Toward a psychology of being*. New York: Van Nostrand Reinhold.

Piaget, J. (1952). *The origins of intelligence in children* (M. Cook, Trans.). New York: International Universities Press.

Power, F. D., Higgins, A., & Kohlberg, L. (1989). *Lawrence Kohlberg's approach to moral education*. New York: Columbia University Press.

Vygotsky, L. S. (1978). *Mind in society*. Cambridge, MA: Harvard University Press.

Websites

Child Development

www.sbec.state.tx.us

Texas State Board for Educator Certification

Includes contact information, certification requirements, testing, and preparation programs.

en.wikipedia.org/wiki/Child

Wikipedia, the free encyclopedia

childdevelopmentinfo.com/development

Child development basics. Site recommended by the American Psychological Association.

www.worldbank.org/education/edstats

Compiles World Bank data on pertinent education topics.

Developmental Delay

http://www.devdelay.org/

Developmental Delay Resources (DDR) publicizes research into determining identifiable factors that would put a child at risk and maintains a registry, tracking possible trends.

Play

http://www.cfw.tufts.edu/topic/4/84.htm

Links to topics by age, sites on play, importance of play.

Middle School

cela.albany.edu/publication/brochure/guidelines.pdf
Six features of effective instruction for teaching middle and high school students.

Adolescence

www.ijpm.org/content/pdf/232/adolescence
A 1-year follow-up study on the persistence of psychological problems in adolescence.

Risk Behaviors

www.apa.org/releases/adhd_drugs.html
Early attention-deficit/hyperactivity disorder and risk for substance use in adolescence.

Competency 2 _

Multiculturalism and Education: Opportunities for All Students

Teri Bingham, EdD
West Texas A&M University

Angela Spaulding, EdD
West Texas A&M University

> **Competency 2:** The teacher understands student diversity and knows how to plan learning experiences and design assessments that are responsive to differences among students and that promote all students' learning.

The beginning teacher:

A. Demonstrates knowledge of students with diverse personal and social characteristics (e.g., those related to ethnicity, gender, language background, exceptionality) and the significance of student diversity for teaching, learning, and assessment.

B. Accepts and respects students with diverse backgrounds and needs.

C. Knows how to use diversity in the classroom and the community to enrich all students' learning experiences.

D. Knows strategies for enhancing one's own understanding of students' diverse backgrounds and needs.

E. Knows how to plan and adapt lessons to address students' varied backgrounds, skills, interests, and learning needs, including the needs of English-language learners and students with disabilities.

F. Understands cultural and socioeconomic differences (including differential access to technology) and knows how to plan instruction that is responsive to cultural and socioeconomic differences among students.

G. Understands the instructional significance of varied student learning needs and preferences.

H. Knows the ELPS in the domains of listening and speaking in accordance with the proficiency-level descriptors for the beginning, intermediate, advanced, and advanced-high levels.

I. Knows the ELPS in the domains of reading and writing in accordance with the proficiency-level descriptors for beginning, intermediate, advanced, and advanced-high levels.

KEY TERMS

acculturation

assimilation

at-risk students

bilingual education

Brown vs. Board of Education

character education

cultural awareness

culturally responsive teaching

culture

curriculum restructuring

demographics

diversity

English language learners

ethnicity

exceptionality

gender

gifted students

home culture

macroculture

microculture

multiculturalism

prior knowledge

Public Law 94–142

self-efficacy

social skills training

socioeconomics

Title IX

For over 200 years Americans have voted in democratic elections, and the vast majority of Americans are proud of the U.S. Constitution and their right to vote. The privilege of voting allows Americans from both genders and from all racial/ethnic and socioeconomic groups to participate in democratic processes; in this respect, all Americans have equal access to participate in government because adults can cast only one vote in any given election. Similarly, our democracy has afforded virtually all American children the opportunity to attend public schools. Although the privilege of a public school education is often taken for granted because it is protected by federal law, the emphasis on equal access in public schools is a relatively recent trend in the United States.

GENDER DIFFERENCES

Like culturally responsive teaching, gender is an important consideration for the classroom teacher, and in terms of academic achievement, there are slight differences between females and males. According to the U.S. Department of Education (2000), girls perform at higher levels on reading achievement tests than boys do at ages 9, 13, and 17. However, on mathematics tests boys score slightly higher than girls do at ages 9 and 13 but score much higher than girls do at age 17. Males score higher than females on Advanced Placement examinations except for those on foreign languages. Similarly, males outperform females on all sections of the ACT and SAT except for verbal. Although males traditionally have excelled more in mathematics than females have, the achievement gap in mathematics between males and females has decreased in the past 20 years. In contrast, females continue to score at much higher levels on achievement tests in reading and writing than males do.

In addition to achievement levels, differences in patterns of participation between females and males are significant. Jovanovic and King (1998), for example, found females are more likely to assume passive roles in science classes as they approach and enter high school. Girls typically are expected to take notes for groups while boys handle equipment for activities. Similarly, Sadker, Sadker, and Klein (1991) found in a sample of 11th graders that only 17% of 11th-grade female students in science classes reported hands-on experiences with lab equipment, in contrast to 49% of male students. The decrease of direct participation of girls in science activities is one reason why boys outperform girls on achievement tests in science, and teachers need to involve girls more actively in labs.

Also, teachers are more inclined to call on boys and expect more from them in mathematics and science classes than they do for girls (Nieto, 2004). Males usually dominate classroom discussions and are more apt to receive both positive encouragement for their work and more negative attention for their misbehaviors than girls are. However, in single-sex classes girls are more likely to ask questions and to be more active participants (Streitmatter, 1994). Female students can excel in mathematics and science classes and have improved their performance on standardized achievement tests in these areas. More female students are taking higher-level mathematics courses, and this is one reason why they are achieving at higher levels in mathematics (Gollnick & Chinn, 2002). Students cannot learn what they are not exposed to or taught, and this is one of the primary reasons why equal educational opportunities for both genders is critical.

Consequently, teachers and parents need to encourage both genders to excel in all content areas. Girls need to receive as much instructional feedback and encouragement as boys do in mathematics, and teachers need to encourage boys to improve their performance in reading and writing. Boys are more likely than girls are to be "at risk" of not completing school. Also, boys are placed in special education and in remedial mathematics or English classes more often than girls are (Willingham & Cole, 1997).

Teachers need to ensure both genders are treated equitably in a classroom context. For example, boys and girls ought to be asked to pass out papers or to assume the role of a group's note-taker. In addition, teachers ought to elicit responses from girls in discussions as frequently as they do for boys, so boys do not dominate classroom discussions. It is also important to highlight the contributions of women in history, literature, science, and mathematics classes (Banks, 2002). If the contributions of women or any group are not part of the curriculum, both girls and boys are not exposed to the contributions of over half the population. In this respect, students are presented a skewed representation of the various academic disciplines (Bennett, 2003; Nieto, 2004).

DIVERSITY

Until the U. S. Supreme Court's *Brown vs. Board of Education* decision of 1954 overturned the *Plessey v. Ferguson* decision of 1896, which previously legalized segregation in all public institutions, segregation in public schools was a way of life. The *Brown* decision became a watershed decision because it opened the doors of public institutions to African Americans and all people of color. Later, Title IX of the 1972 Educational Amendment Act was enacted and more opportunities were provided for women because sex discrimination was prohibited in all public institutions accepting
federal funding. Equally important, Public Law 94–142, the All Handicapped Children Act of 1975, mandated public schools to provide support services for students with disabilities.

© Konstantin Chagin, 2014, Used under license of Shutterstock, Inc.

The *Brown* decision, Title IX, and Public Law 94–142 significantly changed public education and created an equitable but more complex educational system. Teachers now have the responsibility to provide a quality education for children from all groups. Because public schools are becoming more diverse, teachers must increase their understanding of the customs, beliefs, and values of students and parents from many different groups. Understanding cultural diversity is an important part of a teacher's professional knowledge-base because culture profoundly affects learning and social interactions. Equally important, teachers must respect and encourage students from all cultural groups, so that all students have opportunities to excel academically and to belong socially. Accepting and becoming more knowledgeable about cultural diversity is an important aspect of effective teaching and is emphasized in teacher education programs throughout Texas.

Most people agree that a respect for various cultures is important in any democracy, but what do we really mean when we refer to culture and cultural differences? Do we think primarily of race/ethnicity or differences among people from various regions, levels of income, or language groups? Of course, all of the aforementioned examples are important aspects of culture. However, defining culture is a difficult task because culture encompasses every aspect of life and is constantly changing. For example, social scientists consider culture as the shared symbols and values of a group, and every nation has its own shared and overarching values, ideas, and symbols that comprise its macroculture (Banks, 2002). Democratic principles and ideals of justice emphasized in the Bill of Rights are important aspects of the American macroculture, and common American values such as the importance of economic improvement, a strong work ethic, and rugged individualism have influenced the American macroculture for generations (Banks, 2002).

A nation's macroculture, however, is not monolithic in that every macroculture is comprised of many micro-cultures, which are smaller cultural groups. Ethnicity, gender, religion, language, socioeconomics, region, and exceptionalities are examples of common microcultures. Everyone belongs to several microcultures; however, some microcultures influence a person's life more than others do. Two individuals, for example, may belong to the microculture of Italian Americans. One of these individuals may speak Italian, belong to the local Italian club, and retain many customs and traditions of Italy. In contrast, the other Italian American may not speak Italian or know much about Italian customs. In this case the microculture of ethnicity significantly affected the first Italian American much more than that of the other Italian American.

ETHNICITY

Everyone belongs to and is influenced by several microcultures, and race/ethnicity is one of the most impor-tant microcultures. Public schools are becoming more diverse because immigration from all over the world has increased since the 1970s. According to the U.S. Bureau of the Census (2000), the ethnic/racial groups in public schools throughout the United States are as follows: 61.2%, white, non-Hispanic; 16.3%, Hispanic; 17.2%, black, non-Hispanic; 4.1%, Asian/Pacific Islander; and 1.2%, American Indian/Alaskan Native. The demographic data on current birthrates indicates that by 2020 students of color (e.g., Hispanic Americans, African Americans, Native Americans, and Asian Americans) will represent more than half of the public school students in many states, including Texas.

In the past, ethnic groups different from the macroculture were expected to assimilate into American society and to disregard their native language and cultural heritage. However, assimilation was problematic for people of color who often were barred access from many institutions (Gollnick & Chin, 2002). As previous noted, the *Brown* decision changed the social, political, and educational climate in the United States, and today most edu-cators do not emphasize an assimilation model. Instead, most educators prefer an acculturation model, which values diversity and encourages people to maintain their native culture as they learn to live democratically in the American macroculture (Banks, 2002).

CULTURAL DIFFERENCES IN COMMUNICATION STYLES

Even though the student population is becoming more diverse each year, most teachers are from middle-class European American backgrounds (Darling-Hammond, 2001). Consequently, teachers need to become more knowledgeable about cultural differences in patterns of communication, so that misunderstandings are ame-liorated. Consider, for instance, Diller and Moule's (2005) vignette about a dedicated English teacher who encouraged and helped her Korean students to improve their writing. She carefully evaluated students' com-positions, identifying those things they did well and making specific, constructive suggestions about how to improve their drafts. In addition, the teacher wrote each student a paragraph on his or her paper discussing the strengths and weaknesses of his or her composition, and she began each paragraph with the student's name to add a personal touch.

This conscientious and patient teacher even devoted additional time helping students whose first language was not English. So why were the parents of her Korean students upset with her? The answer to this question lies in cultural misunderstandings. Although the Korean parents were grateful that the teacher helped their children to improve their fluency in English, they were horrified that the teacher wrote the names of their children in red. In their Buddhist culture a person's name is written in red after they have died. This innocent mistake on the part of this exemplary teacher caused serious problems between her and her Korean students. Had she known about this Buddhist custom, she would not have used a red pen to evaluate students' papers, and this unpleasant incident would not have occurred.

Nevertheless, miscommunications caused by a lack of cultural knowledge are common throughout the world (Cushner, McClelland, & Safford, 2003). For instance, Asian students are often surprised that American students speak informally and seemingly disrespectfully to their teachers because such speech patterns are considered inappropriate to address teachers in Asian schools. Likewise, many Asian and Pacific Islanders note their shock of the direct communication styles of Russians. Similarly, American businesspeople often appear curt to their Arab counterparts. For example, Arab business personnel consider it respectful to ask about the families of their American business counterparts instead of immediately discussing business. If the Americans ignore these comments and counter with questions related to business negotiations, the Arabs sometimes interpret this as rudeness while the Americans may interpret their own behaviors as respectful and professional.

Likewise, miscommunication is sometimes caused by a lack of awareness about cultural differences in non-verbal behaviors. For instance, Spaulding and O'Hair (2000) note that some cultures avoid direct eye contact when conversing with authority figures as a sign of respect whereas other cultures interpret not looking at an authority figure (e.g., a teacher) in the eyes as disrespect. Most European Americans have been socialized to look authority figures in the eyes as a sign of respectful behavior. In contrast, Japanese Americans usually avoid eye contact with teachers to show respect. Teachers need to be aware of differences in nonverbal behaviors so that signs of respect are not misinterpreted (Cushner et al., 2003).

Unfortunately, during the past 35 years, researchers have found that teachers sometimes do not understand cultural differences in the communication styles of students; as a result of these misunderstandings, they sometimes display more verbal or nonverbal forms of negativity toward students of color than they do toward European American students (Good & Brophy, 2000). Similarly, researchers (e.g., Cornbleth, Davis, & Button, 1974; Rist, 1970; Zeichner & Hoeft, 1996) have found that teachers have fewer quality instructional interactions with and provide less encouragement for students of color than they do for European Americans. These findings are problematic because unless teachers encourage and have high academic expectations for all groups, learning is not maximized in the classroom context (Good & Brophy, 2000; Zeichner & Hoeft, 1996). Since many misunderstandings are caused by a lack of cultural awareness, teachers need to learn as much as possible about the verbal and nonverbal communication patterns of their students.

Research on Cultural Differences in Learning Styles and Background Knowledge

Equally important, researchers have found that some ethnic groups have preferences in their learning styles, and researchers often explain these differences in terms of field-independence or field-dependence (Cushner et al., 1992; Shade, 1989). Field-independent learners are more analytical and goal oriented and often break down concepts into sequential pieces. Field-independent learners usually prefer independent rather than group work. Male European Americans and Japanese Americans usually favor field-independent learning styles.

On the other hand, field-dependent learners prefer to see an overview of content, to work with other people, and to conform to the social context. Research on African American learning styles has found strong field-dependent elements. Many African American students respond more to kinesthetic or hands-on activities and learn more easily if whole concepts are presented instead of parts taught in isolation. In addition, African Americans tend to prefer learning activities that are social and use a variety of ways of knowing or reasoning (e.g., inferential and deductive learning).

Likewise, research on learning styles of Hispanic American and Native American students has found strong tendencies of field-dependent learning styles. Baruth and Manning (1992) found Hispanic Americans prefer group work, hands-on activities, learning by doing, and concrete examples of key concepts rather than abstractions with no practical applications. Native Americans often prefer small group work, private rather than public learning, and the use mental images when trying to remember details and concepts (Baruth & Manning, 1992; Shade 1989). Also, Native Americans like to observe and imitate models rather than proceeding through a given task by trial and error (Bennett, 2003).

"Culturally Responsive" Teaching

The research on learning styles is not without its contradictions and may lead to stereotypes about how students from various ethnic groups learn effectively.

Nevertheless, an important finding of the research on learning styles is that instruction becomes more effective if it matches students' learning styles and cultural backgrounds. Gay (2000) advocates that teachers use "culturally responsive" methods of teaching; in other words, teachers need to use students' prior knowledge in its cultural context when introducing new concepts. McCarty, Wallace, Lynch, and Bennally (1991), for example, found Navajo students to engage more easily in higher cognitive activities and questioning strategies when they are able to connect new learning to their cultural context and background knowledge.

Another reason culturally responsive methods of teaching are effective is because learners are familiar with the overall context for learning. Situating learning activities in real-world tasks has enhanced student learning. Lave (1991), for instance, found that individuals who had significant difficulties learning mathematics in a typical course were able to make accurate calculations in the context of a grocery store as they shopped to determine which product was the best buy.

Similarly, the cognitive apprenticeship model (Collins, Brown, & Newman, 1989) emphasizes the importance of building a real-world learning context, which is congruent with students' background knowledge. Also, the cognitive apprenticeship model stresses the importance of using teacher- or student-made models of the given task to be completed as well as instructional scaffolding to guide students through higher cognitive tasks in a step-by-step process. Knowledge of students' backgrounds becomes an exceptionally effective tool when designing these types of lessons and requires teachers to learn more about the cultural and background knowledge of their students. For the classroom teacher, teaching and learning are reciprocal in that teachers must become learners as well—in this case, learners about their students (Nieto, 1999).

Culturally Responsive Curriculum Restructuring

In addition, educators foster conditions favorable to culturally responsive teaching and an acceptance of diversity through curriculum restructuring. Banks (2002) believes multiculturalism ought to permeate the entire school curriculum and advocates the use of content about various ethnic groups from kindergarten to 12th grade. Teachers in various academic disciplines or content areas, including mathematics, can highlight the contributions of all ethnic groups and both genders to foster an acceptance of diversity. The social studies curriculum is especially helpful in providing representations of contributions from all ethnic groups and both genders in American history. Also, the use of multiple perspectives is critical, so the views of all groups are voiced. For example, if a class is studying the American West, accounts of both women and men, Native Americans, European Americans, African Americans, Hispanic Americans, and Asian Americans ought to be considered. The use of multiple perspectives exposes students to various views and provides opportunities for students to understand how events affect various groups. Equally important, multiple perspectives provide opportunities for critical thinking and evaluation of complex ideas.

School districts also can recognize holidays and festivals of various ethnic and religious groups. Students can learn about the importance of these special occasions from the perspectives of those groups who celebrate them (Bennett, 2003; Gay, 2000). In this respect, students will learn about the values of various groups in their communities and will learn about culture from a global perspective since the United States is comprised of ethnic groups from all continents. Equally important, emphasizing the rights of all ethnic groups to practice their cultural, social, and religious beliefs promotes democratic ideals, which fosters a more positive school climate.

CULTURALLY AND LINGUISTICALLY DIVERSE STUDENTS

As our classroom student composition continues to become more diverse, we as teachers need to update our teaching practices to accommodate these changes. Students whose first language is not English are becoming more prominent in our classrooms and it is the teacher's responsibility to educate them with complete fidelity.

Students who are culturally and linguistically diverse (CLD) bring new challenges to teachers. It behooves teachers to become CLD literate so they can meet the needs of these learners. To become CLD literate begins with understanding our students. This starts by first identifying and reflecting on our own assumptions about individuals who are culturally and linguistically different than us. When a teacher is unaware of a child's culture we may make false assumptions about him or her. A teacher may perceive a student's behavior as inappropriate and consequently the teacher's decisions may inadvertently undermine the student's academic success.

To identify our false beliefs about cultures different than our own we must identify our assumptions about CLD learners' home environments, background experiences, language abilities, and academic potential. These assumptions color teacher expectations for students and impact their perspective on the potential success of CLD learners both in school and in their future.

Understanding our students begins with identifying and reflecting on our own assumptions about individuals who are different than us. According to Herrera (2010), teachers may make well-intended decisions that limit a student's academic success when the teacher's false cultural assumptions lead to erroneous conclusions. What may be normal in a student's native culture may be outside the norm of appropriate behavior in a different culture. For example, when a teacher corrects a Hispanic student, the student may laugh to save face and it is that culture's way of handling the correction. However, the teacher may perceive the laughter as disrespectful and determine that the student isn't taking him seriously. It is imperative for teachers to be aware of their students' cultural differences to avoid making false assumptions. As another example, suppose a Muslim student appears tired and disinterested. The teacher may assume the student is bored or staying up too late videogaming. However, during Ramadan Muslims fast from food. So in all reality the student's behavior may be attributed to the child being hungry.

To better understand our students, teachers need to recognize their own assumptions about a CLD learner's home environment, background experiences, language abilities, and academic potential. These assumptions influence a teacher's expectations of students and impact the potential success of CLD students.

According to Herrera, did you know . . .

1. Assumptions lead to judgments in about 7 seconds after cross-cultural contact?
2. These assumptions are usually ethnocentric and highly resistant to change?
3. We judge others based on criteria that are different than those we apply to ourselves?
4. We judge the behavior of others based on stereotypes?

> Knowing your audience (students) is the best way to connect with them. —*Teri Bingham*

There are many ways for teachers to get to know their students better. Here are just a few ideas: Use a questionnaire or survey to learn about their interests and hobbies, listen to them in whole-group or small-group discussions and one-on-one conversations, ask questions, have them draw pictures to go with the lesson they are learning, complete an "All About Me" poster, bring three small items in a paper sack to show the class as the student introduces him- or herself.

Biocards

A simple and fun way to get to know your students better is to have them complete a biocard. A biocard requires the student to answer questions about him- or herself about interests, hobbies, family, community, culture, native language, and the like. Teachers can use biocards to learn more about each student so as to connect with them and enhance lessons with each learner profile in mind. Also, teachers can learn their students' names faster if they have each student attach a photo to the biocard they turn in.

Name _____

Email _____

Cell _____

Interests _____

_____

_____

_____

_____

Something unique about me _____

_____

_____

_____

_____

What influenced me the most to want to teach _____

_____

_____

_____

_____

One thing I really would like to know about teaching is _____

_____

_____

_____

_____

In my life this situation happened and it really changed the way I view the world for the better

_____

_____

_____

_____

Growing up I was expected to _____

_____

_____

_____

_____

Growing up I was in big trouble if I _____

_____

_____

_____

_____

While growing up the level of support and encouragement from my family was_____

_____

_____

_____

Common Information Teachers May Want to Ascertain from Students

1. Where they were born
2. Native language
3. Prior school experience
4. Family dynamics
5. Values
6. Traditions
7. Preferred groupings
8. How they learn best
9. Assets they bring to the class
10. Incidents of prejudice or discrimination

How to Use the Information Received

1. Influence the teacher's state-of-mind by understanding where the student is coming from.
2. Be culturally responsive.
3. Incorporate more visual aids, cooperative learning, and cognitive processing activities.
4. Engineer grouping practices with a particular task and goal in mind.
5. Put the new knowledge in their context.
6. Document prior knowledge to demonstrate progress.

Ways to Create an Educational Climate to Optimize Learning for Culturally and Linguistically Diverse Learners

A student's ability to learn is influenced by how well the teacher designs his or her classroom to have a climate whereby all learners flourish and thrive.

All students need a rich learning environment, however, for CLD children it is imperative for their academic and social success.

There are five relevant areas to address in order to provide the best possible learning environment for CLD learners. Although these ideas are beneficial for all students, they are essential for CLD learners.

1. The teacher needs to provide an appropriate and student-friendly physical setting. Keep in mind that CLD learners may not know the word for certain items they need in the classroom.

   a. Have student resources readily available and visible to students. For example, have markers, glue sticks, staplers, tape, index cards, pencils, and the like visibly accessible.

   b. Have resources and computers accessible for all learners.

   c. Vary student seating arrangements based on the purpose of the new skill or task. This relates to group work. When students are practicing a new skill or task during the initial phases of learning, they will be best served by sitting with peers that speak their first language. This allows them to effectively communicate during the cognitive processing stages of learning. When students are practicing a new skill or task for mastery it might behoove them to sit with English speakers so they hear the language and the nuances in speaking English.

   d. Include word strips in more than just English to identify common classroom elements (i.e., *door*, *chair*, *window*). Use both English and the CLD students' first language(s).

   e. For wall and bulletin board decorations include artwork from the homelands of your CLD learners.

2. During the planning stages the teacher must organize the scope and sequence of the given curriculum. It is most beneficial for students learning new material to build on prior knowledge, the context in which it was learned, and flow together seamlessly into understanding. Also CLD's benefit when teachers teach from the known to the unknown.

3. CLD students' ability to learn is influenced by how well the classroom climate nurtures the students as a community of learners. It is essential for the community to promote:

   © Monkey Business Images, 2014, Used under license of Shutterstock, Inc.

   a. Trust in each other both emotionally and physically. The classroom needs to be an environment where students feel safe from embarrassment, humiliation, threats, bullying, intimidation, and losing their dignity. The teacher sets the tone and models appropriate, respectful behavior for all students.

   b. Respect for each other and differences. The teacher ought to look for the assets the CLD learner brings to the classroom, not the deficits.

   c. An atmosphere where students learn from one another and build each other up.

   d. A setting where all children are fully engaged in the learning process. This tacitly expresses the teacher's desire for all students to learn and expectation for success.

   e. Student responsibility for his own learning. The classroom is no longer a place whereby the teacher distributes knowledge and students simply absorb it. It is a setting where we all learn together and learn how to learn.

   f. Following classroom rules, procedures, and routines. Every successful teacher knows the value of having effective classroom management. For students to follow rules and procedures they must be aware of and possibly practice the procedures until they become routine.

   g. The celebration of learning. All students, but especially CLD students, need to be aware of their progress. Through celebration students can realize the value of learning.

4. Providing sociocultural support makes a difference to CLD learners. Ways to do this include:

   a. Native language support

   b. Peer assistance (use the buddy system)

   c. Peer assessment

   d. Interactive grouping with a purpose for the ways groups are comprised

5. Providing academic support increases the CLD learner's ability to understand.

   a. Frontload academic vocabulary.

   b. Be a dynamic teacher .

      i. Use concrete objects for students to explore.

      ii. Provide visual aids.

      iii. Incorporate hands-on, engaging activities.

      iv. Act out or demonstrate the meaning of words.

      v. Provide experiments, investigations, and explorations for discovery learning.

   c. Scaffold during the lesson. Scaffolding means to provide systematic, progressive support throughout the initial stages of learning. Some students need support throughout the process of learning to reach mastery. Other students only need support during the initial stages of learning and then they become independent learners as they continue to practice the new skill or knowledge as they attain mastery.

   d. Interactive reading in the CLD learner's new language.

   e. Design lessons with the student's zone of proximal development (ZPD) in mind.

Three Components of Students' Background Knowledge

Before the students come to us they have been part of several communities that have shaped them into a tapestry of who they are.

Highly effective teachers understand the three components that create a student's background knowledge. Only by knowing our students can we provide a learning environment for them to thrive socially and be academically successful.

1. **Family background**—The dynamics, values, ideology, language, and beliefs that students acquired from being part of a particular family. As a teacher you must know this in order to capitalize on it.

   a. Traditions

   b. Native language

   c. Home literacy practices

      i. Reading

      ii. Writing

      iii. Speaking

   d. Family dynamics

2. **Prior knowledge**—A student's prior knowledge is a mixture of what they have learned in the different communities in which they have experienced.

   a. Language brokering

   b. Community environment and expectations

   c. Family employment

   d. Community support systems

3. **Academic knowledge**—Skills and knowledge that a student has acquired during his or her formal education. Typically this is the curriculum that schools and teachers have traditionally valued.

    a. Previous content knowledge

    b. School literacy practices

        i. Reading

        ii. Writing

        iii. Speaking

    c. School-based cooperation and collaboration skills

    d. School dynamics

So the question we as teachers need to ask ourselves is, "How do I become that culturally responsive teacher?" We must begin by reflecting on our own beliefs and identify what has influenced you to have false, unfavorable assumptions about other people. How has your opinion been molded by parents and extended family, the media, and limited exposure to persons who are culturally different from you?

Actively search for evidence to contradict your assumptions and bring this opposing information to your awareness. Use newfound evidence to begin changing your erroneous opinions as you continue to identify evidence that supports your new ideas. You will need to stay open-minded as you try to change the prism you look through in viewing the world. Just as a kaleidoscope changes with each turn, we too must assimilate new information into our thinking process as the facts change. In your mind avoid the common labels or stereotypes our society put on people. Lastly, identify and elaborate on the assets the CLD child brings to the classroom, rather than listing the drawbacks.

Planning Considerations for CLD Learners

To make the best decisions possible when planning their lessons and learning activities, teachers need to be keenly aware of the student's background: sociocultural, linguistic, cognitive, and academic. Teachers should consider these biographies as they plan for content objectives, language objectives, and grouping configurations. Regarding **content objectives**, present the new material within the context familiar to the learners. This may mean using a variety of examples to frame and apply academic concepts relative to the vagaries of students' home, community, and school experiences. By incorporating a context familiar to the CLD student you are supporting him in coming to a thorough understanding and taking ownership of the new information or skill.

Being cognizant of each learner's background while completing lesson plans allows teachers to be mindful to emphasize vocabulary acquisition through clearly identified **language objectives**. The teacher needs to promote academic language development among all students. However, for CLD students conditions that encourage learners to practice and apply new vocabulary and concepts in meaningful and interactive ways need to be employed. For example, suppose a teacher is instructing the students to take the information from a bar graph and convert it into a circle graph. For CLD learners, the teacher may first need to explain bar graphs; for non-CLD students, she is simply building on previous learning.

During the planning stages a teacher needs to create **grouping configurations** based on what the learner is to practice or comprehend during the task. Strategically designed teams of learners will maximize each CLD learners' linguistic, academic, and social development. By engaging students in a variety of grouping configurations, their dialogue skills and vocabulary will develop. In designing cooperative learning groups consider the following:

    a. The assets and needs of the CLD learners.

    b. Grouping students according to the academic knowledge, skills, and vocabulary needed to complete the task.

   c. Devising pairs and groupings that will help each student grow linguistically and academically for that lesson.

   d. How students' academic and linguistic progress will be documented.

Instructional Strategies for Teaching CLD Learners

When preparing and delivering instruction the teacher can best accommodate the CLD learner by understanding the learner's state of mind, designing the presentation of new information by considering the context in which students learned it, and helping students recognize the value of what they have learned and its application.

UNDERSTANDING THE LEARNER'S STATE OF MIND

Would the people living in Amarillo, Texas, have the same state of mind as the people in New York City? Of course not, and so it goes that people from other countries will have a state of mind that is different than ours. Three suggestions include:

1. Students' actions need to be viewed through the eyes and circumstances of the learners' world. Judgments need to be suspended until the teacher understands the student's perspective and ordinary sociocultural behaviors.

2. As teachers we recognize students learn in a variety of ways. Make an effort to observe the CLD student and ascertain how he learns that may be different than you expected.

3. Be aware of and attend to student differences.

CONSIDER THE CONTEXT

In education it is a common practice to build on prior knowledge. However, when working with CLD students, teachers also need to be aware of the context in which the student learned it. This involves more than just linking new knowledge to prior knowledge. It involves the teacher incorporating how the prior knowledge was learned, being perceptive of the depth of student understanding, knowing the context of how it was learned, and appreciating the student's conceptualization of it. For CLD learners, teachers will need to guide students from the known to the unknown. For example, here in the United States a child may learn about jungle animals from children's literature books and cartoon figures. These experiences may leave the child without a true knowledge of the danger of these creatures and lead to unrealistic beliefs. However, a child from Myanmar may have a realistic appreciation of the danger of jungle animals from personal experiences in that environment.

VALUE OF NEW KNOWLEDGE

All students benefit from and value their education more by having opportunities to demonstrate their new skills, and by seeing real-life application. Teachers can increase student motivation by recognizing the student's effort and communicating to him his success and what he learned has value. Performance-based assessment allows students to demonstrate their new skills and convey to the teacher the breadth and depth of the child's comprehension and accomplishment. In many circumstances performance-based practices reveal the child's achievement better than a paper-pencil test. By teachers encouraging students look for real-life applications outside of school and share those events students' value of educational endeavors are likely to increase.

> "When a student knows he will be held accountable for learning it increases his engagement."
> —*Teri Bingham*

English Language Proficiency Standards

In order to increase CLD learners English language acquisition, English Language Proficiency Standards (ELPS) have been created.

§74.4. English Language Proficiency Standards

a. Introduction

   1. The English language proficiency standards in this section outline English language proficiency-level descriptors and student expectations for English language learners (ELLs). School districts shall implement this section as an integral part of each subject in the required curriculum. The English language proficiency standards are to be published along with the Texas Essential Knowledge and Skills (TEKS) for each subject in the required curriculum.

   2. In order for ELLs to be successful, they must acquire both social and academic language proficiency in English. Social language proficiency in English consists of the English needed for daily social interactions. Academic language proficiency consists of the English needed to think critically, understand and learn new concepts, process complex academic material, and interact and communicate in English academic settings.

   3. Classroom instruction that effectively integrates second language acquisition with quality content-area instruction ensures that ELLs acquire social and academic language proficiency in English, learn the knowledge and skills in the TEKS, and reach their full academic potential.

   4. Effective instruction in second language acquisition involves giving ELLs opportunities to listen, speak, read, and write at their current levels of English development while gradually increasing the linguistic complexity of the English they read and hear, and are expected to speak and write.

   5. The cross-curricular second language acquisition skills in subsection (c) of this section apply to ELLs in kindergarten-grade 12.

   6. The English language proficiency levels of beginning, intermediate, advanced, and advanced-high are not grade-specific. ELLs may exhibit different proficiency levels within the language domains of listening, speaking, reading, and writing. The proficiency-level descriptors outlined in subsection (d) of this section show the progression of second language acquisition from one proficiency level to the next and serves as a roadmap to help content area teachers instruct ELLs commensurate with students' linguistic needs.

b. School district responsibilities. In fulfilling the requirements of this section, school districts shall:

   1. identify the student's English language proficiency levels in the domains of listening, speaking, reading, and writing in accordance with the proficiency level descriptors for the beginning, intermediate, advanced, and advanced high levels delineated in subsection (d) of this section;

   2. provide instruction in the knowledge and skills of the foundation and enrichment curriculum in a manner that is linguistically accommodated (communicated, sequenced, and scaffolded) commensurate with the student's levels of English language proficiency to ensure that the student learns the knowledge and skills in the required curriculum;

   3. provide content-based instruction including the cross-curricular second language acquisition essential knowledge and skills in subsection (c) of this section in a manner that is linguistically accommodated to help the student acquire English language proficiency; and

   4. provide intensive and ongoing foundational second language acquisition instruction to ELLs in Grade 3 or higher who are at the beginning or intermediate level of English language proficiency in listening, speaking, reading, and/or writing as determined by the state's English language proficiency assessment system. These ELLs require focused, targeted, and systematic second language acquisition instruction to provide them with the foundation of English language vocabulary, grammar, syntax, and English mechanics necessary to support content-based instruction and accelerated learning of English.

Expectations of Teachers Regarding English Language Proficiency Standards (ELPS)

The primary goal of the ELPS is to make content comprehensible to students and build their academic language. The four domains teachers are accountable for documenting initial skill and progress include *listening*, *speaking*, *reading*, and *writing*. The four proficiency-level descriptors (PLDs) teachers are required to use in documenting the ELPS are *beginning*, *intermediate*, *advanced*, and *advanced-high*. These four proficiency-level descriptors are to be used in all subject areas in the required curriculum at all grade levels. The proficiency levels are not grade-specific and the four ELP domains are independent of one another. For example, a child may be identified as advanced for speaking, but intermediate at writing. Also, a first grader may be advanced-high in speaking but a high school age student may be a beginner.

ELPS are intended to help students become proficient in both social and academic language. Teachers are expected to provide daily social interactions for students and incorporate English language acquisition with quality academic instruction. Quality instruction of the curriculum involves linguistic accommodation using dynamic *communication*, appropriate *sequencing*, and deliberate *scaffolding*.

1. Communication—To be effective with ELL learners the teacher needs to communicate in ways other than just verbal. Dynamic teachers use demonstrations, actions, objects, pictures, motions, experiments, explorations, visual and auditory aids, discovery opportunities, hands-on activities, and student-centered experiences.

2. Sequencing—Be certain to use a developmentally appropriate sequence and start from what the ELL student knows and how he or she learned it.

3. Scaffolding—to scaffold you need to be aware of students' prior knowledge and use that as a springboard for new skills and knowledge. Scaffolding means to systematically and progressively provide adequate support during the learning process.

Student Expectations and ELL Domains

As a teacher you will be accountable for identifying each child's proficiency level according to the PLDs. You will be responsible in documenting each ELL in the following four domains:

1. Listening
2. Speaking
3. Reading
4. Writing

Proficiency-Level Descriptors for ELL Students

1. Beginning
2. Intermediate
3. Advanced
4. Advanced-high

For more information, go to www.elltx.org/proficiency_level_descriptors.html. This website provides detailed information about each of the PLDs.

Sheltered Instruction Observation Protocol (SIOP) Model

The purpose of the Sheltered Instruction Observation Protocol (SIOP) model is to help teachers provide a supportive learning environment for English Language Learners (ELL's). During the planning stages as a teacher is mindful of each element, she will enhance the learning opportunities for all students in her class. Although the tenets of SIOP are effective for all students, they are essential for ELL's to be successful learners.

The eight components of the checklist for sheltered instruction are preparation, building background, comprehensible input, learning strategies, interaction, practice/application, lesson delivery, and review/assessment (Echevarria, Vogt, & Short, 2008).

Lesson Preparation

During lesson preparation, the teacher identifies both the content objective that the students are expected to learn and the academic language objective that is inherent in the lesson objective. As students become familiar with the objectives, they progress toward greater fluency in English. During this planning time, teachers want to consider supplemental resources, activities that bring meaning to the new skill or concept, and design opportunities for verbal interactions during the instruction.

Building Background

Because many CLD learners are unfamiliar with American culture, effective teachers engineer ways to build background knowledge that connects the curriculum with the student's previous learning and experience. While we know the importance of assisting CLD students with learning academic language, these diverse students benefit most when teachers mindfully generate and provide opportunities for the students to orally practice new vocabulary words.

Comprehensible Input

During instruction, teachers provide comprehensible input when they present information in such a way that the ELL's understand. This input relates to rate of speech, simple sentence structure, clear instructions with ample demonstrations of each step of a process or procedure, and a visible finished model. Input also involves being a *dynamic* teacher using models, visual aids, gestures, actions, objects, pictures, and writing down key points. Use of native language support resources also cultivate increased CLD students school achievement.

Learning Strategies

The goal for all students is to become problem solvers who use critical thinking skills or higher-order thinking. For this to occur, students need to practice a variety of learning strategies through discovery activities and creating projects that requires critical thought. Scaffolding instruction provides guidance and support as a student learns and practices the new task or knowledge. As the student masters the new skill or knowledge, the teacher replaces the supports with new ones relevant to the new level or concept. Ultimately, we want ELL's to function independently of the teacher. Teachers who ask higher-order thinking questions and provide complex activities to foster differing depths of knowledge (Webb, 2002) increase students critical thinking skills.

Interaction

Learning takes place as students interact with each other and with the teacher about the academic objective. Learning accelerates when diverse students are given opportunities to rehearse their oral language with their peers in small groups and in whole class discussions. These students also need to practice language functions, such as asking questions, explaining their viewpoint, gaining clarification, and evaluating ideas and opinions. (Be sensitive to a student's cultural norms as they acclimate to their new environment.)

Practice and Application

Practice makes permanent. Therefore, CLD learners benefit when given class time to practice new material with hands-on resources while they employ language skills: reading, writing, listening, and speaking. (Be sure to have students engage in both the social language objectives and the academic language objectives.)

Lesson Delivery

This component addresses the classroom instruction being delivered. Effective, meaningful lessons are usually preceded by thoughtful planning. Quality instruction involves a myriad of elements; however, for the purpose of SIOP lesson delivery, effective lessons are those that have met both objectives, use adequate pacing, provide engaging student-oriented learning activities, and are supported by established classroom management routines and procedures.

Review and Assessment

Because it seems that there is never enough time to get everything completed in class, we need to follow the philosophy that *less is more*. Instead of trying to cram in one more fact or skill at the end of a class, it behooves teachers to review the key concepts and vocabulary taught that day. This may help the students internalize the new learning, thus, increasing retention and recall for the following day. As a result, teachers may spend less time the next day reviewing (or reteaching), and instead, be able to build on the prior day's lesson. Consequently, less content results in more curricula being taught. Teachers who frequently check for understanding throughout the lesson increase the likelihood of students comprehending and processing information. This allows the teacher to routinely provide feedback to students of how well they understand the new task or knowledge. Formal, summative assessments can be used to measure not only the new skills but also language acquisition.

Teachers who use the SIOP model for planning their classroom instruction will increase the likelihood of diverse learners being successful. The decisions made by the teacher attending to each SIOP component will enhance the classroom environment to make it a place where all students can achieve academic success.

© baldyrgan, 2014, Used under license of Shutterstock, Inc.

TIPS FOR COMPETENCY 2: MULTICULTURALISM AND EDUCATION

Diversity

1. Be aware that social interaction patterns vary by culture.
2. Teachers must model appropriate and respectful behavior for *all* students and insist on respectful interactions among students.
3. The best way to foster appreciation of diversity is to have the students work together in a productive group setting. This allows them to get to know each other in a comfortable setting.
4. Be aware of the impact gender stereotyping has on students' self-confidence.
5. Classroom communication skills vary from culture to culture for both verbal and nonverbal communications.
6. Appreciate culture and know individuals differ within a culture regarding interest, strengths, weaknesses, and language.
7. Be familiar with the different ways cultures communicate, both verbally and nonverbally.
8. When a student demonstrates racism do not send an implied message that it is okay by not responding. Address racial comments appropriately. Try not to single out a student, yet don't overlook it either.
9. Communicate to all that inappropriate comments will not be tolerated.
10. To teach to diverse populations make all examples familiar and relevant to all students.
11. Know your students and use examples from their world, interests, hobbies, etc.
12. To increase student participation in a diverse class, level the playing field by introducing new curriculum during instruction. Make it new knowledge for everyone.

English as a Second Language

1. When you have an ESL student the ESL teacher needs to know your lesson objectives and be receptive to the ESL teacher's ideas of how to best accommodate these students.

2. For ESL students meet frequently with the ESL teacher to discuss how to best adapt future lessons for the students to be successful.

Miscellaneous

1. For at-risk students the teacher needs to integrate corrections into the instruction. Build success during the initial stages of learning.

2. Before being critical of others' ideas, first examine your own beliefs.

3. To reach all students use a variety of learning modalities.

4. Be aware that cooperative learning groups help foster appreciation of diversity.

5. Always privately address racial comments (slurs). Do *not* ignore them. This gives the tacit impression that those comments are okay or even worse, that you agree with them.

SOCIOECONOMIC STATUS

Like gender, socioeconomic status or social class is a microculture that has a profound impact on students' background and cultural knowledge. Ruby Payne's (200) work on the culture of poverty is especially helpful for the classroom teacher. Payne found that students from low-income backgrounds understand how to survive intelligently in the context of their community culture but do not have the background knowledge necessary to function acceptably in a public school context. Clarifying expectations for appropriate behavior as well as the parameters of assignments help students to become more successful academically. Consequently, lessons grounded in situated cognition and apprenticeship models are especially helpful here. Students from all income levels are capable of excelling academically if they are given the opportunities to do so.

However, research has shown that many educators have lower expectations for low-income students than they have for students from more affluent backgrounds. For instance, Anyon (1981) evaluated curriculums of various elementary schools (e.g., working class, middle class, affluent professional, and elite executive) and found substantial differences in their quality and emphases. In the working-class school, the curriculum consisted of fragmented, decontextualized pieces of information. Much of that which was considered learning consisted of drill-and-skill activities with few connections to conceptual knowledge. Worksheets were common, and most seatwork activities required students to work alone. There were few collaborative activities. The instructional practices focused on transmission forms of knowledge at low cognitive levels, and students' views were not valued. Most teachers in the working-class school had low expectations for their students. The expectations of teachers—whether they are high or low—become self-fulfilling prophecies and have a profound impact on students' academic self-concepts (Good & Brophy, 2000).

In contrast, the curriculums of the more affluent schools concentrated on conceptual knowledge and on interpreting the significance of key ideas. Teachers required critical thinking and higher cognitive tasks and employed a wider variety of instructional methods than those used in the working-class school. They were not as rigid in an authoritarian way and were more inclined to have positive interactions with students. Students in the more affluent schools excelled academically in contrast to the students in the working-class school who were offered a weak curriculum and little encouragement for academic achievement.

At the secondary levels there also are disparities between the curricula of socioeconomic groups. For instance, studies by Oakes (1992) and Metz (1990) have found that there are three common tracks for most secondary students: vocational, general, and college preparatory. The researchers found that the lower education track primarily consists of students from lower-status backgrounds. This is problematic because the curriculums of the lower tracks at the secondary level typically emphasize few higher cognitive skills and cover less material than is taught in the general and college-preparatory tracks. Consequently, the levels of achievement between the lower and upper tracks become wider each year.

On the other hand, James Comer's (1995) work in improving the achievement levels of traditionally lower-achieving schools and Jaime Escalante's (Escalante & Dirmann, 1990) success in mathematics programs at Garfield High School have shown that students from low-income families can excel academically. Low expectations, not the lack of ability, are largely responsible for the lack of academic achievement of students from low-income backgrounds (Anyon, 1997; Good & Brophy, 2000).

LANGUAGE

Other aspects of cultural diversity concern differences in language and dialects. Many students enter kindergarten or the first grade speaking languages or dialects different from those of their teachers. In some cases teachers have shown preferences for students whose dialects are the same as their own; consequently, teachers must be aware of their own biases (Gollnick & Chinn, 2002). A child's dialect has no relation to his or her innate intelligence or ability and willingness to learn. Children merely learn to speak those dialects they are exposed to during their first few years of life. Language is an important aspect of culture, and respect for differences in languages and dialects prevents linguistic ethnocentrism.

In our increasingly diverse schools, teaching students about linguistic diversity is important (Banks, 2002). Representations of linguistic diversity ought to be employed by teachers. For instance, teachers may present different types of folktales from various cultures. In addition, teachers can present a variety of common words in English adopted from other languages, and students can learn to count in another language such as Spanish (Gay, 2000).

Bilingual and English as a second language programs are becoming more common with the increase of non-English-speaking students entering first grade. If implemented well, these programs have enhanced students' abilities to speak, read, and write English at higher levels of literacy (Bennett, 2003). To determine whether or not a student qualifies for either a bilingual or English as a second language program, specific guidelines must be followed. For example, a Home Language Survey, which documents the dominant language spoken at a student's home, is completed by the student or a parent. Next, an oral proficiency exam is administered by the school district. If it is determined that a student is an ELL, the student is referred to the Language Proficiency Assessment Committee (LPAC) for review. After a student's needs are assessed by the LPAC and recommendations are made for placement in either bilingual or English as a second language classes, a parent must approve the committee's recommendations for placement into these programs.

Classroom teachers can help ELLs by employing a variety of collaborative learning strategies (e.g., reciprocal teaching or cooperative learning) to complete academic tasks. Collaborative activities provide ELLs with opportunities to discuss key concepts with other students who may be fluent in his or her primary language. Also, it is important for teachers to allow ELLs to use their primary language to discuss concepts. Language is a tool that enables us to express our understanding of both lower and higher cognitive ideas (Vygotsky, 1978). If ELLs are unable to complete complex problem-solving activities using English, they need opportunities to use their primary language to develop higher cognitive abilities in disciplines such as mathematics. All languages and dialects need to be respected, and students whose primary language is not English need equal opportunities for academic success (Gollnick & Chinn, 2002).

EXCEPTIONALITY

An important microculture of the school context is exceptionality. The Education for All Handicapped Children Act (PL 94–142) and the Individuals with Disabilities Act (IDEA Act; PL 101–476) mandated that all exceptional children have the right to an education free from discrimination resulting from their disabilities. Public Law 94–142 and PL 101–476 require that students with disabilities are mainstreamed or placed in the "least restrictive environment." In other words, exceptional students ought to be provided opportunities to participate in a regular classroom context. Before PL 94–142 was enacted, most exceptional students were segregated from mainstream classrooms and often shunned by society (Gersten & Baker, 2001).

However, much of the discrimination against exceptional children has been ameliorated by these federal laws. School districts are required to accommodate students for a wide variety of disabilities such as autism, mental retardation, physical impairments, behavioral disorders, or other impairments (e.g., visual, hearing, or speech). Support services also may include transportation for students with physical impairments or psychologists for students with behavioral disorders. In addition, Section 54 of the Vocational Rehabilitation Act provides special services for other disabilities such as dyslexia or attention-deficit disorder (ADD).

Before a student is placed in special education and receives support services, a thorough evaluation is conducted after an initial referral is made by a parent or teacher (Gersten & Baker, 2001). If a parent gives consent for testing, a thorough examination of all aspects of the presumed disability is given by trained personnel such as an educational psychologist. Within 30 days after testing results are available, an Admission, Review, and Dismissal (ARD) Committee meeting is held. ARD Committees are comprised of classroom teachers, special education teachers, one or more parents, assessment personnel, and a representative from administration. Schools are required to have at least one ARD meeting (also called IEP meetings) a year for a child identified as special needs and receiving services. As a teacher with a child with special needs in your class you will be part of the educational team and expected to attend the ARD meeting. It is here that the Individual Education Plan (IEP) document will be created, reviewed, and updated. This legally binding document specifies the goals and objectives for individual students, along with necessary accommodations and modifications the teachers are required to make in order to help the student be successful.

The committee's primary responsibilities are to determine whether or not a student is eligible for special education, and if the student is eligible, then an appropriate placement is made with the necessary services. An IEP is required for all special education students. Every IEP includes specific information about a child's education such as what services a child will receive and when the services will begin and end. In addition, a child's short- and long-term instructional goals as well as the methods used to assess instructional goals are documented. A student's IEP can only be changed during the ARD meeting; a teacher cannot arbitrarily set goals and objectives for a child. If the teacher sees a need to update an IEP he can begin the process to hold an ARD meeting; he or she does not have to wait until the next scheduled meeting.

Information regarding children with special needs must remain confidential and teachers must only discuss issues with others that are currently on the child's educational support team. Outside this sphere, teachers must not identify a child by name or any characteristic that leads another person to know who the student is. For example, suppose the child's previous year's teacher was highly successful and the teacher of the student this year would like to receive ideas of how to best support the student. Do not use the child's name or any identifying characteristic, such as a child with a traumatic brain injury or cerebral palsy. Simply ask for ideas of how to help children be more successful in word decoding during reading. Or ask how the teacher scaffolds his instruction for the class when learning fractions. These answers could easily be applied for many struggling students.

As in most professions there is jargon or a professional vocabulary. One of these vocabulary words regarding special education is the word *identified*. This refers to a student identified with special needs and all that it entails must be adhered to by the teacher. Information regarding these identified children is confidential and many laws and regulations are in place to protect the child and ensure a positive, successful educational experience.

It is always a good idea for the regular education teacher to contact the special education teacher about ways to help children with special needs be successful, and to remedy organization problems a child might be having. Keep in mind, teachers who are certified in special education have received expert training on strategies and techniques to help children with special needs in a variety of cognitive and behavioral ways. Regular education teachers will profit by teaming up with special education teachers to benefit all children.

Giftedness

Another aspect of exceptionality is giftedness. However, because there are no federally mandated definitions of giftedness, the identification of gifted students is decided by local or state guidelines. Many people acknowledge that gifted children have exceptional talents in intellectual activities, academics, creativity, or leadership. Nevertheless, because giftedness is difficult to define, continued debate about that which connotes giftedness is likely to change in the future (Subotnic, 1997)

In Texas the criteria to determine giftedness is determined at local levels, and various assessments can be used to determine giftedness. Many schools use various academic achievement and IQ tests; however, other assessments such as student portfolios, work samples, or interviews are used in some cases. Programs for gifted students are mandated by Texas law for K-grade 12. At the elementary level gifted students typically (1) are in self-contained classes for the gifted, (2) are pulled out of their regular classes and sent to a teacher for the gifted during the regular school day, or (3) stay with their regular teachers who have been trained to teach gifted students. At the secondary levels, most gifted programs consist of one or more classes specifically designed for gifted students.

Public schools have programs to meet the needs of exceptional children. During the past 30 years, many improvements have been made to enhance the education of exceptional students. However, certain inequities raise questions about ways that students are identified for special education and gifted programs. For example, there are a disproportionate number of boys, low-income students, and ethnic minorities in special education class, most gifted students are from European American or upper-middle-class backgrounds (Oakes, 1992). The answers to these questions are extremely complex, and much more research needs to be conducted to study this trend. Nevertheless, these concerns do not negate the increase of opportunities for exceptional children to receive quality educational experiences.

CONCLUSION

The world is now a very small place, and virtually every ethnic group is represented in the American public school system. Consequently, teachers must expand their knowledge base of cultural differences each year and understand how culture affects the school context so that they are more able to design culturally responsive lessons to enhance student learning and positive verbal and nonverbal interaction. If educators value the cultural backgrounds of students and have high expectations for their academic achievement, then students will have more opportunities to succeed academically and socially in schools. In contrast, a lack of cultural understanding of students' backgrounds undermines the instructional effectiveness of conscientious teachers. Therefore, teachers must acquire an understanding of students' cultural backgrounds so all students have opportunities for valuable educational experiences.

Prework

Prework Assignment for CLD #2

To be turned in the next class day.

Explain eight ways of creating an educational climate to optimize learning for CLD learners.

Prework Assignment for CLD #3

To be turned in the next class day.

Be ready to discuss the necessary planning considerations for CLD learners.

> "It is the office of the school environment to . . . see to it that each individual gets an opportunity to escape from the limitations of the social group in which he was born, and to come into living contact with a broader environment." —*John Dewey*

When planning, teachers need to be keenly aware of his or her students' backgrounds (sociocultural, linguistic, cognitive, and academic) in order to make the best decisions possible.

Explain the Meaning of Each Below.

The student's background should influence the Lesson Planning by being considered for:

1. Content objectives
2. Language objectives
3. Grouping configurations

CLASS ACTIVITIES

Classroom Activity #1: "Don't Judge Me Because . . ." snowball fight

On a piece of paper have each student anonymously write things they have been judged about. For example, a student might write, "Don't judge me because I am male, I am Muslim, I come from poverty." Another student might write, "Don't judge me because I am a single mom at 19, I am fat, I am young, and I don't have a job." Have the students go into a large open area (like the hallway) and on the count of three wad up the paper and throw it. Pick up another paper snowball and throw it. After a minute-long snowball fight have each student get a snowball and return to the classroom.

Ask the students to read their paper snowball and then have them report the responses of those that 1. Surprised the reader. 2. Made the reader feel sad. 3. The reader thought 'me too'. Conclude by pointing out that we all feel judged and many of us feel similarly to one another.

Classroom Activity #2: YouTube clip "Dog with a Bone" by Cata Triple X

This clip shows a dog attacking his own paw because he thinks it is going to steal his bone. Use this clip to discuss how we all make false assumptions and how ridiculous they can be; just like the dog making a false assumption about his own paw.

Classroom Activity #3

Divide the class into eight groups. Each group discusses and reports on one of the following questions. Have each group write their response on a large sheet of paper with markers. The instructor acts as facilitator.

1. What are my assumptions about CLD learners' home environments?
2. What are my assumptions about CLD learners' language abilities?
3. What are my assumptions about CLD learners' academic potential?
4. How do my assumptions influence my expectations for CLD or other students?
5. What do you believe about the parents of CLD learners?
6. How do non-CLD students and CLD students get along together?
7. What should be done about CLD learners' education?
8. Is it fair for regular classroom teachers, without specialized training, to teach CLD learners?
   a. Is it fair to the teacher?
   b. Is it fair to the students?

Classroom Activity #4

In small groups have students discuss and list what they would want to know about their future students. Detail what to put on their biocard for future use.

HOMEWORK

Assignment 1

Interview at least two students of color about their school experiences, home cultures, and preferred styles of learning. How does this information help you to provide more culturally relevant lessons? Write a short essay to explain your ideas, and use current research to support your views.

Assignment 2

Interview at least two teachers of color about their school experiences, home cultures, and preferred styles of learning. How have their experiences as students and teachers influenced the ways that they teach? Write a short essay to explain your ideas, and use current research to support your views.

Assignment 3

Require your students to present a research project on cultural holidays and make sure students explain why the holidays are important to those cultural groups that celebrate them.

Sample Test Questions

1. Ms. Jenkins wants all of her students to value their own culture while appreciating the macroculture. The term that best describes this process is

    a. acculturation.

    b. stereotyping.

    c. multiracism.

    d. assimilation.

2. Ms. O'Neill knows that the family backgrounds of her students are very diverse and often different than her own family and of those of her closest friends. She is aware that she must respond to each family respectfully and not view cultural differences as deficits that prevent learning. Which of the following beliefs would *not* be helpful in accomplishing this goal?

    a. All families—like all cultures—have strengths.

    b. Children from low-income backgrounds are not able to learn as much as those students from high-income backgrounds.

    c. Children consider their own family environment to be normal.

    d. A teacher's job is to encourage children from all backgrounds.

3. Mr. Henry, a fifth-year teacher, teaches first-grade students. He knows that he has good teaching skills and that his students are learning effectively. However, he is concerned that he will not con-tinually improve the knowledge and skills associated with children with special needs. Mr. Henry

read an article about "least-restrictive environment." What is the major provision of "least-restrictive environment"?

a. Students with special needs are entitled to be mainstreamed when it will improve their education.

b. Students with special needs should never be restrained.

c. Students with special needs are entitled to participate in physical education classes with regular students.

d. Students with special needs may participate in all athletic programs.

Answers

1. **A is the correct answer.** An acculturation model emphasizes the importance of respecting cultural differences.

   B is not correct. Stereotyping is something to avoid because it often causes tensions among various groups.

   C is not correct. Racism of any sort causes problems and inequities.

   D is not correct. In contrast to the acculturation model, the assimilation model discourages people from retaining and having pride in their cultural heritage.

2. A is not correct. If teachers are to respect cultural differences, they need to recognize the strengths of every culture.

   B is the correct answer. This is something teachers ought to avoid. Assuming that students from low-income backgrounds are not able to learn effectively undermines their academic progress; assumptions like these are destructive.

   C is not correct. Teachers need to understand that students consider their home cultures as natural and normal.

   D is not correct. Students from all backgrounds need encouragement.

3. **A is the correct answer.** PL 94–142 mandates mainstreaming when it will enhance the learning and educational opportunities of students.

   B is not correct. Mainstreaming has nothing to do with restraining students, which is problematic.

   C is not correct. Although students with disabilities may be mainstreamed in physical education classes, such placements are not always appropriate.

   D is not correct. Students with disabilities participate in athletic activities; however, mainstreaming pertains primarily to a classroom context.

REFERENCES

Anyon, J. (1981). Social class and school achievement. *Curriculum Inquiry, 11*(1), 3–42.

Banks, J. A. (2002). *An introduction to multicultural education* (3rd ed.). Boston: Allyn & Bacon.

Baruth, L. G., & Manning, M. L. (1992). *Multicultural education of children and adolescents*. Boston: Allyn & Bacon.

Bennett, C. I. (2003). *Comprehensive multicultural education: Theory and practice* (5th ed.). Boston: Pearson Education.

Collins, A., Brown, J.S., & Newman, S.E. (1989). Cognitive Apprenticeship: Teaching the Craft of Reading, Writing and Mathematics! In L.B. Resnick (ed.) *Knowing, Learning, and Instruction: Essay in Honor of Robert Glasser Hillsdale,*

NJ: Erlbaum, ad in Brown, J.S. Collins, A., and Duguid, P.(1989). Situated Cognition and the Culture of Learning. *Educational Researcher*, 18(1), 32–42.

Comer, J. (1995). *School power: Implications for an intervention project*. New York: Free Press.

Cornbleth, C., Davis, O. L., & Button, C. B. (1974). Expectations for pupil achievement and teacher-pupil interaction. *Social Education, 38*, 54–58.

Cushner, K., McClelland, A., & Safford, P. (2003). *Human diversity in education: An integrative approach (4th ed.)*. New York: McGraw-Hill.

Darling-Hammond, L. (2001). Inequality and access to knowledge. In J. A. Banks & C. A. M. Banks (Eds.), *Handbook of research on multicultural education* (pp. 465–484). San Francisco: Jossey-Bass.

Diller, J. V., & Moule, J. (2005). *Cultural competence: A primer for educators*. Belmont, CA: ThomsomWadsworth.

Echevarria, J., Vogt, M. E., & Short, D. (2008). *Making content comprehensible to English language learners: The SIOP model*. Boston: Allyn & Bacon.

Escalante, J., & Dirmann, J. (1990). The Jamie Escalante math program. *Journal of Negro Education, 59*(30), 407–423.

Gay, G. (2000). *Culturally responsive teaching: Theory, research, and practice*. New York: Teachers College Press.

Gollnick, D. M., & Chinn, P. C. (2002). *Multicultural education in a pluralistic society* (6th ed.). Upper Saddle River, NJ: Merrill/Prentice Hall.

Gersten, R., & Baker, S. (2001). Teaching expressive writing to students with learning disabilities: A meta-analysis. *Elementary School Journal, 101*(3), 251–272.

Good, T., & Brophy, J. (2000). *Looking in classrooms* (8th ed.). New York: Longman.Herrera, S.G. (2010). *Biography-Driven Culturally Responsive Teaching*. New York: Teachers College Press.

Jovanovic, J., & King, S. (1998). Boys and girls in performance-based science classroom: Who's doing the performing? *American Educational Research Journal, 35*(3), 447–496.

Lave, J. (1991). Situating learning in communities of practice. In L. B. Resnick, J. M. Levine, & S. D. Teasley (Eds.), Perspectives on socially shared cognition (pp. 63–82). Washington, DC: American Psychological Association. McCarty, T. L., Wallace, S., Lynch, R. H., & Bennally, A. (1991). Classroom inquiry and Navajo learning styles: A call for reassessment. Anthropology and Education Quarterly, 22, 42–59.

Metz, M. H. (1990). How social class differences shapes teachers' work. In M. W. McLaughlin, J. E. Talbert, & N. Bascia (Eds.), The contexts of teaching in secondary schools: Teachers' realities (pp. 40–107). New York: Teachers College Press.

Nieto, S. (2004). *Affirming diversity: The sociopolitical context of multicultural education* (4th ed.). Boston: Pearson Education.

Nieto, S. (1999). *The light in their eyes: Creating multicultural learning communities*. New York: Teachers College Press.

Oakes, J. (1992). Can tracking research inform practice? Educational Researcher, 21(4), 12–21.

Payne, R.K. (2001). A framework for understanding poverty. Highlands, TX: aha! Process.

Rist, R. (1970). Student social class and teacher expectations: Self-fulfilling prophecy in ghetto education. *Harvard Education Review, 40*(3), 411–451.

Streitmatter, J. (1994). *Toward gender equity in the classroom: Everyday teachers' beliefs and practices*. Albany: State University of New York Press.

Sadker, M., Sadker, D., & Klein, S. (1991). The issue of gender in elementary and secondary education. In G. Grant (Ed.), *Review of Research in education* (Vol. 17, pp. 269–334). Washington, DC: American Educational Research Association.

Shade, B. J. (1989). The influence of perceptual development on cognitive style: Cross ethnic comparisons. *Early Child Development and Care, 51*, 137–155.

Spaulding, A., & O'Hair, M. J. (2000). Public relations in a communication context: Listening, nonverbal, and conflict-resolution skills. In T. J. Kowalski (Ed.), *Public relations in schools* (2nd ed., pp. 137–161). Prospect Heights, IL: Longman.

Subotnik, R. (1997). Teaching gifted students in a multicultural society. In J. Banks & C.

Banks (Eds.), *Multicultural education: Issues and perspective* (3rd ed., pp. 361–382). Boston: Allyn & Bacon.

U.S. Bureau of the Census. (2000). *USA Statistics in Brief: Population and vital statistics*. Washington, DC: U. S. Department of Commerce. Available at http://www.census.gov/stab/www/popart.htm.

U. S. Department of Education. (2000). *Digest of education statistics, 1999.*

Washington, DC: National Center for Educational Statistics.

Vygotsky, L. (1978). *Mind in society: The development of higher psychological*

processes. Cambridge, MA: Harvard University Press.

Webb, N. L. (2002). Depth-of-knowledge levels for four content areas. Language Arts.

Willingham, W., & Cole, N. (1997). *Gender and fair assessment.* Mahwah, NJ: Erlbaum.

Zeichner, K. M., & Hoeft, K. (1996). Teacher socialization for cultural diversity. In J.

Sikula, T. J. Buttery, & E. Guyton (Eds.), *Handbook of research on teacher education* (2nd ed., pp. 525–547). New York: Macmillan.

Websites

http://www.edchange.org/multicultural/teachers.html
Multicultural Pavilion, a site dedicated to equity and diversity in education.

http://www.newhorizons.org/index.html
New Horizons for Learning, a quarterly journal.

http://www.emtech.net/multicultural_education.html
Multicultural education, a wealth of links to many sites about educating immigrant children.

http://www.library.csustan.edu/lboyer/multicultural/lesson2.htm
Lesson plans with a multicultural focus.

http://www.ncrel.org/sdrs/areas/issues/educatrs/presrvce/pe3lk5.htm
16 Key Elements of Effective Teacher Education for Diversity

http://www.emtech.net/multicultural_education.html
Links to multicultural education sites by country.

http://www.edchange.org/multicultural/papers/buildingblocks.html
Building Blocks: The First Steps of Creating a Multicultural Classroom by Larri Fish of Siena College

http://www.education.gsw.edu/johnson/MulticulturalEducation.htm
Articles: Culture, Multiculturalism and Pluralism: The Goals of Multicultural Education

www.kidlink.org/KIDPROJ/MCC
A searchable database of holidays celebrated by peoples around the world.

http://www.child-reading-tips.com/multicultural-books-for-young-children.htm
Multicultural Books for Young Children
http://www.infography.com/content/996029633095.ht
A professor whose research specialty is teaching art in multicultural classrooms recommends these sources.

Competency 3 _

Designing Effective Planning

Teri Bingham, EdD
West Texas A&M University

Competency 3: The teacher understands procedures for designing effective and coherent instruction as well as assessment based on appropriate learning goals and objectives.

The beginning teacher:

A. Understands the significance of the Texas Essential Knowledge and Skills (TEKS) and of prerequisite knowledge and skills in determining instructional goals and objectives.

B. Uses appropriate criteria to evaluate the appropriateness of learning goals and objectives (e.g., clarity; relevance; significance; age-appropriateness; ability to be assessed; responsiveness to students' current skills and knowledge, background, needs, and interests; alignment with campus and district goals).

C. Uses assessment to analyze students' strengths and needs, evaluate teacher effectiveness, and guide instructional planning for individuals and groups.

D. Understands the connection between various components of the Texas statewide assessment program, the TEKS, and instruction and analyzes data from state and other assessments using common statistical measures to help identify students' strengths and needs.

E. Demonstrates knowledge of various types of materials and resources (including technological resources and resources outside the school) that may be used to enhance student learning and engagement and evaluates the appropriateness of specific materials and resources for use in particular situations to address specific purposes and to meet varied student needs.

F. Plans lessons and structures units so that activities progress in a logical sequence and support stated instructional goals.

G. Plans learning experiences that provide students with developmentally appropriate opportunities to explore content from integrated and varied perspectives (e.g., by presenting thematic units that incorporate different disciplines, providing intradisciplinary and interdisciplinary instruction, designing instruction that enables students to work cooperatively, providing multicultural viewpoints, encouraging students' application of knowledge and skills to the world beyond the school).

H. Allocates time appropriately within lessons and units, including providing adequate opportunities for students to engage in reflection, self-assessment, and closure.

KEY TERMS

Bloom's taxonomy
checking for understanding
convergent questions
Depth of knowledge (DOK)

diagnosis
divergent questions
evaluation
instructional objectives

lesson design
Madeline Hunter
task analysis
5-E model

Failing to plan is planning to fail. We would never board an airplane if we thought that the pilot did not know how to fly the plane. We would never agree to a surgery if we thought that the surgeon did not know the proper procedure. Therefore, as teachers we need to know our craft and plan our lessons so that our students get the most out of it, and we need to encourage them to meet their potential.

Teachers in Texas need to understand the importance of the Texas Essential Knowledge and Skills (TEKS) and use them in accordance with their campus and district goals when planning their lessons. The significant components of planning include diagnosis, task analysis, instructional objective, Bloom's taxonomy, lesson design, and effective examples. Each component is thoroughly discussed.

DIAGNOSIS

Suppose you were not feeling well and you went to your family doctor. Upon entering the room, the doctor greeted you, wrote out a prescription, handed it to you, and said good-bye. How would you feel about this encounter? You would probably have some concerns that the doctor neglected to try and find out the problem that brought you in, your symptoms, what you have already tried, and from there determine a protocol. Hopefully, this would be followed with another appointment to assess how well the protocol is working and to make necessary changes. Yet, as teachers, we sometimes take this

© Maridav, 2014, Used under license of Shutterstock, Inc.

approach as we begin each unit with a prepared lesson and teach it to completion without ever "diagnosing" the students. Teachers need to first ascertain what the students know, don't know, and the misinformation they have before determining the starting point of the lesson.

In the classroom, the purpose of diagnosis for the teacher is to determine the students' knowledge base, misinformation, gaps, holes, and where the prior learning leaves off. By diagnosing the students' knowledge, the teacher can decide what needs to be reviewed, what holes need to be filled, what misinformation needs to be corrected during the unit, and where to start teaching the new information.

Conscientious teachers diagnose the students at three distinct points for each lesson. **Diagnosis** is when a teacher identifies the extent of the students' prior knowledge and determines where to start teaching the new material. **Checking for understanding** is peppered throughout the lesson. **Evaluation** is used to determine what the students know at the conclusion of the lesson, chapter, or unit. Evaluation is usually used as a score in the grade book.

Before starting a new lesson, the teacher needs to diagnose students to ascertain what they already know, what they don't know, and what they know incorrectly. From this, the teacher knows where to begin planning the lessons.

It is advisable to monitor learning while teaching the new knowledge or skill. This allows the teacher to check for understanding in order to resolve any possible misunderstanding during the learning process. The purpose of checking for understanding is to determine if the students comprehend the new learning, which will result in increased correct learning. There are several ways to ascertain whether or not the students are keeping up with the lesson. Some techniques include, but are not limited to, asking questions, facilitating a dialogue among students, spot-checking student work, signaling responses, using response cards, and small-group discussion with a spokesperson sharing the groups' main ideas afterward.

Checking for understanding, the teacher is faced with deciding what to do with the feedback. Here are some guidelines to follow:

1. If the students understand, then the teacher should continue teaching. We have all had the experience, as students, when the class easily catches onto the new material but the teacher continues her diatribe until the students are disengaged and disinterested. Avoid this by progressing at an appropriate pace as long as your learners are keeping up with you. Suppose you have taught your students how to add fractions with a common denominator. When you begin teaching subtraction build on the prior knowledge of whole-number addition and the need for a common denominator. The learner may quickly catch on and need less lecture time. Subsequently, it is appropriate for the teacher to move on.

2. If the students are hesitant or reluctant with the new material, they need more practice in order to increase their confidence in the new knowledge or skill. Keeping with our scenario of adding fractions, suppose you have taught the skill, but the students are reluctant to begin their seatwork. Clearly, they need a few more modeled practice problems facilitated by the teacher to build their confidence.

3. If the students are confused, they need a review of the specific area that is misunderstood. It is important for teachers to identify the specific area where the students got lost. Go back and reteach just that part. Seldom does a whole lesson need to be retaught. Furthermore, it is critical for the teacher to reteach the material in the way originally presented and not to fall into the trap of showing the students an alternative way, a shortcut, or an easier way. Avoid reteaching a different way during the initial stages of learning. The students are still trying to figure out the first way it was taught and the new information gets confused with the original.

4. If the students are frustrated, overwhelmed, discouraged, confused, or checked out, the teacher needs to recognize this, acknowledge the students for their effort, and indicate that as a class they will set it aside for now and come back to it later. The purpose for handling it in this fashion is to move the class from having an "unpleasant feeling" to a "pleasant feeling" where learning is more likely to happen. Of course, the teacher needs to be prepared to come back to the material later with the same approach so as not to confuse the learner but to enhance the lesson. Let it be a red flag to the teacher if the class is frequently getting frustrated and confused. You may need to examine your instruction in order to identify the problem. Look at how you are chunking the material. Are you teaching in incremental, small, meaningful chunks of content? Are you checking for understanding frequently enough to clear up any misunderstanding along the way? Are you using practical real-world examples to which the students can relate, building in relevance and making the content meaningful? Are you keeping the students' interest? Are you providing an appropriate amount of examples and are they clear, or are they too confusing to identify the critical attribute?

At the completion of a unit, the teacher needs to assess how well the students learned the material. This is called evaluation. It is for a grade and can be any form of assessment.

TASK ANALYSIS

Suppose you want to make some chocolate chip cookies from scratch. How would you go about it? First, you would need to get the ingredients listed in the recipe. Next, rather than dump all of the ingredients into a bowl and start stirring, you would need to add the ingredients in a specific order. Let's keep this analogy in mind as we discuss task analysis.

Task analysis is the process by which the teacher identifies the components (i.e., the ingredients) of the knowledge or skill essential to the accomplishment of an objective. The task analysis is the organization and step-by-step procedure the teacher will use in teaching. It is *not* how the teacher will teach it, but rather the critical elements and order in which it will be taught. Before a teacher can task-analyze, she needs to know the content. The teacher needs to have a conceptual understanding and break it down into its components. During the first phase of a task analysis, there are two steps. The first step is to break the task into its essential components. The second step is to put these identified components into a sequence of necessary steps that must be learned for achieving a desired outcome or objective (i.e., add each ingredient in order and complete each step as the recipe explains).

An effective task analysis can be completed by pretending to do the skill. Your task analysis easily provides a step-by-step procedure to teach incrementally while checking for understanding at appropriate times. This allows the teacher to correct misunderstandings during the lesson instead of waiting to see the train wreck at the end of the lesson. Student success is the result of an effective task analysis.

The second phase is using the task analysis to decide whether the components are a dependent or an independent sequence. A dependent sequence means the new learning depends on some previous learning, other than the basics. When the content is a dependent sequence, the teacher needs to determine the students' prior knowledge about the content (diagnosis). The teacher is responsible for identifying holes and misinformation in the students' knowledge base in order to teach the missing information. Then ascertain what the students know and where the learning leaves off. This is where to begin the new instruction. Examples of dependent sequences include math, music, and physics.

An independent sequence means the new learning does not rely on previous knowledge; other than basic reading, writing, and mathematics. In some instances, even though a logical sequence may exist, no prior knowledge is requisite for learning the new skill or information. Examples of independent sequence include foreign languages, history, and social studies. It is common for teachers simply to start teaching the new content when it is an independent sequence.

In summary, task analysis is the sequencing of necessary steps for learning new knowledge or skills. To accomplish this, a teacher first determines what needs to be learned and in what order for students to successfully acquire the new content.

INSTRUCTIONAL OBJECTIVES

Quality objectives couple an end product with a level of Bloom's hierarchy of cognition or with a defined complex task according to Webb's work on Depth of Knowledge. The work of both Bloom and Webb will be discussed. However, the starting point for the teacher is to determine what product a student can produce which requires complex thinking, problem solving, and critical thinking, while at the same demonstrates mastery of the new knowledge or skill. The product should be perceived by students as meaningful, relevant, and significant.

To attain the desired outcome teachers need to ask themselves, "how can my students learn this best," rather than, "how will I teach this?" The first question is student-centered the second is teacher oriented. This then changes the responsibility of learning to the teacher's instruction instead of the passive learners' reception of information. Keeping this in mind, the teacher can select a student-centered outcome or product that requires strategic reasoning to produce and reveals the student's degree of understanding. First, Bloom's work will be discussed. Following this will be an explanation of Webb's work with Depth of Knowledge.

Suppose you were handed a plastic baggie filled with jigsaw puzzle pieces. What would you need to facilitate your completion of the puzzle? You would probably want a picture of what the completed puzzle looks like. Although all the pieces are there, you would still want a roadmap of the task of putting the puzzle together. Instructional objectives serve much the same purpose for teachers, learners, and others. The objective gives the picture of where the new learning is leading. *The objective is what the learner will produce at the end of a lesson to demonstrate mastery of the new skill or knowledge.*

The purposes of the instructional objectives are to:
   1. Provide direction for instruction.

2. Provide guidelines for assessment.
3. Convey the instructional intent to others.

Provide Direction for Instruction

As educators, we need to use the objective as our standard when we select the activities the students will complete, the ideas we intend to share with the learners, and all that takes place in the classroom relevant to the curriculum. The objective helps the teacher begin with the end in sight and drives instruction. We need to measure each component of our lesson to the objective and ensure that it supports the objective and isn't something that may be interesting, but not pertinent to the objective. Incorporating too many interesting, yet irrelevant ideas into a lesson can confuse the learners as to how it all ties together, when it really doesn't. The students may become distracted from the intention (objective) of the lesson. Teachers can simply put these "pearls of wisdom" that don't fit under the selected objective under the objective where they do fit. Everything in the lesson needs to be directed at the objective.

Provide Guidelines for Assessment

The instructional objectives are to be used to provide guidelines as teachers create the assessments for the students. When the lesson supports the objectives and the assessment fits the objectives, then clearly we have achieved the goal of testing what we are teaching. Teachers need to be careful to assess according to the objectives, and not to evaluate knowledge or skills that are foreign to the learners.

Convey the Instructional Intent to Others

As teachers, we are responsible for communicating our objectives to parents, students, administrators, colleagues, and substitute teachers. Each group has various reasons for wanting to know our intentions. Depending on the interested party, the teacher either states the objective in formal educational jargon or in layman terms. Parents are often interested in knowing what their child is going to study in class. The students want to know what they are going to learn, and they expect to be told in a casual and nonprofessional vocabulary. Substitute teachers want to know what they are expected to teach and have the students produce at the end of the lesson. Other teachers need to know the objective when they plan together or do vertical alignment. Administrators expect teachers to use professional vocabulary when discussing objectives with others in the profession.

Objectives describe student performance rather than teaching behavior. Instructional objectives are to be stated as learning outcomes. When writing instructional objectives, one should state the objective as a product, not as a process. The objective is what the learner is expected to demonstrate or produce at the end of the learning experience, not what the teacher will do to facilitate the learning.

Begin with "The learner will" followed by a perceivable action verb. Do not write, "The learner will be able to" because that is not perceivable. We want the student to actually *complete* the new skill or task.

Examples

- The learner will identify like terms in an algebraic expression.
- The learner will explain one advantage the northern states had over the southern states in fighting the Civil War.
- The learner will prepare a slide for use under a microscope.
- The learner will compare and contrast *Romeo and Juliet* to gang violence today.

When telling the students the objective, simply inform them what they can look forward to accomplishing at the end of the lesson, or what they will learn that will help them produce the given objective. For example, if the formal objective is "The learner will classify dinosaurs," the teacher could tell the students, "You are going to be so excited about our activity today because after I give you a little bit of information, you each get to sort toy dinosaurs."

STUDENT-CREATED PRODUCTS OR PRODUCTIONS LIST

advertisement	dialogue	map	resume
advice column	diorama	mobile	riddle
anecdote	display	model	rubbing
annotation	drama	monologue	rules and regulations
announcement	dramatic set design	movie title	science-fiction story
application	editorial	mural	score card
art gallery	essay	museum exhibit	scrapbook
award	eulogy	name tag	short story/reports
ballad	experiment	news report	skit
banner	fable	newsletter	song
batik	fairy tale	newspaper article	sonnet
bibliography	family tree	one-act play	stencil
biography	flow chart	oral report	stitchery
board game	flyers	package for a product	survey
book cover	graph	pamphlet	tape recording
booklet	graphic design	pantomime	telegram
bulletin board	greeting card	photo album	terrarium
card game	guess who/what	photo story	textbook
cartoon	haiku	picture dictionary	time capsule
case study	historical scene	picture story	timeline
chart	historical story	placemat	travelogue
cheer	illustrated story	play	tri-board display
collage	illustration	poem	trivia questions
coloring book	interview	poster	T-shirt design
comic strip	job description	puppet	TV documentary
commercial	journal	puppet show	TV newscast
computer game	large-scale drawing	radio show	video game
costume	lecture	rap	video presentation
crossword puzzle	lesson	reader's theater	videotape recording
dance	letter to person	recipe	vocabulary list
debate	letter to the editor	reference file	word search
demonstration	limerick	requests	
diagram	magazine article	response/rebuttal	

Usually, learning will increase if students understand what they are going to learn and why it is important. However, if knowing the objective will have a negative impact on them, the teacher may not want to tell them the objective. Example: The learner will multiply fractions. Many students might be turned off to this. Instead, the teacher would want to engage the learners in an interesting and relevant activity followed by a discussion of the value of knowing what it means to multiply fractions.

According to Terry TenBrink (2003, p. 67), objectives should be:

1. Developmentally appropriate.
2. Completed by the student within a reasonable amount of time.
3. In proper sequence with other objectives.
4. In support of the overall goals of the scope and sequence of the curriculum.
5. In harmony with the goals and values of the institution.

For mastery purposes, or for students identified with special needs, the objective may include conditions and criteria. For example, Jason will complete 15 single-digit multiplication problems with 75% or better accuracy.

We have limited our discussion and illustrations to the cognitive area; however, some curricula are more suited to the affective or the psychomotor domain. The affective domain focuses on attitudes and feelings, while the psychomotor domain lends itself to physical ability and coordination.

BLOOM'S TAXONOMY

Benjamin Bloom (1984) has developed a classification system for the cognitive domain. He has created a hierarchy of thinking skills. Bloom's work was later revised (Anderson, Krathwohl, & Bloom, 2001) changing the order of the last two terms: Synthesis and Evaluation. Also, the noun terms were changed to verbs. It is common for teachers to write instructional objectives and questions using Bloom's taxonomy during their lesson planning. The six levels of cognitive processes starting with the lowest are:

1. **Knowledge**—When the learner recognizes or knows the facts without understanding them. Cognition in this level of Bloom's taxonomy has a student recall or recognize information in a manner similar to how it was learned. For example, a young child may be able to recite the numbers from 1 to 10, but he cannot correctly count a set of objects because he doesn't understand that when counting, each object gets one count.

2. **Comprehension**—When the learner understands the recalled information or new material. This is much more than simply repeating memorized information; the information or material takes on meaning. For example, it explains the concept of evaporation and not just list the steps of water evaporating.

3. **Application**—When the learner takes the new skill or knowledge and applies it to a completely new situation. When a student transfers information or ideas he has learned into solving a realistic problem, he is operating at the application level of Bloom's taxonomy. For example, after a child learns about scientific notation in his math class he then transfers that knowledge into his science class to explain the size of microscopic bacteria.

4. **Analysis**—When the learner separates the whole into its parts then compares the parts to the whole and to each other. Analysis may involve organizing and reorganizing information into categories. This level of cognition requires students to analyze, hypothesize, and classify. For example, when we are creating a budget, we have a specific amount of money to break down into different areas, but we also need to compare each amount within a given area to ensure that we keep our budget reasonable. Consequently, we compare each part to the other parts and compare each line-item to the whole budget.

5. **Evaluation**—When the learner judges, evaluates, or criticizes according to a specific criteria or standard. Opinions are generally not included here unless they are well supported by unbiased information, facts, and supporting evidence. Frequently one's own values, beliefs, attitudes, morals, and perceptions influence the way we evaluate or judge others' ideas or products.

6. **Synthesis**—When the learner combines and integrates different resources or ideas to create one new, original product. An example would be when a student uses many resources to write a research paper. He synthesizes the various pieces of information into one new creation or product.

Knowledge, comprehension, and application are referred to as lower-level thinking skills. Analysis, synthesis, and evaluation are considered higher-level thinking skills. The latter are referred to as HOTS (higher-order thinking skills) in educational circles. Knowledge and comprehension are facts; application, analysis, and synthesis are processes; and evaluation can be metacognition.

As teachers, we use Bloom's taxonomy as we write instructional objectives, construct higher- and lower-order thinking questions for students, and we generate test questions.

As mentioned previously, Bloom's work is used to write instructional objectives and to write questions. Below are sentence-starters for each level of Bloom's taxonomy so teachers can generate questions at all levels of cognition.

BLOOM'S TAXONOMY OF LEVELS OF COGNITION	
Level	**Key Words**
Knowledge/ Remembering	what, when, who, define, describe, where, memorize, narrate, distinguish, identify, list, name, match, how, was, repeat, relate, record, recall, reorganize, show, state, locate, how much, select, choose, tell when, match, label, write, which, indicate, tell how, why, which one, omit, find (locate), make a list, report
Comprehension/ Understanding	explain, summarize, interpret, rewrite, convert, give example, restate, describe, identify, report, discuss, recognize, express, locate, review, compare, conclude, contrast, demonstrate, differentiate, predict, reorder, which, distinguish, estimate, extend, extrapolate, rearrange, rephrase, inform, what, fill in, hypothesize, illustrate, infer, relate, tell in your own words, classify, judge, show, indicate, tell, translate, outline, select, match, represent, paraphrase
Application/ Applying	demonstrate, show, operate, construct, apply, develop, test, consider, build, plan, choose, how would, construct, solve, show your work, tell us, indicate, use/employ, check out, interview, translate, dramatize, operate, schedule, illustrate, interpret
Analysis/Analyzing	debate, distinguish, differentiate, solve, diagram, compare, criticize, experiment, analyze, categorize, describe, classify, discriminate, recognize, support your, indicate the, relate, explain, what assumption, what do you, break down, contrast, deduct, infer
Evaluation/ Evaluating	select, judge, predict, choose, estimate, measure, value, rate, assess, what is, evaluate, decide, check the, which would you consider, defend, check, what is most appropriate, indicate, appraise, justify, debate, criticize, support
Synthesis/Creating	create, suppose, design, compose, combine, rearrange, write, think of a way, purpose a plan, put together, what would be, suggest, how, develop, make up, what conclusion, what major hypothesis, formulate a solution, synthesize, derive, produce, compare, predict, plan, assemble, construct, design, prepare, classify

Sentence Starts and Question Prompts

KNOWLEDGE

- Tell what _____ looks like (describe)
- Point to
- Say
- Tell

- Show
- Write
- Recite

COMPREHENSION

- Tell the main idea
- Tell in order (sequence)
- Show (illustrate)
- Tell how _____ felt
- Give definition
- Tell or write in your own words (rewrite, paraphrase)
- Tell what _____ means (define)
- Tell why
- State in your own words
- What does this mean
- Give an example
- Condense this paragraph
- State in one word
- What part doesn't fit
- What restrictions would you add
- What exceptions are there
- Which is more probable
- What are they saying
- What seems to be
- What seems likely
- Which are facts, opinions
- Is this the same as
- Select the best definition
- What would happen if
- Explain what is happening
- Explain what is meant
- Read the graph, table
- Is this valid
- Which statements support the main idea
- Show in a graph, table

APPLICATION

- Tell how _____ is used in this example
- Use _____ in a new way
- Show how to (demonstrate)
- Draw or paint a picture that shows (illustrate)
- Predict what would happen if

- Choose the best statements that apply
- Judge the effects
- What would result
- Identify the results of
- Tell what would happen
- Tell how, when, where, why
- Tell how much change there would be

ANALYSIS

- Tell how _____ and _____ are alike/different
- Tell why you think _____ did _____ (infer)
- Tell what is true/not true, real/make-believe
- Put into groups (categorize)
- Tell why you think _____ felt _____ (infer)
- Tell what _____ learned from _____
- What assumptions
- What motive is there
- What conclusions
- Make a distinction
- What is the premise
- What ideas apply, not apply
- Implicit in the statement is the idea of
- What is the function of
- What's fact, opinion
- What statement is relevant
- Extraneous to, related
- What is not applicable
- What does author believe, assume
- State the point of view of
- What ideas justify conclusion
- The least essential statements are
- What's the theme, main idea, subordinate
- What inconsistency fallacies
- What literacy form is used
- What persuasive technique
- What relationship between

EVALUATION

- Tell why _____ is better/worse/more fair, etc.
- Tell why you agree or disagree with _____.
- Tell which you choose for first/second/third place (rate)
- Which would you consider
- What is most appropriate

- Which is good
- What is the solution
- Will it work
- Decide which

SYNTHESIS

- Tell something else _____ could do
- Think of a way
- Propose a plan
- Put together
- What would be
- What conclusion
- What major hypothesis
- Formulate a solution
- Tell or write a new story about (create)
- Tell how to make _____ better

Professional Learning Communities

Many school districts are using the Professional Learning Community (PLC) model. In this model, teachers form teams to discuss and implement a variety of ways to increase their pedagogy and ultimately student success. PLC's will be discussed in Chapter 12, but for lesson planning purposes, one aspect will be addressed here. Teams of teachers work in their respective PLC groups to plan their lessons, discuss common assessments, determine strategies to differentiate instruction, and identify projects to enhance student learning.

Four Guiding Questions for Professional Learning Community Lesson Planning

1. What do we want the students to learn?
2. How will we know when they learned it?
3. How will we respond if they don't learn it?
4. What will we do if they already know it?

Question number one refers to the lesson objective. In other words, what new skill or knowledge does the teacher want the students to learn or master. Inherent in this task is the teacher identifying what are the critical attributes and essential knowledge for the learner to know or do.

The second question relates to the teachers using a common assessment for all the students. The teachers working together in a specific PLC group identify or design an assessment to use to determine how well the students learned the new material. It is wise for teachers to start with the goal in mind and teach to the end result.

The third question is crucial to guide the teacher's instruction for those students who need more background knowledge, struggle with learning new material, or learn differently than the typical student. For these reasons, teachers can diagnose the students' degree of prior knowledge and level of understanding with a pre-test, class dialog, or brainstorming session. It is common for teacher to use differentiated instruction so as to reach and interest more students.

The last question refers to those students who already know the new knowledge or task to be taught. For these students, teachers plan enrichment activities to help students think more critically, deeper, and broader. It is reasonable for the teacher to select a project for these students that will require them to use problem-solving strategies. For more Information on Professional Learning Communities see Richard Dufour and Robert Eaker's work.

Below is an illustration of another template for collaborative planning.

COMMON COLLABORATIVE
INSTRUCTIONAL PROCESS
Organized around groups of teachers focused on Professional Learning Community questions.

TARGET	• WHAT IS IT THAT WE WANT ALL STUDENTS TO LEARN? Purpose: To allow students the opportunity to learn at grade level or above.	**OBJECTIVE**
GAUGE	• HOW WILL WE DETERMINE WHETHER EACH STUDENT HAS MASTERED THE ESSENTIAL LEARNING? Purpose: To determine what success looks like.	**ASSESSMENT** · Formative · Summative
PLAN	• HOW WILL WE DESIGN LESSONS FOR STUDENT LEARNING? Purpose: To design lessons that align with standards and that include a critical thinking component.	**LESSON DESIGN**
INVESTIGATE	• HOW WILL WE IMPROVE THE LEARNING EXPERIENCE FOR STUDENTS IN THE FUTURE? Purpose: To determine a lesson's effectiveness or ineffectiveness.	**REFLECTION**
RESPOND	• HOW WILL WE RESPOND WHEN A STUDENT EXPERIENCES DIFFICULTY IN LEARNING OR HAS ALREADY MASTERED THE ESSENTIAL KNOWLEDGE AND SKILLS? Purpose: To meet individual student academic needs.	**SCAFFOLDING ENRICHMENT**

Webb's Depth of Knowledge Levels

In addition to Bloom's hierarchy, there is another model (Webb, 2002), which targets a student's Depth of Knowledge (DOK) used to complete an activity. The DOK model focuses on the type of thinking required complete a task; not the difficulty of an assignment. Therefore, the cognitive demand required in producing the student outcome or product reflects the level of complexity. In other words, the DOK stresses how deep a student has to understand the content in order to interact with it. The DOK categories are designed to ensure that teachers are teaching with a variety of intellectual reasoning levels (degrees of mental rigor) to promote student achievement. DOK levels can be used to guide instructional activities, develop questions, and create assessments; formal and informal and formative and summative.

Depth of Knowledge Levels

1. Recall and Reproduction
2. Skills and Concepts
3. Short-term Strategic Thinking
4. Extended Thinking

Recall and Reproduction

The emphasis of this level is on factual information. It involves simple recall of content; not solving or computing. Student answers are either right or wrong. An example of recall and reproduction would be to have a student locate Amarillo on the map of Texas.

Example of possible student products include recitation, googling, defining, stating facts, and labeling.

Skills and Concepts

This level involves cognitive processing beyond simple recall or reproduction. Rather it requires learners to apply skills or concepts to the curriculum using comparisons and contrasts. Keeping with map reading skills for our example, an activity representing this level of thinking would be to have the students contrast the distance from Amarillo to Plainview with the distance from Plainview to Lubbock.

Examples of projects at this level are dioramas, illustrations, performances, demonstrations, and conceptual journaling.

Short-term Strategic Thinking

Level three goes deeper into the mental processing by requiring reasoning skills and planning to find a practical solution. It requires applying abstract, cross-curricular thinking to knowledge and skills to create novel and unique solutions. This type of strategic thinking requires analysis and evaluation. There is usually more than one way to approach a problem and more than one solution. Again, relating to map reading skills an example of rigor for this category would be to have the students plan and explain their reasoning for the best route to get from Amarillo to San Antonio.

Student-oriented outcomes to demonstrate cognitive rigor at this level include flowcharts, debates, persuasive writings or speeches, podcasts, and judging.

Extended Thinking

At this level, students investigate real-world problems that require critical thinking skills. Curricular content for this level require students to engage in problem-solving over an extended period of time. To complete the objective, students will engage in complex reasoning processes such as analysis, evaluation, and synthesis. This level of strategic thinking involves; brainstorming solutions, selecting a viable plan and put it into action, and make informed decision based on data. A variety of creative and innovative solutions are possible. This research will require students to draw upon many curriculum areas and multiple resources. Building on the previous example, a project that would require the cognitive complexity to generate a solution at this level of higher-order thinking would be having the students create a new highway system for connecting most major cities in Texas. Students would need to defend which cities they selected, the cost of constructing each intercity highway, and predict how many people this new system would serve.

© Hasloo Group Production Studio, 2014, Used under license of shutterstock, inc.

Objectives targeting this extended level of complex thinking could include products such as research projects; novel stories; a multi-media presentations; raps or songs; and graphs, tables, and charts.

As students cognate at this level, they may still use the first three levels of reasoning skills as building blocks during the complex thinking process. For example, during this project, the learners may need to study population facts of different cities; thus, representing level one thinking. Furthermore, they will need to use mathematical calculations to compute the cost of each highway (level two). And they will evaluate their data to judge which cities would benefit most from new highways (level three). This example demonstrates how learning activities and assessments can incorporate all DOK levels as part of a greater, more complex activity. A teacher could ask herself, "What kind of project could my students create to demonstrate their new knowledge and skills (DOK levels 1 and 2) yet would require them to operate on DOK level 3 or 4?"

Keep in mind the length of time to finish a project is not the key indicator of any level, nor is the verb used in the lesson objective. But rather, the mental processes, that must occur to complete the objective, determine the level of rigor, hence, the DOK level.

Hess' Cognitive Rigor Matrix & Curricular Examples:
Applying Webb's Depth-of-Knowledge Levels to Bloom's Cognitive Process Dimensions

Revised Bloom's Taxonomy	Webb's DOK Level 1 Recall & Reproduction	Webb's DOK Level 2 Skills & Concepts	Webb's DOK Level 3 Strategic Thinking/ Reasoning	Webb's DOK Level 4 Extended Thinking
Remember Retrieve knowledge from long-term memory, recognize, recall, locate, identify	• Recall, observe, & recognize facts, principles, properties • Recall/ identify conversions among representations or numbers (e.g., customary and metric measures)			
Understand Construct meaning, clarify, paraphrase, represent, translate, illustrate, give examples, classify, categorize, summarize, generalize, infer a logical conclusion (such as from examples given), predict, compare/contrast, match like ideas, explain, construct models	• Evaluate an expression • Locate points on a grid or number on number line • Solve a one-step problem • Represent math relationships in words, pictures, or symbols • Read, write, compare decimals in scientific notation	• Specify and explain relationships (e.g., non-examples/examples; cause-effect) • Make and record observations • Explain steps followed • Summarize results or concepts • Make basic inferences or logical predictions from data/observations • Use models /diagrams to represent or explain mathematical concepts • Make and explain estimates	• Use concepts to solve <u>non-routine</u> problems • Explain, generalize, or connect ideas <u>using supporting evidence</u> • Make <u>and justify</u> conjectures • Explain thinking when more than one response is possible • Explain phenomena in terms of concepts	• Relate mathematical or scientific concepts to other content areas, other domains, or other concepts • Develop generalizations of the results obtained and the strategies used (from investigation or readings) and apply them to new problem situations
Apply Carry out or use a procedure in a given situation; carry out (apply to a familiar task), or use (apply) to an unfamiliar task	• Follow simple procedures (recipe-type directions) • Calculate, measure, apply a rule (e.g., rounding) • Apply algorithm or formula (e.g., area, perimeter) • Solve linear equations • Make conversions among representations or numbers, or within and between customary and metric measures	• Select a procedure according to criteria and perform it • Solve routine problem applying multiple concepts or decision points • Retrieve information from a table, graph, or figure and use it solve a problem requiring multiple steps • Translate between tables, graphs, words, and symbolic notations (e.g., graph data from a table) • Construct models given criteria	• Design investigation for a specific purpose or research question • Conduct a designed investigation • Use concepts to solve non-routine problems • <u>Use & show reasoning, planning, and evidence</u> • Translate between problem & symbolic notation when not a direct translation	• Select or devise approach among many alternatives to solve a problem • Conduct a project that specifies a problem, identifies solution paths, solves the problem, and reports results
Analyze Break into constituent parts, determine how parts relate, differentiate between relevant-irrelevant, distinguish, focus, select, organize, outline, find coherence, deconstruct	• Retrieve information from a table or graph to answer a question • Identify whether specific information is contained in graphic representations (e.g., table, graph, T-chart, diagram) • Identify a pattern/trend	• Categorize, classify materials, data, figures based on characteristics • Organize or order data • Compare/ contrast figures or data • Select appropriate graph and organize & display data • Interpret data from a simple graph • Extend a pattern	• Compare information within or across data sets or texts • Analyze and <u>draw conclusions from data, citing evidence</u> • Generalize a pattern • Interpret data from complex graph Analyze similarities/differences between procedures or solutions	• Analyze multiple sources of evidence • Analyze complex/abstract themes • Gather, analyze, and evaluate information
Evaluate Make judgments based on criteria, check, detect inconsistencies or fallacies, judge, critique			• <u>Cite evidence and develop a logical argument</u> for concepts or solutions • Describe, compare, and contrast solution methods • <u>Verify reasonableness of results</u>	• Gather, analyze, & evaluate information to draw conclusions • Apply understanding in a novel way, provide argument or justification for the application
Create Reorganize elements into new patterns/structures, generate, hypothesize, design, plan, construct, produce	• Brainstorm ideas, concepts, or perspectives related to a topic	• Generate conjectures or hypotheses based on observations or prior knowledge and experience	• Synthesize information within one data set, source, or text • Formulate an original problem given a situation Develop a scientific/mathematical model for a complex situation	• Synthesize information across multiple sources or texts • Design a mathematical model to inform and solve a practical or abstract situation

Webb Leveling: Expectations for Student Performance

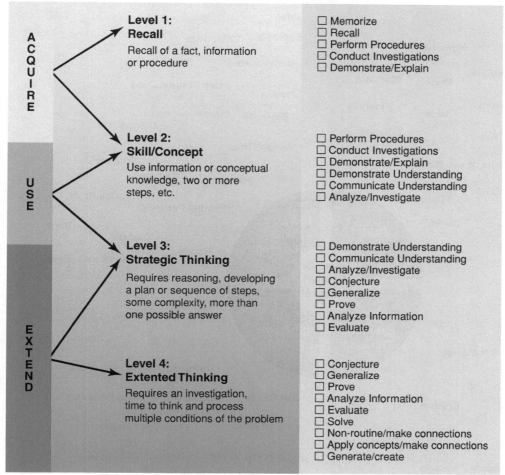

ACQUIRE

Level 1:
Recall

Recall of a fact, information or procedure

- ☐ Memorize
- ☐ Recall
- ☐ Perform Procedures
- ☐ Conduct Investigations
- ☐ Demonstrate/Explain

USE

Level 2:
Skill/Concept

Use information or conceptual knowledge, two or more steps, etc.

- ☐ Perform Procedures
- ☐ Conduct Investigations
- ☐ Demonstrate/Explain
- ☐ Demonstrate Understanding
- ☐ Communicate Understanding
- ☐ Analyze/Investigate

EXTEND

Level 3:
Strategic Thinking

Requires reasoning, developing a plan or sequence of steps, some complexity, more than one possible answer

- ☐ Demonstrate Understanding
- ☐ Communicate Understanding
- ☐ Analyze/Investigate
- ☐ Conjecture
- ☐ Generalize
- ☐ Prove
- ☐ Analyze Information
- ☐ Evaluate

Level 4:
Extented Thinking

Requires an investigation, time to think and process multiple conditions of the problem

- ☐ Conjecture
- ☐ Generalize
- ☐ Prove
- ☐ Analyze Information
- ☐ Evaluate
- ☐ Solve
- ☐ Non-routine/make connections
- ☐ Apply concepts/make connections
- ☐ Generate/create

NOTE: Although verbiage may indicate a lesson is written at a higher cognitive level, one must also consider the rigor (cognitive demand) and engagement expected of students. Examples:

Example 1: Students asked to create a list during a lesson would be demonstrating understanding at a Level 1, not a Level 4 as the verb create would indicate. A lesson written at a Level 4 would ask the students to create an original artifact that demonstrates higher order thinking skills.

Example 2: Asking students to solve a problem would be a Level 2 sample of communicating understanding. Having students solve a problem, explain the sequence of steps and prove their solution would be a Level 3 sample of communicating understanding.

Refer to the Descriptors and Questions for Webb Leveling guide for further details.

Depth of Knowledge (DOK) Levels

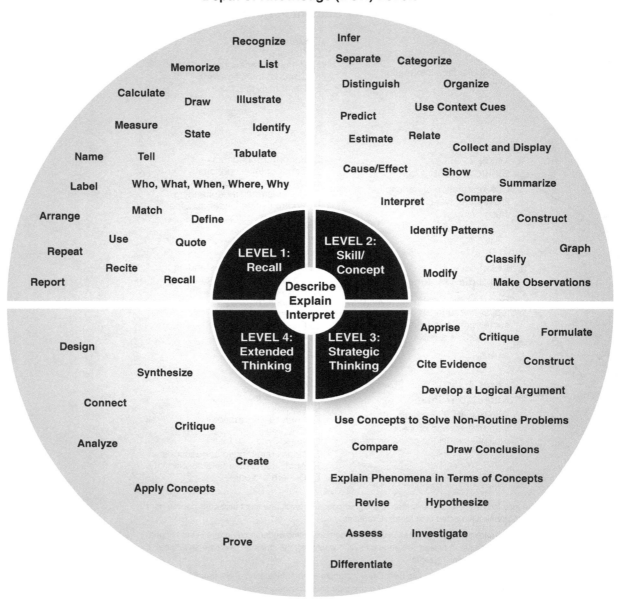

Level 1 Activities	Level 2 Activities	Level 3 Activities	Level 4 Activities
Recall elements and details of story structure, such as sequence of events, character, plot and setting.	Identify and summarize the major events in a narrative.	Support ideas with details and examples.	Conduct a project that requires specifying a problem, designing and conducting an experiment, analyzing its data, and reporting results/solutions.
Conduct basic mathematical calculations.	Use context cues to identify the meaning of unfamiliar words.	Use voice appropriate to the purpose and audience.	Apply mathematical model to illuminate a problem or situation.
Label locations on a map.	Solve routine multiple-step problems.	Identify research questions and design investigations for a scientific problem.	Analyze and synthesize information from multiple sources.
Represent in words or diagrams a scientific concept or relationship.	Describe the cause/effect of a particular event.	Develop a scientific model for a complex situation.	Describe and illustrate how common themes are found across texts from different cultures.
Perform routine procedures like measuring length or using punctuation marks correctly.	Identify patterns in events or behavior.	Determine the author's purpose and describe how it affects the interpretation of a reading selection.	Design a mathematical model to inform and solve a practical or abstract situation.
Describe the features of a place or people.	Formulate a routine problem given data and conditions.	Apply a concept in other contexts.	
	Organize, represent and interpret data.		

LESSON DESIGN

There are several models of direct instruction, and most share several common elements. Madeline Hunter's (1994) approach has been remarkably popular over the years, and when used as she intended, it is highly effective. Hunter's lesson design includes seven elements. However, not all lessons lend themselves to inclusion of all seven.

Seven Elements of Lesson Design

1. **Anticipatory Set**—The purpose of the anticipatory set is to focus the learners at the beginning of a lesson. It may be as simple as a review, dialogue, or something eye-catching (a story, poem, video clip, music, object, etc.) Suppose the students were going to study rainbows. The teacher could start the lesson by playing the song "Somewhere Over the Rainbow" and project a colorful rainbow from the overhead onto the screen. The anticipatory set is not behaviors to simply get the students' attention such as flashing the overhead lights. It is deliberate and well planned to the students engaged in the learning process.

2. **Objective**—This is the same as the instructional objective, which has already been discussed. *The objective is what the learners will produce to demonstrate mastery of the new skill or knowledge.* It is best to tell the students the objective, unless it causes them to lose their motivation. (Everything you have already learned about *objectives* fits here!)

3. **Input**—How the learner receives the new skill or knowledge. Commonly, it is the teacher and all models of instruction. However, it could be from a video, a guest speaker, the Internet, a book, etc. This is the time for the teacher to provide any necessary background information as the new concept is introduced. During input the teacher begins to teach the new material. It is common for the input to overlap with the demonstration of the new skill or knowledge, referred to as modeling.

4. **Modeling**—When the teacher demonstrates the new skill or knowledge systematically. During this step-by-step demonstration the teacher continually checks for understanding. During the initial stages of learning the teacher guides the students. As the teacher continues to demonstrate more examples he gradually releases the responsibility for learning to the students. The teacher should have samples of the finished product visible. Each step needs to have the critical element demonstrated and labeled. In addition, the examples need to be clear and pure, allowing the learners to focus on the essential factors and not be distracted by nonrelevant elements in the process or product creation. As a rule of thumb show three to five examples. "Watch as I do it" becomes "Let's do it together" as students learn the skill during modeling. (Everything you have already learned about task analysis fits here!)

5. **Checking for Understanding**—As the teacher, you are intermittently checking for understanding throughout the lesson. Before continuing on to the next step of a process or chunk of new learning, the teacher needs to know if the students are understanding and are cognitively still with him. Checking for understanding is also important at the end of the lesson before the students practice the new skill or knowledge. Students must be completing the task nearly error-free before beginning the guided-monitored practice.

Checking for understanding may be employed in different ways based on whether the new material is skill- or knowledge-based. Focusing a microscope is a skill, remembering the water cycle is knowledge. Checking for understanding of a new skill will consist of the students trying the new skill with teacher feedback and questioning. If the students are learning the skill long division they will work a few sample problems while the teacher will identify their degree of understanding by determining if they know the step-by-step process accurately. Teachers may also check for understanding by ascertaining if the students can correctly answer questions. During this phase the class is still working as a whole group under the teacher's supervision. Checking for understanding of new knowledge commonly consists of asking questions regarding the new material. These questions can be at a variety of cognitive levels according to Bloom's taxonomy.

As a teacher plans the questions be aware there are two types of questions: **convergent** and **divergent**. Convergent questions promote narrowly focused thinking; typically there is a specific answer the teacher is expecting. Convergent thinking is when ideas come together. This type of question usually has one correct answer. Examples of convergent thinking are what is the square root of 81, name the common types of volcanoes, or explain the life cycle of frogs.

Divergent questions require students to compose their own ideas. Divergent thinking is utilized in open-ended questions where there is more than one right answer. Examples of divergent thinking are what might technology look like 10 years from now, look at this photograph and decide what you would name it and why, or should schools require student uniforms and explain your reasoning.

There are many ways to check for understanding; some are observing the students as they work, response cards, signaling, choral response, single student response, short written response, reporting a collective answer, spot-checking the students' work, pair and share, and sampling or dip-sticking.

Response Cards

Response cards are cards that are either two-sided or divided into sections, each section displaying a different response. Each child uses a response card to visual display his or her answer to the teacher as the teacher poses questions to the class. For example, the teacher could ask a question about government and the students would display either Senate or House of Representatives. Suppose the class was studying parts of speech. The teacher could say a word or phrase and the students could point to one of six sections on their response card indicating if the answer is a noun, adjective, verb, adverb, preposition, or pronoun. During a math class when students are deciding which operation to use to solve a word problem, they could use a response card with four sections showing the four primary math operations: addition, subtraction, multiplication, and division.

Questions to Ask Yourself as You Plan a Lesson

1. What are you going to teach?
   a. Identify the TEKS objective(s)
   b. How are you going to teach it?
      i. How will you start to get the learners interested, curious, and engaged? (Anticipatory set)
      ii. How will you know if the students learned it? (Objective)
      iii. What is the step-by-step process to be demonstrated and how will you organize your instruction? (Task analysis, which becomes your input and modeling when you decide how to teach the new material). Differentiated instruction may be used to teach the same skill or knowledge using different activities.
      iv. How will you know if the students are "getting it"? (Checking for understanding)
      v. Are they ready to try it on their own? (Guided-monitored practice)
      vi. Choices for the students to choose from to demonstrate mastery. (Independent practice and differentiated instruction)
2. What is the knowledge base of your students?
   a. What do they need to know and be able to do prior to being introduced to the new material?
   b. What will you do if they do not have the requisite skill or knowledge?

6. **Guided-Monitored Practice**—Commonly called seatwork. The students practice the new task while the teacher monitors the work. As a general rule, the students complete five to eight practices or problems. "You do it, I'll watch, prompt, praise, and leave."

7. **Independent Practice**—Commonly called homework. Students do it without the teacher being available, but at the same range of difficulty they have been exposed to in guided-monitored practice.

You may also find it useful to list the materials you need for your lesson.

For preservice teachers who are still learning how to plan and design lessons the following outline of questions will help facilitate their thinking. As a neophyte responds to each of the elements listed in the table, he will be forming a lesson.

Teachers may find it beneficial, especially for their culturally and linguistically diverse learners, to consider elements of SIOP (Sheltered Instruction Observation Protocol) during their planning. Although SIOP is explained in Competency #2, some features are reviewed as they relate to lesson design. The primary purpose of SIOP is to provide a lesson plan model and delivery system to promote student language acquisition during content instruction. The SIOP model includes an instructional content objective as well as language objectives. Language objectives relate to having the students practice and apply new concepts coupled with academic language using reading, writing, speaking, and/or listening skills. Include language objectives with key vocabulary and supplemental materials as a significant part of daily lessons. The SIOP model provides eight components and a checklist for teachers featuring 30 elements.

5-E Model

The 5-E model is more of a discovery approach that is commonly used in science. It is an excellent model to provide an environment of exploration and experimentation for students.

Engagement—Mentally engage the learners and motivate with an event or question.

Exploration—Hands-on activities that require the students to cognitively engage in the experience.

Explanation—Encourage students to generate reasonable solutions and answers for the experience. Students are expected to listen and pose more questions.

Elaboration—Activities that help the students apply the new skill or concept as they investigate new and unique situations.

Evaluation—Students demonstrate mastery of the new skill or knowledge. Events help students to continue to elaborate on their understanding of the new material.

Sample Lesson Plan

This sample lesson plan is designed for post-high school students to demonstrate elements of a lesson plan.

Anticipatory Set—Have two-color counters (chips) on the students' table and ask the question, "What happens if you owe someone more money than you have?"

Objective—The learner will add single-digit integers.

Input—Explain the meaning of the different-colored chips. Red represents negative numbers and yellow represents positive numbers. The chips will be used to represent quantities, both positive and negative.

Modeling—Demonstrate the following problems explaining the process of adding integers. Gradually release responsibility to the students.

1. $4 + 3$
2. $-4 + (-3)$
3. $4 + (-3)$ Here introduce the concept of zero pairs. A red counter and a yellow counter make a zero pair and cancel each other out.
4. $-4 + 3$

Checking for Understanding—During the input and modeling the teacher will ask questions such as the following during the appropriate step in the process.

- "How would you start this problem?"
- "What would you do next?"
- "What do the yellow counters represent?"
- "What do the red counters represent?
- "What is a zero pair?"
- "What can you take out?"
- "What do you get when you add two negative numbers and why?"

If the teacher perceives that the students understand the skill, they can start practicing it ergo guided-monitored practice.

Guided-Monitored Practice

1. $-2 + (-5) = -7$

2. $6 + (-4) = 2$

3. $-3 + 2 = -1$

4. $-1 + (-8) = -9$

5. $5 + 6 = 11$

6. $-4 + 6 = 2$

7. $5 + (-1) = 4$

8. $-1 + (-1) = -2$

9. $3 + (-5) = -2$

Independent Practice
Assign problems of the same level of difficulty as those during the guided-monitored practice.

KEYS FOR EFFECTIVE EXAMPLES

As teachers create lesson plans, they will generate examples to help the students understand the concept. To assist in writing effective examples, there are four keys to keep in mind:

1. *Focus on the essence.* Identify and elaborate on the distinguishing feature on which you want the students to focus their attention. Emphasize the critical attribute and its significance.

2. *Hook onto long-term memory.* Build on the students' prior knowledge and experience. Help the students make connections with things they already know to the new content.

3. *Keep examples unambiguous, clear, and precise.* Remember the student is learning this for the first time, so don't pack too much into one example.

4. *No emotional distracters.* When the learning experience evokes some emotion in students, it helps them remember it. However, if it is so emotionally charged that the example becomes distracting to the learner, we have done a disservice. You wouldn't want to bring a zebra into the room to teach the concept of stripes. The students would get so distracted by zebra sounds and smells that they may forget they are learning about stripes.

© baldyrgan, 2014, Used under license of Shutterstock, Inc.

TIPS FOR COMPETENCY 3: DESIGNING EFFECTIVE PLANNING

TEKS, Curriculum and Instruction

1. Use the TEKS to know what content to teach and choose how to teach it based on achieving student success.

2. Use TEKS to know the knowledge students should have from prior years and what to currently teach.

3. Readiness assessments are used to determine if instruction and curriculum are developmentally appropriate.

4. When planning:
   - Organize the unit of study so it follows a logical or natural sequence.
   - The teacher should have student success be the primary concern. Avoid selecting activities that are self-serving (i.e., less grading, more free time, easier).

5. Take advantage of teachable moments by being responsive to student interests.

6. Chunk and check (from your task analysis), teach a little (chunk), check for understanding (use four if-thens), do it again. Teach a little then check for understanding throughout the entire lesson.

Field Trips

1. Prior to taking a field trip generate learning goals with the students.

2. To better prepare students for field trips they should have certain questions in mind, and perhaps goals and objectives of what they are to get out of the experience.

3. Volunteers need to be aware of the objectives for the field trip.

4. Each student must have a permission slip signed by their parent or guardian.

Learner Behaviors

1. Give students control over their own learning. They can create their own action plan. Students can define their learning goals for a given content and develop an action plan so they are purposeful in their work.

2. Create multiple opportunities to construct meaning.

3. The instructional objective helps students judge their work and direct their efforts appropriately.

4. Create opportunities for students to practice convergent thinking and divergent thinking.

Cooperative Learning

1. Cooperative learning roles need to vary to develop skills.
2. Opportunities for group work establish norms of a positive supportive environment.

DISCUSSION OUTLINES AND ACTIVITIES

Diagnosis

Diagnosis is done at three different times for each lesson and each has a unique name. Fill in the following information.

Before is called _____.

During is called _____.

Complete the four if-then decisions a teacher makes intermittently during a lesson.

     * If   then

     * If   then

     * If   then

     * If   then

After is called _____ .

Task Analysis

A task analysis is the process by which the teacher identifies the essential components of the knowledge or skills essential to the accomplishment of a task. This task leads to accomplishing the learning objective.

Phase 1

Step 1:

Step 2:

Phase 2

Decide if the task is a dependent or independent sequence. Explain each.

Dependent sequence:

Independent sequence:

Task Analysis Exercise

Complete a task analysis for teaching how to make singular nouns into plural nouns. You may want to consider the following types of words when generating your examples and decide how you would chunk this.

hat	show	fairy
shelf	knife	kite
strawberry	penny	porch
church	chair	foot
baby	horse	cherry
mouse	bench	woman
toe	goose	wolf
pants	calf	moose
dog	goat	leaf
child	sheep	

Instructional Objectives Outline and Exercise

1. The purposes of the instructional objectives are:

    a. Provide direction for _____.

    b. Provide guidelines for _____.

    c. Convey the instructional intent to _____.

2. Teachers need to state the objective as a _____, not as a _____. It is about what the _____ will do or produce, not what the teacher will do to facilitate the learning. Describe student performance rather than _____ behavior.

3. How does the teacher determine whether or not to tell the learners the objective?

4. Begin with "The learner will _____."

Exercise for Bloom's Taxonomy

Explain each of the words below.

Knowledge

Comprehension

Application

Analysis

Synthesis

Evaluation

Writing Objectives Using Bloom's Taxonomy

Write six instructional objectives, one for each level of Bloom's taxonomy. Then trade papers with a friend and circle the perceivable action verb.

1.

2.

3.

4.

5.

6.

Seven Elements of Lesson Design

In small groups explain each of the following terms and give an example.

- Anticipatory set
- Objective
- Input
- Modeling
- Checking for understanding
- Guided-monitored practice
- Independent practice

Sample Test Questions

1. Mrs. Lee is teaching a unit on photosynthesis and wants to teach appropriate goals for her students' grade level, but several of her students' reading skills are below grade level. How should she decide what to teach?

   a. Mrs. Lee needs to plan lessons that support state instructional goals for her grade level and provide extra assistance to those students with poor reading skills.

   b. Mrs. Lee needs to plan lessons on objectives taught in lower grades so her students can learn the material before moving on.

   c. The students with poor reading skills need extra reading assignments so they can improve their skills.

   d. It is more important that Mrs. Lee teach lessons that the students are interested in so they will want to read rather than follow the Texas essential knowledge and skills guidelines.

2. Mrs. Lee is notified that she will soon be receiving a student who is identified as special education. As Mrs. Lee prepares her future lesson plans, it would be beneficial for her to:

   a. Call the student's mom to make sure she approves of the curriculum.

   b. Expect the student to perform with the rest of the students and plan accordingly.

   c. Find out the students' interests and design her instruction around those areas.

   d. Be informed of the students IEP (Individual Education Plan) and make appropriate accommodations and modifications in her lesson plans.

3. As Mrs. Lee is teaching, she notices that many students are having difficulty maintaining interest. She should:

   a. Remind the students that this material is important to their future.

   b. Generate examples that the students are familiar with and are relevant to the students and the content being taught.

   c. Stop and have a discussion of why it is important for students to pay attention in class.

   d. Make the content more interesting by studying what the students' like.

Answers

1. **A is the correct answer**. The significant part of this vignette is appropriate goals for the students and that comes from the TEKS. A secondary effort needs to be made regarding the poor reading skills.

   B is not correct. The objective isn't the problem; the reading ability is the major issue.

   C is not correct. It focuses on a poor way to improve reading skills. The reading ability clearly needs to be addressed, but the question is in respect to curriculum, not student reading levels

   D is not the correct answer because it is important to align learning objectives with the state curriculum. The teacher is responsible for making the content meaningful and relevant. The TEKS indicate what is to be taught, not how to teach it. The quality of the instruction is determined by the teacher.

2. A is not correct. No one determines the curriculum. The curriculum comes from the TEKS.

   B is not correct. This is illegal and unethical. Teachers must follow the student's IEP.

C is not correct. Effective teachers weave in all students' interests when planning instruction.

D is the correct answer. The teacher needs to attend future ARD meetings and follow the student's IEP.

3. A is not correct. Most students are more interested in the here and now; not the distant future.

B is the correct answer. The best way to get students' interest and maintain it is to build on their prior knowledge and familiar experiences. Also, make the material meaningful and relevant to the students.

C is not correct. This type of discussion will cause students to tune out.

D is not correct. Although students may want to study only those areas that are of interest to them, the TEKS drives instruction.

REFERENCES

Anderson, L. W., Krathwohl, D. R., & Bloom, B. S. (2001). A taxonomy for learning, teaching, and assessing: A revision of Bloom's taxonomy of educational objectives. Allyn & Bacon.

Bloom, B. S. (1984). *Taxonomy of educational objectives handbook*. New York: Longman.

Hunter, M. (1994). *Enhancing teaching*. New York: Macmillan

TenBrink, T. (2003). *An educator's guide to classroom assessment*. Boston: Houghton Mifflin.

Webb, N. (1997). Research Monograph Number 6: "Criteria for alignment of expectations and assessments on mathematics and science education. Washington, D.C.: CCSSO.

Webb, N. (August 1999). Research Monograph No. 18: "Alignment of science and mathematics standards and assessments in four states." Washington, D.C.: CCSSO.

Competency 4 _

How Learning Occurs

Teri Bingham, EdD
West Texas A&M University

> **Competency 4:** The teacher understands learning processes, factors that impact learning, and demonstrates this knowledge by planning effective, engaging instruction and appropriate assessments.

The beginning teacher:

A. Understands the role of learning theory in the instructional process and uses instructional strategies and appropriate technologies to facilitate student learning (e.g., connecting new information and ideas to prior knowledge, making learning meaningful and relevant to students)

B. Understands that young children think concretely and rely primarily on motor and sensory input and direct experience for development of skills and knowledge and uses this understanding to plan effective, developmentally appropriate learning experiences and assessments.

C. Understands that the middle-level years are a transitional stage in which students may exhibit characteristics of both older and younger children and that these are critical years for developing important skills and attitudes (e.g., working and getting along with others, appreciating diversity, making a commitment to continued schooling).

D. Recognizes how characteristics of students at different developmental levels (e.g., limited attention span and need for physical activity and movement for younger children; importance of peers, search for identity, questioning of values and exploration of long-term career and life goals for older students) impact teaching and learning.

E. Stimulates reflection, critical thinking, and inquiry among students (e.g., supports the concept of play as a valid vehicle for young children's learning; provides opportunities for young children to manipulate materials and to test ideas and hypotheses; engages students in structured, hands-on problem-solving activities that are challenging; encourages exploration and risk-taking; creates a learning community that promotes positive contributions, effective communication, and the respectful exchange of ideas).

F. Enhances learning for students by providing age-appropriate instruction that encourages the use and refinement of higher-order thinking skills (e.g., prompting students to explore ideas from diverse perspectives; structuring active learning experiences involving cooperative learning; problem solving, open-ended questioning and inquiry; promoting students' development of research skills).

G. Teaches, models, and monitors organizational and time-management skills at an age-appropriate level (e.g., establishing regular places for classroom toys and materials for young children, keeping related materials together, using organizational tools, using effective strategies for locating information and organizing information systematically).

H. Teaches, models, and monitors age-appropriate study skills (e.g., using graphic organizers, outlining, note-taking, summarizing, test-taking) and structures research projects appropriately (e.g., teaches students the steps in research, establishes checkpoints during research projects, helps students use time-management tools).

I. Analyzes ways in which teacher behaviors (e.g., teacher expectations, student grouping practices, teacher-student interactions) impact student learning and plans instruction and assessment that minimize the effects of negative factors and enhance all students' learning.

J. Analyzes ways in which factors in the home and community (e.g., parent expectations, availability of community resources, community problems) impact student learning and plans instruction and assessment with awareness of social and cultural factors to enhance all students' learning.

K. Understands the importance of self-directed learning and plans instruction and assessment that promote students' motivation and their sense of ownership of and responsibility for their own learning.

L. Analyzes ways in which various teacher roles (e.g., facilitator, lecturer) and student roles (e.g., active learner, observer, group participant) impact student learning.

M. Incorporates students' different approaches to learning (e.g., auditory, visual, tactile, kinesthetic) into instructional practices.

N. Provides instruction to ensure that students can apply various learning strategies (e.g., using prior knowledge, metacognition, graphic organizers) across content areas, in accordance with the ELPS.

O. Provides instruction in a manner that is linguistically accommodated (communicated, sequenced, and scaffolded) to the students' level of English-language proficiency to ensure that the student learns the knowledge and skills across content areas in accordance with the ELPS.

P. Applies knowledge of the implications for learning and instruction of the range of thinking abilities found among students in any one grade level and students' increasing ability over time to engage in abstract thinking and reasoning.

KEY TERMS

advanced organizers	*metacognition*	*negative transfer*
David Ausubel	*relationship*	*mass practice*
Graphic Organizers	*sequencing*	*distributed practice*
information processing	*transfer theory*	
meaning	*positive transfer*	

In recent years, neuroscientists have discovered more about how the brain learns. This is useful to us as teachers so we can use these findings to increase our students' learning, retention, and recall. We begin with a simple yet germane overview of how the brain learns.

Our senses are constantly bombarded with stimuli. We simultaneously see, hear, touch, smell, and perhaps taste things. Our brain operates as a filter to quickly decide which of these sensations are significant enough to be noticed and which to disregard. For example, if you live in a busy home environment with people coming and going, you might not pay attention to a door closing. However, suppose it is 3:00 A.M. and you hear the front door close. It is likely your brain would immediately attend to this, and you would wonder who was there and whether you should grab a baseball bat or hide under the bed. Suppose you are meeting a friend for lunch at a busy restaurant and as you scan the crowd looking for your friend, there exists a sea of faces. Your brain instantaneously disregards many of the faces until you spot your friend; then once you recognize your friend, the brain locks onto it. However, while your brain is sifting through all the visual stimulation, someone or something else may "catch your eye." Suppose you see your favorite aunt; your brain will focus on her rather than disregard her with the plethora of other faces.

Now let's apply this to your classroom. Your students' brains are sorting through a multitude of stimuli, deciding which are important and which are not. The sensory register is that part of the brain that acts as a filter. As a teacher, somehow you need to ensure that the students' attention is on you or the activity rather than becoming part of the background noise that is being filtered out. Therefore, we first need to get the students' attention, in other words get them engaged, to get through the sensory register and not be filtered out with the "noise."

When the student attends to the stimuli, they are operating with what is called the working memory or short-term memory. The information in your working memory exists for approximately 15-30 seconds before it begins to fade. The working memory is much like the desktop on your computer. It is where you are currently focused. Once you save the file it is the same as shifting what is in your working memory into your long-term memory. When a student cognitively processes information, it helps save it in their long-term memory, much like saving a file to your hard drive. If material is not attended to in working memory, it fades and is gone, just like turning off your computer without saving the file. For all practical purposes, the new information is gone. Teachers experience this when they have taught a lesson, not knowing the students were not processing the information, and the next day when they review the material, the students behave as though it is brand new and they have never seen it before. A frustrated and confused teacher can easily become disgruntled and think her students are not living up to her expectations, when in fact, they never saved the skill or content in their long-term memory but only worked with it for a short time within their working memory. If a teacher doesn't understand how the brain learns, this can be a very frustrating situation for her and the students.

Now let's briefly review what a teacher needs to do to help students learn, retain, and recall. First, we need to get the students to attend to the skill or activity to get it through the filter into working memory. Next, they need to process the material in such a way as to save it into long-term memory. Once it is in long-term memory, the problem becomes one of retention and recall. The information is in the students' brains; we just need to assist the students in knowing how to recall it. Going back to our computer example, we now have to locate a file and bring it back to our desktop so we can work on it.

With this overview in mind we will discuss:

1. How to get students focused on the skill or activity so as to engage the working memory.
2. Ways to save the content in short-term memory into long-term memory.
3. Building retention and recall.

As a teacher plans his or her lesson, it is important to keep in mind that most people can process seven plus or minus two bits of information at a time. For example, if we are teaching the state capitols, we need to chunk the information into seven plus or minus two bits of information at a time. So depending on our learners we can teach anywhere from five to nine state capitols at a time. However, if we exceed this number, we risk having some students forgetting some and perhaps becoming frustrated at their lack of success and give up. All 50 capitols will be taught, just not together. Suppose you want the students to learn the periodic chart, the causes of World War II, or weekly spelling words. Rather than give the students all the material to be memorized on Monday and have them begin studying, break the material into appropriate chunks and give a smaller yet meaningful amount each day. Although it seems that this will take longer, it is likely that it will go faster because the students will retain the information and you will have less reteaching to do.

There are two variables in determining how much material to teach at one time. In other words, do you teach toward the seven minus one or two or plus one or two bits of information at a time? The first variable is the ability level of the students. If they are less able, break the information into five, six, or seven bits of information. If the students are more able, you can use larger quantities of information. It is important to note at this point that a chunk of information can be very specific or very inclusive and general as long as it all relates.

The second variable in deciding how to chunk the new content is the difficulty level of the material. If the material is relatively easy, you can use larger portions. If the material is difficult, use smaller quantities.

There are four strategies to get your learners' attention and engage their working memory. They are use of self, emotion, a discrepant event, and mand.

STRATEGIES TO ENGAGE WORKING MEMORY

Self

It is human nature to be interested in anything that relates to us. Think of a time when you were looking at photographs of you and your friends. Who did you look at first in the picture? We tend to identify ourselves first to determine whether we like the picture, then we look at the others in the photograph. When we glance at a newspaper and it is open to the horoscope section, whose horoscope do we read first? As humans, we like and are interested in things about us, our interests, hobbies, careers, and the like. Therefore, as a teacher we can incorporate into our lesson ideas about our students—sports, musical interests, what movies they like to see, what books they like to read, what they do in their spare time, what goals they have for their future, their career aspirations, current jobs, etc. By doing this, we activate their short-term memory.

Emotion

Another technique to get the learners' attention is by eliciting emotion in our students during our instruction. Emotion is a very powerful way to involve students and help move the new content into long-term memory. Our lessons need to be emotionally engaging but not so emotionally charged that it becomes distracting. This can be a fine line to walk. Suppose that, as part of the curriculum, a high school literature teacher decides to assign *West Side Story*. If she teaches in a school with a high amount of gang-related activity this could be so emotionally charged that it becomes distracting. On the other hand, it could be a vehicle to discuss the negative impact of gangs. There are no clear-cut answers, just guidelines for teachers to follow. Again, try to make the lesson emotionally engaging, but not so emotionally charged that it becomes distracting.

Discrepant Event

A third method to engage students' short-term memory is by using a discrepant event. A discrepant event is something different or unusual that stands out to create cognitive disequilibrium and get the learners' attention. A discrepant even goes counter to students' predictions, experiences, or intuition. For instance, children enjoy helium balloons because they operate in an unexpected way. Children are accustomed to objects dropping to the ground. A balloon filled with helium going up makes a child curious and interested so he enjoys playing with it. Cognitive disequilibrium is when a student becomes intellectually off-balance and hence curious because it challenges their previous way of thinking. A discrepant event can be a foreign object, an unusual piece of music, a curious smell, an uncommon event, an atypical demonstration, and so forth.

Mand

Using mand, a teacher can engage the students' working memory. Mand is a nonverbal way to indicate "pay attention, this is important." Examples include raising or lowering your voice, tapping on the board, underlining a certain word, pausing in your speech, standing in a certain part of the room, repeating yourself, gesturing, and many other nonverbal cues. When teachers haphazardly use mand, they inadvertently give the students the message that one idea may be more important than another when they are simply trying to get the students' attention. Therefore, it is critical that a teacher deliberately uses mand to give the correct message of importance regarding an idea, not merely to quiet down a class.

Once the students' working memory is activated, it is necessary for them to process the skill or knowledge such that it enters long-term memory. There are many ways to do this. Practice and rehearsal, both rote and elaboration, helps students remember. Any kind of activity requiring the students to cognitively process the material will assist their retention level.

For students to remember the new material, it must be stored in long-term memory. Seven factors that increase the probability that our students will remember what they have learned in our class are meaning, feeling tone, degree of original learning, schedule of practice, transfer theory, use of examples, and organization.

1. **Meaning**—To make the material meaningful to the student we need to relate it to their past experience and knowledge base. We can use this prior knowledge as a springboard for the new skill or information. A teacher can also make the material meaningful by connecting it to students' interests, hobbies, sports, musical abilities, careers, etc.

2. **Feeling tone**—A pleasant feeling tone in our class helps students want to learn the material and retain it. Ways to generate a pleasant feeling tone include positive comments, encouragement, a sense of humor, greeting the students as they enter the room, and being kind and caring. Feeling tone is about the positive climate created by the teacher; not necessarily the appearance of the classroom.

3. **Degree of original learning**—The degree to which a student originally learns the knowledge and skills requisite to the new material. Subsequently, the new content influences a student's retention level for the forthcoming material. For example, when a student has learned arithmetic skills well, he is better prepared for learning further mathematics. However, if he struggles, he is less prepared and it will impact his retention. A high degree of original learning increases student retention and decreases the time it takes to learn the new information.

4. **Schedule of practice**—Two types of schedules of practice are useful in increasing retention. During the initial stages of learning, a student needs **mass practice**. Mass practice is frequent repeated practice for the purpose of quick learning. It is often short bursts of practice and often with different approaches. For example, suppose the teacher is having the students practice their spelling words. The first time she may have the students write each word on a piece of paper. The next time, which may be later that same day, the students may again practice them by writing them on small individual dry-erase boards and simultaneously show the teacher their response. A third time, again later that day or the next day, the teacher could put shaving cream on each student's desk and they write their spelling words in the shaving cream. Another idea is to have the students spell the words with letter magnets on a magnetic board. Another idea is to have the children work in pairs with letter cards and spell their words on a small clothesline. Frequent, short sessions are more effective than a few long ones.

After the students have learned the material, the teacher switches to **distributed practice**. This is where the students continue to practice, but it is spread out over time. They may rehearse their spelling words once a week, then once a month, then every 6 weeks, etc. The purpose of distributed practice is to build long-term retention.

5. **Transfer theory**—When prior learning influences the acquisition of new learning. Positive transfer is when prior knowledge accelerates the acquisition of new learning. The more a student knows about the new material the shorter the learning time. Negative transfer is when prior knowledge interferes with new learning. Teachers' effective use of transfer theory can help students understand new concepts easily by relating them to things they already know or by cutting off ideas that may confuse the students if accurate prior knowledge is incorrectly applied to a new idea.

Let's examine the impact of positive transfer as it relates to teaching operations of fractions. When a student learns to add fractions, a common denominator is necessary. Consequently, as the teacher introduces subtraction of fractions he could accelerate the students' understanding by explaining that subtraction is similar to addition in that the student still needs to find a common denominator before subtracting the fraction. This is positive transfer.

Now let's analyze an example of negative transfer. When the students begin to learn multiplication of fractions, they may erroneously think they first need to find a common denominator. They are taking accurate information (the common denominator) and applying it to a situation where it does not fit. In this case, the teacher needs to point out the potential of negative transfer during the introduction and cut off these ideas. The teacher should discuss why students need to find a common denominator for addition and subtraction but not for multiplication. Furthermore, if the teacher involves the students in hands-on activities, the students are more likely to remember it. As teachers gain experience in their profession, they will begin to recognize areas of potential negative transfer so they can steer the students away from it. If a student is not likely to make a wrong connection (negative transfer), do not bring it up. Suppose a teacher was going to have the students do an art project with beans, colored macaroni, and paste. When teachers tell the students not to put the beans up their noses and not to eat the paste, the teacher may actually be planting these ideas in the students' heads. If it is likely the student will exhibit a certain behavior or make a wrong connection, the teacher needs to bring it up and cut it off. If it is unlikely that the students will have negative transfer, then do not bring it up.

There are three techniques to promote transfer. These include similarity, association, and degree of original learning.

Similarity

The three ways concepts can be similar is through knowledge and skill, thoughts and feelings, and learning methodology or style. Teachers can accelerate learning by connecting the new skill or knowledge to previous learning that is similar. One concept that some students struggle with is the names and sounds of letters. Some letters name and sound match. Examples of these letters include *A*, *E*, *I*, and *O*. Whereas the sound of other letters can be heard in the name of the letter. For example, the letters *B*, *D*, *F*, *L*, and *S* have the sound of the letter heard in its name. Other letters have no audible connection between the letter's name and sound. This can be found in the letters *H*, *W*, and *Y*. For example, the name of the letter *H* and the sound of the letter *H* differ greatly. Consequently students can be challenged by this. However, a clever teacher would connect letters names and letter sounds with the fact that animals have names and sounds. Making this connection to the students' prior knowledge about animals having a name and making a sound that may or may not sound like their name will help children learn and understand letters better. Teachers also can positively transfer ideas that are not necessarily similar but have been associated together in past experience.

Another use of similarity is through thoughts and feelings. When the new material can be bridged to prior thoughts and feelings it will accelerate the learning. Suppose the teacher was introducing the four seasons. She could have the students identify with each season by relating the temperature with what it reminds them of and how it made them feel. For example, winter may remind them about snow and how it feels cold. When discussing summer the students may recall eating ice cream, the smell of sunscreen, and how great it feels to get into a swimming pool.

The last way similarity can be used is through instructional/learning methodology. If a student is already familiar with a particular instructional strategy it will not distract from the content and he can focus all his energy on the new content. Oftentimes the first encounter with a science lab can be overwhelming for a student. This may be because of the new learning environment rather than the actual science curriculum. Another example has to do with field trips. The idea of leaving the school can be so exciting that it distracts from the actual learning opportunity.

Association

As human beings we have lots of associations with former experiences. Think of a time when you heard a particular song on the radio and associate it with a time, place, or person from your past. Did you turn up the volume or change the station? The song at one time was a neutral stimulus but has been associated with a time, place, or person and now is associated with previous experiences and feelings.

Using association teachers can expedite the acquisition of the new curriculum. For example, a teacher could associate gang violence today when teaching Shakespeare's play *Romeo and Juliet* so the students understand the dilemmas and issues involved in the play.

Another way to employ association uses students' past successes to help remind them that they can achieve. It is useful for teachers to remind students of prior success to elicit a pleasant feeling tone as they begin a new activity or challenging experience. Past achievements can serve as a morale booster as we face new growth opportunities.

Degree of Original Learning is the degree to which the learner mastered the new skill or knowledge. A high degree of original learning can expedite new knowledge. The last way to promote transfer is through using examples that tap into prior knowledge, making connections to familiar experiences and skills, and emphasizing the similarity of critical attributes.

6. **Use of Examples**—As a rule of thumb, students need three to five examples to help them understand a new concept. There are four keys for generating examples that help glue the new skill and knowledge into the students' long-term memory:

   1. Focus on the essence—This means to create examples that highlight the critical attribute and delineate the germane characteristic of the concept. It is also important to keep the essence constant and vary the situation. For example, when teaching the concept of a triangle, the critical attribute is a closed figure with three sides. Next, the teacher would vary the examples as she demonstrates different-looking triangles.

   2. Connect to prior knowledge—Use examples that are familiar to the students and build on their prior knowledge.

   3. Use unambiguous examples—Keep the examples clear and narrowly focused on the concept. Too often teachers muddy the example with too many ideas or wordiness.

   4. No emotional distracters—Examples should be emotionally engaging but not emotionally distracting. When an example elicits emotions it helps drive it into long-term memory; however, if it is too distracting and the student gets caught up in the emotion we have lost their attention.

7. **Organization**—David Ausubel (1960, 1963) addresses the need for students to have advanced organizers. The purpose of advanced organizers is to help the students have a mental system in which they can easily store and retrieve information. It is much like having many items that need filing. The individual labels the file folders so he has a system in place for filing and retrieval. A teacher provides this to students by giving them an overview of the content, having the students read the subtitles in a chapter, or reading the questions at the end of a chapter before they begin reading the chapter for comprehension.

Sample Graphic Organizers

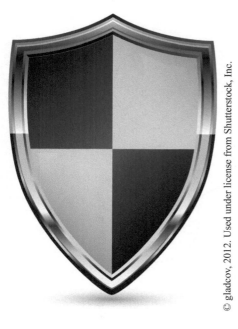

© gladcov, 2012. Used under license from Shutterstock, Inc.

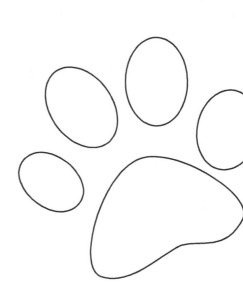

© HitToon.com, 2012. Used under license from Shutterstock, Inc.

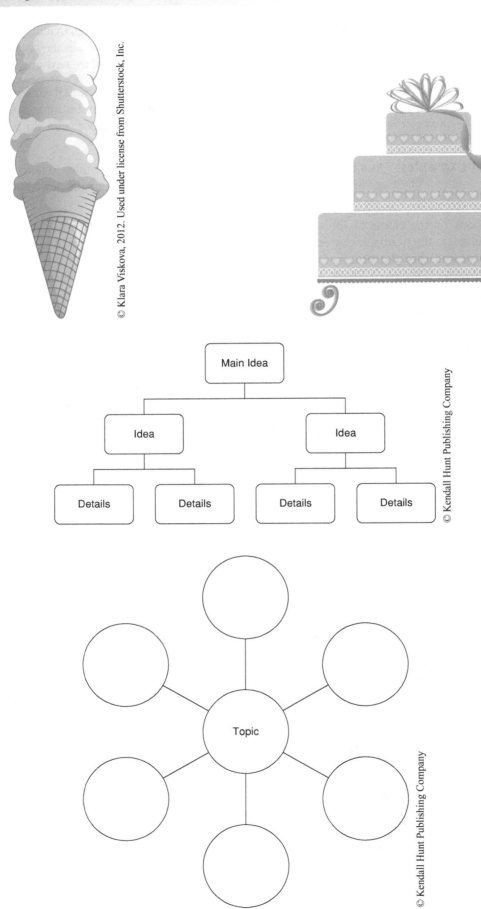

Main Idea

Idea

Idea

Details

Details

Details

Details

Topic

Another way to help students organize information is to use graphic organizers. The purpose of graphic organizers is to provide a visual way to organize information. The teacher can provide the graphic organizer or the student can make one up.

WAYS TO REDUCE THE NEED FOR PRACTICE

As with any new skill or knowledge practice is necessary for improvement. The purpose of practice is to increase speed and accuracy. Knowing this, teachers spend a lot of class time having students practice. However, as teachers, if we can spend less time on practice, yet students still learn and retain the information or new skill effectively, we can have more time for the remaining curriculum. According to Madeline Hunter (1982), there are ways to reduce the need for practice, including meaning, transfer theory, relationship, and sequencing.

Meaning—When teachers make new material meaningful to students, it increases the effectiveness and retention rate of the lesson. Relate new skills and knowledge to the students' hobbies, interests, talents, sports, music, food, money, and ambitions.

Transfer theory—Through appropriate use of positive transfer, teachers can accelerate learning; and being aware of negative transfer in order to distinguish the difference between prior knowledge and current ideas, teachers can reduce the probability of error and the need for practice.

Relationship—There exists three ways that teachers can increase student learning by proper use of relationship. The first way is using thematic units. Thematic units are powerful learning strategies because many content areas can be tied together through a common theme. Consequently, this relates many domains together, much like students will encounter in real life. Another use of relationship is remembering that position equals relationship. As teachers write on the board or display visual aids, they need to know that students will tacitly assign relation to the position. For example, suppose a teacher has the students name four types of clouds. The children say stratus, cumulus, nimbus, and cirrus as the teacher randomly writes them on the board. The children may misinterpret position as relationship and think each type of cloud is written in its respective position in the sky. The third use of relationship is teaching content in context. Much of this relates to authentic learning. For example, if the students are learning about ratio, rather than have them work purely computational problems, have the students find real ratios of things that interest them and are meaningful.

Sequencing—The last way to reduce the amount of practice a student requires involves sequencing. There are ways the teacher can sequence material for student practice to help build retention quickly. The five ways include review, chunking, change in sequence, extra practice, and chaining.

1. **Review**—It is common for teachers to begin a new lesson with a review of the previous day. This helps students refresh their memory and bring up prior knowledge. The end of a lesson is another strategic place for a review. To increase retention it is extremely beneficial to review the more difficult parts of the new material at the conclusion of a lesson. At this point the review can be as simple as a brief dialogue with the students or a reinforcement activity to glue the new content into students' long-term memory.

2. **Chunking**—Keep in mind the idea that the brain can process seven plus or minus two bits of information at a time. Therefore, by decreasing the size of each learning chunk, students can more easily digest the new concept. Remember, it takes a lot of mental energy to learn and internalize something new.

3. **Change in sequence**—When first introducing a concept, it is beneficial to place the more difficult learning in the front position of the lesson. This allows students to focus on the hardest part first when they have the most mental energy available. This may be followed with easier material. As the students mass-practice the new material over the subsequent days, the teacher may change up the sequence for variety. For example, when music students are learning to play a new song on their instruments, the teacher may have the students learn a more difficult part first. Then the students may begin playing the new song from the beginning. As the students practice, it would not be uncommon for them to first review the difficult section of the new song. This would then be followed by the measures that are frequently repeated in the piece; then the students would play the entire song from beginning to end. This is one example of how a teacher might change the sequence. However, when it is important for a student to learn the material in a specific sequence, this strategy would not be appropriate. Examples of this would be when students are learning to recite the alphabet, memorize their counting numbers, or steps in a mathematical procedure.

4. **Extra practice**—It is tempting for teachers to have students practice new material in one long session immediately following the lesson. Although it is important to mass-practice the new material, students learn more and retain it longer when they practice small amounts in short episodes. Students also benefit when teachers maintain the skill to be practiced but change the experience. During the practice period provide a little extra practice on the more challenging parts of the content.

Let's combine the ideas of chunking, review, and practice as a teacher has the students learn all the state capitols. The teacher would introduce seven plus or minus two (chunking) capitols at a time, keeping in mind the difficulty of the task and the students' ability level. Some capitols may be easier for students to memorize than others. Next, the teacher would have the students practice this chunk as part of the mass practice. Then the teacher would go on to another subject and return to practicing the introduced capitols later. He would continue this pattern over the course of the day. In this way, the students will practice the same capitols perhaps five different times throughout the day experiencing a different activity each time. Ideas for practice could be recitation, matching the name of each state to its capitol using a map, having the children write the capitol on a dry-erase board as the teacher says the state, play concentration with cards where the students have to turn over two cards and match the correct state and capitol, and have 10 students volunteer to each hold up a card identifying a state or a capitol and the rest of the class has to match up the correct students. Using creativity, the ideas are endless.

The next day the teacher would review the previous chunk and introduce a new chunk of capitols. Again she would have the students practice immediately and throughout the day in a variety of ways. Remember, children learn best in a play environment.

5. **Chaining**—Chaining is backward buildup. When reading a magazine, some people start at the back and read to the front cover. This is an example of chaining. It is where the teacher starts at the last position, then the second to the last, and so forth until she is at the beginning. Suppose the theater department of a school is beginning to practice the school play. Perhaps the actors learn and practice the third act first, then the second act, and finally, the first act. By the time they have memorized their lines for the first act, they know the entire play. Another example would be when the choir is learning a new song. They could start by learning the fourth verse first and work backward to the first verse. This strategy does not lend itself to all lessons but it can add novelty to the learning experience.

One last note on practice: Practice may not make perfect, but it does make permanent.

To summarize, when teachers understand how the brain attends to, sorts, and processes information, teachers can effectively design and implement their lessons to help students be academically successful. Understanding how students learn, teachers can then assist them in learning, retaining, and recalling the new material.

METACOGNITION

Metacognition is the brain monitoring itself. It is when you think about what you are thinking about while you are thinking about it. A student metacognates when he is aware of his cognition during a task. Students benefit by metacognition so they are more purposeful, monitor, and make improvements in their work.

Forms of self-monitoring include planning and evaluating one's work. Examples of this are reading responses, journals, learning logs, and student portfolios.

INFORMATION PROCESSING

As the teacher presents information, it is important to know that some students are field-dependent learners and others are field-independent learners. Field-dependent learners are active learners when the big picture is being discussed. For example, applications of ideas, overviews, and narratives of the overall idea engage field-dependent learners. Field-independent learners take a passive role during these times. However, field-independent learners are actively engaged during the details of the discussion. They prefer systematic procedures, specifics, and directions. Therefore, teachers need to incorporate both strategies into their instructional repertoire to reach as many students as possible.

© baldyrgan, 2014, Used under license of Shutterstock, Inc.

TIPS FOR COMPETENCY 4: HOW LEARNING OCCURS

- Use instructional strategies that promote student learning.
- Linking new information to prior experiences helps students make connections between the new material and what they already know.
- Foster a view of learning as a purposeful pursuit so students view it as meaningful.
- Promote a sense of responsibility for one's own learning so that students become self-directed and self-starters.
- When possible, give students control over their own learning. Allow them to define their learning goals within the given context, create their own action plan, and monitor their own progress and performance so they are focused and purposeful in their work.
- Facilitate activities to encourage students to be critical thinkers and problem-solvers.
- The Benjamin Franklin method of decision making involves making a list of pros and cons for both sides of a decision.
- To keep students focused and progressing, set goals, interim deadlines, and timetables. Meet with individuals or groups of students to provide help. Interim deadlines promote student achievement while doing projects.
- Students gain ownership and have a sense of control over their learning when they create a plan of action. This is especially true of struggling students.
- Foster individual talents and special abilities in students.
- Nurture divergent thinking in students. An example of a question to get students thinking differently would be, "Suppose you had to live without electricity, how would life be different?" or "How would you organize and pack for a 3-day hike in the desert?"

Discussion Activities and Outlines

Teachers need to ensure that students first attend to the correct stimulus as their senses are being bombarded with stimulation. Next, the idea presented needs to be such that it gets through the sensory register and into the working memory (short-term memory). The new skill or knowledge then needs to be stored in long-term memory for retention and recall.

Draw a sketch representing this process.

A person can process _____ + or – two bits of information at a time.

Explain the two variables that determine plus or minus two bits of information.

Ways to Engage Working Memory

1. Self

2. Emotion

3. Discrepant event

4. Mand

Two Types of Rehearsal to Help Students Retain the New Material

1. Rote

2. Elaboration

Four Ways for Students to Elaborate to Increase Their Retention

1. Image

2. Paraphrase

3. Summarize

4. Use of an example

Teaching for Retention

1. Meaning

2. Feeling tone

3. Degree of original learning

4. Schedules of practice
   a. Mass practice

   b. Distributed practice

5. Transfer (three things that transfer):
   a. Knowledge
   b. Thoughts or feelings
   c. Actions

6. Examples

7. Organization

Transfer Theory

<u>Transfer</u>—The process of prior knowledge influencing the acquisition of new learning.

<u>Positive transfer</u>—Previous learning accelerates the acquisition of new learning. The more you know about the new material, the shorter the learning a time.

<u>Negative transfer</u>—Prior knowledge applied inappropriately interferes with new learning.

For negative transfer, cut off ideas that interfere with new learning.

Two Factors to Promote Transfer

1. Similarity

    a. Knowledge and skill
    b. Thoughts and feelings
    c. Learning methodology

2. Association

Two Ways to Increase Transfer Effectively

1. Degree of original learning

2. Effective examples
    a. Tap long-term memory
    b. Make connections to the new material
    c. Identify critical attributes

Four Keys When Generating Examples

1. Focus on the essence

2. Hook onto long-term memory

3. Use unambiguous examples

4. No emotional distracters

Four Ways to Reduce the Need for Practice

The purpose of practice is to increase speed and accuracy.

1. Meaning

2. Transfer theory

3. Relationships
   a. Thematic units
   b. Position equals relationship
   c. Teach content in context

4. Sequencing

Ways to Sequence

1. Review

2. Chunking

3. Change in sequence

4. Extra practice

5. Chaining

Four Questions and Answers about Practice

1. How much material should the students practice at one time?

2. How long should a practice period last?

3. How often should the students practice?

4. How will the students know how they performed?

Answers

1. A small amount (7 plus or minus 2) with maximal meaning. Use meaning to determine quantity, not math. Divide the content into short, meaningful chunks. As the teacher presents a chunk, give several examples to increase the probability of more students learning. Also, check for understanding and have the class practice that chunk of material sufficiently before moving onto the next chunk.

2. A short period of time with students applying intense effort to learn. Several short, intense practice periods will increase learning more than one long practice period. Furthermore, students often have the mindset that they can complete anything if they can see the end in sight. Therefore, short periods lend themselves to students exerting more effort in learning. Consequently, teachers need to stress the learning of the material, not just putting in a certain quantity of time. Most of us can simply wait out the clock; it takes effort to learn. To maintain continuity but break the monotony of practice, the teacher can have the students practice in short episodes throughout the day. Each practice period will involve the same objective but change the approach.

3. For new material, the students need mass practice. Mass practice involves frequent repetition and is for quick learning. Once the material is mastered, the teacher can switch to distributed practice. This practice is spread out over time for the purpose of long-term retention.

4. The teacher should give immediate and specific feedback. The students should know the teacher's grading criteria before they begin the product to be assessed.

Metacognition

Metacognition—when the brain monitors itself. It is when you think about what you are thinking about while you are thinking about it.

A student metacognates when …

Students benefit by metacognition so they will

    a. Be more purposeful in their work.

    b. Monitor their work.

    c. Make improvements to their work.

Forms of self-monitoring of one's work include:

    a.

    b.

    c.

Examples of these are:

    a.

    b.

    c.

    d.

Sample Test Questions

1. Mrs. Stewart teaches a sixth-grade social studies course that is currently focusing on map-reading skills. At the beginning of the unit she plans to ask the students to tell her what they already know about maps and reading maps. Then she intends to give them an overview of the unit on maps. By finding out what the students already know about maps and map reading, Mrs. Stewart can:

   a. identify those areas of the map-reading skills she can skip.

   b. accelerate their learning by building on prior knowledge.

   c. write a challenging test to adequately assess them.

   d. motivate the students by showing them how much they have learned at the end of the lesson.

2. Mrs. Stewart tells the students that next Friday they will be going on a field trip to the Science Center, then eat lunch at Burgerville on 10th Avenue and Wilshire Boulevard, visit the zoo after lunch, then return to school. She gives each group of students a map of their community and tells them to use the map to create directions of how to get from school to the Science Center, from there to Burgerville, then on to the zoo, and back to school again. Mrs. Stewart probably uses this activity to:

   a. foster diversity in the classroom.

   b. get shy learners to participate.

   c. allow children with a bad home life to have a happy day.

   d. make the content meaningful and relevant.

3. Mr. Bates teaches high school mathematics. Veronica is a student in his class with a field-dependent processing style. Mr. Bates might expect Veronica to experience particular difficulty paying attention:

   a. in social situations.

   b. during detailed explanations.

   c. working in groups.

   d. during discussion of the applications.

4. Which of the following would best prepare Mr. Bates's students to understand a lesson finding the areas of geometric figures?

   a. The day before the lesson, have the students write down and discuss in small groups all the things they already know about geometric figures and their areas.

   b. The day before the lesson, give the students a handout that shows the different geometric shapes and the formulas for the areas of each and tell them to review the formulas before they come to class the next day.

   c. The day before the lesson, distribute a worksheet the students will have to complete after Mr. Bates goes over the formulas the next day in class.

   d. The day of the lesson, begin by drawing large diagrams of the geometric figures on the board, then write the formula and an example of its application underneath each figure.

5. During the geometric areas unit Mr. Bates has the students keep a journal of their new knowledge. This serves the purpose of:

   a. students needing to log their progress.

   b. getting students to apply what they have learned to a new situation.

   c. getting students to think about their new knowledge.

   d. students helping others catch up after they have been absent.

Answers

1. A is not correct. It is better to briefly review a skill than to skip it altogether.

   B is the correct answer. This is effective use of positive transfer.

   C is not correct. Diagnosis is used for identifying what the learners already know, including gaps, holes, and misinformation. It also identifies where the learning leaves off and where the new instruction should begin. It is not used for writing tricky tests that the teacher knows the students will not know the answers.

   D is not correct. There are better ways to motivate learners. It is fine to point out how much they have learned, but motivation is woven through all instruction.

2. A is not correct. Group work can foster appreciation of diversity but the focus of the question is about the benefit of students making a map of their own community.

   B is not correct. Again, the focus is not about learner profiles but making the content relevant and meaningful to the students.

   C is not correct. The purpose of a field trip is educational, not to give kids a break from reality. However, if this is a byproduct, that is fine too.

   D is the correct answer. By having the students use a map of their own community and places they are interested in visiting will make map reading skills meaningful and relevant.

3. A is not correct. Information processing is not necessarily related to the vagaries of social situations.

   B is the correct answer. Field-dependent learners are active learners during discussions of the overall concept and passive learners during specifics or details.

   C is not correct. Again, field-dependency is not related to working in groups.

   D is not correct. Discussing the applications broadens the perspective and this is field-dependent learners' strength.

4. **A is the correct answer**. Having the students generate and discuss their prior knowledge regarding geometric figures will prepare them for the next day and allow Mr. Bates to build on that prior knowledge.

   B is not correct. It is not reasonable for students to understand formulas that have never been introduced or explained. Furthermore, it would probably intimidate them.

   C is not correct. There is no viable purpose to showing them a worksheet they know little about. Also, it would probably demotivate many students.

   D is not correct. This would be too much information at one time. It would be better to teach one shape, show how the formula is derived using hands-on activities, have the students generate the formula through inquiry, then provide examples of its application. Each shape would be a different lesson.

5. A is not correct. Although it may behoove students to recognize their progress, journals are better used for metacognitive purposes.

   B is not correct. This answer addresses *application*, which is not requisite for journal entries.

   C is the correct answer. Journals are a beneficial vehicle for metacognition.

   D is not correct. It is the teacher's job to help students catch up after being absent, not the student's.

REFERENCES

Ausubel, D. P. (1960). The use of advance organizers in the learning and retention of meaningful verbal material. *Journal of Educational Psychology, 51,* 267-272.

Ausubel, D. P. (1963). *The psychology of meaningful verbal learning.* New York: Grune & Stratton.

Hunter, M. (1982). *Mastery teaching.* El Segundo, CA: TIP Publications.

Creating a Positive, Productive Classroom Environment

Domain 2

Competency 5

The Importance of a Positive Classroom Environment to Enhance Academic Achievement and to Promote Effective Social Interactions

Teri Bingham, EdD
West Texas A&M University

Angela Spaulding, EdD
West Texas A&M University

> **Competency 5:** The teacher knows how to establish a classroom climate that fosters learning, equity, and excellence and uses this knowledge to create a physical and emotional environment that is safe and productive.

The beginning teacher:

A. Uses knowledge of the unique characteristics and needs of students at different developmental levels to establish a positive, productive classroom environment (e.g., encourages cooperation and sharing among younger students; provides middle-level students with opportunities to collaborate with peers; encourages older students' respect for the community and the people in it).

B. Establishes a classroom climate that emphasizes collaboration and supportive interactions, respect for diversity and individual differences, and active engagement in learning by all students.

C. Analyzes ways in which teacher-student interactions and interactions among students impact classroom climate and student learning and development.

D. Presents instructions in ways that communicate the teacher's enthusiasm for learning.

E. Uses a variety of means to convey high expectations for all students.

F. Knows characteristics of physical spaces that are safe and productive for learning, recognizes the benefits and limitations of various arrangements of furniture in the classroom, and applies strategies for organizing the physical environment to ensure physical accessibility and facilitate learning in various instructional contexts.

G. Creates a safe, nurturing, and inclusive classroom environment that addresses students' emotional needs and respects students' rights and dignity.

KEY TERMS

caring	*conflict-resolution strategies*	*Maslow's hierarchy of needs*
character education	*cooperative learning*	*self-efficacy*
classroom climate	*environmental factors*	*self-fulfilling prophecy*
conflict contaminants	*high expectation*	*social skills training*

If you had the opportunity to work for bosses who clarify their expectations, help you to successfully complete major tasks, and provide positive feedback when you performed well, would you enjoy coming to work every day? In all probability you would find satisfaction in your work. In contrast, would you want to work for bosses who were sarcastically demeaning, unclear in their expectations, and never complimentary when you worked long hours to complete important deadlines? Probably not, because when the climate of the workplace is considered, most adults usually prefer a positive atmosphere in which people are valued and accepted. Workers are much more inclined to enjoy their jobs if their workplaces are not overshadowed by negativity.

Similarly, students are more apt to value their school experiences if their classroom teachers are encouraging and create conditions that foster academic achievement and positive social interactions. The climate of a classroom has such a significant impact on students' education that educators in the state of Texas have devoted Competency 5 to classroom climate and its effects on learning.

CLASSROOM CLIMATE AND TEACHER EXPECTATIONS

Upon entering a restaurant, we easily become aware of the climate. It may be loud and rambunctious like a sports bar after a score, it may be romantic with soft music and low lighting, or it may be family-oriented with plenty of booths, candy machines at the entrance, and bright lights. Our classrooms also have a climate that students become aware of upon entering. This perception is then reinforced through the teacher's actions or negated by them. The ideal classroom climate is one where students have a pleasant relationship with the teacher, want to learn, and know the teacher believes in them. Students quickly pick up on the degree to which their teacher supports them and has high, yet reasonable expectations. A teacher's expectations of a student influence the way that student views him- or herself (Tavani and Losh, 2003).

Teachers who care about their students want them to achieve academically. Caring teachers encourage their students to excel academically and to develop their intellectual gifts and potentials; however, in doing so, it is critical that teachers have high yet attainable expectations for their students. In contrast, teachers who consistently accept poor work from capable students are not exhibiting concern for them. Instead, their actions are telling their students that they are not interested in their academic achievement (Stipek, 2002). The expectations that teachers have for students profoundly affect student learning. Students live up to or down to a teacher's expectations (Rubie-Davies, 2006; Weinstein, 2002). For children who have low levels of ability, or come from a home or community environment that is less than desirable, a teacher who holds high expectations and provides academic support and is responsive to that child makes a difference (Klem & Connell). Researchers have found that teacher expectations trump student background and ability. Teachers who have high, yet reasonable expectations of students play a vital role in helping a child begin to believe in him- or herself and perform at higher academic levels of proficiency (Lieberman & Miller, 2004).

Students often respond to teachers according to the expectations they have for students' levels of academic achievement. For example, if teachers do not expect their students to learn at higher cognitive levels, then they will not do so. In such cases, teachers probably have decreased the cognitive demands of the curriculum, which is unfortunate because students cannot learn what they are not taught and expected to learn. On the other hand, students often learn much more effectively when they are expected to do so and when teachers provide suitable guidance to enable students to perform well academically.

Unfortunately, many students who are presumed to be low achievers or to be categorized in the low-ability groups often are not given as much attention and encouragement as students who are considered high achievers. For example, Good and Brophy (2000) found that teachers often treat high-achieving students differently than they do other students. Many teachers tend (1) to call on high achievers more often than other students and are more apt to give them adequate time to answer questions, (2) to praise high achievers more for their academic successes than they praise lower-achieving students for their successes, (3) to provide high-achieving students with more feedback when they ask questions than they do for lower-achieving students, and (4) use positive nonverbal communications more often with high than with low achievers. This differential treatment is problematic for many students who are cognizant of both the positive and negative ways that they and other students are addressed by their teachers. Persell (2004) notes that:

> *Students report being aware of the different expectations teachers have for them, and they notice differences in the way that teachers treat them. For example, students studied by Ferguson (2001) reported that when they asked the teacher a question, they received only a brief one-sentence reply, but when other students (for whom the teacher had high expectations) asked the same question, the teacher spoke at length in response. (pp. 99–100)*

Such inequitable treatment creates a negative classroom climate and discourages many students from asking teachers for help and, therefore, not only decreases the learning opportunities for these students but also undermines a teacher's effectiveness. The unfortunate irony is that those students who are more inclined to need encouragement and academic help are less likely to receive it even when they elicit it.

Rosenthal and Jacobson (1968) studied the impact of positive teacher expectations and found that teacher expectations profoundly affected the academic achievement of first through sixth graders. At the beginning of the school year, the researchers told teachers that average students had high levels of intellectual potential and probably would show unusual levels of academic achievement gains in the coming year. Consequently, the teachers believed that their students were extremely talented, and they had high expectations for student learning, which seemed to substantially increase students' levels of academic achievement.

It is critical for teachers to have high expectations for students and to encourage them to excel academically. Academic success is important for both present and future learning because students' levels of achievement have a profound impact on their academic self-efficacy (Stipek, 2002). If students have low self-efficacy, they are much less inclined to persevere in challenging, higher cognitive tasks whereas students with high self-efficacies are more likely to stick with and complete higher cognitive activities. Students with high self-efficacy expect to achieve academic success. Consequently, building students' self-efficacy is an extremely important aspect of motivating students to learn because students are more inclined to persevere in challenging academic work as their self-efficacy increases and because academic success often is a wide door to future academic success (Baron, 1998; Schunk, 1995).

Fifty years ago, Merton (1954) developed the concept of self-fulfilling prophecy. He stressed that students often behave and perform academically in the way that teachers expect from them. Concerning expectations for student behavior, teachers need to establish and clarify reasonable classroom rules and routines and expect students to follow them so that instructional activities unfold smoothly. Rules, policies, and procedures need to be taught, modeled, and practiced at the beginning of the year. When teachers take time to teach students their expectations for classroom interactions, students are more inclined to accept and meet teacher expectations.

© Tomasz Trojanowski, 2014, Used under license of Shutterstock, Inc.

Through experience most of us know this to be true. Many of us have had a teacher who believed in us and really made an impact in our life. Caring teachers who are student-centered and provide motivating, engaging learning experiences cultivate an environment where students can flourish. In an emotionally safe classroom students understand we are all learning together and are expected to support each other. Children do not laugh at others' mistakes, but rather help each other learn and be successful; together we celebrate one another's accomplishments. When students work in collaboration toward a common goal, there can be genuine concern for each other and greater appreciation of one another's diversity and assets. Classrooms where the students feel safe, accepted, competent, and productive offer fertile ground for them to achieve academic and social success.

EMOTIONAL AND PHYSICAL SAFETY

In order for students to thrive academically they need an atmosphere where they feel emotionally and physically safe (Cohen & Geier, 2010; Rutter, Giller, & Hagell, 1998). Emotionally safe means the students know they will not be embarrassed, humiliated, intimidated, threatened, bullied, or caused to lose their dignity. There are other ways for teachers to motivate students than using these negative tactics. Students feel safe when their physical needs are met. This means they are allowed to use the restroom and get a drink of water at reasonable times and frequency. It also means they are not afraid of physical threat or harm on the playground, in the halls, in the bathroom, or walking home after school. Students with physical impairments need access to resources to feel comfortable in the classroom. Teachers need to make certain that learning centers, computers, and resource materials are accessible by all learners. Furthermore, classroom spaces need to provide safety from physical harm. By arranging the furniture with the students' needs in mind, learners can have physical access to all communal areas. Various instructional contexts may require teachers to get creative in their arrangement of the students' desks, small-group areas, and classroom furniture. For example, if the teacher meets with small groups of learners at a horseshoe-shaped table for a specific learning experience, ensure that children with physical handicaps can safely participate too.

RESPECT AND ACCEPTANCE

A supportive classroom environment is one where the teacher models equity for all (Lieberman, 2011). He or she is aware of the erroneous stereotypes and gender issues that can lead to false beliefs about students. An equitable teacher treats all students with respect and dignity and holds reasonable expectations of all learners regardless of gender, ethnicity, religion, culture, socioeconomic status, sexual orientation, or disabilities. When the teacher sets high standards of excellence for all students, they may achieve self-efficacy. When the teacher models and expects respectful behavior from his or her students, the classroom is a place where students feel accepted and not judged.

STUDENT COMPETENCE

Students increase their self-efficacy, believing that they can accomplish tasks and be successful, when they demonstrate competence (Bandura, 1993; Goddard, Hoy, & Woolfolk, 2000; Schunk, 1990). Teachers can support the initial stages of learning by providing scaffolding, guidance, and assistance. Teachers can provide engaging learning opportunities for students to practice new skills and knowledge, increasing the likelihood that the students will feel proficient (Levesque, Zuehlke, Stanek, & Ryan, 2004). A student who has experienced numerous successes in his past predicts success in future endeavors. A student who has experienced much failure in his past predicts failure in his future. Ergo, it is imperative for teachers to design learning activities where students experience competence. This does not mean we dilute the curriculum. Rather, we engineer activities where students will practice the new skill or knowledge at an appropriate level of difficulty then steadily increase the degree of complexity. By using readiness assessments teachers will know the student's zone of proximal development and plan accordingly.

STUDENT PRODUCTIVITY

Students value their educational experiences when they create products that are meaningful. There are a plethora of methods students can use to demonstrate mastery of their new skill or knowledge. Those products or assessments are of significance when they are connected to real-world applications. It is these meaningful activities that generate a feeling of productivity in students, thereby reinforcing the idea that education is a valuable experience. Differential instruction lends itself to students having opportunities to demonstrate mastery of new skills and knowledge using various forms of alternative assessments.

TEACHER ENTHUSIASM, ATTITUDE, AND NURTURING

The classroom climate is impacted by the teacher's attitude, enthusiasm, and level of nurturing for students. Although teachers are human and have their own trials in their personal lives, students still need for their teacher to exude a positive attitude with a pleasant disposition. Much like actors know the show must go on, teachers must temporarily set aside their problems for the benefit of students. Of course, it is fine for students to see that teachers have good days and bad days, but hopefully there are a lot more good days than bad. A teacher's enthusiasm for education and even a specific content can be contagious. One of the best ways to get students excited about new material is to demonstrate that passion yourself. Students ascertain how their teacher tacitly feels about a topic. So, effective teachers create their own excitement and love of learning so they can share that with the children.

In early childhood classes it is common for teachers to be nurturing toward their students. However, older students still need nurturing and compassion too. We as teachers need to expand our operational definition of nurturing to include supporting, encouraging, cherishing, and cultivating. Nurturing goes beyond giving a small child a hug or an emotional bandage; teachers in upper elementary, middle school, and high school also need to exercise nurturing skills. This doesn't mean to pamper a student or excuse him from his responsibilities. Nurturing means to support and encourage the student as he learns new skills and knowledge; to let a child feel cherished and cared about; to cultivate a positive identity within the student and to notice each student. Students are not small adults, they are children and youth who need to be nurtured in appropriate ways no matter what grade they are in. Think about it, even as an adult, don't we all appreciate a kind word or gesture occasionally?

To inspire and promote a classroom where all children feel accepted, dignified, respected, and safe, teachers need to reflect on the students' interactions. By analyzing student-student and teacher-student interactions, the teacher can engineer a better environment. The classroom climate transcends all learning, student relations, teacher-student communications, and student development. As the majority of the day is spent in school, we want it to be a place where students feel comfortable and can develop both cognitively and emotionally.

CARING AND ITS EFFECTS ON THE CLASSROOM CLIMATE

It is especially important that teachers foster an atmosphere of acceptance in which students feel that they are valued by their teacher and class. Noddings (1992) and Wentzel (1997) have emphasized the importance of caring in the classroom and school environment. How one defines caring varies from person to person and from culture to culture. Students, parents, and guardians want caring teachers. Typically, when educators refer to caring in the classroom, they typically are not just referring to a pleasant disposition, although this is important. Noddings (2001), for example, explains it this way:

> *If one supposes that caring is merely a nice attitude, an attitude that ignores poor behavior and low achievement in favor of helping students feel good, then, of course, caring will be seen as antithetical to professional conduct. But this is wrong. A carer, faithfully receiving the cared-for over time, will necessarily want the best for that person; that is part of what it means to care. (p. 101)*

Caring teachers help students understand that they are accepted and belong and that their academic abilities are respected and valued. For example, children in the lower elementary grades need opportunities to express themselves during sharing types of stories and other activities. These sharing events help the student to develop a sense of belonging if the teacher is empathetic and is attentive to the student. Similarly, some students have difficulty making the transition from elementary school to the middle school environment. When they were in elementary school, they typically had one to two teachers in self-contained classrooms. It is a shock for some students to have multiple classroom locations and teachers that they do not know. With all these changes, middle school students especially need to know that they belong and are valued by their teachers so that their self-esteem and level of academic achievement do not decline. Likewise, teachers foster belonging in high school classes when they value the opinions of their students and when they create an academic and social environment in which they are not ridiculed if they make mistakes. When teachers accept students as individuals and create a positive and caring classroom environment, students are much more inclined to learn effectively (McCombs, 1998).

PRAISE

Praise, encouragement, and acknowledgment can feel like a verbal hug to the recipient. This demonstrates care and concern about students. When praise is sincere, earned, and specific it can motivate a student; however, there are some guidelines to follow to maximize the value of praise and minimize the unintended messages we sometimes send. Here are some suggestions to follow when using praise and encouragement.

1. Only praise when the student has earned it, otherwise it can appear as, and probably is, manipulation. When praise is used to manipulate a student into completing a behavior he or she may be resentful and possibly nonresponsive. Be specific in detailing the behavior you are praising and would like to see more of. For example, "Zane, thank you for holding the door open for the other students" or "Ben, it was great of you to show the new student where the cafeteria is located. Thanks."

2. Make your comment about the student's effort and success, not on his or her character. For example, rather than saying, "You are a terrific student," try saying, "Thank you for picking up all the homework, you are a great helper."

3. Express your feelings to the student about what he or she did. "Jake, you make me proud to have you in class" or "Your kindness is greatly appreciated."

4. Recognize the student's effort and progress; do not wait for perfection. "Wow, knowing your fours times table! You have come a long way!" or "Look at that score, you should be proud of how well you did."

5. Children generalize our comments so we need to phrase them in such a way that the student draws positive conclusions about him- or herself. For example, a child throws his trash toward the garbage can at a distance and the teacher says, "Jaime, don't be lazy, walk over to the trash." The student doesn't isolate our comment to this instance, but rather interprets it and generalizes it to his character that the teacher believes he is a lazy person. Instead, say, "Jaime, I know you could make that shot if you go up close to the trash can." Then follow it with a nod or a wink so he knows you are actually giving him instruction. Another example is, "Thank you for feeding the class pet, you are a super helper" or "Great job putting away all the art materials. Thanks for being responsible and for all your help."

6. When we give praise we need to keep two things in mind. First, do not follow praise or encouragement with a "but." It gets interpreted that our praise was to simply mask or soften our criticism. For example, "Becca, you did a great job on your spelling test, now you need to work harder on your book report." Rather than combine the two statements, separate them by time. And the second idea dovetails with the first: After giving praise, stop talking and allow the comment to sink in.

© baldyrgan, 2014, Used under license of Shutterstock, Inc.

TIPS FOR COMPETENCY 5: A POSITIVE CLASSROOM ENVIRONMENT

1. An effective classroom climate provides physical access to all students for resources, learning areas, and community areas.
2. A student feels emotionally and physically safe from harm or hurt feelings.
3. During group work, advanced learners can deepen their understanding by teaching the concept to others.
4. Classrooms with a positive atmosphere feel welcoming and pleasant to students and the class works together for the benefit of the whole.

THE APPEARANCE OF A POSITIVE CLASSROOM

The physical environment of classrooms also influences the classroom climate. For instance, if teachers decorate the walls and bulletin boards with colorful pictures and posters with motivational messages and if they exhibit student work to show students they are proud of their achievements, they are creating a positive milieu for their classroom. This creates a much more positive climate than a classroom with four blank walls and no displays of students' efforts and achievements. Some teachers also choose to add rugs, lamps, or other furniture to make their classroom more inviting for students. Other teachers add aquariums and classroom plants to brighten their rooms. Of course, there are many ways to create a positive and colorful environment for students, and teachers usually do so according to their personal interests and those of their students (Sadker & Sadker, 1997). Students can also contribute to the appearance of their classroom.

In addition, teachers must organize classroom seating in ways that are conducive for instructional activities. If teachers intend to use cooperative learning strategies or to employ collaborative learning activities, seats may need to be arranged in clusters, or teachers may use work tables positioned strategically. This will enable students to work together in the same physical space. Furthermore, teachers need to make sure that all workstations and materials are easily accessible for all students. Teachers will eliminate many classroom management problems and minor conflicts if there are clear avenues for student movement from one key work area to another as well as specific rules and procedures about student movement and materials. Establishing an orderly classroom helps to maintain a positive classroom environment and contributes to students' perceptions of competence (Connell & Wellborn, 1990).

Another way that teachers can create a positive environment for the students is to be aware of ways to help students with special needs. For example, students in wheelchairs need open access to all work areas so that they are able to move freely throughout the classroom. If workstations are difficult for them to reach, they may feel left out or may become frustrated. Furthermore, other students may not be as accepting of students with special needs if teachers do not model inclusion and involve all students (Parkay & Stanford, 1995).

INSTRUCTION THAT PROMOTES A POSITIVE CLIMATE

In addition to having high expectations, there are other important aspects of a positive classroom climate. As noted by Good and Brophy (2000), teachers who develop positive classroom environments have clear expectations for student work, offer reasonable support to guide students through challenging academic tasks, develop activities that are meaningful, and provide opportunities for collaborative learning activities. Students want to know what is expected, how they are to complete their work, and how and when to obtain guidance and feedback from their teachers. Also, it is important that students understand what they are supposed to be learning and why the learning activities are important so that they know their learning is significant and that it is, therefore, important for them to work conscientiously (Good & Brophy, 2000). Furthermore, students need to know how they will be assessed and what steps they need to take to complete a given academic task successfully. Teachers enhance student learning when they direct students through these processes in a step-by-step manner.

Instructional scaffolds, which allow students to work in the zone of proximal development, are efficacious instructional ways for teachers to guide students through academic work. Vygotsky (1986) referred to the zone of proximal development as the difference between what students are able to do working alone and what they can learn with some assistance. For example, providing students with structured overviews, using prereading activities, providing opportunities to use the writing process to complete a writing assignment, modeling the process to be completed (e.g., solving of a word problem in mathematics), or giving positive and specific feedback are ways to enhance students' capacities to learn within the zone of proximal development. The zone of proximal development is an instructional scaffold to guide students through academic tasks, especially higher cognitive tasks.

For instance, cooperative learning activities provide opportunities for students to learn in the zone of proximal development, and these effective instructional methods have had positive effects on learning and on classroom climate because students must work together to succeed both individually and as a group (Slavin, 1990). In other words, the emphases of students' work and accountabilities are on cooperation in learning rather than competition. Cooperative learning groups are employed by teachers at the elementary, middle, or high school levels, and research has shown that cooperative learning often leads to higher levels of academic achievement for low-, middle-, and high-ability groups (Slavin, 1990). In addition, studies across grade levels and in various content areas have shown cooperative learning to be an effective way to foster academic achievement (Johnson & Johnson, 1987).

Another important finding about cooperative learning and classroom climate is that cooperative learning has improved race relations and has fostered strong friendships among students from different racial groups (Slavin & Oickle, 1981). Acceptance and tolerance are necessary to build a classroom climate that is conducive to collaborative learning activities and an equitable and respectful social structure in which all students are valued (Schofield, 2001).

Equally important, using students' background knowledge of their home cultures also creates a more positive classroom environment and increases learning. It makes sense that learning will increase for students as they make connections between the new material and their life experiences from their cultural community. Consequently, students were able to link their background knowledge to new learning and became successful mathematics students even though they previously struggled to learn mathematics.

CONCLUSION

A positive classroom climate is established by the creation of a physically appealing work environment for students as well as by teacher caring, high expectations for learning, effective instructional practices, and the development of positive social skills.

Creating a positive learning environment does not guarantee maximum learning will occur; however, a positive environment ameliorates the negative factors that impede learning and productive social interactions. Students are much more inclined to learn effectively in the classroom context if they believe they are valued. Of course, everyone—children, adolescents, and adults—want to be valued and accepted; as noted by Maslow, these needs are just part of being human. In terms of the classroom environment, teachers need to create a reasonably comfortable and physically safe environment, communicate high but attainable expectations, use effective instructional strategies to enhance student learning and to increase students' self-efficacy, and employ social skills training and conflict-resolution strategies. The creation of a positive and productive classroom environment is complex because it is multifaceted in that the classroom has its own ecology. Each factor impacts the other, and all of the aforementioned factors have a significant impact on students' perceptions of the classroom environment and on their abilities and desires to learn. Students learn in the classroom context, and like adults in the workplace, students are happier and more productive in a positive atmosphere than in an environment laced with negativity.

Activities

1. Visit a school in your neighborhood and interview at least one teacher about how to establish a positive classroom climate. Next, write a summary of your findings. Your conclusion ought to discuss how you intend to employ some of these methods in your first teaching assignment. Also, concerning the theme of learning to teach, make sure that some of your questions focus on various problems that are common to beginning teachers.

2. Based on your reading, create your own classroom conflict framework. Include the following in your framework:

    a. The contaminants you will protect your classroom from and how you will do so.

    b. The types of conflict you expect to occur in your classroom.

    c. The factors you will consider before selecting a resolution strategy.

    d. Possible resolution strategies you will utilize in your classroom (begin a list that you will continually modify and add to).

Sample Test Questions

1. A third-grade teacher has observed that one of her students has great difficulty learning across all subjects. Choose one of the following instructional methods that best communicates high expectations to the student.

    a. Assist the student individually in setting appropriately challenging learning goals and provide the child with the necessary resources.

    b. Provide a plan for the student that focuses on areas of individual strength and discard those weak areas that may frustrate the student unrealistically.

    c. Praise the student frequently and give rewards, even when the student does not do well.

    d. Organize the class, providing the student many opportunities to work cooperatively with others, earning group recognition and individual responsibility.

2. A new middle school teacher is aware of problems in her seventh-grade classroom. She thinks it might be the climate she has provided since she previously taught elementary school. Which of the following questions might assist her as she investigates the situation?

    a. Have I established a classroom structure that promotes individual student accountability for learning?

    b. Are the lessons I plan providing enough opportunities for students to participate in a variety of ways to demonstrate their learning?

    c. Have I provided an environment that demonstrates my educational philosophy so that students can succeed?

    d. Am I planning lessons that provide learning experiences and opportunities for all students as they actively engage in the content?

3. The diverse student population in a high school classroom causes the ninth grade history teacher to realize that not all her students have come to her class with the same level of knowledge of her curriculum. Therefore, she has decided that she needs to assess differently this year in order to provide the challenging but supportive environment she likes to have in her class.

   a. She decides to include peer assessment as a part of her testing in the class.

   b. She decides that she needs to consider how students learn as well as the product to determine progress.

   c. She decides to vary the levels of difficulty of questions on her exams.

   d. She decides to set up separate standards of learning for the diverse group of students, therefore allowing them to experience success in her classroom.

Answers

1. **A is the correct answer.** Teachers need to have high, yet reasonable expectations for all students and provide ample resources to support their learning.

   B is not correct. It does not address the areas of the student's weaknesses, leaving the student with gaps in education.

   C is not correct. It does not address the learning needs at all, but rewards a student for nothing. This is poor practice.

   D is not correct. The teacher is placing the responsibility for the student's progress completely on students in the cooperative group. Although the student is accountable to the group and as an individual, the accountability is minimal and cannot address all learning needs for the student appropriately.

2. A is not correct. It only addresses one component of climate, that of student accountability for learning.

   B is not correct. It only addresses the variety of ways students can participate in class.

   C is not correct. It addresses the teacher's personal educational philosophy, which, while it is important and lays the foundation for what occurs in the classroom, it is not the only issue at hand.

   D is the correct answer. It addresses the climate of student involvement and active engagement in the classroom activities.

3. A is not correct. The teacher uses peer assessment, and this is problematic to some extent. In a high school classroom this has to be used judiciously.

   B is the correct answer. It provides an overall solid approach to both student learning and assessment, taking into consideration the way they learn and the outcome of the learning.

   C is not correct. It is a good strategy, but not enough to truly change the environment to account for diverse learners.

   D is not correct. It standardizes the gap between students, making such inequities seem acceptable.

REFERENCES

Bandura, A. (1993). Perceived self-efficacy in cognitive development and functioning. *Educational Psychologist, 28*(2), 117–148.

Baron, J. (1998). Using learner-centered assessment on a large scale. In N. Lambert & B. McCombs (Eds.), *How students learn: Reforming schools through learner-centered education* (pp. 211–240). Washington, DC: American Psychological Association.

Cohen, J., & Geier, V. K. (n.d.). *School Climate Research Summary: January 2010.* Available from http://www.schoolclimate.org/climate/research.php.

Connell, J., & Wellborn, J. (1990). Competence, autonomy, and relatedness: A motivational analysis of self-system processes. In M. Gunnar & L. Sroufe (Eds.), *Minnesota Symposia on Child Psychology* (Vol. 22, pp. 43–77). Hillsdale, NJ: Erlbaum.

Ferguson, R. F. (2001, December 13). *Closing the achievement gap: What schools can do.* Presentation, New York University.

Filley, A. (1975). Interpersonal *conflict resolution.* Glenview, IL: Scott Foresman. Good, T. & Brophy, J. (2000). *Looking in classrooms* (8th ed.). New York: Longman.

Goddard, R. D., Hoy, W. K., & Woolfolk, A. (2000). Collective teacher efficacy: Its meaning, measure, and effect on student achievement. *American Education Research Journal, 37*(2), 479–507.

Harvey, T. & Drolet, B. (1994). *Building teams building people: Expanding the fifth resource.* Lancaster, PA: Technomic.

Huse, E. (1975). *Organizational development and change.* New York: West. Johnson, D. W., & Johnson, R. T. (1987). *Learning together and alone* (2nd ed). Englewood Cliffs, NJ: Prentice-Hall.

Klem, A.M. & Conell, J.P. (2004). Relationships Matter: Linking Teacher Support to Student Engagement and Achievement. *Journal of School Health, 74(7), 262–273.*

Lieberman, A. (2011). *Mentoring teachers: Navigating the real-world tensions.* New York: Wiley.

Lieberman, A., & Miller, L. (2004). *Teacher leadership.* San Francisco: Jossey-Bass.

Levesque, C. S., Zuehlke, N., Stanek, L., & Ryan, R. M. (2004). Autonomy and competence in german and u.s. university students: A comparative study based on self-determination theory. *Journal of Educational Psychology, 96,* 68–84.

Maslow, A. (1970). *Motivation and personality* (2nd ed.). New York: Harper & Row.

McCombs, B. (1998). Integrating metacognition, affect, and motivation in improving teacher education. In N. Lambert & B. McCombs (Eds.), *How students learn: Reforming schools through learner-centered education* (pp. 379–408). Washington, DC: American Psychological Association.

Merton, R. K. (1954). The self-fulfilling prophecy. *Antioch Review, 8,* 193–210.

Meyer, D. G. (1987). Social *psychology.* New York: McGraw-Hill.

Noddings, N. (2001). The caring teacher. In V. Richardson (Ed.), *Handbook of research on teaching* (4th ed., pp. 99–105). Washington, DC: American Education Research Association.

Noddings, N. (1992). *The challenge to care in schools.* New York: Teachers College Press.

Osgood, C. E. (1962). *An alternative to war or surrender.* Urbana: University of Illinois Press.

Parkay, F. W., & Stanford, B. H. (1995). *Becoming a teacher* (3rd ed.). Boston: Allyn & Bacon.

Persell, C. H. (2004). Social class and educational equality. In J. A. Banks & C. A. M. Banks (Eds.), *Multicultural education: Issues and perspectives* (5th ed.). Danvers, MA: Wiley.

Roberts, M. (1982). *Managing conflict from the inside out.* San Diego, CA: Learning Concepts.

Rosenthal, R. & Jacobson, L. (1968). Pygmalion in the Classroom. *The Urban Review, 3(1), 16–20.*

Rubie-Davies, C. M. (2006). Teacher expectations and student self-perceptions: Exploring relationships. *Psychology in the Schools, 43*(5), 537–552.

Rutter, M., Giller, H., & Hagell, A. (1998). *Antisocial behavior by young people.* Cambridge, UK: Cambridge University Press.

Sadker, M. P., & Sadker, D. M. (1997). *Teachers, schools, and society* (4th ed.). New York: McGraw-Hill.

Schofield, J. W. (2001). Improving intergroup relations among students. In J. A. Banks & C. A. M. Banks (Eds.), *Handbook of research on multicultural education.* (pp. 597–616). San Francisco: Jossey-Bass.

Schunk, D. H. (1990). Introduction to the special section on motivation and efficacy. *Educational Psychology, 82,* 3–6.

Slavin, R. E. (1990). *Cooperative learning: Theory, research, and practice.* Englewood Cliffs, NJ: Prentice-Hall.

Slavin, R. E., & Oickle, E. (1981). Effects of cooperative learning teams on student achievement and race relations: Treatment by race interactions. *Sociology of Education,* 54, 174–180.

Spaulding, A., & O'Hair, M. J. (2000). Public relations in a communication context: Listening, nonverbal, and conflict-resolution skills. In T. J. Kowalski (Ed.), *Public Relations in Schools* (2nd ed., pp. 137–161). Prospect Heights, IL: Longman.

Stipek, D. (2002). *Motivation to learn: Integrating theory and practice* (4th ed.). Boston: Allyn & Bacon.

Tavani, C. M., & Losh, S. C. (2003). Motivation, self-confidence, and expectations as predictors of the academic performances among high school students. *Child Study Journal*, 33, 141–151.

Vygotsky, L. (1986). *Thought and language.* Cambridge, MA: MIT Press.

Weinstein, R. S. (2002). *Reaching higher: The power of expectations in schooling.* Cambridge, MA: Harvard University Press.

Wentzel, K. (1997). Student motivation in middle school: The role of perceived pedagogical caring. *Journal of Educational Psychology*, *89*, 411–419.

Websites

http://www.effectiveschools.com

Learning for All website featuring the latest Effective Schools research and professional development opportunities done with Lawrence Lezotte.

http://www.tea.state.tx.us/nclb/

Texas Education Agency site for Titles I through 6 and 9, including Parent Involvement in the Title I program. In Title I, Policy Guidance, a search in the pdf file that opens locates parental involvement in numerous locations in the document.

http://www.tea.state.tx.us/comm/page2.html

TEA site for *Texas Education Today*, the state's official education communication for the public. Various editions of the publication are accessible using Adobe Reader.

http://www.tea.state.tx.us/comm/page1.html

TEA site with current press releases listed by topic and archives available back to 1999.

http://www.sbec.state.tx.us/SBECOnline/default.asp

TEA State Board of Education and Certification site devoted to information about becoming a teacher in Texas and includes the Educators' Code of Ethics and No Child Left Behind.

http://www.responsiveclassroom.org/

Website devoted to the responsive classroom with free newsletter and brochures about child development.

http://cte.udel.edu/TAbook/climate.html

Website focused on a positive classroom climate and addressing individual student differences.

http://www.education-world.com/a_curr/curr155.shtml

Website devoted to a plethora of educational issues including classroom climate and classroom management.

Competency 6 _

Managing Student Behavior

Teri Bingham, EdD
West Texas A&M University

Sheryn Johnston, EdD
Private Consultant

> **Competency 6:** The teacher understands strategies for creating an organized and productive learning environment and for managing student behavior.

The beginning teacher:

A. Analyzes the effects of classroom routines and procedures on student learning, and knows how to establish and implement age-appropriate routines and procedures to promote an organized and productive learning environment.

B. Demonstrates an understanding of how young children function in groups and designs group activities that reflect a realistic understanding of the extent of young children's ability to collaborate with others.

C. Organizes and manages group activities that promote students' ability to work together cooperatively and productively, assume responsible roles, and develop collaborative skills and individual accountability.

D. Recognizes the importance of creating a schedule for young children that balances restful and active movement activities and that provides large blocks of time for play, projects, and learning centers.

E. Schedules activities and manages time in ways that maximize student learning, including using effective procedures to manage transitions; to manage materials, supplies, and technology; and to coordinate the performance of noninstructional duties (e.g., taking attendance) with instructional activities.

F. Uses technological tools to perform administrative tasks such as taking attendance, maintaining grade books, and facilitating communications.

G. Works with volunteers and paraprofessionals to enhance and enrich instruction and applies procedures for monitoring the performance of volunteers and paraprofessionals in the classroom.

H. Applies theories and techniques related to managing and monitoring student behavior.

I. Demonstrates awareness of appropriate behavior standards and expectations for students at various developmental levels.

J. Applies effective procedures for managing student behavior and for promoting appropriate behavior and ethical work habits (e.g., academic integrity) in the classroom (e.g., communicating high and realistic behavior expectations, involving students in developing rules and procedures, establishing clear consequences for inappropriate behavior, enforcing behavior standards consistently, encouraging students to monitor their own behavior and to use conflict-resolution skills, responding appropriately to various types of behavior)

KEY TERMS

discrimination	*negative reinforcement*	*shaping*
extinction	*positive reinforcement*	
generalization	*schedule of reinforcement*	

Teachers need to understand the importance of classroom organization, procedures, and routines, establishing classroom rules and consequences, planning transitions, and managing student behavior.

Providing a safe and secure environment in school is a basic condition that must be satisfied before students can benefit from the learning experience. One of the most important aspects of teaching focuses on the teacher's ability to effectively organize and manage the classroom. Effective classroom management can increase the amount of time spent in learning activities and decrease time spent dealing with inappropriate behaviors. When volunteers and paraprofessionals understand their role and responsibilities they can support the behavior standards, policies, and procedures. This chapter addresses some of the most important aspects of effective classroom management.

ORGANIZING THE CLASSROOM

Deciding how the physical space in the classroom should be organized is a task teachers often take for granted. Individual teacher preferences, age of the students, and instructional needs of the classroom contribute to these decisions. Student desks can be arranged in a variety of ways. Traditionally students sit in rows and columns. This arrangement makes it easier for students to focus on individual tasks and for the teacher to interact with each student. Experience tells us, however, that if the teacher does not move around the entire room and make a concentrated effort to include all students, those in the front of the class typically interact more than those in the back and sides of the room.

Some classrooms have desks arranged in groups or clusters. This encourages student interaction and facilitates cooperative group work. However, because this arrangement does provide opportunities for students to interact, the teacher should not expect complete silence when students are doing individual work.

Traditional Seating Arrangement

Groups of Four Desks

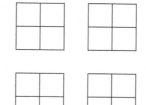

Groups of Five Desks

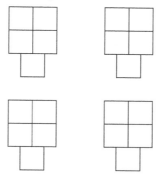

Horseshoe Arrangement

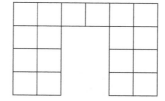

As the teacher plans the arrangement of the classroom, there are several factors to keep in mind. Areas for small-group activities, computer stations, pencil sharpeners, water fountains, and restrooms should be out of the flow of traffic for the classroom. The teacher should sit facing the classroom so all students are visible while interacting with small groups or individual students. Make sure there are paths throughout the room for the teacher to have easy access to all students and supplies. The placement of student desks and work areas should allow the teacher to clearly see all students. Orientation of each area should allow clear vision of chalkboards/white boards, smart boards, document camera projections, etc. Make sure materials and supplies that are used regularly are easily available. Remember that the purpose of the room arrangement is to facilitate instruction and optimize student learning.

Procedures and Routines

One of the keys to effective classroom management is the establishment of age-appropriate procedures for daily or regular activities and transitions. These procedures allow the teacher to teach the skills students need so they know exactly what is expected of them in given situations. Clear procedures advance a systematic, productive learning environment. Once the procedures are established and students have opportunities to practice, the procedures become routines. In order to develop procedures the teacher should look at the daily schedule of academic and nonacademic activities and decide how the students should perform each activity.

Also, teachers need to plan and communicate transition activities to the students. Procedures should have approximately three to five steps that enable the students to successfully complete the activity. Harry and Rosemary Wong in their series *First Days of School* (1988) provide an excellent discussion of the use of procedures and routines.

Although not an exhaustive list, suggestions for needed procedures could include the following:

- Entering the classroom in the morning
- Doing morning seatwork
- Taking attendance
- Taking the lunch count
- Going to the restroom
- Getting a drink of water
- Turning in homework
- Turning in completed assignments
- Working in centers
- Passing out papers
- Passing in papers
- Putting headings on papers
- Sharpening pencils
- Going to the nurse
- Going to the library
- Working in cooperative groups
- Fire drills
- Keeping the classroom clean
- Leaving the classroom

The teacher should look at the daily schedule and determine which activities will require procedures for efficient, smooth operation of the classroom. Procedures should be written and posted in the classroom. Giving a copy to each student and to his or her parents helps ensure that everyone knows exactly what is expected. When the teacher establishes routines for the daily running of the classroom, questions can be easily answered and confusion over details is avoided. A copy of the procedures will also help substitutes to maintain smooth and consistent operation of the class. The majority of the daily procedures should be taught during the first few days of school, with the remainder being taught and rehearsed as the situations arise in the daily activities (library, fire drill, etc.).

Remember that failure to follow a procedure is not a discipline matter, but rather an opportunity for re-teaching and positive support for the student. If a student does not follow a procedure, the teacher should ask him to repeat the procedure, practice the procedure, and perform the procedure the next time an opportunity arises.

Examples of Procedures

Entering the Classroom

- Enter the classroom quietly.
- Put your coat/backpack in its place.
- Sharpen your pencils.
- Begin your morning/bell work.

Lining Up

- Stand up behind your desk.
- Push your chair under the desk.
- Walk quietly to the end of the line.
- Stand quietly behind the person in front of you.
- Walk quietly with your hands at your sides.

Sharpening Your Pencil

- Sharpen your pencils first thing in the morning.
- If you break a point, raise your hand.
- Wait for the teacher to recognize you.
- Quietly walk to the pencil sharpener.
- Sharpen your pencil and quietly return to your seat.

Transitions

- Getting ready for recess or lunch
- Changing from one activity to the next
- Switching from one content to another
- Having groups change centers
- Using guided reading groups dynamics

ESTABLISHING CLASSROOM RULES AND CONSEQUENCES

Learning how to behave in the classroom should not be a guessing game for students. Establishing age-appropriate rules for behavior standards in the classroom can be accomplished by the teacher or in collaboration with the students. Teachers can provide the general format and guide the students in determining which rules will create an optimized learning environment. Some students may feel a sense of ownership when they are involved in the rule-making process. Rules should be reasonable, clearly understandable, and consistent with the school's guidelines for behavior. Discipline plans for the classroom must not only include rules but also consequences (both positive and negative) for compliance or noncompliance. Also, students should be held accountable for monitoring and managing their behavior.

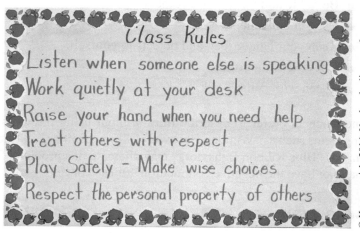

© Hannamariah, 2014, Used under license of Shutterstock, Inc.

As teachers the more we can do to create a learning environment where students feel safe, accepted, competent, productive, and successful, the fewer behavior problems we have. There are several proactive steps that teachers can take to maximize a smooth-functioning classroom and minimize the need for discipline.

Rules

- Most authorities agree that three to five rules are sufficient. More rules become difficult to remember, especially with younger children.

- Rules should be broadly stated. Teaching students to be respectful of others is more inclusive than setting a rule for "no hitting."

- Rules should be stated positively. They should inform students what they "should" do, not what they "shouldn't" do. Many teachers set rules that include a laundry list of what not to do—"don't talk," "don't hit," "no running," etc. These tend to focus the students' attention on the negative or inappropriate behaviors and by their nature result in negative consequences or punishment. By stating rules positively and letting students know what is expected of them, consequences for compliance provide an opportunity for positive behavior supports.

- Including students in making the classroom rules gives them a sense of ownership. It helps them to feel as if they have a stake in the running of the classroom. Very young children may have more difficulty participating in this process, whereas older students may tend to be more "punishing" than the teacher would like. It is the teacher's responsibility to guide them through the process of establishing rules as appropriate.

- Rules should be consistent with and support the school's Student Code of Conduct. Some campuses will have a systemwide discipline plan that includes classroom rules and consequences. If this is the case, the teacher should fit his or her rules into the campus plan.

- Make sure rules are reasonable, easy to understand, and within the students' repertoire of behaviors. If rules are unreasonable, they will be ignored. ("No talking" is an unreasonable rule and is not enforceable.) If students do not understand the rule, they cannot follow it. ("Respect others" may not be meaningful until the teacher gives examples and nonexamples to convey the general meaning of the rule.) At times, especially with very young children just beginning school, the teacher will have to directly teach the behaviors addressed in the rule. (Teachers may have to teach students how to take turns talking by raising their hand in order to "respect others.")

- Rules, like procedures, should be written, posted, and distributed to students and parents. Enforce rules fairly and consistently.

Examples of positively stated rules include:

- Be respectful of others and their property.
- Be respectful of school property.
- Be responsible for your own work and materials.
- Be prepared to learn.
- Be polite and respectful to others.
- Use good manners.
- Keep your hands, feet, and objects to yourself.
- Obey all school rules.
- Listen while others talk.

Some teachers prefer to describe rules without using the word "rules," which may invoke noncompliance. Using terms such as "Winning Behaviors," "Expectations," "Principles to Live By," "Code of Conduct," "Game Plan," or "Blue Ribbon Behaviors" may alleviate this problem. Students will know rules are still implied, but it may not have the negative connotation "rules" conveys.

Consequences

Once the rules are established the teacher needs to determine specific consequences for when a student follows or breaks the rules. Consequences should not be confused with punishment. When a student follows the rules they may receive positive consequences or rewards. When the student breaks the rules, negative consequences or penalties are applied.

When determining rewards, it is important to consider the age of the student. While tangibles (items that can be seen, touched, tasted, held, etc.) are extremely effective with younger children, they may not be valued as much by older students. One of the most efficient ways to determine what students are willing to work for is to ask them. Another way is to provide a list of rewards for students to choose from. Observation can also provide possible rewards to include in the classroom discipline plan.

Token Economy

Some teachers' consequences are tied to a token economy. Tokens are used to reinforce appropriate student behaviors. Tokens can be used to improve both academic and social behaviors. Begin by telling the students what behaviors will earn them a token and how the tokens can be used. The teacher gives the token when a student performs the necessary task or behavior. Tokens can be given to students for raising their hands, turning in homework, completing assignments, contributing to a discussion, walking quietly in the hall, etc.

One way to award students is to have them write their name on the token and place it in a jar or basket at the appropriate time. On a regular basis (daily, weekly, monthly, etc.) a drawing is held and the student whose name is drawn receives a prize. An alternative to this is to have a student store where students use their tokens to purchase items at certain time intervals, for example on Fridays. It is important to remember to offer tokens to all students who exhibit the target behavior, even those who do it all the time.

GENERAL PRINCIPLES

- Create effective lesson plans that are meaningful, interesting, engaging, and relevant. If your "discipline" is more entertaining than your "lessons," you will spend more time dealing with student behaviors.

- Establish consistent procedures for daily activities. When students know how they are expected to perform daily activities, they will generally be more successful.

- Treat all students with respect all the time and communicate that expectation for student behavior. Teachers should model respectful behavior and support this behavior in students.

- Provide sincere, specific, and frequent PRAISE for student behavior. There is no more powerful tool than telling students what they do well and specifically describing what they did. (Example: "Charlie, you did a great job of coming into the classroom quietly and going directly to your seat, thank you.")

- Balance the schedule for young children between active movement and restful activities. This schedule can include whole-class instruction and activities, small-group experiences, learning centers, reading or literature circles, individual computer time, and working in pairs.

- When students are aware of the expected product, outcome, and time limits it will increase time-on-task and work productivity.

- Manage transitions with the end in mind. Students will do what the teacher wants when they know what it is the teacher expects of them. So be certain to tell the students what to do and continue with the flow of the class. When a teacher instructs the students to put away their math books, the students will do that but then they will naturally start talking because they have no other task. However, when the teacher tells them to put away their math books and get out their learning logs and explain what they learned about triangles, it is reasonable for there to be some talking but it will quiet down because they have moved on to the next task. In the first example the teacher will have to work hard to get the students on task because she first has to get their attention. In the second example she simply has to get them engaged in what they already know.

- In order for students to maintain productivity, teachers need to provide meaningful learning activities while they attend to administrative, noninstructional duties (e.g., lunch counts, attendance, collecting homework). Ideally, teachers should use technology to simplify these tasks when possible.

- When the students get resources and supplies, have one student responsible for getting the materials for a group of students. This will minimize the amount of student traffic and congestion.

- As a teacher, if you are lucky enough to have a volunteer or paraprofessional in your classroom, inform them of the learning objectives and have them assist student learning or provide enrichment for more advanced students.

Behavioral Modification

Pavlov is known for classical conditioning. Classical conditioning is when a naturally occurring *involuntary* response becomes associated with a previously neutral stimulus. Three tenants in his work include:

- Extinction
- Generalization
- Discrimination

Skinner is known for operant conditioning. Operant conditioning is when a *voluntary* response is strengthened as it is reinforced.

The basic principles of operant conditioning results in reinforcement theory.

Reinforcement Theory

Reinforcement is the strengthening of a behavior. The principles of reinforcement theory are:

- Positive reinforcement
- Negative reinforcement
- Schedule of reinforcement
- Extinction
- Shaping

In contrast to behavior modification is punishment. *Punishment* is when a student has to endure the consequences as a result of his behavior. It is something the student perceives as aversive to him; it is undesirable and the student is no longer in control of his choices.

POSITIVE REINFORCEMENT

Positive reinforcement strengthens a behavior through *addition*. A positive reinforcer is determined by the receiver wanting or desiring something.

Three types of positive reinforcers are:

1. Praise (written or verbal) is the *most powerful form of positive reinforcement*. Needs to be:
   a. Specific.
   b. Earned.
   c. Sincere.
2. Privilege
3. Something tangible (e.g., rewards, including token economies)

Keep in mind that low-SES students and low-ability students quickly respond to tangible items and it is difficult to get them to perform without the use of tangible items or privileges in the future. Furthermore, as time goes on the students will require greater privileges or more rewards for the same amount of productivity. If they don't receive them they may stop working altogether.

Examples of Positive Reinforcers

- Tangibles (food, stickers, pencils, small toys, etc.)
- Free time pass
- Homework pass
- Ten extra minutes of computer time
- Run errands for teacher

- Choose activity for unstructured time
- Extra recess time
- Sit by a friend
- Use of special supplies (markers, colored paper, crayons, etc.)
- Help the custodian
- Eat lunch with a friend
- Spend time with favored adult
- Play a game with a friend
- Be group leader for the day
- Earn pizza/popcorn party for the class
- Good notes home
- Phone call to parents for "brag session"
- Earn certificates for appropriate behavior
- Movie tickets
- Tickets/tokens to trade for desired items
- Tickets to local sporting events
- Care for class pet
- Take a stuffed animal home for the night
- Small container of bubble blowing liquid
- Yo-yo
- Temporary tattoo
- Balloon
- Coloring book
- Bookmark
- Grab bag
- Water a plant
- Work with the custodian
- Tutor a younger student
- Sit at the teacher's desk
- Clean the pet cage
- Sharpen class pencils
- Get a pass to do sharing time
- Get a school T-shirt
- Decorate the bulletin board
- Trip to the library
- Quiet time to yourself
- Lead the class in a song

NEGATIVE REINFORCEMENT

Negative reinforcement strengthens a behavior through subtraction. A negative reinforcer is determined by the receiver wanting something to be taken away. The threat of punishment can be a negative reinforcer.

Because the student is still in control, he or she may find an alternative way of removing the negative reinforcer other than what the teacher had in mind.

Both positive and negative reinforcement leaves the student in charge of determining a more pleasant state. When control is taken away it results in punishment.

Examples of Negative Reinforcers

- Frown or "teacher look"
- Loss of recess time
- Loss of lunch with friends
- Loss of free time
- Loss of privileges
- Loss of preferred activity
- Restitution of item
- Office referral
- Time-out
- Detention
- Suspension
- Expulsion

SCHEDULE OF REINFORCEMENT

There are two types of schedules for reinforcing behavior. The first is continuous reinforcement where the behavior is reinforced each time it is demonstrated. This makes for very fast learning. The second type of schedule is intermittent reinforcement, where the behavior is rewarded over increasingly longer segments of time. This makes for durable and long-term behavior.

EXTINCTION

Extinction is when the teacher ignores an undesirable student behavior in hopes of extinguishing it. Although this technique may work, it is important that teachers are aware that the student behavior may get worse before it gets better. Never use extinction when the behavior is dangerous to the student or another individual.

SHAPING

Shaping is when the teacher positively reinforces successive approximate behaviors. Students need encouragement as they develop new behaviors. Just like a baseball coach wouldn't wait for a player to hit a home run before praising him, a teacher shouldn't wait for a student to behave perfectly before reinforcing or acknowledging him.

To Maintain Positive Behaviors, Use:

1. Proximity
2. Student's name in a positive way
3. Physical movement
4. Signaling (nonverbal)
5. Private record

MANAGING STUDENT BEHAVIOR

Building a relationship with students based on mutual respect and genuine caring is probably the most important factors to managing student behavior. Students want to know they are cared about and shown respect. It all begins with the teacher and how she interacts and communicates with the learners. When a teacher shows sincere care for the students and treats them with dignity and respect, the students have an increased desire to behave appropriately. The best way to begin a relationship with anyone is with a firm handshake, a pleasant greeting coupled with eye contact, and a smile. Try it!

Managing student behavior in the classroom usually occurs on a continuum from very authoritarian to very permissive. Teachers who establish an authoritarian management style may create an atmosphere that is tense and intimidating, and may lead to rebellious behavior and lack of discipline unless the teacher is present and leading the class. This style does not promote creativity, self-control, or optimal learning. At the other extreme, a style that is too permissive can lead to an out-of-control classroom with few and insufficient boundaries, lack of student motivation, and frustration for students and teachers. A management style that is somewhere toward the middle of the continuum is more conducive to learning. Although the teacher is ultimately responsible for the smooth running of the classroom on a daily basis, collaboratively involving students promotes cooperation and leads to a smooth-functioning classroom that encourages students to participate responsibly in the process. A well-managed classroom is one in which the students manage their behavior appropriately.

Some language to use with students in addressing a problem include:

1. Starting with I'm sorry.

Example: I'm sorry you did not earn enough points for the popcorn party.

2. Giving the student the Teacher's eye and simply saying, "No ma'am" and gently shake your head or simply saying, "NO sir" while looking him in the eye.
3. Keeping small problems small.

Example: "Sarah, right now this is a small problem. We can keep it a small problem or you can make it into a bigger problem. Are you willing to work together to keep it a small problem?"

How Do I Decide What to Do about Misbehavior?

When deciding how to respond to a behavior it is best to choose a strategy that stops the behavior promptly, has the smallest negative effect on the class, and causes the least disruption. Behaviors can be classified into three categories: *nonproblems, level one problems, and level two problems*. Nonproblems are common behaviors that are brief and do not interfere with learning or teaching. Examples of nonproblems are brief inattention, talking during transitions, small periods of inattentiveness, and short pauses during seatwork. It may be best to ignore, use proximity, or a very gentle touch on the student's shoulder. To react to them would waste instructional time, fragment the lesson, and decrease a pleasant classroom climate.

Level one problems are mildly annoying, limited to one or a few students, and are brief in duration. These behaviors go against class rules or routines, but do not seriously interfere with learning. However, if unaddressed they could get worse, become persistent, spread, or affect the learning of others. Some of these behaviors are calling out, leaving his or her desk without permission, passing notes, eating, throwing trash, tapping (pen, pencil, foot), excessive talking, or off-task conduct.

Level two problems can be minor problems that have grown to become frequent or chronic for an individual, disrupting the class. These include failure to complete tasks or assignments, defiance, noncompliance with rules, policies, or procedures frequently off task, excessive uninvited talking, or hurting or threatening another student.

© Franck Boston, 2014, Used under license of Shutterstock, Inc.

In deciding a strategy to handle the inappropriate behavior, several objectives must be considered. The teacher needs to weigh the long- and short-term effects of his or her response. Simultaneously consider the negative side effects of misbehaving student(s) and the entire class. There are numerous interventions for a teacher to choose from including both level one and level two interventions.

Level One Interventions

- Nonverbal cues—eye contact, signaling, a light touch
- Get the activity moving—avoid dead time and plan transitions so they are smooth and have materials ready
- Use proximity
- Use group focus—draw them back in kindly
- Redirect the behavior
- Provide needed instruction
- Issue a brief desist—tell the student to stop the undesirable behavior, you can combine with redirection, and monitor for compliance
- Give the student a choice

Level Two Interventions

- Withhold a privilege or desired activity
- Isolate or remove student
- Use a penalty
- Assign detention
- Office referral

Three Components to Include when Correcting a Student

1. Stay focused on the original problem
2. Label the student's behavior
3. Tell the student the rationale for your decision

As a teacher, when you need to visit with a student about his or her behavior choices there are a few ideas to keep in mind. Stay focused on the original problem. When confronted, it is a normal human reaction for students to try and distract the teacher from the student's behavior. A student may complain about your instructional style, personality, prejudice or bad breath. Do not go down this road; remain centered on the misbehavior.

When discussing the inappropriate actions label the student's behavior. It seems to help teachers when they can give the student behavior a label. For example, "Sarah, you are trying to negotiate with me. I will not break your trust by going back on my word."

Set limits and boundaries and do not negotiate with students after the fact. It helps teachers to stand firm when they have a positive rationale for remaining firm with their resolve.

Helpful rationales to explain our decisions to students include telling the students…

1. "Being inconsistent hurts the relationship."
2. "If I go back on my word you learn that my 'no' doesn't mean no."
3. "Consistency builds trust and strengthens our relationship."
4. "My responses need to stay predictable and consistent."
5. "You can rely on me to keep my word."

Discipline Programs

There are numerous theories as to how best to establish an effective classroom management plan.

- Assertive Discipline (Canter, 1976; Canter & Marlene Canter, 1992)
- Behavior Modification (Skinner, 1953, 1971)
- Cooperative Discipline (Albert, 1992)
- Discipline as Self-Control (Gordon, 1989)
- Positive Classroom Discipline (Jones, 1987, 2001)
- Discipline with Dignity (Curwin & Mendler, 1988)
- Noncoercive Discipline (Glasser, 1998)

These programs along with others provide a starting point for the teacher as he or she develops an individual plan for classroom management. It is not necessary to follow one plan in its entirety, but all programs have elements that might be included in an effective classroom management plan that fits the given age, community, and culture in question.

Basic Guidelines

When determining what works best for a given situation, the teacher might consider the following generalizations:

- Behavior does not occur in a vacuum. It is important to look at all things within the classroom that can influence student and teacher behavior. Everything is cause and effect.
- Overreliance on negative consequences or punishment can escalate problem situations instead of promoting appropriate behaviors.
- Parents and administrators should always be aware of and understand the overall plan.
- The system should include a documentation component. Teachers should be able to tell parents and administrators exactly when a behavior occurs, under what circumstances, and specific consequences that were utilized.
- Most importantly, remember that if a system is not working, teachers need to "modify and adjust" the plan until students are experiencing success in the program.

Some Specific Behavior Management Cautions and Suggestions

- Teachers cannot control student behavior but they can control their own reaction to it.
  - ＊ Use a calm, quiet voice when redirecting student behavior.
  - ＊ Maintain a calm facial expression when addressing inappropriate behavior.
  - ＊ Do not take student behavior as a personal affront.
- Ensure consistent use of consequences across settings and times to lessen the possibility of reacting in anger.
- Avoid trying to talk students into "being good." As adults we spend an exceptional amount of time trying to get students to do what they're "supposed to do." In the classroom, the teacher should calmly state the request and expect student compliance. If necessary repeat the request again and then apply the consequence.
- Try to establish eye contact with students when redirecting behavior. This helps ensure they are listening.

Imposing Penalties

1. If you are angry with the student, *delay* the discussion.
2. Impose penalties privately!
3. Penalties should be imposed calmly and quietly.

   4. Always reestablish a positive relationship.

   5. Separate the behavior from the child.

Steps to Planning Student Conference

   1. One behavior to change.

   2. A replacement behavior, when possible.

   3. A positive reinforcement plan.

   4. A negative reinforcement plan (remember the threat of punishment is a negative reinforcer).

   5. How the teacher can increase performance of the new behavior.

Note: When conferencing with a student, keep it private, focus on only the student with whom you are visiting, and be sure the conversation remains confidential.

The One-, Two-, or Three-Finger Signaling Technique

The finger signaling technique helps a teacher manage student questions from across the room when they are working with another student or group of students. When a student raises his hand he also signals his type of question by holding up one, two, or three fingers. This strategy allows the teacher to continue teaching or working with a student and still direct other students from a distance. The major benefit of this strategy requires students to raise their hands to indicate their needs to the teacher.

The first type of question is one in which the student is comfortable asking in front of the whole class. The student indicates this by raising a hand and holding up the index finger. The teacher then knows she can stay where she is and call on the student without embarrassing him.

The second type of question means the student needs to get out of his seat for some reason (i.e., sharpen a pencil, throw away trash, get a drink, go to the restroom, etc.). The student indicates this by raising a hand and holding up two fingers. The teacher then can decide to mouth to the student and ask him quietly what he needs or go over to the student and ask.

The third type of question is one in which the student wants to talk to the teacher privately without the rest of the class hearing. In this case the student holds up three fingers when he raises his hand. This communicates to the teacher that the student has a comment or question he would like to ask the teacher privately. The teacher now knows she needs to go to the student or wave for the student to come to her.

This technique allows the teacher to continue working with a student and still respond from across the room to another student.

Allowing the Class to Establish Rules for Behavior

One way to have students support the class rules is to have them take the lead in the decision-making process. This gives the students ownership and helps them buy into the system. Divide the class into groups of four to five students and describe the group's assignment. Follow the listed guidelines:

   1. Choose group leaders.

   2. Group leaders designate a spokesperson, a secretary, and a time keeper.

   3. Explain to the class that they will be designing a contract that delineates how they will treat each other and how they will deal with problems.

   4. Explain the four questions that need to be answered in each group.

Pose the following questions: (Allow 2 minutes of discussion for each question.)

   1. How do you want me, your teacher, to treat you?

   2. How do you want to be treated by each other?

3. How do you think I, your teacher, want to be treated by the class?

4. How should we handle problems that arise in class?

Response to Questions: (Teacher calls on each group to respond to each question.)

- List answers to develop a contract for classroom behavior.
- Write the contract using the class consensus.
- Allow each student to sign the behavior contract.

Note: Always post the rules in the classroom so they are visible reminders of expected behaviors.

Reinforce:

- Initially the contract should be referred to routinely, focusing on what the class is doing appropriately and what they need to work on.
- Remember to modify as necessary after discussion with students.
- When new students are placed in the class, have other students introduce the contract and then ask the new student to sign the contract if they agree.

Sample 1 of Classroom Behavioral Expectations (Class Rules):

These should be posted in the classroom.

Expectations:

- Have respect for others.
- Come to class <u>prepared</u>.
- <u>Listen</u> to the teacher's instructions.
- Be a <u>positive</u> role model.
- Use <u>appropriate language</u>.
- Come to class with a <u>positive attitude</u>.
- <u>Do your best</u> in everything you do.

Sample 2 of Classroom Behavioral Expectations (Rules):

Classroom Principles:

- Speak respectfully to everyone.
- Keep hands and feet to yourself.
- Listen quietly while others are talking.
- Happily follow directions.
- Bring all needed materials to class.
- Follow all school rules.

Examples of a Behavior Management Systems

Blue and Red Ticket System:

1. First offense—Eye contact and/or proximity control
2. Second offense—Private verbal warning from teacher

3. Third offense—Blue ticket is given to student; student has to talk to teacher after class and this is written on the ticket.

4. Fourth offense—Red ticket is given to student; student has to complete an action plan, which is written on the ticket (see action plan and behavior journal below for two variations of same idea).

5. Fifth offense—Student is given consequence according to school policy.

6. For severe behavior problems, student is referred directly to the office.

ACTION PLANS AND BEHAVIOR JOURNALS

Action plans or Behavioral Journals are different types of forms to be completed by the student. These can serve as documentations of the inappropriate student behavior.

Action Plan

Student Name: _____

What's the problem?

_____

_____

What plan will you use to solve the problem?

_____

_____

_____

_____

Behavior Journal

Student Name: _____ Class/Period: _____ Date: _____

The rule I chose to break was: _____

_____

I chose to break this rule because: _____

_____

_____

_____

This is what I could have done instead: _____

_____

_____

_____

_____

Student Signature: _____ Date: _____

© baldyrgan, 2014, Used under license of Shutterstock, Inc.

TIPS FOR COMPETENCY 6: MANAGING STUDENT BEHAVIOR

1. Include the students in making the classroom rules so they feel a sense of ownership.

2. Plan and introduce to your students your systems, procedures, routines, and especially transitions. Then PRACTICE them with the students until they know them.

3. Ensure group work productivity and increase time-on-task delineate expected product, outcome, and time limits.

4. Enforce rules fairly and consistently.

5. Seating arrangements should optimize learning for all students.

6. When conferencing with a student, keep it private and confidential.

7. Make sure paraprofessionals and volunteers understand their roles and responsibilities in the classroom.

Communication Steps to De-escalate and Problem-Solve

1. Observe

2. "**I see you** (behavior)." (*State two or three obvious behaviors.*)

3. Ask — "**Are you feeling** (emotion)?"
   "What are you feeling?" (If you guessed wrong)

4. Validate and acknowledge — "**I can see you're [emotion].** "

5. Get the details — "**What are you [emotion] about**?"
   Who, What, When, Where, How (Avoid asking, "Why" - Why is an emotionally charged word.)

6. Connect the feeling to the source—restate for clarification and understanding — "**So, you're [emotion] about [source]. Is that right?**"

7. Depending on the circumstances you can say, "**How do you want it to be?**" or "**You must have expected something different, what was it?**"

8. "**What have you already tried?**"

9. "**How did that work out**?" or "**How did that go?**"

10. Have the child generate solutions and decide on one. — "**What can you do differently to have a positive outcome?**"   (What are you willing to do? Who, What, When, Where, How)

11. Check back if appropriate to see how the plan worked — "**Would you mind letting me know how things work out?**"

12. End with a handshake. A handshake strengthens a relationship

Prework

Assign a Case Study on Classroom Management

Directions for the case study:

1. Read the *Case Study* at least twice.

2. In writing, explain the following:

   a. What are the problems?

   b. What would you try first to resolve each one?

   c. If that did not work, what would you try next?

CLASS ACTIVITIES

Class Activity #1: As a whole class generate a list of student behaviors that are troublesome. After you discuss **How Do I Decide What to Do About Misbehavior?**, go back to this list and label them as nonproblem, level one problem, or level two problem.

Class Activity #2:
WRITE YOUR RESPONSES ON A SEPARATE SHEET OF PAPER
In your small group, read each classroom scenario and decide:

   a. If it is a nonproblem, a level one problem, or a level two problem.

   b. What your first response strategy would be to handle it.

   c. An alternative response if your first approach does not produce good results.

   1. Jennifer and Melissa talk and pass notes as you conduct a class discussion. Several other students whisper and daydream.

   2. Desi and Brice talk constantly. They refuse to get to work, and they argue with you when you ask them to open their books.

   3. Dylan manages to get most of his work done, but in the process he is constantly disruptive. He teases the girls sitting around him, keeping them constantly laughing and competing for his attention. Dylan makes wisecracks in response to almost anything you say. When confronted, he grins charmingly and responds with exaggerated courtesy, much to the delight of the rest of the class.

   4. When someone bumped into Marc at the drinking fountain, he turned around and spit water at the other child. Later Marc ordered a boy who was standing near his desk to get away and then he shoved the boy. On the way back from the cafeteria, Marc got into a name-calling contest with another boy.

Class Activity #3: Watch the DVD "More Time to Teach: Responding to Student Behavior" (Child Sense Seminars for Parents and Educators, Produced by R.E.M. Productions, Distributed by ChildSense, New Brighton, MN 2007, **www.childsense.net**)

Instructions: Complete the following outline (below) and complete homework assignment #2 by synthesizing all the information in this chapter with the information on the DVD.

Purpose: Demonstrate ways to decrease time-wasting behaviors and increase learning time.

OUTLINE
Four Levels of Response and Intervention

   1. Planned ignoring

      a. How to decide? Ask yourself 2 Q's

         i. Can I keep teaching?

         ii. Can others keep learning?

   2. Minimal intervention or subtle reminder

      a. Proximity

      b. Gentle signals

      c. Gestures

      d. Wait time

3. Offering choices

   a. Goal—keep small problems small

   b. Be calm and respectful

   c. Speak with a firm voice

   d. Say "Your choice is to _____ (desirable behavior) and or to _____ (consequence), I hope you decide to _____ (desirable behavior)."

4. Following through

   a. Be consistent

Student Tactics to Try to Get Teachers to Change Their Mind

   1. Beg and plead

   2. Promise and negotiate

   3. Guilt and threat

   4. Rebel and isolate

Teachers, set consequences and follow through.

Homework

Homework Assignment #1: For homework each student selects the three inappropriate student behaviors they are most concerned about and decide how they might handle each one.

Ideas to include:

- Defiance
- Rudeness
- Aggression
- Unresponsiveness

Homework Assignment #2: Create a newsletter explaining what you have learned about misbehaviors and responding to student behaviors.

Sample Test Questions

1. When a teacher is considering the effectiveness of his classroom management strategies, he needs to know which of the following is *least* effective:

   a. Help students understand the reasons why inappropriate behavior is unacceptable and cannot be tolerated

   b. Organize the classroom and instruction to eliminate conditions conducive to misbehavior.

   c. Teach and model appropriate behavior.

   d. Expect students to behave appropriately during transitions and lulls in instruction when they are unfamiliar with the procedures.

2. Which of the following would be an inappropriate first activity for a teacher to use the first day of class?

    a. Make the first lesson fairly difficult to ensure that students understand how hard they will need to work in the class.

    b. Spend time introducing procedures and discussing expectations of the class.

    c. Make the first lesson engaging, fairly simple, and enjoyable to help students have a positive attitude about the class.

    d. Have a seating chart and help the students find their seat before beginning an "ice breaker" activity in which they learn each other's names.

3. While Ms. Kellinger's students are working in their groups it is important that she actively monitor the groups in order to:

    a. Keep the students from talking too much.

    b. Identify who the troublemakers are.

    c. Monitor, assess, and guide individual and group collaborative skills.

    d. Direct student plans for displaying completed work.

4. On the first day of school Mr. Balderas told the students his rules, policies, routines, and procedures that he expected the students to follow. Over the next few days he noticed the students failed to follow the procedures he had explained for turning in their homework and getting started on the days warm-up activity. He should:

    a. Go over the rules again.

    b. Explain the penalties for not following directions.

    c. Have the class sign a contract that they will follow the classroom rules, policies, and procedures.

    d. Review the procedures, guide the students through them, and practice them.

Answers

1. A is incorrect. It is a good idea to discuss this with the students.

    B is incorrect. An organized classroom is conducive to learning.

    C is incorrect. It is the teachers' responsibility to teach and model appropriate behavior.

    D is the correct answer. This answer is the noneffective one. Students are less likely to behave appropriately when they are unfamiliar with the expectations. Lulls during instruction and transitions are likely places where students do not know what to do so they become "creative" with their time.

2. **A is the correct answer.** An inappropriate activity would be to set up the students for a difficult or possibly failing experience. The first day needs to set the tone that the teacher has high yet reasonable expectations, and provides a classroom with a pleasant and safe tone.

   B is incorrect. It is a good idea to introduce procedures and expectations.

   C is incorrect. This is a great idea for the first lesson.

   D is incorrect. This too is an effective way to start the first class day.

3. A is incorrect. It is important for the teacher to circulate the room and keep students on task.

   B is incorrect. Although the teacher might identify a student who is more active than others, this isn't the best reason for monitoring students working in groups.

   C is the correct answer. As students are working in groups the teacher is charged with monitoring their progress, collecting informal data concerning their skills, guiding their thinking, answering questions, and being aware of their overall productivity.

   D is incorrect. It has little to do with the purpose of monitoring students.

4. A is incorrect. The students need to know and practice the procedure for turning in homework, not the rules in this case.

   B is incorrect. The students need time to learn the procedure before there are penalties executed.

   C is incorrect. The students are being malicious, they just need to learn the procedures.

   D is the correct answer. Students need to internalize and practice new procedures so they become habitual routines.

REFERENCES

Albert, L. (1992). *An administrator's guide to cooperative discipline.* Circle Pines, MN: American Guidance Service.

Canter, L. (1976). *Assertive discipline: A take-charge approach for today's educator.* Seal Beach, CA: Lee Canter & Associates.

Canter, L., & Canter, M. (1992). *Assertive discipline: Positive behavior management for today's classroom.* Santa Monica, CA: Lee Canter & Associates.

Curwin, R., & Mendler, A. (1998). *Discipline with dignity.* Alexandria, VA: Association for Supervision and Curriculum Development.

Glasser, W. (1998). *The quality school: Managing students without coercion.* New York:Harper & Row.

Gordon, T. (1970). *Discipline that works: Promoting self-discipline in children.* New York: Random House.

Jones, F. (1987). *Positive classroom discipline.* New York: McGraw-Hill.

Jones, F. (2001). *Fredric Jones's tools for teaching.* Santa Cruz, CA: Fredric H. Jones & Associates.

Skinner, B. (1953). *Science and human behavior.* New York: Macmillan.

Skinner, B. (1971). *Beyond freedom and dignity.* New York: Knopf.

Wong, H., & Wong, R. (1988). *First days of school.* Mountain View, CO: Authors.

Implementing Effective, Responsive Instruction and Assessment

Domain 3

Competency 7

Principles and Strategies for Effective Communication

Teri Bingham, EdD
West Texas A&M University

Amy Andersen, EdD
West Texas A&M University

> **Competency 7:** The teacher understands and applies principles and strategies for communicating effectively in varied teaching and learning contexts.

The beginning teacher:

A. Demonstrates clear, accurate communication in the teaching and learning process and uses language that is appropriate to students' ages, interests, and backgrounds.

B. Engages in skilled questioning and leads effective student discussions, including using questioning and discussion to engage all students in exploring content; extends students' knowledge; and fosters active student inquiry, higher-order thinking, problem solving, and productive, supportive interactions, including appropriate wait time.

C. Communicates directions, explanations, and procedures effectively and uses strategies for adjusting communication to enhance student understanding (e.g., by providing examples, simplifying complex ideas, using appropriate communication tools).

D. Practices effective communication techniques and interpersonal skills (including both verbal and non-verbal skills and electronic communication) for meeting specified goals in various contexts.

KEY TERMS

dialectical thinking	*divergent questions*	*think time*
convergent questions	*Bloom's taxonomy*	

Teaching and communicating go hand-in-hand as teachers explain directions, pose questions, demonstrate procedures, build knowledge bases, and explore activities with their students. It is imperative for teachers to perform all of these behaviors well and make adjustments as necessary to enhance student understanding.

As teachers contemplate the role effective communication plays in running a smooth and productive classroom, there are many ideas to consider. These ideas include dialectical thinking, questioning techniques, how to dignify a students' incorrect verbal answer, and when and how to repeat students' answers.

DIALECTICAL THINKING

Dialectical Thinking is when you can reasonably, responsibly, and respectfully examine a position different than your own that you feel strongly about. You may not agree with another's opinion but you can understand where he is coming from based on his experience, values, and culture. This is very difficult to do when one has strong emotions tied to the opinion.

QUESTIONING TECHNIQUES

Asking good questions before, during, and after learning is imperative for effective teaching and successful student learning. Questions are an effective tool for bridging the gap between presentation of content and student understanding. Other bridging strategies that function to promote and stimulate thinking include advance organizers, guided practice, feedback and correctives, self-evaluation, and discussion. Questions are intended to elicit student responses and engage all students in the thinking process. Questions should require thoughtful response and reflection. Effective questions are ones for that students actively compose a response and thereby become actively engaged in the learning process. Therefore, the goal of questioning is to ask questions which actively engage all students in the learning process while moving children from the knowledge and comprehension levels of **Bloom's taxonomy** toward application, analysis, synthesis, and evaluation. Utilize all levels of Bloom's taxonomy when writing questions to stimulate all levels of student cognition. Include **convergent questions** and **divergent questions**. Convergent questions have one correct answer. For example: "Name the current President of the United States." Divergent questions are open-ended questions that have more than one answer. An example of a divergent question is, "If you were the author of the book *The Hunger Games*, how would you have ended the story?"

The three phases of the questioning cycle consist of writing effective questions, properly asking questions, and responding appropriately to student answers.

Guidelines for Writing Questions

1. Questions should be clear and not too wordy.
2. Questions should be used to stimulate thinking and to produce an extended answer.
3. Questions should rarely call for a yes or no answer.
4. Try to anticipate questions that you will use and write key questions into the lesson plan.
5. Design questioning so that the whole class benefits from both the questions and responses.

Guidelines for Asking Questions

1. **Conduct questioning so all students, not just a few, feel a responsibility to participate**. Only call on a student after you have given everyone ample think time.
2. **Word questions to make all students become engaged in the thinking process**. It is a common practice for teachers to begin questions with the following phrases: "Who can . . . " "Can you . . . " "Does anyone . . . ". An alternative to this frames the questioning technique to increase students'

feelings of accountability, place the students in the context, and get them started thinking. Notice the psychological twist when a question begins with

a. "Think of a time when . . . "

b. "Be ready to explain (state, list, paraphrase, defend, justify, restate) . . . "

c. "Tell me . . . "

d. "Be thinking of . . . "

e. "Remember when as a child you . . . ".

3. **Address questions to the whole class so all students feel accountable for thinking**. There is a three-step process used in asking questions so all students feel responsible for knowing the answer.

   Step 1. Ask the question. Do not say a student's name before or immediately following the question. Doing so gives the other students a pass on thinking.

   Step 2. Allow at least 8 seconds for quality think time, also called wait time. More time for students to think often results in better responses, deeper thought, and critical thinking.

   Step 3. Call on a student you feel confident will know the correct answer.

   Because all the students will hear the student's response, the teacher wants to increase the likelihood that all students learn it correctly. Therefore, it is important for the students to hear correct answers as often as possible. We want to minimize the occurrence of students hearing incorrect knowledge or information. This does not mean as teachers we only call on the "smart" students or those we perceive as more capable. But rather, we create several questions that will capture the range of learner abilities in the class. Asking thought-provoking questions, using appropriate wait time that fosters children's reflective thought, and asking children to elaborate and justify their responses promotes critical thinking. Using Bloom's taxonomy for higher-order thinking, a teacher can generate several questions at various levels of cognition. Interestingly, evaluation, the highest level of cognition according to Bloom, could elicit a response from an academically less-able student yet one who has strong support for his judgment.

4. **Provide ample think time**. In our society, we are uncomfortable in silence. Think about how frequently we turn on noise: radio, TV, iPod. It is not uncommon for teachers to be uncomfortable with silence as they wait for a student to respond. This discomfort in silence leads teachers to call on students too quickly or simply answer the questions themselves. Students stop thinking once they realize the teacher will respond to his own question if no one raises his hand to answer. After asking a question, allow for quality think time by waiting for at least 8 seconds before calling on a student. The best advice for teachers, regarding think time, is to slow down and pause longer between questions and calling on a student than what at first seems comfortable. Also, use nonverbal skills to indicate to the students that you are giving them time to think. For example, you can fold you hands in front of you, step to the side of the room so you no longer appear to be in instruction mode, or briefly spread your arms wide to demonstrate they have the floor. The greatest benefit of giving sufficient think time is the students' answers will be broader, deeper, and well thought out. That is worth a few seconds of silence.

5. **After a student responds initially to a question, wait a few seconds again before responding**. Often a student will continue to respond without the teacher prompting. After the student answers, acknowledge him and when appropriate encourage or support him in continuing. A simple nod of the head or smile can help a student feel confident that he is on the right track and continue to build upon his answer.

6. **Respond appropriately to partial answers**. If a partial answer is given, allow sufficient think time for the student to reconsider or add to the response, and then prompt, probe, or pose another question to expand his answer. You may need to nod, smile, or acknowledge to the student his thinking is correct in order for him to feel confident enough in his response to continue.

7. **Do not call on students in order**. Ask randomly, evenly distributed questions or students will recognize patterns and not pay attention until they know it is getting close to their turn.

8. **Do not make students guess**. When a teacher calls on a student and the student does not know the correct answer, he has given his answer: he doesn't know. Making a student guess is embarrassing and humiliating. Use the skill of dignifying an incorrect verbal response (discussed later in this chapter) and answer the question yourself seamlessly. Sometimes the best way to illustrate absurdity is to use absurdity. If I asked you what type of a car my mom drives and you didn't know, it would be futile for me to tell you to guess. If a student does start taking guesses he is simply filling his and the other students' minds with wrong information. This unmistakably illustrates the reason for not having students guess at answers. Instead, dignify them and respectfully answer it yourself. If a student does not know an answer then it is the teacher's responsibility to provide the correct information.

9. **Do not use questioning to get a student's attention**. The purpose of questioning is to engage all students in the learning process, not to catch a student who is inattentive. There are better, more positive ways to get a student to attend to the teacher rather than calling on him to answer a question the teacher knows the student did not hear. This simply results in the student being embarrassed and/or humiliated. Furthermore, it misleads the students into thinking that when the teacher calls on a student he is disciplining the student for being off-task. This is made evident when a teacher calls on a student and rather than giving an answer, the student replies, "I was paying attention" or "I was taking notes" or "I was listening." Clearly it confuses students when questions are employed for both ascertaining if a student knows an answer *and* as a discipline technique to get a student on-task.

QUALITY RESPONDING

The manner in which the teacher responds to student answers affects the feeling tone in a classroom. When teachers respond in a positive, supportive manner, students are more likely to participate again in the future. Children feel safe to express their ideas in a risk-free learning environment where the teacher fosters a sense of community. When teachers humiliate, intimidate, embarrass, threaten, use sarcasm, or cause a student to lose his dignity, members of the class are less likely to participate.

1. **Acknowledge a good response**. Always tell the learner when he is correct. Teachers can use both verbal and nonverbal communication to recognize the student's accurate answer. Nonverbal messages can include a thumbs-up, smile, nod, quiet clapping, okay sign with thumb and index finger, or a high-five.

2. **Handle incorrect responses positively**. Try to rephrase the question in such a way that the student will arrive at an acceptable response. Reinforce any correct part of a partially correct response. Build on student responses, whether correct, incorrect, or partially correct. See the next section for more details.

3. **Clarify incomplete or wrong answers**. Make necessary corrections to incomplete or incorrect answers to avoid leaving students thinking the wrong answer is acceptable. Clarify misleading impressions of what is accurate and what is erroneous.

4. **To foster the class's dialogue on open-ended questions, teachers can recognize a student's correct response and ask for others' ideas**. Teachers can validate and acknowledge a student's contribution and use it to stimulate additional discussion.

Three Steps to Dignify and Correct Students' Incorrect Verbal Answers

When a student gives a wrong answer to a question it means he does not know two things. First, he doesn't know the correct answer to the question and second, he doesn't know the question to his answer. If he knew the question to his answer he would know that his answer doesn't go with the question posed. Therefore the teacher needs to do three things:

1. Dignify the student's incorrect verbal response by providing the question to which the student gave the answer. This requires quick thinking on the teacher's part. However, with experience it becomes an easier and a more natural response.

2. Ask the question again or rephrase the question in such a way as to increase the likelihood that the student will answer it correctly.

3. Stay with the student and provide clues, prompts, or hints to help coach him to be right. Do *not* go on to another student.

Two Pointers to Keep in Mind

1. **If the student does not know the answer or his mind has gone blank the teacher should answer the question himself.** This strategy should be invisible to the students. After the teacher calls on a student and the student blanks out, the teacher simply and casually rephrases the question and answers it himself. Suppose the question was, "What were the issues surrounding the Persian Gulf War?" followed by quality think time. Next the teacher calls on a student he believes knows the right answer. Let's say the student appears to have gone blank. The teacher could then say, "Let's first think of the countries involved in this conflict and determine what issues each faced . . . " then complete his explanation of the issues.

Some physiological characteristics and behaviors indicating that a student's mind has gone blank include red or white discoloration in the face, frantically looking around at peers, looking down, hunching over the desk, sliding down in the chair, glazed eyes, etc.

2. **When a student says the wrong answer stick with him, do not go on to another child.** Do not call on another student or request the student to call on someone he thinks knows the right answer. This gives the tacit message that you lack confidence in the student's ability to get the accurate answer. Instead, give him cues, prompts, or visual aids to lead him to the correct response. If the student still appears not to understand or too mentally anxious to respond, then seamlessly and imperceptible to the other students answer the question yourself. For example, suppose the teacher asked, "What is the difference between a vein and an artery?" Then he calls on a student who doesn't know the answer or shuts down, the teacher could rescue him by saying, "Veins and arteries are similar because they both carry blood. Veins carry blood to the heart and arteries carry blood away from the heart." Then casually continue the lesson.

REPEATING STUDENT ANSWERS

It is not uncommon for teachers to repeat students' answers. It is as though there is an echo in the classroom. When teachers unknowingly repeat students' answers it decreases the probability that students will listen to each another. Instead the students simply wait for the teacher to repeat it before attending to the information. This can start bad habits of students not listening the first time something is said. According to Madeline Hunter (1994), there are invalid and valid reasons for repeating students' answers. Both are discussed.

Invalid Reasons for Repeating Student Answers

1. It has been modeled in previous school experience.
2. It has become a habit.
3. Repeating an answer gives the teacher time to think up the next question or statement.
4. It is believed that hearing something twice facilitates learning and retention. To achieve this it is actually more beneficial for the students to cognitively process the information, as discussed earlier.
5. It makes the student feel good about him- or herself.

Valid Reasons for Repeating Student Answers

1. The teacher needs to clarify or extend an answer.
2. To handle an incorrect answer.
3. To encourage a shy learner during the initial stages of learning.

When a student quietly answers a question the teacher needs to get the student to speak a little louder. However, when a teacher replies, "Say it louder," the student is often reluctant to do so. This is because the student first wants to know whether or not she is right. Therefore, the teacher needs to first validate the answer by saying, "That is right, now say it so the others can learn it." This gives the students needed feedback and kindly "invites" the student to speak up so he feels more confident.

HELPING A STUCK STUDENT

Another important skill for educators is how to give effective help to students who are having difficulty on a task. Unsolicited assistance from the teacher can make students feel that the teacher lacks confidence in their ability or judged to be incapable of doing the task independently. When helping a stuck student we want the student to feel in charge of the assistance. We also want to provide an environment where each student feels responsible for his learning and experiences competence. To increase student understanding during instruction, think aloud as you demonstrate the skill or process. This helps students learn the cognitive processes that precede each action.

Begin by observing the student to decide if he is thinking or if he really is stuck and needs to be jump-started. If you believe he needs assistance, walk over to him and bend down so as to be less visible by the class. The student may be sensitive and not want his peers to know he needs help. A good way to start the communication is to ask, "So, what are you working on?" Then praise him for what he knows or has accomplished. Next, ask questions to get the student moving; sometimes it just takes getting him engaged with the material again. Questions that help the student recognize what he does know and pinpoint where the confusion lies include:

- What have you done so far?
- What are you suppose to do next?
- What part do you understand?
- What part isn't very clear?

Once you identify what is confusing the student, ask questions that will help the student focus on the next step or relevant information to support his success. Examples include:

- What information are you given and what are you looking for?
- Who is the main character?
- What is the problem or dilemma in the story?
- Think aloud for me as you do each step.
- Let's look at an example together.

If he is still stuck, ask simpler questions that direct the student's focus. Keep narrowing your questions until he is able to understand what you are teaching. On the other hand, if the student lacks information, the teacher should supply the answer to the question. Students cannot generate that which is not in their brain and wild guesses lead to more confusion.

Praise, Prompt, Leave

In general, there are three types of receptions a teacher receives when giving unsolicited assistance. However, the teacher's behavior remains the same regardless of the student response: praise, prompt, leave. The first type of response comes from a student who needs help, but doesn't want help. He doesn't want to interact with the teacher, or perhaps he is uncomfortable with the idea that his peers know he can't do the work. Being keenly aware of this type of student, the teacher approaches carefully and bends down to be less visible. However, position yourself so you can still observe the rest of the class. Then you praise the student for what he has accomplished, even if it is only writing his name at the top of the page. Prompt with questions as discussed above. Then smile and walk away.

The second type of student not only wants your help, but wants to exploit you. Once you walk near this student he wants you to be his private tutor, coach, and cheerleader. Although he wants you to stay and watch him do every problem or complete every task, you still praise, prompt, leave. However, for this student you leave him with a challenge to do a certain amount of work while you check on others and see how far he can get before you return. Really do return so he continues to trust you. This might sound like, "Ben, you got the hang of it. I'm going to check on others, see if you can get to #9 before I get back." Then smile and walk away.

The third reception you may encounter is actually the easiest. It is the child who knows he needs help and is open to assistance. The difference here is he does not want you to stay after you get him back on track. The process is still praise, prompt, leave.

For each student, after he does the work correctly you need to decide whether you should stay and guide him through one or two more until you feel he can do it independently or if you should move away and let the student continue working. To maximize the amount of students you can monitor or assist, don't stay too long with any one student. If it appears a student needs a great deal of time and aid, check the assignment to see if it is appropriate for his ability level and stage of cognitive development.

Even if the students do not need assistance the teacher should circulate the room checking on student progress, accuracy, maintaining proximity and presence, and being readily available to answer the shy or quiet child's question. Always reinforce effort and compliment growth. It can be tempting to return to your desk to catch up on some work or to put up your bulletin board. However, resist doing these things; it makes you less approachable to your students.

The personal interaction a teacher encounters with each child significantly contributes to the student's self-direction, motivation, and achievement. Positive interactions between the teacher and student can result in increased student self-esteem and feelings of competence.

TIPS FOR COMMUNICATING

- When teaching, consider communicating the new material in accordance to the students' learning styles.
- When conferencing with a student take into consideration their communication style in respect to their culture.
- Use language that is appropriate to students' interests, ages, and experiences.
- Be aware of the positive effects of think time.
- Classroom communication skills vary from culture to culture.
- Exercise effective verbal, nonverbal, and electronic communication skills and interpersonal skills.
- Be keenly aware of your body language and what the students' body language may be communicating. Respond appropriately.
- For identified students it is important to communicate the lesson objectives to the appropriate resource personnel.
- Be a reflective listener.

DISCUSSION OUTLINES AND ACTIVITIES

Explain "dialectical thinking."

Questioning

1. What is the purpose for a teacher's asking the class questions?

2. List three ways teachers can begin questions so students feel accountable to respond.

3. What is the best advice for teachers regarding think time?

4. When should the teacher generate the questions that correspond to the lesson?

5. What are the three steps in asking students questions?

6. Who should the teacher call on?

Dignifying and Correcting Students' Incorrect Verbal Answers

List the three steps to dignify a student's incorrect verbal response.

1.

2.

3.

What are the three tips for correcting a student's wrong, or partially wrong, answer?

1.

2.

3.

Sample Test Questions

1. Mr. Morales is going to give his students a 10-minute writing assignment for the first time. What should he consider as most helpful to the success of his students?

   a.   Effective teachers appreciate the cultural vagaries of communication.

   b.   Effective teachers use a variety of communication techniques.

   c.   Effective teachers shape the classroom into a community of learners monitoring their own progress.

   d.   Effective teachers communicate instructional tasks clearly to students.

2. As the students watch a video, Ms. Chang occasionally stops the tape and asks questions about the ideas presented. Ms. Chang probably uses this strategy because she knows which of the following?

   a.   Students stay on task better when they are monitored.

   b.   Effective teachers use verbal and nonverbal cues to stop inappropriate behavior.

   c.   Effective teachers ask questions that promote divergent thinking.

   d.   Teachers' efforts to maintain student involvement through dialogues and questions help students cognitively process the information better.

3. Mrs. Cicone finds that her students rarely answer questions that require deeper thought. To encourage students to think and promote problem-solving skills, what types of questions should Mrs. Cicone ask?

   a.   Divergent questions

   b.   Who, what, where, and when questions

   c.   Convergent questions

   d.   Group dynamics questions

4. Ms. Hilderbrandt frequently asks questions as part of her instructional strategy. She probably knows that when asking questions, effective teachers:

   a.   call on students so that they will be prepared.

   b.   ask more convergent questions.

   c.   provide supportive feedback to responses.

   d.   provide the right answer when no one immediately responds.

5. After Mr. Parker poses a question to the students he allows sufficient think time. However, some teachers struggle with waiting three seconds or more before calling on a student. Which of the following is probably the *main* reason for this?

   a. The teacher is concerned that the students will misbehave.

   b. The teacher believes no one will answer anyway so it is best to go on.

   c. There is a cultural norm in the United States where teachers become uncomfortable with silence.

   d. The teacher understands that if the students can't answer the question right away they probably don't know the answer.

Answers

1. A is incorrect. This question is not about cultural diversity.

   B is incorrect. This question is not about communication techniques, but rather a writing assignment.

   C is incorrect. This question is not about building a community of learners or students monitoring their progress.

   D is the correct answer. When students are beginning any new task they need to first have clear instructions.

2. A is incorrect. She is not monitoring the students' behavior. She is trying to keep the students focused and cognitively engaged.

   B is incorrect. It does not relate to the question. However, it is a true statement.

   C is incorrect. Again, it does not relate to the question. However, it is a true statement.

   D is the correct answer. There is a strong correlation between student involvement and students' cognitive engagement. Therefore, teachers strive to keep students focused and involved.

3. **A is the correct answer**. Divergent questions help students to broaden their thinking, foster higher-order thinking, and increase problem-solving skills.

   B is incorrect. These questions only require simple recall and do not require higher-order thinking.

   C is incorrect. Convergent questions have one correct answer.

   D is incorrect. Although she may ask a question for students to discuss as a group, it still may not be a divergent question.

4. A is incorrect. To keep all students involved teachers need to call on them out of sequence.

   B is incorrect. Teachers should ask both convergent and divergent questions.

   C is the correct answer. Students will feel better about themselves and participate when the teacher provides positive and supportive feedback to the students' response.

   D is incorrect. It is the teacher's responsibility to coach students to be correct and guide their thinking. When a teacher frequently answers her own questions, students do not feel accountable.

5. A is incorrect. Although this may be true, the teacher needs to maintain student behavior and train the students to be patient as they wait for others to respond.

   B is incorrect. Teachers need to hold the students accountable for answering questions.

   C is the correct answer. In our society many people are uncomfortable with silence so it becomes difficult to provide sufficient think time for students.

   D is incorrect. The students need think time to ponder and form quality answers.

REFERENCES

Hunter, M. (1994). *Enhancing Teaching.* Pearson College Div

Websites

http://www2.edutech.nodak.edu/ndsta/gill.htm

Contains an article about the importance of effective communication in the classroom.

http://www3.uakron.edu/education/safeschools/COOP/comm.html

Contains a different perspective on classroom communication with additional links to how communication affects classroom management and conflict resolution.

http://www.education-world.com/a_tsl/archives/02-1/lesson020.shtml

Contains lesson plans to help foster communication skills in your classroom.

http://www.adprima.com/lesson.htm

Provides an article on how good lesson planning can improve your communication skills in the classroom. It includes links and explanations on how to improve your lesson-planning skills.

http://honolulu.hawaii.edu/intranet/committees/FacDevCom/guidebk/teachtip/teachtip .htm#communication

Has several links that take you to information including culturally effective communication tips and how to improve nonverbal communication.

Competency 8

Student Motivation and Engagement

Teri Bingham, EdD
West Texas A&M University

Judy Lopez-Kutcher, EdD
Dallas Independent School District
Alternative Teacher Certification

> **Competency 8:** The teacher provides appropriate instruction that actively engages students in the learning process.

The beginning teacher:

A. Employs various instructional techniques (e.g., discussion, inquiry, problem solving) and varies teacher and student roles in the instructional process and provides instruction that promotes intellectual involvement and active student engagement and learning.

B. Applies various strategies to promote student engagement and learning (e.g., by structuring lessons effectively, using flexible instructional groupings, pacing lessons flexibly in response to student needs, including wait time).

C. Presents content to students in ways that are relevant and meaningful and that links with students' prior knowledge and experience.

D. Applies criteria for evaluating the appropriateness of instructional activities, materials, resources, and technologies for students with varied characteristics and needs.

E. Engages in continuous monitoring of instructional effectiveness.

F. Applies knowledge of different types of motivation (e.g., internal, external) and factors affecting student motivation.

G. Employs effective motivational strategies and encourages students' self-motivation.

H. Provides focused, targeted, and systematic second language acquisition instruction to English language learners in grade 3 or higher who are at the beginning or intermediate level of English-language proficiency in listening and/or speaking in accordance with the ELPS.

I. Provides focused, targeted, and systematic second language acquisition instruction to English language learners in grade 3 or higher who are at the beginning or intermediate level of English-language proficiency in reading and/or writing in accordance with the ELPS.

J. Develops the foundation of English language vocabulary, grammar, syntax, and mechanics necessary to understand content-based instruction and accelerated learning of English in accordance with ELPS.

KEY TERMS

active learning	*feeling tone*	*continuous assessment*
attribution theory	*inductive teaching*	*prior knowledge*
authentic assessment	*inquiry method*	*role of the student*
cognitive prompts	*intrinsic motivation*	*role of the teacher*
convergent questions	*knowledge of results*	*scaffolding*
deductive teaching	*level of concern*	*success*
discussion method	*locus of control*	*wait time*
divergent questions	*metacognition*	
extrinsic motivation	*ongoing assessment*	

A student's academic success relies heavily on teacher effectiveness. The instructional techniques and processes within a given classroom are established by the teacher and directly impact the academic progress made by each student in the classroom.

Competency 8 centers upon the teacher's method of instruction and motivation that actively engages students in the learning process. What does this imply? As educators, one of our challenges of remaining effective is that we constantly stay abreast of current educational research and effective instructional practices. Although no one can "make" a student learn, there are techniques teachers can employ to create an environment where students desire to learn is increased. All students are motivated to do something. It is the creative teacher who can channel that motivation in positive directions to help students want to learn and be academically successful.

Effective teaching strategies that are developmentally appropriate and motivational techniques that engage students in active learning are the gist of this competency.

STUDENT AND TEACHER ROLES

The roles of student and teacher have dramatically changed within my lifetime. Reflecting upon my years as a student, I realize how disengaged I was in the learning process. In all of my school years, I remember two teachers who actively challenged me to think. One was a high school American history teacher and the other was a college political science instructor. What was different about them? They weren't afraid to "push the envelope" and challenge responses. They created in me a desire to ask "why" and not be afraid to seek out the answers. They effectively lead me down the path of Bloom's levels of analysis, synthesis, and evaluation and I didn't even know it at the time!

The **role of the teacher** in today's educational setting is that of facilitator rather than dispenser of information. **Active learning** transforms students from passive listeners to active participants by requiring them to think, read, write, listen, brainstorm, debate, discuss, and create in order to solve the task at hand. Students are engaged in learning because they are the ones doing most of the work involved in the learning task. They are the ones being challenged to work and think at the upper levels of Bloom's taxonomy. In turn, the teacher's role is that of facilitator and guide. A teacher facilitates learning by designing lessons that allow students the freedom to create and develop learning experiences. The teacher structures instruction in such a way that students are guided down a predetermined path, but allows students the freedom to design, research, and develop activities and products that demonstrate the desired learning has occurred. Instructional techniques such as small groups and cooperative learning are types of activities that actively engage students while allowing the teacher to monitor and facilitate learning. Small-group activities that require students to discuss and produce a final product are prime examples of this. For example, while studying a unit about the rainforest, students in a language arts class may be asked to turn a section of the classroom wall into a rainforest. This activity calls for students to work together to research the different layers of the rainforest and the type of vegetation found at each level, as well as the animals that inhabit the different layers. This type of activity produces a product that is the result of research and discussion among group members. Group members must work together to create a final product that accurately reflects their research. This type of project results in learning that is internalized by students and endures over time. This product demonstrates understanding in a very different way than simply reading several books on the topic and turning in a report. Students must apply what they have researched and discussed to create the final product, which demonstrates mastery of the subject matter.

Cooperative learning is an instructional technique that uses small groups of students who work together to maximize both their own learning and that of others. The entire group benefits from the individual efforts of each group member. Cooperative learning works in today's classrooms because it provides students with opportunities to act in a positive interdependent manner. Positive interdependence occurs when students recognize the fact that they succeed not as individuals, but as a group. An individual student succeeds when the group succeeds. Cooperative learning also facilitates the development of accountability, both individually and as a group. These are lifelong skills that all students need to be successful participants in today's society and workforce.

Another of the teacher's roles is that of guide. This occurs when the teacher designs lessons and activities that allow students to gather information on their own. In this role, the teacher guides students along the path of discovery, but does not "give" students the information outright. The long-held role of teacher as the sole imparter of knowledge gives way to that of teacher as guide and encourager. These instructional activities allow for **discussion and inquiry methods** as integral parts of the learning process.

What implication does this hold for the **role of the student**? The student's role in active learning is that of knowledge seeker and gatherer. Under the structure established by the teacher, the student engages in activities that transform them from someone who merely knows something to someone who has learned something. Students not only gather information, but harvest it in a way that allows them to store what they have learned into a deep level of understanding that endures. Knowledge becomes deep-seeded and students understand the relevance of what they have learned and accomplished.

INSTRUCTIONAL ACTIVITIES THAT FOSTER STUDENT ENGAGEMENT AND ACTIVE LEARNING

The concept of active learning has already been defined in this chapter, as has the instructional strategy known as cooperative learning. Active learning transforms students from passive listeners to active participants by requiring them to think, read, write, listen, brainstorm, debate, discuss and create in order to solve the task at hand. Active learning engages students in higher-order thinking processes and challenges them to go above and beyond what is necessary to merely "pass." Cooperative learning provides instructional strategies for active learning. The beauty of cooperative learning is that it is, in effect, an umbrella for many types of student-centered group activities. Cooperative learning activities such as Jigsaw, Student Team Learning, and Cooperative Integrated Reading and Composition (CIRC) are but a few of the structured types of activities found under the umbrella of cooperative learning. A list of Internet resources on cooperative learning is provided for the reader at the end of this chapter.

Instructional activities that actively engage students in higher levels of thinking are the very foundation of Competency 8. Students must be challenged to think, to become proactive learners and problem-solvers. To accomplish this, the teacher must structure lessons in ways that incorporate various models of teaching designed for this purpose. One such model of thinking is that of inductive rather than deductive teaching.

Deductive teaching is a model of teaching/learning that is most familiar to us. A typical example of deductive teaching is the tried-and-true lecture model. In deductive teaching, the teacher gives students the information to be learned, asks a few questions related to the topic, and then assigns some sort of task in which the students demonstrate their understanding of the topic. Little, if any, creativity or use of higher-order thinking skills occurs in deductive learning. Deductive teaching is teacher-centered, as opposed to inductive teaching, which is student-centered. **Inductive teaching** is an instructional strategy in which the teacher gives students bits and pieces of the information to be learned and students must draw conclusions on their own. In order for inductive teaching to be effective, teachers must provide students with enough pieces of information to peak their interest and then guide them through higher-order cognitive processes to acquire the desired information. Both deductive and inductive models of teaching have a legitimate purpose. An effective combination of these methods can create lessons that result in student learning. Effective teachers know how to use deductive teaching to convey needed information and follow this with inductive activities that take students beyond lecture notes and into realms of drawing conclusions and making inferences. **Inquiry-based teaching** is another strategy used by effective teachers to engage students in active learning. Problem solving is taught via questioning and discovery. The role of the teacher in inquiry learning is that of a catalyst. Inquiry-based teaching is composed of the following steps: formulating a problem, observing, investigating, analyzing, communicating, and considering solutions. Through the use of carefully constructed open-ended questions, teachers are able to guide students into a discussion that allows students to do most of the talking. The teacher carefully guides the students into discussing the topic at hand and leads them to the point of discovery. There is no greater satisfaction for a teacher than to see the "light bulb" expression on students' faces as they solve the problem posed by the teacher.

There are other types of instructional activities that foster student engagement. Among these are activities such as role-playing, simulations, discussions, and debates. **Role-playing** requires the student to assume the role of another person and think and act as that person would. They "become" that person. In order to do this, a great deal of research and questioning must occur in order for the student to be able to assume the role of another individual. An example of this would be a project in a science class in which a student role-plays Thomas Edison and describes what was involved in the creation of the light bulb, the challenges he experienced, and the obstacles he faced and surmounted. **Simulations** are scenarios that require the use of skills in order to achieve a goal. An example of this would be a problem-solving activity such as asking students to design a subdivision in which the houses are all underground and are powered only by solar and wind power. After the students have researched and completed the project, it is presented to the class and the teacher leads a debriefing session in which students reflect upon and explain what they did, why they did it, and what they learned. **Class discussions** can also be a source of student engagement so long as the teacher serves as the "host" of the discussion forum and allows the students to be the center of the discussion. The teacher carefully guides the discussion in the desired direction while allowing the students to do the bulk of the discussing. This strategy empowers students to take an active role and sends the message to them that everyone has a valued place in the discussion. **Debate** is another instructional strategy that actively engages students by forcing them to do the detailed type of research that will allow them to answer whatever questions are asked of them. Debate not only requires higher-order thinking skills, but demands that students be able to think on their feet and express themselves in an eloquent and convincing manner. An example of this would be holding presidential debates prior to an "election." Students would assume the roles of the various candidates and would address a number of political topics based on the stand on the issues held by the actual political candidates.

For learning to be meaningful and engaging, students must be made responsible for their own learning. This results in students who are problem-solvers because they have learned how to think through situations. Engaging instruction is also authentic because it confronts students with real-world situations that they will have to face throughout their lives. It allows students to understand that what they are studying in the classroom transcends the school walls and carries them into the future. It equips students to be lifelong learners, critical thinkers, and active problem-solvers.

FACTORS THAT AFFECT EFFECTIVE TEACHING AND ACTIVE STUDENT ENGAGEMENT

Much has been said about grouping and its value in active learning. However, grouping students is much more complicated than merely putting four to six students together and calling them a group. In order to group effectively, teachers need to make sure that groups contain students of mixed abilities. The research done regarding cooperative learning touts the value of mixed-ability groups and praises the academic outcomes derived from the proper use of this technique. As learners, we all acquire knowledge both in different ways and at different rates. A learner who has mastered a given topic is a valuable asset to a student who is struggling with that concept because, oftentimes, the student who possesses mastery is able to explain the concept to the struggling student in a way that clarifies it for that student. Any classroom teacher can attest to trying to explain something several different ways to no end. The teacher becomes frustrated because numerous ways of explaining something have been tried and the student becomes frustrated because the student still doesn't get it. Suddenly, a fellow student pipes in with a simple phrase that usually starts with "What Ms. Jones is trying to say is that . . ." The mystery is solved!

Grouping is a powerful educational tool, but it is also a dangerous practice if used to group students by ability. Student grouping should, in most situations, not be done in a manner that puts students of similar abilities together. Rather, groups should be composed of mixed-ability groups. Struggling students benefit and learn from students who have already demonstrated mastery of a topic. Conversely, students who have demonstrated mastery receive practice and reinforce this mastery by teaching it to a peer.

Effective student grouping is never stagnant. Effective teachers do not assign groups at the beginning of the year and maintain those same groups throughout the year. Students have different skills and different educational needs. The teacher addresses this by using flexible and fluid grouping. Students are grouped together for a particular learning task or assignment. Once that task or assignment is completed, that learning group is dissolved and a new one replaces it when a new task or assignment is given. Students should be told from the beginning that they will move in and out of groups and that they should expect to work in many different types and sizes of groups throughout the academic year. Good grouping is determined by the task at hand and by the number of students needed to successfully complete any given assignment.

Instructional pacing is another important component of effective instruction. Instructional pacing is an art acquired by reflective teachers. We have all had teachers who move at lightning speed without ever realizing that they have left most, if not all, of the class behind. And, sadly, we have all had teachers who have moved at a snail's pace and have been oblivious to students' boredom and misbehavior. Good instructional pacing comes with keeping a pulse on the class. It is the ability to know that the instructional pace is neither too fast nor too slow, but "just right." Effective instructional pacing also includes questioning students along the way to ensure that student interest is maintained and that subject-matter comprehension is occurring. Teachers who question effectively understand the value of using wait time in their classes. **Wait time** is the time that a teacher waits from the end of the question to the beginning of a student's response. Generally, a good rule of thumb is 8 seconds before intervening, prompting, or re-asking the question. Finally, the importance of constructive feedback and positive reinforcement cannot be left unstressed. Constructive feedback provides students with information that either reinforces their learning or helps correct any misconceptions. It does not allow mistakes or misconceptions to be internalized by the student. Positive reinforcement provides students with the satisfaction of knowing they have acquired new knowledge and skills.

THE ROLE OF THINKING IN THE LEARNING PROCESS

Effective teachers challenge students to think. These teachers know that asking a student to construct a model of an energy-efficient home and explain how and why it works is a more challenging assignment than asking a student to write a three-paragraph paper on the value of conserving energy. Effective teachers also know the value of asking divergent questions as opposed to convergent questions. Divergent questions are open-ended questions that have more than one solution, whereas convergent questions are questions that have one correct answer. An example of a convergent question is "How many states are in the Union?" The only correct answer is "50." An example of a divergent question, however, is "What are the political and economic ramifications of California and Texas seceding from the United States?" Whereas the first question only has one answer, the second question lends itself to research, discussion, and possibly debate about the effects that such an action would have on the political power base and the economy of the United States. It also lends itself to more than one correct answer.

Because effective teachers challenge students to think, a word or two must be said about two basic reading processes. The first is that of building background. Good teachers always take the time at the beginning of a new lesson to establish background and to make sure that students have a foundation on which to build. Establishing **prior knowledge** refers to the process of building upon what is already there. For example, what are the prerequisite skills that students must know in order to be successful in an assignment about genetics? What do they already need to know? What happens if they don't have these prerequisite skills? An effective teacher knows to check that the foundation is in place and on solid ground. This is most easily done by asking questions before beginning a lesson that tap into the students' prior knowledge about a subject. If the necessary prior knowledge is not there, then the teacher backs up and provides that foundation, which ensures a basis for successful learning. **Scaffolding** is a term that refers to providing support for a student for as long as it is needed and removing that support when the student no longer needs it. Good teachers automatically do this by knowing how and when to help as well as how and when to withdraw that assistance. A practical example of scaffolding is the use of training wheels on a bicycle. Scaffolding helps ensure successful learning by providing assistance where needed and then setting the student free to engage in active learning that is both independent and interdependent.

Effective teachers model and teach **metacognition**. Metacognition is simply thinking about one's thinking. Good readers constantly ask themselves questions as they read. Good readers know how to monitor their reading and adjust their reading as well as self-correct when necessary. Struggling readers do not always possess these skills. As an effective teacher, regardless of the subject matter you will teach, you need to understand the role that reading plays in any given content area. Effective content-area teachers are aware of the value of metacognition and take the time to model it in their teaching. Students learn to think by being challenged to do so. Metacognition provides the vehicle to promote thinking skills and challenge students to become lifelong knowledge seekers.

HOW ARE STUDENT ENGAGEMENT AND ACTIVE LEARNING ASSESSED?

Although Competency 10 deals with assessment, several notions dealing with assessment bear addressing in this chapter. For assessment to be a valuable and useful learning tool, it must be both ongoing and authentic. **Ongoing assessment** occurs when the teacher continuously has a pulse on the instructional activities and the students involved in these activities. It consists of monitoring and adjusting the instructional cycle so that students are successful in their learning. Ongoing assessment can be as simple as a teacher who walks around the classroom and monitors the discussions held within small groups or a teacher who watches and reads the body language and puzzled looks of students. Ongoing assessment is the ability of a teacher to read the pulse of the students and design instruction that leads to students' enduring learning. It is continuous in nature and serves not only to inform that teacher about what the students have learned, but, more importantly, tells the teacher how effective the instruction has been. (This allows the teacher to monitor and adjust along the way and make the necessary modifications to maximize learning and ensure students' success.) **Authentic assessment** refers to the types of assessment that require students to make a product that demonstrates the real-life connection to what they have learned. Authentic assessments can include, but are not limited to, such projects as panel discussions, models, experiments, or assembling a product to demonstrate understanding of how something works.

Engaged learning and authentic assessment occur in classrooms in which the teacher views his or her role as that of facilitator, guide, and partner in the learning process. In turn, students see themselves as investigators and partners with both the teacher and fellow students in the learning process.

WHAT ROLE DOES MOTIVATION PLAY IN STUDENT LEARNING?

Motivation can be defined as the course of actions that move someone towards a goal. Motivation can be extrinsic (outside of oneself) or intrinsic (within oneself). Examples of extrinsic motivation are money and praise. Students who are paid a certain amount of money for each "A" they earn on their report card are being extrinsically motivated. Students who are publicly praised for an accomplishment are also receiving extrinsic motivation. If praise is to be effective it must be immediate, authentic, and age/grade appropriate. Extrinsic motivation depends on the completion of a task and can be seen as a way of controlling behavior. Intrinsic motivation, in contrast, is internal and can be seen as the sense of satisfaction that someone feels when they know they have done something well or have successfully completed a project.

© Poznyakov, 2014, Used under license of Shutterstock, Inc.

As individuals, we all need to be recognized. Teachers who only reward students extrinsically run the risk of making external praise and recognition meaningless. They also run the risk of never acknowledging those students who, by nature, are intrinsically motivated and for whom extrinsic motivators are of little value. Each type of motivation has its purpose. An effective teacher knows how to recognize the value of each and how to use them effectively within their classrooms to maximize learning and increase student engagement.

There are several different theories regarding motivation. The first one we will discuss is B. F. Skinner's (1979) behaviorist model, which holds that motivation serves to reinforce a desired behavior. This can occur through positive or negative reinforcement. **Positive reinforcement** occurs when an action is rewarded immediately after the desired behavior has occurred. On the other hand, **negative reinforcement** occurs when an undesirable stimulus is removed immediately after the desired behavior has occurred. In each case, the goal is the same, that is, the strengthening of a desired behavior.

Albert Bandura's (1986) social learning theory presents the view that changes in behavior occur as a result of observing and imitating a model. For changes in behavior to occur, the subject must be willing to accept the model and imitate the desired behavior. After this occurs, the subject must then encode the learned behavior into memory.

Bandura was very much aware of the relationship between motivation and behavioral changes. Bandura believed that behavior is motivated in one of three ways: direct reinforcement, vicarious reinforcement, or self-reinforcement. **Direct reinforcement** takes place when the subject watches and imitates the desired model and is immediately rewarded for having done so. **Vicarious reinforcement** takes place when a subject anticipates being rewarded for implementing the same behavior for which someone else has been rewarded. Lastly, **self-reinforcement** takes place when a subject sets and accomplishes a personal goal or standard. Self-reinforcement does not depend on any external factors.

Jean Piaget's (Piaget & Inhelder, 1969) cognitive view of motivation centers around the idea that how people think about themselves and their environment influences their development. According to Piaget's theory, people possess a need for balance in life. This balance (equilibrium) occurs when what we understand about the world is in balance with our experiences. An imbalance (disequilibrium) occurs when something new is introduced that unbalances what a person knows about the world and the experiences this person has had. Because the mind has a need for equilibrium, the learner seeks out the needed information to resolve the imbalance. Once this is accomplished, equilibrium is restored.

The final view of motivation that we consider is that of Abraham Maslow. Maslow's (1968) hierarchy of needs states that individuals have certain needs and attempt to fulfill those needs in a certain order. Maslow sorted these needs into two groups: deficiency needs and growth needs. Deficiency needs are the lower-level needs of survival, safety, belonging, and self-esteem. Growth needs are the higher-level needs of intellectual achievement, aesthetic appreciation, and self-actualization. According to this theory, growth needs cannot be attended to unless an individual has fulfilled all deficiency needs.

Regardless of the theory one espouses, as teachers, it is critical that we understand the role that motivation plays in the academic success of our students. Teachers must constantly find techniques to motivate students and foster positive self-esteem in ways that are appropriate and meaningful for each individual.

CREATING A RISK-FREE LEARNING ENVIRONMENT THAT MAXIMIZES STUDENT ENGAGEMENT AND ACTIVE LEARNING

About 10 years ago, an eighth-grade student approached her ESL teacher at the beginning of class and told her she had a question. The teacher asked her what it was. The student's question was "How do you say 'foot fingers' in English?" Think about this for a second. This was an eighth grader in front of a group of adolescents. No one laughed or made any sort of a comment. The teacher, understanding that the student needed a label for a concept she already knew, simply replied "Toes." That is a risk-free learning environment! It is an atmosphere established from the very first day of school that allows students to be comfortable taking academic risks. It is an environment that fosters learning and that will not allow anyone to ridicule or be ridiculed by others. If student learning is to be maximized, teachers must create classroom environments that honor and celebrate situations such as the one mentioned above. As teachers, we hold an enormous power in our hands. We have the power to shut down a child's natural sense of wonder and thirst for learning by how we treat that child and how we rise to the challenge of attending to his academic needs. We also have the ability to empower that student to develop into a lifelong learner who understands the inherent value and impact of learning. The choice is ours.

SEVEN STUDENT VARIABLES OF MOTIVATION

Madeline Hunter (1989) has identified seven student variables for motivation. These variables that teachers control can increase the likelihood that students will want to learn. They include attribution theory, knowledge of results, level of concern, success, feeling tone, interest, and intrinsic and extrinsic rewards. Each of these variables are discussed.

Attribution Theory

Attribution theory is to whom or what the learner attributes his success or failure. There are two types of **locus of control**: internal and external. Internal locus of control is when the learner takes responsibility for his success or failure. External locus of control is when the learner blames someone else or the circumstances for his success or failure that are within his control.

Locus of Control	Success	Failure
Internal	Effort	Lack of effort
External	Luck, easy task	Too hard, bad day, teacher doesn't like me

GOAL OF ATTRIBUTION THEORY

For teachers the goal of attribution theory is to emphasize the effects of effort to transfer the locus of control from external to internal and maintain internal locus of control.

To do this:

1. Identify the negative attributions you most often hear a student make.
2. Create a positive alternative to the negative attribution.
3. When you hear a student use a negative attribution, take a moment to introduce your alternative, and discuss with the student how to use it. Model the use of a positive attribution.

4. Create opportunities for the student to use the positive attributions and praise their use.

5. Monitor for students' spontaneous use of positive attributions. Call these to the students' attention and praise them.

Knowledge of Results and Cognitive Prompts

There are two different times students receive feedback of how well they are progressing. When it is interactive feedback such as questions and answers it is called *cognitive prompts*. Cognitive prompts indicate to the student what he or she does and doesn't know.

When the feedback is after the fact such as returning a test or homework assignment it is called *knowledge of results*. Knowledge of results needs to be *timely* (as soon as possible) and *specific* to be most powerful and motivating.

Knowledge of results needs to be specific in four ways:

1. What the learner did right.
2. What made it right, or well done.
3. What the learner did wrong.
4. How to fix it.

Letter grades or prosaic teacher comments such as "good work" or "nice paper" do not have any specific information for students to use for improving or to continue doing what was done well.

However, a few verbal or written remarks indicating a specific way to improve or why it was well done will provide a student with useful information that he or she is more likely to use in the future.

Level of Concern

Level of concern is the degree to which a student is concerned or feels anxiety in a learning situation. An effective teacher deliberately (not haphazardly) raises and lowers the students' level of concern to increase their motivation (intent to learn).

There are three levels of concern: high, moderate (ideal), and low. A high level of concern is when the student experiences a great deal of anxiety and stress about his or her learning. This can actually impede learning. Some concern is motivating, but not when it becomes paralyzing. A moderate level of concern is when the student is concerned about their learning, but not so much that it interferes with his or her acquisition of the new skill or knowledge. A low level of concern is when the student is apathetic about his or her academic success. It is the teacher's responsibility to monitor and adjust the students' levels of concern to maintain a moderate level that is ideal for learning.

When a student's level of concern is too high it can be lowered by the teacher explaining that students will be successful if they come to class, pay attention, take notes, do the homework, ask questions, study, and get help when they do not understand something. Students can then mentally check off these behaviors, recognize their effort, and feel more confident that they are doing what it takes to be successful. Simultaneously, students can recognize they have not put forth their best effort and they need to do more in order to accomplish a desirable grade. Consequently, with the same comment, the teacher can raise and lower students' level of concern as needed.

In general there are four categories of ways to raise and lower concern. The first category deals with visibility of the teacher or student work. A teacher's proximity can be used to increase a student's concern during instruction or while doing seatwork or decrease the concern by circulating the room instead of hovering. Another way to increase students' degree of effort put forth is to observe them while they are working. When students are aware that tests or homework papers with excellent grades may be displayed on the class bulletin board, it can encourage students to try harder. However, if a child prefers for his or her quality work not to be made visible, teachers should respect that position.

A second technique to influence level of concern is for the teacher to increase or decrease the consequences of student work. For instance, when an assignment is worth more points, most students will make more of an effort. Oftentimes in college the class final is counted as a large percentage of the final letter grade. Because of this it is common for students to "cram" for the final in order to get a good grade, especially if they need to bring up their overall grade.

The variable of *time* impacts the level of anxiety a student feels about an assignment. When students perceive they have a lot of time to accomplish a task they are not as anxious about it. However, when they believe they do not have much time to complete the work they have increased concern. Amount of *assistance* can also play a role in students' anxiety or concern about a task. Typically when students are allowed to work in cooperative learning groups they have more confidence in their productivity. But when students have to work individually, it may raise their level of concern. It seems many teachers intuitively know this and allow students to work together unless they get off task; then they must work alone. This threat resonates with students' level of concern and is intended to motivate the students to stay engaged with the assignment to its conclusion. However, it is interesting to note, at the collegiate level many students would rather not work in groups but instead do their own work. They have learned through bitter experience that sometimes they do most or all of the work and another student exploits them to get a good grade without putting in time and effort.

Success

Another way students are motivated is by experiencing success. To feel successful there exist two factors that must be present: effort and uncertainty.

Effort + Uncertainty = Success

Effort—The amount of effort necessary for success varies from student to student.

Uncertainty—Students predict future performance based on their past performance. Consequently, levels of uncertainty vary from student to student. Students who have experienced a lot of *success* in the past will predict success in the future. Students who have experienced a lot of *failure* in the past will predict failure in the future.

A teacher needs to maintain just the right level of uncertainty so students will be confident enough to try, but not make it so easy that it does not require much amount of effort on the students' part. To do this the teacher controls the level of difficulty by raising and lowering the academic bar. Adjusting the academic bar creates high, yet reasonable expectations for each individual student.

To help students be successful the teacher controls two factors as it relates to their instruction. First is the *level of difficulty* of the content. Teachers can use certain strategies to make the content easier for students to understand. The absence of these techniques can result in the material being difficult for the students to grasp. One example is the amount of material the teacher covers during an instructional period. Another example is the number of samples or illustrations the teacher provides. A third example is the professionalism, or lack thereof, in which the teacher responds to student questions.

The second factor a teacher controls to increase student success is the teacher's *skill at teaching*. It is crucial for teachers to continue their professional growth during their tenure in the teaching profession.

Feeling Tone

Feeling tone is the climate in the classroom. Feeling tone affects the amount of effort a student will put forth toward learning. It exists on a continuum from pleasant through neutral to unpleasant. Pleasant and unpleasant are both motivating. Neutral is used to transition from unpleasant back to pleasant. A pleasant feeling tone is established through the use of praise, encouragement, a positive attitude, and the like. It is a place where students feel emotionally safe and want to be. An unpleasant feeling occurs when teachers threaten negative consequences or criticizes a student. This can temporarily motivate some students to perform, but can have detrimental effects in the long run. If a teacher uses an unpleasant feeling tone it is important to switch back to a pleasant feeling tone once the student has demonstrated the desired task or behavior.

Five Ways to Promote Student Interest

The ways to peak students' interests involve relevance, novelty, vividness, use of self, and labs. Relevance means to make it meaningful from the students' perspectives. Novelty means to teach differently from time to time. To make one's instruction vivid, use stimulating examples, appropriate personal experiences, colorful stories, and the like. As humans we are interested in ideas that have to do with us personally. For example, when someone buys a new calendar they are likely to turn the month of their birthday to see what picture is attached. There are five methods to interest students through the use of self:

1. Use the student's name in a positive statement or example.
2. Call on the student to provide data for a hypothetical problem.
3. Relate the material to the students' interests and use examples that are familiar.
4. Make the content meaningful to the students' life or future.
5. Use a positive statement about the students or the class regarding the content

Intrinsic and Extrinsic Motivation Revisited

Intrinsic motivation—When someone is intrinsically motivated they complete a task because they enjoy the process.

Extrinsic motivation—When someone is extrinsically motivated they complete a task because they want the end result. Rewarding student behaviors, or positive reinforcement, is an example of extrinsic motivation.

Neither is necessarily good or bad. But in education we want students to become intrinsically motivated so they will take responsibility for their learning, become lifelong learners, and enjoy the pursuit of learning.

CLASSROOM DISCUSSION QUESTIONS

1. Mrs. Jones is developing an intradisciplinary unit on weather for her third graders. Ms. Jones teaches in a school located in south Texas.

   a. Considering the geographical location of the school and the age of her students:
      i. Develop two activities that can be used to activate her students' prior knowledge about the weather.
      ii. Develop an opening activity that will hook students' interest in this unit.

   b. Mrs. Jones discovers that her students only know about rain and sunshine but have never seen fog, sleet, or snow. Discuss the instructional implications that this has on her planning, lesson delivery, activities, and assessment.

2. Design a lesson that uses both the deductive and inductive model of teaching. Identify the following components in your lesson plan:

   a. Grade level
   b. Subject
   c. Topic
   d. Learning objectives/TEKS
   e. Deductive components of the lesson
   f. Inductive components of the lesson
   g. Activities/methods of authentic assessment both within and at the end of the unit

3. What prerequisite knowledge and skills are required for fifth graders to successfully study the election process in the United States? Develop a concept map detailing the needed prerequisite knowledge and skills. Include activities that can be used to teach this topic. (If needed, information about making concept maps can be found at sites such as

http://classes.aces.uiuc.edu/ACES100/Mind/CMap.html and

http://users.edte.utwente.nl/lanzing/cm_home.htm.)

4. Mr. Jimenez has just finished a unit on ocean life with his sixth-grade students. In response to student interest, Mr. Jimenez is now preparing to begin a unit on the migration patterns of whales. Brainstorm a list of activities and strategies that Mr. Jimenez can use to monitor and assess his students' learning. Create a t-chart that identifies activities/strategies that measure ongoing and authentic assessment.

Sample Test Questions

K-GRADE 4

The students in Mrs. Fielding's second-grade class are gathered around Jorge, a student in the class. Jorge is telling his classmates about a kitten he found on the way home from school yesterday. Jorge tells how the kitten can barely walk and how it still has some trouble eating. Mrs. Fielding observes the interest that the class expresses and decides to prepare an interdisciplinary unit dealing with the care of baby animals and the responsibilities of pet ownership. Mrs. Fielding begins to plan her unit by identifying the goals and objectives found in her grade-level TEKS. She will begin the unit by bringing in pictures of her own cat during different stages of its growth. Mrs. Fielding will also bring in age-appropriate books on kittens and other young animals. She will integrate various activities, such as bringing toy baby animals to the class. The class will generate a list of pet-care responsibilities. Mrs. Fielding will also have a person from the local animal shelter bring in a baby kitten and speak to the class about care and responsibility. Students will also create a "Baby Animal" book, which they will develop and illustrate in small groups.

1. When sitting down to plan the unit, Mrs. Fielding first needs to consider:

   a. how many activities should be covered in the unit.

   b. at the end of this unit, what she wants the students to have learned.

   c. what type of test to administer at the end of the unit.

   d. how many groups should be formed and which students should be in each group.

2. Mrs. Fielding brings in several age-appropriate books dealing with baby animals and how to care for them. In small groups, students produce a booklet titled "How to Care for a Baby Animal". Students in the groups work together to write the captions and draw the illustrations. Which of the following best describes the instructional purpose behind Mrs. Fielding's activity?

   a. The activity will enable all students to participate by either writing or illustrating a page in the book.

   b. The activity will activate students' prior knowledge and allow them to build upon what they already know.

   c. The activity will allow for students to practice higher-order thinking skills.

   d. The activity allows young learners an age-appropriate way to show what they have learned.

3. Mrs. Fielding can best ensure maximum student learning by addressing which of the following issues prior to the visit from the animal shelter worker:

   a. The students' prior knowledge about kittens.

   b. Determining what the previous year's teacher taught them about being responsible caregivers.

   c. Meeting with the animal caretaker and discussing the developmental level of typical second graders.

   d. Having students learn how to spell *animal*.

GRADES 4–8

1. Students in Mr. Martinez's fifth-grade class is going to begin a chapter on photosynthesis. Mr. Martinez notices that the students are restless and seem unable to concentrate, even though he has provided them with prereading questions meant to set a purpose for reading this chapter. Based on students' reactions, what can Mr. Martinez conclude about the effectiveness of this activity?

   a. Students are naturally disinterested in the topic and probably do not have a desire to learn about it.

   b. Students have little, if any, background on the topic and Mr. Martinez needs to step back and check for prior knowledge.

   c. Students already know everything about the topic and are ready to move on.

   d. Photosynthesis is a topic that is not developmentally appropriate for fifth graders.

2. Mr. Martinez goes home and restructures his unit. He designs a few questions in order to see what the students know about the topic.

- What is photosynthesis?
- What would happen to the environment without photosynthesis?
- How do seasonal changes relate to photosynthesis?

Mr. Martinez can best use the information acquired from the questions to:

   a. decide which worksheet pages to assign the students.

   b. design the format that best fits the end-of-unit test.

   c. design grade-appropriate activities that will help the students learn about photosynthesis and how it affects our lives.

   d. decide how many days will be necessary to cover the topic.

3. An age-appropriate activity that Mr. Martinez use with his class is:

   a. Have students research the topic of photosynthesis and write a five-page research paper that will be due at the end of the unit.

   b. Show a film on photosynthesis and answer 10 teacher-made questions about what they saw.

   c. Divide the class into groups, assign pages from the book to each group, and have each group report on what they read.

   d. Bring in light-sensitive paper. Take the class outside on a sunny day and again on a cloudy day. The class will report on their observation of the effect of sunlight.

GRADES 8–12

An eighth-grade ESL teacher, Mr. Pulliam, is preparing a unit using a book by Gary Soto as a focus. On the first day, he reads one of his children's books as a focus activity. The class participates in a lively discussion about the story and illustrations. Then the class will read about the author and access a website with information about him and his books. Some of the activities Mr. Pulliam will use as the unit progresses include lecture, a video, a guest speaker, and several group activities.

1. Mr. Pulliam's main reason for presenting these activities with his mostly Hispanic teenagers is to:

   a. increase vocabulary in English.

   b. increase motivation.

   c. familiarize the teenagers with a Hispanic author.

   d. increase reading comprehension.

2. For the group activities, Mr. Pulliam will change the groups for different projects.
   What is the main reason he does?

   a. He is trying to group students with similar abilities together because he feels this is a benefit of small-group activities.

   b. Students will have a chance to make a better grade as they rotate to different groups.

   c. Some students are more outgoing and some students are quieter.

   d. Changing groups is more effective because students have different skills and educational needs, and groups need to be changed as tasks are changed.

3. Mr. Pulliam's main reason for using a wide variety of activities rather than one type of activity (i.e., lecture), is:

    a. Using a variety of activities increases student motivation and participation.

    b. It allows students with different skill sets to have a greater chance of achieving success.

    c. It challenges students to think about the topic in various ways, leading to a deeper understanding of the topic.

    d. All of the above.

Answers

K-GRADE 4

1. A is not correct. The quantity of activities should be driven by the lesson objective. Everything in the lesson plan is centered around the objective.

    B is the correct answer. Effective instruction is designed with the end in mind, the objective. Effective teachers always keep in mind what it is they want students to have learned at the end of a unit. With this in mind, lessons, activities, and assessments can be structured.

    C is not correct. The test or alternative forms of assessment should be a direct outcome of the instructional objective. Consequently, teachers need to start with the lesson objective.

    D is not correct. Again, grouping is a result of the lesson and what the learners are to produce to demonstrate mastery at the conclusion.

2. A is not correct. Although this is a true statement, it is only one aspect of the instructional purpose.

    B is not correct. It is important for students to draw upon their prior skills and knowledge as they assimilate new information. This answer is not the best support for the instructional purpose.

    C is not correct. Again, this may be a true statement, but is not the best answer to the question.

    D is the correct answer. Writing and illustrating a booklet is an age/grade-appropriate activity for this grade level to show mastery of the material. It is also an activity that engages learners at this age.

3. A is not correct. Although Mrs. Fields may want to do this for her own instructional benefit, it is not relevant to the animal caretaker specifically.

    B is not correct. Again, this may be helpful for planning purposes, but it doesn't relate to the guest speaker.

    C is the correct answer. By meeting with the animal caretaker, the teacher can explain the age group of the audience and help the speaker direct his information and answers to students in a way that is appropriate for their age and level of cognitive development.

    D is not correct. It may behoove the students to know how to spell the word animal. However, it does not maximize student learning.

GRADES 4–8

1. A is not correct. When approached correctly by tapping into the students' interests and making it relevant, students can be motivated to learn.

   B is the correct answer. Student boredom and misbehavior is very often the result of students' lack of understanding during a lesson. An effective teacher watches for these cues and responds to them by stepping back and reconsidering the structure and nature of the lessons. Modifications can then occur to make it relevant, interesting, and meaningful.

   C is not correct. There is no evidence to substantiate this answer. It is more likely that students are not motivated to learn by the prereading questions.

   D is not correct. Photosynthesis is grade-level appropriate, especially if it is taught with hands-on experiences.

2. A is not correct. Worksheets are not the best instructional strategy.

   B is not correct. The end-of-unit test should be a result of the instructional methodology.

   C is the correct answer. Once a teacher is aware of the level of prior knowledge a class has about a topic, he is able to effectively modify and adjust his lesson plans, activities, and assessments to maximize learning. The students' prior knowledge influences the teacher's planning for the unit.

   D is not correct because these questions have no bearing on how long the unit will take. Generally, the instruction and learning activities determine how long the unit will take to complete.

3. A is not correct. This is not an age-appropriate activity.

   B is not correct. This probably will not involve higher-order thinking. Also, it is not engaging and motivating to the students.

   C is not correct. Although this strategy may be used in some classrooms, there are more effective teaching techniques.

   D is the correct answer. This is the only activity in this cluster that actively engages students and requires any use of higher-order thinking.

GRADES 8–12

1. A is not correct. These activities may result in an increase is English vocabulary, but an effective teacher has a better reason for activities as engaging as these.

   B is the correct answer. Effective teachers know that students must be engaged with a cognitive "hook" at the beginning of a lesson that will make them eager learners. This type of activity serves to spark interest in students because it is something that they can relate to.

   C is not correct. It is a good idea to familiarize the ESL students with a Hispanic author, but that is not the purpose of the activities.

   D is not correct. Reading comprehension may be increased, but only because the activities are motivating.

2. A is not correct. Teachers should use homogeneous grouping sparingly.

   B is not correct. It is more important that students get good grades as a result of an effective learning experience than grouping practices.

   C is not correct. This is a true statement, but a very limited answer.

   D is the correct answer. Grouping, for the most part, should be flexible and fluid so that students maximize their learning in these situations.

3. A is not correct. It is only a partial answer.

   B is not correct. It is only part of the whole answer.

   C is not correct. Again, it is only part of the reason to use a wide variety of activities.

   D is the correct answer. The activities described in this vignette address student motivation, student success, and instructional challenges that result in enduring learning.

REFERENCES

Bandura, A. (1986). *Social foundations of thought and action: A social cognitive theory.* Englewood Cliffs, NJ: Prentice Hall.

Hunter, M (1989). *Mastery teaching: Increasing instructional effectiveness in elementary, secondary schools, colleges and universities.* El Segundo, CA: TIPS Publications.

Maslow, A. (1968). *Toward a psychology of being* (2nd ed.) Princeton, NJ: Van Nostrand.

Maslow, A. (1987). *Motivation and personality* (3rd ed.). New York: Harper & Row.

Piaget, J. (1952a). *The language and thought of a child.* London: Routledge & Kegan Paul.

Piaget J. (1952b). *The origins of intelligence in children.* New York: International Universities Press.

Piaget, J. & Inhelder, B. (1969). *The psychology of the child.* New York: Basic Books.

Skinner, B.F. (1979). *The shaping of a behaviorist.* New York: Knopf.

Slavin, R.E. (1990). *Cooperative Learning: Theory, research, and practice.* Boston: Allyn & Bacon.

Websites

Cooperative Learning

http://www.cde.ca.gov/iasa/cooplrng2.html

http://www.jigsaw.org/

http://www.coe.missouri.edu/~vlib/Joan%27s.stuff/Joan%27s.Page.html

http://www.ed.gov/pubs/OR/ConsumerGuides/cooplear.html

Role-Playing/Simulation

http://www.blatner.com/adam/pdntbk/rlplayedu.htm

http://www3.roleplaysim.org/papers/cache/tompkins.htm

Authentic Assessment

http://www.eduplace.com/rdg/res/litass/auth.html

http://jonathan.mueller.faculty.noctrl.edu/toolbox/tasks.htm

http://www.bgsu.edu/organizations/ctl/aa.html

Grouping

http://www.kimskorner4teachertalk.com/classmanagement/organizingtips/4grouping.html

http://ruby.fgcu.edu/courses/80337/McAvoy/HETERO~1.html

http://www.education-world.com/a_admin/admin009.shtml

Authentic Assessment/Performance Assessment

http://www.ascd.org/cms/index.cfm?TheViewID=916

http://www.ed.gov/pubs/OR/ConsumerGuides/perfasse.html

http://www.ericfacility.net/ericdigests/ed381985.html

Prior Knowledge

http://www.ncrel.org/sdrs/areas/issues/students/learning/lr100.htm

http://www.ericfacility.net/ericdigests/ed328885.html

Instructional Scaffolding

http://condor.admin.ccny.cuny.edu/~group4/

http://cela.albany.edu/newslet/fall02/scaffolding.htm

http://www.ncrel.org/sdrs/areas/issues/students/learning/lr1scaf.htm

http://userwww.sfsu.edu/~ching/personal/Learning/theorists/vygotsky.html

Metacognition

http://www.gse.buffalo.edu/fas/shuell/cep564/Metacog.htm

http://www.ericfacility.net/ericdigests/ed376427.html

http://www.ncrel.org/sdrs/areas/issues/students/learning/lr1metn.htm

http://www.teachers.net/gazette/JUN03/marshall.html

Graphic Organizers

http://www.ncrel.org/sdrs/areas/issues/students/learning/lr1grorg.htm

http://www.graphic.org/goindex.html

http://www.eduplace.com/graphicorganizer/

http://www.ttac.odu.edu/Articles/Graphic.html

Competency 9 _

Using Technology as an Effective Instructional Tool

Jim Rutledge
West Texas A&M University

> **Competency 9:** The teacher incorporates the effective use of technology to plan, organize, deliver, and evaluate instruction for all students.

The beginning teacher:

A. Demonstrates knowledge of basic terms and concepts of current technology (e.g., hardware, software applications and functions, input/output devices, networks).

B. Understands issues related to the appropriate use of technology in society and follows guidelines for the legal and ethical use of technology and digital information (e.g., privacy guidelines, copyright laws, acceptable use policies).

C. Applies procedures for acquiring, analyzing, and evaluating electronic information (e.g., locating information on networks, accessing and manipulating information from secondary storage and remote devices, using online help and other documentation, evaluating electronic information for accuracy and validity).

D. Knows how to use task-appropriate tools and procedures to synthesize knowledge, create and modify solutions, and evaluate results to support the work of individuals and groups in problem-solving situations and project-based learning activities (e.g., planning, creating, and editing word-processing documents, spreadsheet documents, and databases; using graphic tools; participating in electronic communities as learner, initiator, and contributor; sharing information through online communication).

E. Knows how to use productivity tools to communicate information in various formats (e.g., slide show, multimedia presentation, newsletter) and applies procedures for publishing information in various ways (e.g., printed copy, monitor display, Internet document, video).

F. Knows how to incorporate the effective use of current technology; use technology applications in problem-solving and decision-making situations; implement activities that emphasize collaboration and teamwork; and use developmentally appropriate instructional practices, activities, and materials to integrate the Technology Applications TEKS into the curriculum.

G. Knows how to evaluate students' technologically produced products and projects using established criteria related to design, content delivery, audience, and relevance to assignment.

H. Identifies and addresses equity issues related to the use of technology.

KEY TERMS

application software
AUP
blog
cloud
constructivism
copyright
database software
email
fair use

graphic software
hardware
input/output devices
interdisciplinary lesson
Internet
LAN
presentation software
server
social media

software
spreadsheet
system software
TEKS
WAN
word processor
World Wide Web (WWW)

Before 1990, most of what we consider "technology" did not exist in the education environment. Since that time, the use of technology in the classroom has since expanded exponentially, and seems to change almost daily. Since technology is now an important part of the educational environment, new teachers are expected to demonstrate competence regarding technology in the Texas Examination of Educator Standards: **Pedagogy and Professional Responsibilities (PPR)** for teacher certification.

As a teacher, you are expected to use technology:

- As an administrative tool for such tasks as attendance, grade book, various forms and resources, discipline reports, training, and communication
- As a teaching tool to improve teaching and learning and to supplement other teaching tools

This chapter is designed to assist the new teacher in the successful completion of the Competency 9 Technology questions on the PPR teacher certification exam. Additionally, information in this chapter aids the new teacher in social studies, language arts, and science content-area exams.

Competency 9 states that *The teacher incorporates the effective use of technology to plan, organize, deliver, and evaluate instruction for all students.* Another way of saying this is that a teacher must have the skills to utilize technology as a tool to assist in the learning process.

TERMINOLOGY

The advent of modern computer technology has brought with it a new language of strange words and acronyms. Who among us has not gone to a computer store and listened as the salesperson seemed to be speaking another language! It is important that teachers have a basic understanding of the language of technology; it is also important that they know where to find the meaning of technology terms they may not recognize.

Here are some of the common terms all teachers should know:

- Hardware—physical electronic technology equipment. Examples are your computer (sometimes, but mistakenly, called a CPU); various peripherals such as your printer or scanner; mouse; storage devices; etc.
  - ∗ Peripherals are any type of hardware that is connected, with wire or wirelessly, to your computer
- Software—the set of instructions, or programs, that make your computer (hardware) work. Examples are Windows, Word, Excel, Acrobat, and games. Software may be classified into two types:
  - ∗ System software—runs behind the scenes and makes your computer work correctly. Examples are operating systems such as Windows, Mac OSX, Linux, Unix, etc.
  - ∗ Application software—programs that help you do something on your computer. Examples are Word and Acrobat.

- Input/output devices—another way to classify hardware. Input devices help you put information into the computer; examples are a keyboard, mouse, modem, or router. Output devices are that which comes from a computer; examples are a printer, external storage device, or monitor.

- Network—defined as two or more computers (or other devices such as printers) that are connected to each other with wires or wirelessly. Networks often include the ability to view and share information among locations. Networks may include printers, scanners, and other hardware in addition to computers.

  * LAN—Local area network. Connects computers in a small area. Example is an elementary school network or a college network

  * WAN—Wide area network. Usually connects more than one LAN. Texas A&M System or Canyon ISD networks are examples

- Internet—Also known as the Net, Web, or World Wide Web (WWW), the Internet is a WAN in itself, a system that connects computers and networks, facilitating data transmission and communication worldwide.

  * WWW/the Web—The World Wide Web is a loose network in which servers communicate with each other and allow the exchange of data throughout the entire world. Most "WWW" Web addresses are "public" in that anyone with Internet access can view most of the material on that site. The so-called "public" WWW sites use HTTP—Hyper Text Transfer Protocol—to communicate with each other, and most Web documents are created using Hyper Text Markup Language, or HTML.

  * Secure servers use HTTPS (Hyper Text Transfer Protocol Secure), which protects the information on the server and the exchange of information with sophisticated encryption that has allowed for the secure storage of information and the secure exchange of information. Without HTTPS, we would not be able to do things such as shop on the Web using a credit card as payment. Generally, HTTPS servers require a password to verify the user and, as such, are not "public."

- Server—A server is a computer that has the necessary software that will allow it to talk to other computers over a network.

The terms listed above are only a few of the technology terms commonly used in technology communications in the schools. You will undoubtedly encounter a great many more technology terms, some of which you will know or can figure out from context, and others that will stump you. One great source for technology terminology is the *NetLingo Lingo Internet Dictionary* (http://www.netlingo.com/dictionary/all.php).

APPROPRIATE AND LEGAL USE

The advent and usage of technology by teachers and students has resulted in the need to establish policies and guidelines for issues such as employee and student privacy, copyright, accuracy of information, website appropriateness, citation formats, plagiarism, and a whole host of ancillary issues.

The Internet has indeed brought access to the entire world to the classroom, which while on the surface seems to be highly desirable, it can also create serious issues. For example, the same Internet that allows students to see the paintings of the Louvre also can allow them to see pictures of indescribable violence; the Web provides students with videos of almost any science lab experiment imaginable, but also could provide them access to pornographic videos; and the audio files of FDR's Fireside Chats are invaluable in social studies, but students do not need to hear the voices of hatred and bigotry.

Acceptable Use Policies (AUPs)

All public schools are required by law to have an Acceptable Use Policy for students (more on AUP's for employees later). Generally, students must sign an AUP before they are allowed to use the school's technology. The student agrees in advance to the consequences for violating the AUP, which can range from reprimand, to not being allowed to use the school's technology, to appropriate legal action. An AUP will typically cover areas such as:

- Misuse of equipment—such as breaking or damaging equipment or software; another example would be using a school printer to print personal copies
- Misuse of the network—such as using the network to spread a virus or to forward inappropriate emails; a common misuse is using the network for private, non-school business
- Discourteous behavior—such as using the technology to bully another student
- Illegal activities—such as using the network or computers to sell illegal substances or to make terroristic threats
- Accessing inappropriate information—such as the intentional action of a student to view or download pornographic, violent, or other such material

Use of school computers is a privilege and not a right under the law. Should a student violate the school AUP, the student might be reprimanded, reported to an administrator, banned from using the technology, or reported to legal authorities. Teachers are obligated by law in Texas to report violations of the school AUP to the appropriate school administrator, and teachers will generally also contact parents.

Students are somewhat protected from accessing inappropriate material on the Internet by the use of Internet filtering software, which by law must be operational on all school networks. Filtering software works by rendering websites inaccessible if they contain "key words" and other data that the software recognizes as inappropriate. Teachers should be aware that the software is not infallible and "enterprising" students may find ways to bypass the software; therefore, it is the teacher's responsibility to monitor student behavior while students are using the school computers and network.

Employee AUP—In most cases, all school employees, including teachers, are obligated to accept the terms of the school district AUP. Teachers are generally required to follow the same rules as students (listed above). Additionally, teachers should note that the courts have consistently maintained that there is *no* right to privacy as concerns teacher use of school equipment and networks. In other words, a teacher's school email account and emails may be accessed by school administrators as well as law enforcement. Also, any other personal files a teacher may have on a school computer or the school network are not privacy-protected.

Possibly the most common misuse of a school's network and equipment occurs when a teacher uses them for personal business. Generally, schools permit teachers to access their personal email accounts and use the network to access nonschool websites so long as these activities are purely personal and occur outside of class time, such as before or after school. However, such activities are limited by the content and the purpose of the private usage. Examples of actions that are prohibited under teacher AUPs are:

- Using school items that have a direct cost tied to them such as printer paper. Teachers should never print a personal copy on the school printer.
- Accessing websites that are inappropriate, even if this action occurs during "nonclass" time.
- Using the email or network for nonschool business. When there is money or potential profit involved, you may not use the school network or equipment.

Common sense must rule in the usage of school computers and networks by teachers. Generally, it is fine to reply to an email from your mother, or to remind others of church choir practice; it is *not* fine to print an invitation to your daughter's birthday party or send an email to the teachers about buying Avon products from you!

Copyright

The advent of the Internet has brought about a whole new world of potential issues surrounding copyright law. Now, with the click of a mouse, one can copy a manuscript, "rip" or download music, download a movie, scan sheet music, copy software code, copy a picture, or take any number of other actions, all of which could be violations of copyright law.

In layman's terms, copyright simply means that when a creator/author creates a work product with the mind (known as intellectual property), that person "owns" the work product and has the exclusive right to sell, lease, publish, distribute, copy, license, franchise, etc., that work product. Most work products may be copyrighted, but the most common are books, music, art, movies, video, software, games, periodicals, research, and television programming. Intellectual property is considered to be protected by copyright law even if the author has not completed the copyright process required under Federal law.

To understand copyright law, we need to go back a bit in history. Of course, the "copy machine" as we know it has roots back to the 1700s and there were the "ditto" machines in the early 20th century. However, it was not until the invention of the copy machine that it became "easy" to copy the work of others. Frankly, it used to be hard to violate copyright laws before the advent of the copy machine. To violate copyright laws one had to sit down with pen and paper and actually *copy* something!

The invention of the modern, electronic photo copier (Xerox) changed all that when it began to appear in offices in the early 1960s. The newfound ease of copying anything on paper, and other issues, led to the passage of the Copyright Act of 1976. This law has remained the law of the land since 1976 despite the fact that the Internet has completely changed the access to and copying of protected intellectual property. Even though the advent of Internet use by the public in the early 1990s has made it incredibly easy for anyone to copy almost any copyrighted work product, this 1976 law is still the applicable law for copyright protection. Let's examine this law.

The Fair Use Statute, Section 107 of the Copyright Act of 1976 says:

> *the fair use of a copyrighted work, including such use by reproduction in copies or phonorecords or by any other means specified in that section, for purposes such as criticism, comment, news reporting, teaching (including multiple copies for classroom use), scholarship, or research, is not an infringement of copyright.*

Again, in plain English, the law says that a copyright owner has exclusive rights to copyrighted works *except* for certain uses, which are loosely defined in the law. The exceptions to copyright exclusivity are "for purposes such as":

- Criticism
- Comment
- News reporting
- Teaching (including multiple copies for classroom use)
- Scholarship
- Research

The law seems to say that a teacher might use copyrighted material for such educational uses as teaching, scholarship, and research. Such uses are indeed allowed, but many questions remain about using copyrighted works in education, such as:

- Exactly *how* can they be used?
- *How much* can be used?
- *How often* can one use these works?
- *For what purposes* can the works be used?

The courts have developed a body of law since 1976 that spells out how copyrighted works can be used in education without violating the Fair Use statute. In other words, the courts have spelled out in great detail the meaning of fair use. Below are the four factors the courts have used to determine if copyright law (fair use) has been violated:

- **Purpose**—Courts ask the question, "What is the purpose for using the copyrighted material?" If the purpose is *purely* educational, such usage may not violate fair use; any other use than "purely educational' is probably a violation

- **Nature**—Courts ask the question, "What is the nature of the use of copyrighted material?" Nature usually refers to the type of media in question. Copyrighted material that is, *by its nature*, educationally oriented, such as research or papers, get more latitude than, for example, fiction. Public domain works—items whose copyright has expired—are, by nature, useable by anyone. Items that are not educational by nature such as movies get much less latitude from the courts.

- **Amount**—Courts ask the question, "How much of the copyrighted material is used?" Courts have consistently said that the *use of samples* of copyrighted materials in education is fine, but the use of entire works without permission violates fair use. Therefore, copying a few paragraphs of fiction from Faulkner and Hemingway to compare and contrast the two writing styles is fine; copying most or all of a work by either is not.

- **Effect**—Courts ask the question, "What is the Effect of the use of the copyrighted material on the copyright owner?" If it is determined the use of a copyrighted work has a *negative monetary effect*—costs the author money—such usage violates fair use. In other words, if a teacher copies something to keep from having to buy that work, that's probably a violation of fair use. A common effect violation is using pages from an old workbook to keep from having to buy new workbooks.

Teachers should understand that if they copy or download copyrighted materials, and *any* of the four factors above are violated, they will have committed a violation of the Fair Use statute. Violations of fair use can cost the teacher and the school district hundreds of thousands of dollars and considerable embarrassment. Some well-known instances are:

- Many individuals were sued and fined for downloading music from music "sharing" sites like Napster.

- A West Coast school district had software licenses for common productivity software, but copied the software to many more computers than for which were licensed and was fined hundreds of thousands of dollars

- A 20th-century literature teacher had the students buy several books for the class, but partway through the class, they decided to add Hemingway's *Old Man and the Sea* to the class. After having the book copied in a local copy shop, the teacher and the copy business were both successfully sued.

So, what is a teacher to do to avoid violating the Fair Use act? First, stop and think before you copy or download. Some materials are posted on the Internet by teachers and others and it is pretty clear they put the material on the Web for teachers to use. Use it! For example, there are thousands of websites for such things as lesson plans, WebQuests, graphic organizers, science experiments, etc. Use these sites for your classes. If you have any doubts, you can even email the author in many cases, but generally, you are good to go!

If you are not sure about using the material on a website, compare your intended usage against the four factors: purpose, nature, amount, and effect. if your intended usage clearly violates any of the four factors, don't do it. You want your name to be in the local newspaper for Teacher of the Year, not for being sued!

USING TECHNOLOGY TO ACCESS INFORMATION/DATA

The Internet has brought the world into the classroom! This almost instant access to information has changed schools forever. For example, libraries no longer order encyclopedias, which are out-of-date the second they are printed, but instead subscribe to online encyclopedias and dictionaries. The same thing is happening with other resource books. Additionally, there is a world of material available on the Internet that simply was not available before in print. For example, one can find the video for almost any science lab on the Web; students can see the paintings in the Louvre or the British Museum online; videos of wildlife and natural phenomena are readily viewable; audio of FDR's Fireside Chats are available with one click; and one can scan the U.S. Census databases for any number of social studies projects. The list of digital information available to schools on the Internet is inexhaustible! It is fair to say that students not only *should* use the Internet in school, but I admit students *must* use the Internet in school. In education, we stress the utilization of different strategies to help our students learn, including constructivism. You will remember that constructivist theory as expounded by Dr. Jean Piaget stresses that learning occurs best when the learners "construct" their own knowledge and when they build their knowledge through experience. We also stress learner-centered instruction.

An important element of both constructivist theory and learner-centered instruction is student research in which students delve into a subject on their own. Individual and group research and learning activities can also play an important part in differentiated instruction. Therefore, the Internet can and should play an important role in student learning.

Unfortunately, the Internet differs from school libraries in one very important way: librarians, and others, have traditionally screened printed, audio, and video material to ensure that the material was accurate and appropriate for students. Additionally, librarians and media specialists have been available to assist teachers and students in finding appropriate materials, thus saving time and energy. There is no "Internet Librarian" or Internet Dewey Decimal System" to guarantee that material is appropriate and accurate, or that it can be accessed efficiently and effectively.

© racorn, 2014, used under license of Shutterstock, Inc.

Therefore, it is the teacher's job and responsibility to ensure that this world of digital information is used by students in the proper way. Teachers must make sure that Web material is accurate and safe; and teachers must make Internet use effective and efficient. Said another way, the teacher in the digital classroom has these responsibilities:

1. Make sure students are safe when using the Internet (discussed above).
2. Make sure information accessed by students on the Internet is accurate.
3. Make sure Internet use is effective and efficient.

As noted earlier, safe Internet usage is usually accomplished by a school's AUP, Internet filter, and teacher monitoring. However, making sure students only go to websites that contain accurate, appropriate information and that Web use is efficient timewise requires specific teacher intervention. Below, we discuss the process teachers should use with their students when the Internet is used in the classroom.

The most important teacher action to ensure that student use of the Internet is safe, effective, and efficient is stated below, and should be memorized by new teachers.

Teachers should always preselect the websites their students will use.

This means that students should *not* be allowed to use "open-ended" searches for websites. Teachers must choose the websites students will use, and restrict their access to any other websites. This means the teacher is, in effect, the "Internet policeman" and the teacher directs the Internet traffic.

Most technology teachers agree that the preselection of websites by teachers is an absolute. I would agree and emphasize to new teachers that the *only* way to guarantee your students see accurate information on the Web and that the information is accessed in a timely manner is for you to preselect the websites for student use.

Some will argue that students need to learn to safely search the Web for information and for the teacher to choose their websites for them, especially in upper grades, is not the best procedure. I respectfully disagree. We *can* all agree that students need to learn to use the Web safely and effectively, but this learning can be accomplished with specific curriculum in a variety of ways. However, if the teacher plans to have the students use the Web for math, language arts, social studies, science, art, health, or any other subject, the teacher should select the websites those students will use. Period.

It is fair to ask the question, "Why should the teacher preselect websites for students instead of allowing students to do their own Internet searches?" The answer is simple: A teacher is much more mature and more able to evaluate the quality of a website than a student. Additionally, the teacher is responsible for the information students see in the classroom, and that responsibility requires a modicum of control.

Any experienced teacher who is a regular Internet user knows that some websites are not what they seem to be at first glance. As educated adults, most of us can make a discerning judgment when we see a site that is obviously extremely biased, filled with hate, or obviously a hoax. However, most students have neither the experience nor the ability to make informed decisions about biased, inaccurate websites.

If a school or a teacher allows students to do open-ended Internet research, that school and teacher runs the risk of having students find sites that are, at best, completely inaccurate or, at worst, dangerous. We all hear of the hoaxes that are on the Web; we all know that everyone who has any belief system, crazy or not, can set up a website espousing that system; and for far too many students, the statement, "It was on the Internet, so it is true" rings correct.

For example, let's assume students are asked to do a research project on the Holocaust and are sent to the computer lab without being guided to preselected websites. What are you going to say when that student reports on material found on many white-supremacy websites? These sites say things like the Holocaust never happened; the Jews died from cholera and other diseases; the crematories were used to burn bodies to prevent the spread of typhus.

Can your 14-year-old students tell one of the above-mentioned websites from an authoritative historical site? I doubt it. As an example, a now defunct website, http://pubweb.acns.nwu.edu/~abutz/index.html, used to come up when one searched the Web for information on the Holocaust. On the surface, this website appears to be owned by a prestigious institution, Northwestern University, so it would be incredibly easy for a young student to believe the information on this site. However, as a teacher, you should know that when there is a tilde and name at the end of a URL, this indicates that there is a personal website attached to a public site. In this case, a Dr. Butz, who is a Holocaust denier, attached his Nazi lies and filth to the Northwestern University site!

In summary, when you have your students do Internet research, *you* need to select the websites they can use. This will protect you, the school, and most importantly, the students.

To clarify the importance of preselecting websites for student research, go to this active site, http://www.natvan.com, and look at it closely. You will see it is a very racist white-supremacy site that is actually pretty well disguised, and would be believed by many young students.

It is also fair to ask, how can teachers select accurate and safe websites when teachers are already overwhelmed with lesson preparation, meetings, testing, and a general lack of hours in the day?"

There is no guaranteed, quick, and easy way to choose great websites for your students. There are many articles and websites out there that purport to tell you how to find great websites, but frankly, many of these involve the teacher using processes that are too detailed and time-consuming to be practical—they are neither quick nor easy. However, there are shortcuts to expedite the process. Just remember that there is no substitute for taking some time to read and study each website.

Here are some tips and guidelines teachers can use to make the process of website evaluation a bit quicker:

- Choose websites that are owned by a known person or organization. In every field there are well-known experts and organizations. Start with the ones you know!
- Use the top-level domain name to help you (you still have to look at them!). Top-level domain name is that which comes right after the "dot" in a Web address, like .com or .net.
  * As a general rule, .gov and .edu sites are reserved for government and education use, and can be trusted. A quick look at these is usually enough to ensure accuracy and appropriateness.
  * Other domains such as .org often are used by nonprofits and public interest groups. Look at these for bias, as they may be focused on single issues or are trying to raise money, but they often have great information.
  * Domains such as .com or .net don't really tell you anything so you have to look at them carefully to determine their accuracy and appropriateness.
  * Some .com sites such as those of large, publicly traded companies are usually fine because they are regulated by the SEC and FTC, but do be careful.
  * If you see a /~ after the domain name, this means a personal website attached to another site. Be careful of these.

In summary, there is no foolproof way to qualify a website, but you can use the shortcuts listed above. Don't take any chances—take charge of your classroom and preselect all websites that your students will use.

TECHNOLOGY AS A LEARNING TOOL

Here we look at two parts of Competency 9 together: using the appropriate technology tool for the task and using these same tools to communicate information. We study these together to avoid repetition.

New teachers must know how to effectively use technology in the classroom with their students. They must have a basic knowledge of both software and Web applications. The information below describes some of the software and Web applications used by teachers and students, and the various tasks for which each is utilized.

Software

As noted earlier in this chapter, software is the set of instructions, or programs, that make your computer (hardware) work. Software may be classified into two types:

- System software—runs behind the scenes and makes your computer work correctly. Examples are operating systems such as Windows, Mac OSX, Linux, Unix, etc. In the near future, teachers will be using Android OS and various cell phone OSs, but we will save that for another time!

- Application software—programs that help you do something on your computer. Examples are Word, Acrobat, and games. New teachers must be proficient with several types of application software, which are discussed below.

It is important to understand the different types or classes of application software, and to understand how each of these is most effectively used in the classroom with students. For the PPR test, students should know the function of each software type or class. Below is a list of different classes or types of application software with accompanying discussion of how each is often utilized in the school environment:

- **Word processing**—Word processors such as Word, WordPerfect, and others are normally used for writing tasks at all grade levels. Students as young as Pre-K can use a word processor and secondary students use the software for everything in which writing is required such as research papers.

- **Spreadsheet**—Spreadsheet software is most commonly used for tasks involving rows and columns of numbers where data calculations will be done. Common functions for spreadsheets are numerical formulas, small databases, graphs, and charts. Math and science students must use spreadsheets beginning at the lower levels. Common spreadsheet programs are Excel and Lotus. Many lower elementary schools have specialized spreadsheet software whose primary function is to help students make graphs and charts.

- **Presentation software**—Presentation software such as PowerPoint is used for making group presentations by both students and teachers. Presentation programs are utilized to present text, audio, and video as well as a means to access websites for group viewing through hyperlinks. A general rule for presentation software is not to use too much text. This class of software is best used for small amounts of text, and lots of graphics. If one needs to present large amounts of text use word-processed handouts.

- **Database**—Database software such as Access is designed to hold large amounts of information (data) in a format that will allow the data to be sorted and classified by the user. They are best understood by understanding the word *query*. In a database, one can "query" the database, almost like asking a question such as, "Show me number of people in Texas who had college degrees according to the 1980 census versus those with similar degrees in the 2010 census." Students will need to access database information for various research projects.

- **Graphics**—Graphics software ranges from a simple Paint program in Windows to Photoshop to edit pictures to Illustrator and other sophisticated applications that create and modify graphics. Generally, one uses graphics software to paint, draw, and edit graphic objects. Simple graphic creation and editing can be done on word processors and presentation software.

- **Desktop publishing**—Several publishing programs such as Microsoft Publisher helps students with communication devices such as newsletters, flyers, banners, posters, and other graphic publications. These work products are often saved in a format that can be published on a class or school Web page.

- **Learning games and education software**—Most schools have a variety of learning game and content area–specific software to help students learn and master certain subject matter. Most common ones are math and reading software. Some of the programs are remedial in nature to help the student who is behind to catch up while other programs are used in learning stations to reinforce whole-class instruction. Some schools use software to help students prepare for state tests—this software is commonly known as "drill-and-kill" software.

The Internet

In addition to the traditional software applications, students must also be proficient with various Web applications and resources. For the PPR test, students should know the function of several Web applications and resources. Below is a list of Web applications and resources with accompanying discussion of how each is often utilized in the school environment:

- **Resource applications**—Teachers must be familiar with various resource applications available to the students such as subscriptions to online encyclopedias and dictionaries and other resource materials. When there are questions in class, students should be encouraged to "look it up" using these digital resources.

- **Email**—Students use email to communicate internally and with the outside world. Many schools have student email systems that are much more controlled than regular email clients for student use in the classroom.

- **Blogs**—School and class blogs are becoming more and more a part of many curricula. These blogs are tightly controlled with student safety in mind, but are great tools to allow students to write about what they are doing and to allow parents to interact digitally with their child's class.

- **Social media**—Many schools and classes are now using vehicles such as Facebook and Twitter to communicate both internally and externally. Again, these are tightly controlled for student safety, but they allow students to interact with student groups around the world.

- **Web authoring software/Web pages**—Many classes have students using Web authoring software to make their own student and class Web pages. Sophisticated Web pages require the use of specific Web authoring software, but most word-processing, publishing, spreadsheet, and presentation software can be saved in a manner that can be published on the Web. This allows students to interact with other classes worldwide through such activities as publishing school newsletters.

- **Cloud applications**—In technology, the word *cloud* means, more or less, "available on the Internet." Many software applications including word processing, spread sheets, presentation programs, desktop publishing programs, and much more, are available on the Cloud. Such well-known sites as Google, Yahoo, and Microsoft Live provide a full range of free software applications on their Cloud sites, along with large amounts of storage on which to store your Cloud application files. The Cloud is also an excellent place to store important files for backup should your computer hard drive fail. Cloud computing also is important in schools because it is an easy way for students to collaborate by being able to access each other's files over the Internet.

INTEGRATING TECHNOLOGY INTO THE TEKS CURRICULUM

In many ways, an understanding of how to integrate technology into the TEKS curriculum is the most important part of Competency 9. To fully grasp the skills that a new teacher must have in terms of technology integrations, it may be helpful to study the concept under these headings:

- Technology as a tool (not a subject area)—For our purposes on the PPR, we must think of technology as a tool we can use to improve instruction and learning. Of course, we all know that there are specific technology courses such as Business Computer Information Systems, keyboarding, and other secondary courses designed to actually teach technology skills, which fall mostly under the vocational umbrella. For the rest of us, we utilize technology to help our students learn.

  Common examples of how we use technology in schools as a tool to improve student performance are using a word processor for student writing; a publishing program for student posters, newsletters, etc.; presentation software for students to make oral, video, and audio presentations; spreadsheets to make student tables, graphs, and charts; email, blogs, and Web pages for student communication within the school and with the outside world; the Internet for constructivist and learner-centered activities; and Cloud applications to support student collaborative efforts.

- The Technology TEKS—The Texas Essential Knowledge and Skills, which are the curriculum for schools in Texas, requires that teachers ensure students learn the basic technology competencies. Remember that we teach technology competencies to improve student performance in all subject areas, not simply to learn technology. For example, a new teacher helps students learn word processing not for its own sake, but so the student can use word processing for writing.

  There are TEKS about technology in all subject areas—either specifically stated or implied. We refer to the technology TEKS we find in subject-area TEKS as "embedded TEKS." Examples of embedded TEKS are as follows:

  * "Sixth-Grade Science—Scientific Processes—"construct graphs, tables, maps, and charts using tools including computers to organize, examine, and evaluate data . . . "; or

  * "Seventh-Grade Social Studies—Social Studies Skills—"organize and interpret information from . . . databases and visuals including graphs, charts, . . .

  The Technology Applications TEKS are in groups: K–grade 2, grades 3–5, and grades 6–8. Teachers do *not* teach these TEKS in specific technology lessons; rather, teachers teach the Technology Application TEKS when they teach the subject material in their subject area or grade level. For example, referring to the Sixth-Grade Science TEKS in the paragraph above, a teacher would teach sixth-grade students how to make a spreadsheet and graph when teaching a lab lesson in which the student is to evaluate his/her lab data. A careful understanding of how technology is embedded into subject-area TEKS will also ensure that the technology taught is age-appropriate.

- Interdisciplinary lessons—Interdisciplinary lessons are a great vehicle to utilize technology and thereby cover Technology Application TEKS. An interdisciplinary lesson is defined as a lesson in which students learn TEKS from more than one subject area in one lesson. An example would be a student project in social studies about population changes between the pre-Civil War era and the 20th century in which students would study population data from both eras, use a spreadsheet to make graphs showing the change from an agrarian to an industrial economy, then use word processing to write about the effects of the economic and cultural shift. You can see that this interdisciplinary lesson covers TEKS in social studies, math, language arts, and technology.

EVALUATING STUDENT TECHNOLOGY PRODUCTS

The utilization of technology in the classroom brings with it the necessity of understanding how to evaluate student usage of technology. Keep in mind that we use technology as a learning tool, so the evaluation process should focus mainly on the subject area but also would include some evaluation of the technology. In other words, include technology in the evaluation of the subject-area material, not as a separate evaluation.

A common way to effectively include the evaluation of technology within the evaluation of the learning that has occurred in the subject area is to include technology as part of a lesson rubric. For example, in language arts, a common lesson to fulfill a Speaking/Listening Strand TEKS is to have students make an electronic presentation about some language arts subject. As part of the rubric for such a presentation, students might be graded on the "readability" of their slides, slide design, etc. Of course, as part of the lesson, students would have to learn about the presentation software, about how to make a readable slide, about slide design, etc.

An important part of using technology in the classroom is making sure the students use the appropriate technology for the intended outcome. Below are some examples of what software applications are most appropriate for the delivery of particular content and audiences:

- Word processing is the most appropriate tool for text-heavy documents when the audience will read hard copy.
- Spreadsheets are the most appropriate tool to record data, especially numerical data, and are often used when the data will be presented visually, as in graphs and charts.
- Desktop publishing tools are most appropriate for designing flyers, posters, banners, and newsletters. (Word processors may be used for simple flyers and newsletters, especially in lower grades.)
- Presentation software is most appropriate for electronic presentations to whole class and larger audiences and also for presentations that include video, audio, animation, or links to Web material. A good rule is that if one has a lot of text that is germane to the presentation, use presentation software to show an outline and put the text on a word-processed handout. Never put a lot of text on presentation slides as the audience cannot read it anyway.
- Cloud applications are the most appropriate tool for students to collaborate on documents. Using a Cloud application allows students to see and modify documents over the Web, which not only allows collaboration inside the classroom, but even with students elsewhere in the world.
- Web pages, blogs, and other social media are the appropriate tools for students to utilize to present information to the outside world; email is the most effective way for students to communicate between themselves and the outside world.

EQUITY ISSUES

The beginning teacher needs to be aware of the various equity issues that are brought about when utilizing technology in the classroom, which are gender issues, socioeconomic issues, and disability issues.

These issues are addressed below along with suggestions on how to avoid any inequities.

Gender—Studies show that female students statistically tend to utilize computers less than male students because, in part, of the attitudes of parents, teachers, and gender stereotypes. As a teacher, you can easily prevent any potential gender inequity. The use of technology in your classroom should and must be the same for all students. Gender equity is easily reached by requiring the use of technology by all students, male and female. In other words, we are either all going to make an electronic presentation to the class or none of us are. Additionally, do not allow technology as an "option": either require the use of technology for everyone or don't allow it for anyone on a particular assignment.

Socioeconomic issues—One of the most commonly discussed issues concerning technology usage in public schools surrounds what is commonly known as the "Digital Divide." The Digital Divide refers to the perception that those families with greater economic means are likely able to provide a much higher level of access to quality technology than families with lesser economic means. For educators, the Digital Divide means we must be cognizant of these issues when we have students from low-income families:

- The likelihood of an Internet connection in the home decreases.
- Computer equipment in the home, if available at all, is likely to be older and less functional.

- There is less chance students have started using technology at a young age.
- Parents/guardians are less likely to use email or have email access.
- The likely inequity precludes teachers from assigning technology-related homework.
- More training and practice in the classroom may be necessary before using technology.

The Digital Divide is real and must be dealt with by teachers. Of course, this issue is just one of the many issues that arise from teaching low-income students, so it is incumbent on teachers to always take the socio-economic status of their students into account when making any instructional decision.

The Digital Divide is somewhat mitigated by the fact that many schools with mostly low-income student populations actually have better/newer technology in their schools than some other schools! Federal Title I funds that are available to low-income schools have leveled the playing field in many instances. In fact, it is anecdotally reported that both low-income schools (with Title I funds) *and* upper-income schools—who often get technology funding from parent groups and fundraising—have a decided advantage over middle-income schools, which have neither Title I funding nor parent financial support.

Students with disabilities—The use of technology by students with disabilities has two important facets: (1) ensuring that students with disabilities have access to the same technology as all students; and (2) providing technology solutions to help a disabled student learn, which a nondisabled student would not require.

It is a requirement of the Individuals with Disabilities Education Act (IDEA) that schools provide disabled students with the same learning opportunities provided to all students. This means that schools must make appropriate modifications in order for a disabled child to be able to use the same technologies as all students. Here are some examples of modifications often made for students with disabilities:

- Adaptive furniture—Schools have adjustable desks that raise and lower to accommodate wheelchairs. Similarly, a clear path to the computers must be available.
- Adaptive input devices—Students with hand or sight impairments should be provided with such adaptive assistance as a touch-pad mouse to replace a button mouse, a keyboard for the visually impaired, etc. For more severe physical disabilities, input devices range from the common speech-to-text (Dragon, ViaVoice, etc.) to highly specialized breath or head movement keyboard-control devices
- Adaptive output devices—Students with vision or hearing impairments need adaptive devices such as text-to-voice software, and operating systems can adjust monitors to make large text, high contrast, or other adaptations. Similar text-to-voice is often helpful for dyslexic students

In addition to providing adaptive technology to make sure disabled students have equal access to technology, many of these same technologies actually can be used to replace nontechnology activities. For example, speech-to-text software such as DragonDictate can be used by students who cannot write with a pen or pencil (kids with cerebral palsy often utilize this software). Student who cannot speak can utilize voice synthesis software to communicate in the classroom.

The list goes on and on, but the point is this: Schools are obligated to provide adaptive technology for disabled students to be successful in school Sometimes such technology allows the disabled student equal access to technology and at other times, technology can help a disabled student do things other students can do such as write, speak, or see.

If you have a student who needs adaptive technology, talk to a school administrator or your campus technology coordinator. Larger school districts have personnel in the special education department who work with adaptive technology and smaller districts use outside resources, often from regional education centers. Either way, your responsibility is to make sure your students have equal access to technology and have the technology they need to succeed in the classroom.

Sample Test Questions

1. Eighth-grade students in U.S. History to 1877 are assigned to do an Internet research project on Sectionalism as a cause of the Civil War. Which of the instructions below is the correct set of instructions for this project?

    a. Use an approved search engine, Google or Yahoo, to find three websites to use as references for your research project. All three sites must be quality websites based on what you learned in our lesson on Internet searches.

    b. Use an approved search engine, Google or Yahoo, to find three websites for your research paper. All three sites must be .edu sites or sites that are written or owned by a well-known author.

    c. Find three websites to use for your research project that are listed in the handout from the teacher. Do not use any other sites or go to any links from the websites.

    d. All of the above.

2. Sixth-grade students are assigned to do a science lab experiment, graph the data for the experiment, make a presentation to the class that includes the highlights of the experiment (including the graph) and write a four-page paper that describes the entire process of the experiment, including all the steps and results. What software should the teacher instruct the students to use for this project?

    a. Since it is a presentation, students should use a presentation software such as PowerPoint.

    b. Four pages is too much text to put on presentation software so students should use a word processor such as Word.

    c. Students should use spreadsheet software such as Excel to make the graph; presentation software such as PowerPoint for the presentation; and a word processor such as Word for the four-page paper.

    d. None of the above.

Answers

1. **C is the correct answer.** For Web research projects, the teacher should always choose the websites for students and restrict them to *only* those sites

2. **C is the correct answer.** Excel would be best for the graphing task and the graph can be pasted into PowerPoint and Word; a four-page paper is too much text for a presentation tool, so A is not correct; Word would not be appropriate for the graphing or presentation part of the assignment, so B is not correct.

Competency 10 _

Assessment

George Mann, EdD
West Texas A&M University

Teri Bingham, EdD
West Texas A&M University

E. W. Henderson, EdD, JD
West Texas A&M University

> **Competency 10:** The teacher monitors student performance and achievement; provides students with timely, high-quality feedback; and responds flexibly to promote learning for all students.

The beginning teacher:

A. Demonstrates knowledge of the characteristics, uses, advantages, and limitations of various assessment methods and strategies, including technological methods and methods that reflect real-world applications.

B. Creates assessments that are congruent with instructional goals and objectives and communicates assessment criteria and standards to students based on high expectations for learning.

C. Uses appropriate language and formats to provide students with timely, effective feedback that is accurate, constructive, substantive, and specific.

D. Knows how to promote students' ability to use feedback and self-assessment to guide and enhance their own learning.

E. Responds flexibly to various situations (e.g., lack of student engagement in an activity, the occurrence of an unanticipated learning opportunity) and adjusts instructional approaches based on ongoing assessment of student performance.

KEY TERMS

alternative assessment	*content validity*	*evaluation*
authentic assessment	*criterion referenced*	*formal assessment*
bell curve	*curriculum-based assessment*	*formative assessment*
bias	*error*	*generalizability*

informal assessment	*percentile*	*subjective test*
measurement	*reliability*	*summative assessment*
norm referenced	*standardized scores*	*teacher-made test*
normal distribution curve	*standardized test*	*true measure*
objective test	*stem-and-leaf plot*	*validity*

Effective teachers know that the decisions they make can impact their students' lives significantly and that good decisions require accurate information. According to Anderson and Krathwohl (2001), teachers struggle daily with four critical questions in making sound decisions about the processes of teaching and learning. These questions are as follows:

1. An example of a learning question would be "What is important for students to learn in the limited school and classroom time available?"

2. An example of an instruction question would be "How does one plan and deliver instruction that will result in high levels of learning for large numbers of students?"

3. An example of an assessment question would be "How does one select or design assessment instruments and procedures that provide accurate information about how well students are learning?"

4. An example of an alignment question would be "How does one ensure that objectives, instruction, and assessment are consistent with one another?"

While all of the aforementioned questions are critically important, this chapter focuses on question 3, about assessment. Teachers must not only learn to assess their students' academic progress accurately, but must also learn to analyze the assessment data so that their students will receive maximum benefit from assessment activities.

OVERVIEW OF ASSESSMENT

Effective educators know that the assessment techniques they employ must be congruent with the goals and objectives of their instruction. For example, if an educator is teaching students to memorize multiplication facts, certain instructional strategies will be utilized, which require students to encounter each fact repeatedly, followed by a speed test to determine if students have memorized the facts. Generally, when constructing a speed test, a teacher gives students many multiplication problems and provides limited time for them to answer. In this way, the teacher determines which students have learned their multiplication facts and which students are counting out the answers.

While the speed test is effective in some situations, as the goals, objectives, and instructional strategies change, the assessment techniques must also change. For instance, a teacher who has taught students to analyze a short story might construct a power test and provide ample testing time for students to demonstrate their knowledge, understandings and skills, or the teacher might lead a classroom discussion to informally assess students' learning.

As teachers develop formal and informal assessment techniques, they must learn how to assess frequently without overusing their limited instructional time. Ongoing assessments, which are a natural component of the instructional process, allow teachers to monitor their students' performance and to adjust their classroom activities based on the needs of their students as they progress through the state-mandated curricula. Assessments designed to measure how well students have mastered state-mandated or district-mandated content are said to be **curriculum-based assessments** (CBA). Teachers align the curriculum when they teach the state-mandated or district-mandated objectives and then assess students' mastery of that content.

Teachers must be able to utilize effective assessments to provide clear and accurate feedback to their students, both individually and collectively, enabling their students to use the feedback to improve their learning. The teachers, in turn, can use the same information to improve their knowledge base and instructional practices.

By assessing students and considering the state-mandated curricula, teachers can identify and sequence the knowledge and skills that should be taught. To make effective curricular decisions based on continuous assessments, teachers must understand the theory and vocabulary of assessment and know how to apply them in their daily instruction.

Formal and Informal Assessment

What is assessment? According to Hoy and Gregg (1994), assessment is an ongoing process in which teachers systematically collect data, analyze the data, and use that analysis to help students learn. Assessment includes everything that a teacher does to collect and analyze information about students' learning, and can be gained by formal or informal assessment procedures. When teachers are skilled assessors, they improve the learning opportunities for their students and obtain the information needed to improve instruction and student achievement.

FORMS OF FORMAL ASSESSMENT

Skilled teachers will use **formal assessments** that employ systematic methods to determine how well students are progressing academically and assign grades. Formal assessments can include standardized achievement tests and teacher-made tests. For example, a teacher may need to determine how well students have learned science-related concepts and skills. In this situation, the teacher could construct a test that requires students to demonstrate mastery of requisite concepts and skills. The test results then can provide the teacher with information needed to plan future instruction, assign grades fairly, and to identify the concepts and skills that need to be taught again.

While testing provides information needed for teachers to make sound instructional decisions, informal assessments are also effective ways of determining students' instructional needs. Teachers frequently rely on less formal procedures to assess their students' learning. **Informal assessments** can be as simple as observing students as they work, asking pertinent questions, listening to students' dialogue about the subject material, or scrutinizing a homework assignment. As teachers circulate the classroom and spot-check students' work, the teacher is receiving feedback; this is a form of informal assessment. By using both formal and informal assessment techniques, teachers gain the information needed to help students learn more effectively.

Informal assessments are those assessment activities that can be used to determine students' instructional needs without relying on formal testing procedures and are generally not graded. Informal assessments can be implemented as a teacher is providing instruction to identify the needs of individual students or groups of students. Additionally, when informal assessments are employed, students become actively involved in the assessment process.

FORMS OF INFORMAL ASSESSMENT

Checking Homework There are many ways to informally assess students to gain the information needed to alter instructional plans. One of the most obvious informal assessment techniques is the grading of homework or seatwork assignments. If teachers look only at the answers, little information can be gathered and analyzed; however, by examining missed items carefully, teachers can identify what content has been learned and what content needs to be stressed during subsequent instructional periods. For example, error patterns can be identified when checking long division problems, so that an elementary teacher might see that students are making errors in the estimation of partial quotients. When this information is known, the teacher can plan for instructional activities designed to remediate student errors.

Summary Writing Many teachers routinely post the learning objectives for each lesson that they teach on the chalkboard. When the objectives are posted, teachers can require that students write a summary of what they have learned at the conclusion of each class, and they can compare student learning to the objectives that were posted. By scrutinizing these summaries, the teacher or the students can identify what students have learned and what they have failed to learn. As this occurs, the teacher, with the help of the students, can plan activities that will help students master the content that has not been learned.

Learning Logs A way for teachers to ascertain information about students' study habits and learning processes is learning logs. This involves students keeping a log of their learning experiences and reactions to the curriculum. Timely questions from the teacher, followed by a classroom discussion, help students to improve study habits.

Brainstorming When teachers ask students to brainstorm, they must allow all ideas to be presented without criticism. As this occurs, students identify what they know about a content area and in what part of the content area they have an interest. Some teachers report success when they pair brainstorming activities with a teacher-prepared graphic organizer.

Teacher Observation As teachers observe students in the process of learning, carefully worded notes can provide a wealth of information about the students. In all cases, observations should be recorded without judgmental language. For example, "John participates freely in discussion of the story" or "John did not appear to be interested in this topic." With time, patterns will emerge that will provide direct information for the teacher and indirect information to the student.

Checklists School districts are increasingly identifying benchmarks for students at differing grade levels that detail the content to be taught at differing times throughout the academic year. These checklists identify what a student should know, feel, or do in every subject during their progression through the curriculum. The teacher observes students as they progress through the checklist and mark off those objectives as they are mastered. The checklists are generally reliable and easy for teachers to use.

Likert Rating Scales The Likert rating scale is similar to the checklist, but indicates the relative degree that an objective has been mastered. Where the checklist identifies that an objective has been mastered, the Likert scale indicates the degree of proficiency. For example, a student could have most multiplication facts memorized, but still have trouble on some. With a checklist, the teachers can mark each student as having mastered specified content, or the student has failed to do so. Using a five-point Likert scale a teacher indicates the degree to which each student has mastered the content.

Miscue Analysis Miscue analysis is a process in which students are given a reading selection of approximately 250 words. The student is asked to read the passage orally while the teacher listens and marks all mistakes or miscues by circling the errors. As the student completes his or her reading assignment, the teacher asks comprehension questions about the passage. When this is accomplished, the teacher assesses the student's mistakes inductively and identifies the reader's strengths and weaknesses. This information is then used to develop instructional strategies that build upon the reader's strengths and minimize the weaknesses.

An excellent description of miscue analysis may be found at the following website:
http://www.readbygrade3.com/miscue.htm

FORMATIVE AND SUMMATIVE ASSESSMENTS

Assessments may be formative or summative. **Formative assessments** typically occur during the instructional process and provide immediate and contextual feedback needed to help teachers teach more effectively and students to learn more readily. Formative assessments are usually informal and interactive. For example, as a teacher observes students' reactions to the content being taught, they can adjust instruction practices as needed or provide information to students that enables them to learn more effectively.

Summative assessments are more formal and occur at the conclusion of an instructional unit or at the end of a course, often using a standardized test or a teacher-made test. Teachers use summative assessment procedures when they need to summarize student learning. While summative tests are not employed to provide data that can be used immediately by teachers or students, the information can provide data necessary to help teachers identify changes that can be made to help their students be academically successful. Both formative and summative assessments are needed at different times.

TEST, MEASUREMENT, AND EVALUATION

Standardized Test

Standardized tests are paper-and-pencil tests that are administered to large groups of students and scored in a consistent manner. Assessment items, testing conditions, and scoring is uniform for all test-takers. Results of standardized tests are frequently used to compare different groups of students within a state or around the country. Standardized assessments are conducted at the district, state, and national levels. Examples of common standardized tests include the Scholastic Assessment Test (SAT), ACT Assessment (ACT), Iowa Test of Basic Skills, and Graduate Record Exam (GRE).

Bell Curve

A **normal distribution curve**, also called the **bell curve**, is a mathematical concept that represents a hypothetical bell-shaped distribution of scores or data. Such a perfectly symmetrical distribution rarely occurs in real life. The bell curve deliberately sorts scores or data into percentages by standard deviations. The highest point on the curve is located at the mean, and the scores are divided into groupings by the standard deviations above and below the mean. As it relates to letter grades, one standard deviation above and below the mean represents 68% of the data and are assigned a C letter grade. The scores between one and two standard deviations above the mean, approximately 14% of the population, are assigned the letter grade of B, and the scores higher than this, representing about 2% of the data, become As. Fourteen percent of the data falls between one and two standard deviations below the mean and represent the letter grade of D, with the last group receiving F, which fall below two standard deviations less than the mean.

Grading on a curve means that the highest score gets pushed into the top two percent area representing the A's and the remaining scores are sorted according to the percentages assigned to each standard deviation above and below the mean. In this way the bell curve deliberately spreads out the scores. Letter grades that are assigned by grading on a curve do not necessarily represent mastery according to a standard, but rather how each student performed compared to his or her classmates. For instance, suppose, as a whole, a class performed very poorly on a test, with the highest score being a 64%. Without grading on a curve the top score of 64% would reflect a letter grade of a D. However, if the teacher grades on a curve, the highest score, in this case a 64%, would become an A letter grade. If this happened the entire semester and a student received an A in that class on his or her transcript, how might that misrepresent his or her true knowledge to a potential employer? On the other hand, suppose all the students scored very well on a test, with the lowest score being an 83%. Without using a normal distribution the student earning an 83% would receive a B letter grade. However, if the teacher wanted to spread out the scores to assign letter grades, this same student would get an F. It is easy to see how the normal distribution, or

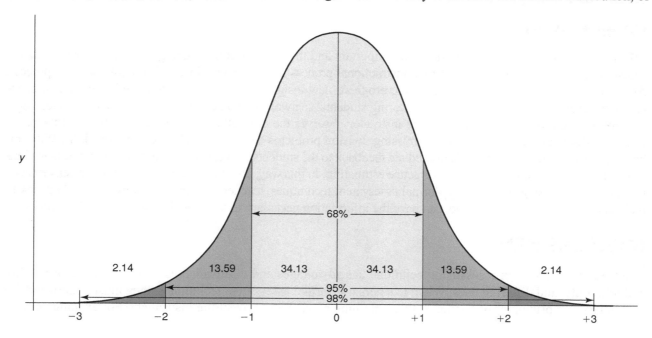

bell curve, can distort letter grades. As a classroom teacher, use the bell curve very judiciously with a deliberate purpose in mind. It is prudent for a teacher to understand the uses of the normal distribution before using it.

Bias

Test **bias** means that the wording of a test question is skewed in favor of a particular group of people. The most common form of bias is cultural bias. An assessment instrument that is culturally biased may unfairly penalize a student based on gender, ethnicity, technological awareness, or socioeconomic status. For example, suppose a state standardized test requires the students to write a persuasive essay using the prompt, "Would you rather take a walk in the woods or on the beach?" This could be a potentially biased question for some students with limited exposure to different environments.

Generalizability

Results from an assessment, survey, or research findings can only be **generalized** to like populations. Suppose you read about a new classroom management technique that works well in a large inner-city school and you teach in a small rural town. Although parts of the new strategy may work in your environment, we cannot assume your students will respond the same way the students in the study did. Sometimes an absurd idea helps to illustrate a point. If women over 70 years old were surveyed to ascertain the degree to which they value and use technology, the findings would not represent the opinion of males under 25 years old. Consequently, because these are not like populations, we cannot generalize our results from one to the other.

Alternative Assessment

Essentially there are two forms of assessment: paper-pencil tests and **alternative assessment**. Paper-and-pencil tests are your traditional forms of classroom tests: true–false, multiple-choice, fill-in-the-blank, solve, and essay. Alternative assessments require students to demonstrate mastery of the new skill or knowledge using a method other than paper and pencil. Examples of alternative assessments include demonstrations, oral reports, lab experiments, debates, performances, authentic assessment, map reading, making a bar graph, making a newsletter, presentations, and the like.

Authentic Assessment

Authentic assessment is a form of alternative assessment whereby the student actually performs the task under realistic conditions. Examples of authentic assessment include creating a personal budget, designing a circle graph depicting data, twirling a baton, or using a ruler to measure length. It involves the student executing the desired skill.

When to Assess

Effective teachers know that assessments are important and that they must be ongoing; therefore, teachers should assess students early and often during the instructional process and at the conclusion of the instructional process. As teachers monitor their students' academic progress, new insights into student learning and instructional needs typically emerge. For example, while monitoring students' seatwork in mathematics, a fourth-grade teacher might observe a pattern of student errors. As the instructor observes the class attempting to divide whole numbers, the instructor discovers several students are missing division problems because of lack of estimation skills. With this knowledge, the teacher can provide immediate feedback to the students, and can adjust current or future lesson plans so that time is provided for students to practice estimating. In this way, both the students' and teacher's performance is improved. By using formal and informal assessment techniques, teachers can provide constructive feedback to their students, and at the same time, can have the information necessary to improve their instructional practices.

MEASUREMENT

Teachers know that each assessment technique has advantages and disadvantages, differing levels of validity and reliability, and differing uses. When teachers use formal assessment techniques, they must understand the vocabulary and principles of testing. A test is nothing more than a measuring instrument. For example, a ruler is a testing instrument that can be used to determine the length of an object and a bathroom scale is a measuring instrument to determine weight. Likewise, a **teacher-made test** is a measuring instrument that is designed to determine how much a student knows and understands about the specific content of a subject.

Measurements are derived from tests and are a mathematical process. Measurements have two elements: a number and a scale. For example, a person's weight is a measurement that can be a number (150) and a scale (pounds). For example, a teacher administers a spelling test to a fifth-grade student and found that the student spelled 75% of the words correctly. After an accurate measurement has been calculated, it can be used in the evaluation process.

While measurement is a mathematical process, **evaluation** is a philosophical process involving the examination of a measurement and drawing of appropriate inferences. For example, the student who scored 75% on the spelling test could be evaluated differently according to other considerations. If the student was exceptionally bright, the teacher might be disappointed with the test performance and conclude that the student's performance was not at an acceptable standard for the student's ability. However, if the student had a learning disability, the teacher might evaluate the student's performance as being quite commendable. The measurement could be the same for both students, and the evaluation could differ dramatically.

TRUE MEASURE AND ERROR

Tests are created and administered to get accurate measurements, which provide teachers with valid and reliable information that can be employed in the decision-making process. However, every measurement contains both **true measure** and a degree of **error**. For example, if two people measure the height of a child, they often get two different measurements. One person might measure the height of the child to the nearest inch and the other person might measure to the nearest quarter-inch. Both measurements would be similar, but neither would be exact. The teacher must strive to minimize the errors in their measurements, so that their assessments will be fair and accurate.

When teachers are measuring students' academic performance, they must recognize that the measurements will never be totally accurate, and they should not make important decisions about students based on a singular assessment. Teachers need to make their measurements as accurate as possible and consider other types of assessment so appropriate decisions may be made about students. The best way to maximize true measurement and minimize error is to have an accurate measuring instrument and carefully check the assessment. An accurate measuring instrument is both reliable and valid.

Test Reliability

Before making evaluations, teachers need to ascertain that the measurements used were as accurate as possible. To be accurate, the testing instrument must be **reliable**, which means that the test must render the same results each time it is administered. For example, a bathroom scale can be used if it consistently measures a person's weight even if it measures 5 pounds more than the person actually weighs. The person can simply subtract 5 pounds from the measurement that is rendered on the scale and still know his or her accurate weight. However, if the scale is not consistent, it cannot be used to determine weight and has no value as a measuring instrument.

There are several ways of establishing the reliability of a test. An example of one type of reliability is called test–retest reliability. To establish test–retest reliability, one group is tested and then tested again later, using the same test. Teachers would not expect students to make exactly the same scores on a test both times it was administered. Some students could have learned content that was tested and others may have forgotten content during the time between the two administrations of the test. However, teachers would expect the students who scored well the first time the test was administered to score well the second time the test was administered. Conversely, students who did not perform well the first time would not be expected to score well the second time they took the test. If this pattern is found, the test is considered to have test–retest reliability.

Test Validity

An assessment instrument has two types of validity. The first type is referred to as test validity and to what is being measured and inferences drawn from the results. The second type, content validity, ensures that the content domain being measured is representative of the skills and knowledge taught. A **valid** test measures what it was designed to assess and appropriate inferences can be drawn from the results regarding the characteristic or ability being measured. **Content validity** measures what was taught and tests the content in proportion to the time that was spent teaching the content. For example, a teacher taught a 5-day unit on division. On day 1, the content focused on division being an inverse operation of multiplication; on day 2, students learned how estimation can be used in division; on days 3, 4, and 5, the steps used in the division process were taught. If this content was taught, it should be tested in proportion to the instructional time spent on each topic. Because 20% of the teaching time was spent studying that multiplication and division are inverse operations, 20% of the test should be devoted to this topic. Likewise, 60% of the test items should be based on the steps used in division. For a test to be valid it must measure how well students mastered the content that was taught. In this way, teachers can determine if students have developed the conceptual knowledge of division and test students' computational skills in other ways.

PLANNING FOR TESTING

Teachers must be careful as they construct tests, for there are many ways to build error into the measuring instruments. For example, a fourth-grade student could love science and have a considerable knowledge base of this subject, yet be a poor reader. After taking a science test, it might appear that the student knows little science when the student might have known most of the content but was unable to comprehend the test questions. The teacher might believe that the test was measuring science content; however, the test was measuring both science content and reading skills.

How can teachers construct tests that are valid and reliable? Test construction should begin as a teacher identifies the goals and objectives of a teaching unit. A teacher needs to build the test prior to teaching a unit. In this way, the teacher's knowledge of the upcoming assessment tends to encourage and focus on the content that was identified as being important. However, the test will need to be revised to include changes in the initial planning. In this way, the teacher will test what is taught, and with careful planning will test the content proportionally to the time spent in instruction.

The structure of a test is also important. When constructing a power test, which provides ample time for a test to be completed, the initial items on the test should be the simplest items, with the remaining items becoming increasingly difficult. In this way, students develop a positive response reaction to the test and do not become overly stressed, which can be a source of error in the measurement.

Students should be given ample time to complete the test unless the teacher wants to use a speed test to determine if students have developed certain skills such as keyboarding or memorization of certain facts. The vocabulary of the test should be developmentally appropriate to ensure that reading is not the primary determinant of students' performance.

The administration of the test should also be carefully planned. Students should be informed of the test dates early and have unit objectives posted to facilitate effective study. Teachers should make efforts to maintain a quiet testing environment by turning off the intercom and posting "testing" notices on the outside of the classroom door.

PROCESSING AND RECORDING TEST SCORES

An efficient way to initially sort scores while simultaneously organizing data is to use a **stem-and-leaf plot**. This technique makes it simple to read data from the plot. It is easy to identify the lowest and highest score, where most scores cluster, and the most common score(s). To create a stem-and-leaf plot make a column of numbers starting with 10 and go down to the 10's place value of the lowest score. Next, draw a vertical line to the right of the column of numbers. On the right side of the vertical line list the digit in the ones place of each student score in the approximate placement numerically, leaving space for lower ones place digits. For example, if the first four student scores are 87, 94, 83, and 72, the stem-and-leaf plot would look like

How do you record test scores in your grade book and how do you process the scores into grades? The simplest way to process scores is usually the best way because complex methods used to process and record scores usually corrupt the accuracy of students' grades. Assume that a teacher has constructed a test that he or she believes to be valid and reliable. The teacher administered the test carefully and scored the test accurately. The next task for the teacher is to record each student's score using a systematic method.

There are many ways to convert test results to scores, but the best way is to use the simplest way while maintaining the raw score for as long as possible. For example, teachers may record a 4 if they think the grade is an A, 3 for a B, 2 for a C, and continue the process through F. By using this process, however, the marks lose some of their meaning. To illustrate this, assume that a student received an A on a major test and an F on a daily assignment. Using the process described above, both grades would have the same weight and a C would be assigned.

The simpler process is to count homework assignments as 20 points and a test as 100 points. In this way, one test is weighted as heavily as five homework assignments. Additionally, the grades maintain their individual identity. Consider a student who took five major tests and did not have homework counted as part of the grade. The student scored:

Test 1: 100   Test 2: 89   Test 3: 89   Test 4: 89   Test 5: 89

Assume the teacher records grades based on the criterion-referenced scale: 90–100% = A, 80–89% = B, 70–79% = C, 60–69% = D, and 59% or below = F. The student would receive the grades of A, B, B, B, and B. The grades would be averaged and the student would receive a B.

However, examine the scores again. The student accrued 456 points out of 500 points possible, which is 91% average for the five tests. By retaining the raw scores, more accurate measurements are made. Typically, teachers can develop their own processes for maintaining grades; nevertheless, some school districts have policies about how grades will be maintained and reported. Some secondary schools require that teachers assign marks to students using norm referencing.

TYPES OF TESTS

Norm-Referenced Tests

All teachers have had the experience of being graded on the curve in their university classes where an instructor assigns grades based on how well a student scored in comparison to other students in the class. For example, if a student scored 80% and that was the highest grade in the class, the student would receive an A. If, however, a student scored 80% and that was the lowest score in the class, the grade would be an F. In **norm referencing**, students' scores are compared to the norm, which is established by the scores of their classmates. Simply put, the score from a norm-referenced test is a reflection of how that person did in comparison to the other test-takers. It is *not* a measurement of skill and knowledge mastery. The purpose of the norm-referenced test is to discriminate between high and low achievers. Consider for example, a college that has spaces for 100 students, but 200 people applied for admission to the university. If the college wanted to ensure that the best students were allowed to matriculate, it might administer a norm-referenced test. The purpose would be to discriminate between high achievers and low achievers, as evidenced by the norm-referenced test. To make sure that the test discriminates, or separates, the students by achievement levels, the test must measure extensive content and be very rigorous. Consequently, it is common for scores of norm-referenced tests to be reported as a percentile rather than a percentage.

A test score reported as a **percentile** indicates the percent of people that scored at or below the test-taker's raw score. For instance, if a student is in the 84th percentile he or she scored the same as or above 84% of the other students taking the test. It could be worded that 84% of the students scored the same as or below the student being discussed. It bears repeating that a percentile score is in comparison to the other test-takers; it is not a percentage of the questions answered correctly.

Criterion-Referenced Tests

Criterion-referenced test scores are not dependent upon how well a student performs compared to other students. Rather, a criterion is established and students' grades are determined by how well each student performs compared to the criterion. The criterion is usually specific instructional objectives or standards. For example, in an English language arts class the teacher may give the students a reading passage followed by a series of questions to measure their reading comprehension. The students' level of reading comprehension is the criterion being measured and the raw score indicates the number of questions they answered correctly. This raw score can be converted to a percentage to reflect their performance in comprehending the passage. If a student answered 9 out of 10 questions correctly, the raw score is 9 and calculates to a 90%.

The teacher is responsible for assigning letter grades to percent ranges. Most people are familiar with the letter grade designation being in increments of 10. Ninety percent to 100% would be an A. Eighty percent to 89% would be a B, and so forth. However, teachers have the prerogative to assign different percent ranges. For example, a preset standard of 94–100% might be the established to receive an A while 87–93% would be a B.

The purpose of a criterion-referenced test is to determine if a student has mastered specified skills or concepts and is not concerned with how well a student performs compared to a norm group. A criterion-referenced test can be administered prior to instruction to determine what a student knows before instruction. Then it is administered again after the teaching has occurred to ascertain what a student learned. When criterion-referenced tests are administered, students' scores are typically reported in percentages and is solely an indication of an individual student's performance.

For teachers to make accurate assessments, they must learn how to develop tests that measure students' learning. This will allow teachers to make accurate judgments and thereby make informed decisions that affect their students.

Objective and Subjective Tests

Tests can be either objective or subjective. A test is **objective** or **subjective** based on the methods used to grade the test. Multiple-choice tests, true–false tests, and matching tests are objective tests; if two teachers, using the same answer key, check a student's objective test, the teacher will not affect the score. This is not true when a teacher uses a subjective test format. The most common type of subjective test is the essay examination. A student's grade could vary dramatically if more than one teacher scores the same subjective test because teachers must make judgments about the quality of each response. Although using a scoring rubric can help minimize the subjectivity of grading, it is still subjective for any type of tests other than multiple-choice, true–false, and matching.

Many teachers use both objective and subjective test formats because both types of tests have advantages and limitations. The choice of using an objective test or subjective test is usually determined by the purpose of the assessment. Experienced teachers know that objective tests are more difficult to construct, but can be scored much more easily than essay examinations.

OBJECTIVE TESTS

There are two types of objective tests: supply-type and select-type. Select-type test formats include multiple-choice tests, matching tests, and true–false tests in which students are presented with both the test items and possible answers. The examinee must read each test item and select one of the alternatives that are provided as being the best answer. An example of a select-type is the multiple-choice test. An elementary teacher might include the following multiple-choice test item:

_____1. *In what year was the United States Declaration of Independence signed?*

     A. 1492   *B. 1776*   *C. 1812*   *D. 1941*

Students would be expected to select the correct answer from those provided. However, if the teacher wanted to develop a supply-item test item that tests the same content, a completion test format could be employed. The completion question testing the same content might be as follows:

_____1. *In what year was the United States Declaration of Independence signed?*

Using the completion test format, the student must supply the correct answer rather than selecting the correct answer from the alternatives provided. It is generally easier to recall an answer if you can select it rather than supply it; therefore, scores on completion tests tend to be lower than scores on matching or multiple-choice tests.

Multiple-Choice Tests

One of the most effective objective test formats is the multiple-choice test, which has several advantages and limitations. Being an objective test format, multiple-choice tests can be checked quickly and accurately. The items can be structured to measure higher levels of cognition, which requires students to study more effectively than when test items are measuring rote memorization. A primary limitation of the multiple-choice test is the difficulty in constructing good multiple-choice items, as each of the alternatives must be attractive to students who do not know the answer. Typically, a teacher can develop two or three good alternatives, but it is difficult to create a fourth alternative that is a viable choice for students, yet incorrect.

Examine the following multiple-choice test format:

_____1. *In what year did Columbus first reach the new world*? (stem of the item)

Alternative A. 1492 (keyed response or correct answer)

Alternative B. 1066 (distractor, an attractive but incorrect alternative)

Alternative C. 1776 (distractor)

Alternative D. 1812 (distractor)

The test alternatives are a combination of the keyed response and the distracters. Please note that the stem is written as an interrogative sentence that can be answered best by one of the four alternatives. Multiple-choice test items must never have blanks and only rarely use an incomplete sentence format because a question format provides a context that helps students to understand what is being asked. The following suggestions will assist teachers to construct multiple-choice questions that render more valid and reliable measurements.

What are the characteristics of a well-conceived multiple-choice test item? An effective multiple-choice test item presents a concise and clearly written question and an effective way for students to select the keyed response. The vocabulary used in the item should be developmentally appropriate. Negatives should be avoided in the stem; and if this cannot be avoided, negatives such as *no*, *not*, or *never*, should be highlighted or underlined.

Typically, each multiple-choice test item has four alternatives, each of which should be reasonable to students who do not know the answer. In this way, students cannot eliminate unreasonable distractors. However, the keyed response must be the best alternative presented to students taking the test.

True–False Tests

True–false tests are widely used and useful to teachers; however, effective teachers will use the multiple-choice, matching, or completion formats extensively because these testing formats tend to be more valid and reliable than are true–false tests. Nevertheless, true–false test items are easy to construct and effective teachers may use true–false items to test content that needs to be tested when it is not possible to use one of the more valid and reliable testing formats.

Examine the following format for the true–false test:

_____ 1. *Columbus first arrived in the New World in the year 1492.*

Note that the test item is a declarative sentence with a method for students to register their agreement or disagreement with the accuracy of the statement. The easiest way to register agreement is to write either *true* or *false* in the space provided to the left of each item's number rather than using other symbols. Inform the students that they must spell the words correctly and that if you cannot read the words easily, they will be scored as incorrect responses.

As previously noted, true–false items are relatively easy to construct, and students can answer a large number of true–false items in a relatively short period of time. Therefore, the true–false format makes it possible to sample a wide range of content material. However, there is a 50% chance of guessing the correct answer to a true–false item. The disadvantage of this is that students will appear to know more of the content tested than they actually understand. For example, if a teacher constructed a true–false test over advanced organic chemistry and administered the test to third-grade students who were instructed to guess the answers, the expected average score for the students would be 50%. Although the students did not know any of the content, by guessing wildly, they would appear to know one-half of the content. Had the students been tested using a multiple-choice test with four alternatives, the average score would be approximately 25% had the students guessed at random.

How then can a teacher construct a true–false test that is somewhat valid and reliable? When constructing a true–false test, teachers must take precautions to ensure that each item is completely true or completely false. Students do not know how to answer a true–false item that is partially true and partially false. Effective test constructors know that the likelihood of an item being totally true or totally false is improved if the item is concise and focused on only one idea.

Also, each item on a true–false test must be free of clues. Students soon learn that if a test item contains one of the words *none*, *all*, *always*, and *never*, the item is generally false. Conversely, if the item contains one of the words *sometimes*, *may*, and *generally*, the item is generally true. As students mature, they recognize that if they do not know the answer to a true–false question, the item is more likely to be false because it is more difficult to construct an item that is true under every circumstance. Therefore, teachers should make efforts to ensure that one-half of the items are true and one-half of the items are false.

Completion Tests

A completion test item is a written question that requires the examinee to supply the correct word or short phrase in response to a question. This format is not a fill-in-the-blank test. The completion format is much like a multiple-choice item with the distraction omitted. Typically, the format asks a question and provides space for the answer to be written. For example:

_____ 1. *What is the symbol for a "set union"?*

By structuring a complete question, the student knows what the item is asking and responds accordingly. When fill-in-the-blanks are used, students do not have a context for answering the question. For example, a teacher in a neighboring state structured the following fill-in-the-blank test item:

1. *The _____ of _____ provided _____.*

This question would be nearly impossible to answer correctly even if a student knew all of the material being tested. The fill-in-the-blank test format is not a completion item and is generally not recommended by effective teachers.

However, many teachers use the completion test format extensively. This format is commonly used in biological and physical sciences and other subjects that employ esoteric terms and stress vocabulary development. It is a useful format, but it is difficult to construct items that can be answered by one word or a short phrase.

Additionally, it is difficult to construct completion tests that measure higher levels of cognition such as analysis, synthesis, or evaluation. Lastly, it is difficult to communicate exactly what you want for a response to a completion question. For example, consider this question:

_____ *2. Who fought at the Battle of the Bulge?*

While the teacher has an answer in mind, the students are not privy to this information. Therefore, answers that the teacher would be required to count as being correct might be allies, Nazis, Germans, Americans, French, or Britons, or a student could name an obscure foot soldier. By structuring a better question, the answer desired is more evident for students who know the content. For example, the same content could be written as follows:

_____ *2. Who was the Allied commander of the cavalry at the Battle of the Bulge?*

How should a completion test item be constructed? The format used in completion tests generally provides students with a complete question and an underlined blank space to the left of the item number. Typically, a completion item asks one question; however, it is appropriate to have more than one underlined blank space for questions that require more than one answer if the answers are highly related. For example, a test item might be, "What are the two types of cell division?"

Furthermore, consider the following recommendations to construct completion test items that are valid and reliable. Completion items should be relatively short and concise and developmentally appropriate. In this way, students have a better understanding of what is being asked and can provide more accurate responses. Avoid clues that would provide hints about the answer to the question. For example, if the length of the line for the answer varied according to the length of the desired response, a clue has been provided.

Matching Test

The matching test item is a modification of the multiple-choice form; however, rather than listing alternatives under each individual stem, a series of stems called premises or cues are listed in one column, column A, and the responses are listed in column B. Please remember that the cues and responses should be arranged in alphabetical or chronological order. In this way, students can find answers easily when taking the test. Teachers need to be careful in providing explicit directions for taking the matching test. In addition, teachers should tell students what information is in both columns, how the matches should be made, and if one response can be used more than once or may not be used. For example:

Directions:

Famous wars and battles are listed under column A. Under Column B, dates of these wars or battles are listed. Place the letter of the appropriate date in the blank to the left of the war or battle. You may use a letter in Column B more than once or a letter might not be used.

	Column A (Cues)	Column B (Response)
A	1. Battle of Hastings	A. 1066
B	2. Crimean War	B. 1759

When constructing a matching test, teachers need to remember to keep each section homogeneous. In the example above, the cue column lists the names of wars or battles and the response column lists the dates of the war or battle. Note that the items in the response column are short; usually limited to a word, number, or short phrase; and that the lengthier parts of the test item are in the cue column. The test should not extend from one page to the next, and should not have more than 10 cues and 11 responses.

SUBJECTIVE (ESSAY) TESTS

Subjective tests are powerful ways for identifying students' knowledge and understanding as well as their abilities to use this knowledge and understanding to synthesize a coherent response to an essay test item. The essay test provides an opportunity for students to organize extended answers to questions posed by the teacher. While many teachers use essay items extensively, others hesitate to administer essay items because of the time it takes to construct and score the test. A well-developed essay item must communicate clearly (1) the information that the teachers want to see on the essay, and (2) the ways they want students to organize the response. Examine the following essay test item:

1. Compare and contrast the presidential leadership styles of Bill Clinton and George W. Bush. Frame your responses around their social, military, and economic policies. Please limit your response to one page. You will be graded on the accuracy of your responses, the organization of your writing, and the clarity and conciseness of your responses. This item is worth 30 points.

Please note that essay items should require higher-level thinking. Often, the items contain a word or phrases such as "compare and contrast," "why," "predict," "create," or "describe and give examples of _____." As the essay question is being formulated, a scoring rubric should also be created with potential points being designated for each part of the essay response.

The test requires considerable time to score even when the teacher has developed a scoring rubric. The most efficient way of creating a scoring rubric is for the teacher to answer each essay item written. In this way, a specific issue that the teacher believes is required to answer the essay completely is identified and the number of points can be identified for each issue described. Additionally, points are reserved for the organization of the essay. The last advantage of teachers answering their own essay items is that when reacting to each item, the teacher can identify changes that might be needed to communicate the intent of the question.

Due to time requirements for checking essays, many teachers hesitate to use the essay format. Often, it may take up to an hour to check each student's essay; and if the teacher has four sections of a class with 25 students in each section, then assessing the essays would take considerable time and energy that could be spent on improving future class presentations.

Student Portfolios

Student portfolios provide a way for students to provide evidence of their learning by organizing work samples into a collection illustrative of their experiences. A portfolio contains several pieces of a student's self-selected work to showcase exemplary samples representative of his or her work or performance. It may include a variety of works relevant to the course curriculum, and usually a rationale explaining why each selection was chosen for inclusion. For instance, a student's portfolio in a writing class may include a business letter, a fictional story, a poem, a "how to" paper, a persuasive paper, and a research paper. Inherent in the creation of a portfolio is student self-assessment.

There are several types of common portfolios: growth, showcase, and evaluation. A growth portfolio shows growth or change over time by contrasting an early work with a later work. This type of portfolio helps develop process skills such as self-evaluation and goal-setting. It also identifies strengths and weaknesses of each artifact and allows the student to track the development of a particular skill, product, or performance.

Showcase portfolios exemplify end of semester/year accomplishments, and can communicate a student's aptitude to future teachers. This type of portfolio showcases a student's perception of his or her favorite, best, or most significant work. Sometimes this form of portfolio can be used for employment or college admission for specific programs.

The evaluation portfolio demonstrates achievement for grading purposes and illustrates progress toward mastery of learning objectives or state standards. This style of portfolio can be used for student placement in some educational environments.

Sample Test Questions

1. Ms. Ladd knows that the TAKS test was designed to ensure that students think critically and creatively. She knows that many of the questions that she asks in class are structured to require only the lowest levels of cognition. She is committed to ask divergent questions that require students to think at higher levels of cognition. Which of the following questions or commands would be best for requiring the highest levels of cognition?

    a. Explain the concept in your own words.

    b. Why does this concept help students?

    c. Solve the following problem using this concept.

    d. How would you create a better model of this concept that might be easier to understand?

2. Mrs. Lynch is concerned with her students' achievement. She knows that educational theorists report that teachers should assess their students both as they are studying a unit and at the conclusion of each unit. Therefore, she decided to construct and administer a combination of:

    a. formative and summative tests.

    b. subjective and objective tests.

    c. standardized and teacher-made tests.

    d. short-answer and essay tests.

3. Ms. Ladd attended a workshop that was designed to improve her students' performance on state-mandated tests. She learned that many of the questions now require students to demonstrate not only that they know content, but that they can apply the content in problems that require higher levels of cognition. The workshop instructor recommended that teachers use the Bloom model of cognition in their questioning techniques. Which of the following test formats would be best for measuring the highest levels of cognition?

    a. Multiple-choice tests

    b. Matching tests

    c. Essay tests

    d. Completion tests

4. When Ms. Carpenter gives a test to determine what she should reteach or teach next, she is administering what type of test?

    a. A power test

b. A speed test

c. A formative test

d. A summative test

5. When Ms. Carpenter develops a test, she reviews it to make sure that the test is measuring what she thinks it is measuring. She is attempting to ensure that the test is:

   a. valid.

   b. reliable.

   c. usable.

   d. Achievement-rated.

6. Ms. Havens wants to help her students learn to think critically and creatively as required for the TAKS test. Therefore, which of the following teaching methods will she use whenever possible to help her students prepare to think critically and creatively?

   a. Teaching that emphasizes the lecture.

   b. Teaching that emphasizes the demonstration.

   c. Teaching that emphasizes discussions.

   d. Teaching that emphasizes discovery.

Answers

1. D is the correct answer because it is the only question of the choices that requires the students to think critically and at a higher level of cognition.

2. A is the correct answer because it is the only one that corresponds with the *timing* of the tests. Formative tests are those given during the unit as the students are forming new knowledge and learning new skills. Summative tests are given at the conclusion of a unit to determine the level of student mastery.

3. C is the correct answer because essay tests lend themselves to recalling information and can tap into higher levels of cognition. The other answers are tests where students are only required to recognize and answer, not recall, or they can even guess and possibly get it right. Furthermore, the other tests required convergent thinking, not divergent thinking.

4. C is the correct answer because it is the only test with the distinct purpose of identifying how well the students are learning the new skill or knowledge. From the test results a teacher can identify those concepts needing to be reviewed, retaught, or determine if the students have attained mastery and are ready to move on.

5. A is the correct answer because test validity is when a test measures what it is suppose to measure.

B is incorrect. Reliable means the test results are consistent and stable.

C and D are distractors and not part of assessment vocabulary; they are made up.

6. D is the correct answer because it is student-centered and requires the students to be problem-solvers and critical thinkers. A, B and C are teacher-centered and require less of the students.

REFERENCES

Anderson, L.W. & Krathwohl, D.R. (eds.) (2001). *A Taxonomy for Learning, Teaching, and Assessing: A Revision of Bloom's Taxonomy of Educational Objectives.* New York: Longman

Hoy, C., & Gregg, N. (1994). *Assessment: The special educator's role.* Pacific Grove, CA: Brooks/Cole.

Websites

http://www.ericfacility.net/databases/ERIC_Digests/ed470206.html
An excellent overview of formative assessment.

http://books.nap.edu/html/classroom_assessment/ch4.html
An excellent article that describes the relationship between summative and formative assessment.

http://www.cals.ncsu.edu/agexed/aee735/ppt8/tsld004.htm
Good insights into test construction.

http://www.fairtest.org/facts/nratests.html
Additional information about norm-referenced tests.

http://www.fairtest.org/facts/csrtests.html#anchor264525
An excellent description of criterion-referenced testing.

Fulfilling Professional Roles and Responsibilities

Domain 4

Competency 11

Increasing Parental Involvement: A Key Component of School Improvement and Reform

Angela Spaulding, EdD
West Texas A&M University

Teri Bingham, EdD
West Texas A&M University

> **Competency 11:** The teacher understands the importance of family involvement in children's education and knows how to interact and communicate effectively with families.

The beginning teacher:

A. Applies knowledge of appropriate ways (including electronic communication) to work and communicate effectively with families in various situations.

B. Engages families, parents, guardians, and other legal caregivers in various aspects of the educational program.

C. Interacts appropriately with all families, including those that have diverse characteristics, backgrounds, and needs.

D. Communicates effectively with families on a regular basis (e.g., to share information about students' progress) and responds to their concerns.

E. Conducts effective conferences with parents, guardians, and other legal caregivers.

F. Effectively uses family support resources (e.g., community, interagency) to enhance family involvement in student learning

KEY TERMS

community support   parental involvement plans   service learning technical jargon

funds of knowledge   parent–teacher conferences

home culture   Parent–Teacher Organization

A national debate about the importance of parental involvement to increase the academic success of elementary, middle school, and high school students began in 1966 with the publication of *Equality of Educational Opportunity Report* (Coleman, Campbell, Hobson, McPartland, & York, 1966). In his extensive study of schools across the United States, James Coleman found that parental involvement is an important predictor of academic achievement in schools. Coleman found that schools with high levels of parental involvement typically had much higher levels of academic achievement than did those with little parental involvement, and his research sparked three decades of debate about educational reform and the importance of parental involvement.

More recently, Bianchi and Robinson (1997) found that parental expectations of academic achievement significantly affect children's attitudes toward and success in academics. In other words, parents who expected their children to excel academically and who took a positive roll in actively helping their children with schoolwork significantly contributed to the academic success of their children. Similarly, other researchers (e.g., Henderson & Berla, 1994) have found that increasing parental involvement in schools has resulted in higher graduation rates, better attendance, and higher completion of homework. In brief, parental involvement is an important aspect ensuring and increasing the academic success of students; consequently, the State of Texas has devoted Competency 11 to the theme of parental involvement in schools.

© Rob Marmion, 2014, Used under license of Shutterstock, Inc.

THE CAUSES OF LOW LEVELS OF PARENTAL INVOLVEMENT

As previously noted, the *Equality of Educational Opportunity Report* became a springboard of debate about family effects on children's education. However, there was little mention about why some parents participated in school communities whereas others chose not to do so. Research has shown that it is not uncommon for school officials to become frustrated by the lack of parental involvement, and many educators assume that many parents are not concerned about the education of their children (Anyon, 1997; Mansbach, 1993).

However, most parents want to become more involved in school activities but do not do so for a variety of reasons. Clark (1995), for example, interviewed many parents who noted they wanted to be more involved in the education of their children but that their work schedules conflict with school activities. Some parents work evenings or odd hours, which prevent them from helping their children with homework (Finders & Lewis, 1994). Although some educators may assume that many low-income parents do not support education, they often are the strongest supporters of education because they realize that education provides opportunities for economic advancement and possibilities for a higher quality of life for their children (Banks, 2001, 2002). If parents are struggling financially to maintain their household, it is understandable why they are not willing to miss work because doing so may decrease their earnings.

Other parents avoid schools because they have low levels of education. Some parents note that for them schools are places of failure and negative memories, and it is not uncommon for people to avoid negative experiences, especially when they feel inadequately prepared to participate (Clark, 1995; Comer, 1988). Equally important, some parents believe they are not prepared academically to help their children with homework, and this causes them embarrassment. Similarly, parents who are not fluent in English may experience frustration in their attempts to communicate their concerns about their children's education. In some cases, parents may perceive that teachers and administrators are indifferent to them and their children's education.

Most educators are concerned about their students' learning and well-being; however, since perceptions sometimes are stronger than reality, negative perceptions of school personnel cause many parents to avoid schools (Comer, 1988). Some parents assume that their input is tolerated but not taken seriously by school personnel, and these misunderstandings create obstacles in improving home–school relationships (Comer, 1995). In addition, parents from diverse cultural groups often perceive that they are not accepted by school personnel; this is especially problematic because schools are becoming more diverse each year (Cushner, McClelland, & Safford, 2003). Parents also have noted that they are frustrated with and alienated by educators who use technical jargon in discussions (Clark, 1995). For example, if teachers refer to standard deviations or norm-referenced tests, parents may not understand the significance of these terms any more than teachers may understand the technical language of lawyers.

The misunderstandings caused by technical jargon are problematic for teachers (Clark, 1995). Parents who are not well educated may not understand the teacher's main ideas and may feel too embarrassed to ask questions to clarify key points. In addition, meetings with parents may cause more confusion and distrust and may alienate parents. As a result, some may avoid conferences with teachers in the future. When teachers fail to learn how to help their students from the unique perspective of parents, teachers miss valuable opportunities to gain insights about their students' **home cultures**, knowledge that enables them to work more effectively with their students.

OPENING THE DOORS OF COMMUNICATION FOR PARENTS

Research has shown that many educators inadvertently have closed doors of communication between parents and school. However, if this is the case, how can the doors of communication be opened in productive and lasting ways? Opening closed doors of communication with parents is possible and, of course, necessary. If teachers listen patiently and respectfully to parents from all backgrounds and try to understand their perspectives, most parents will support teachers' efforts. School officials need to encourage such parents to participate in school activities, especially by showing them that their help and input is valued (Kaplan, Liu, & Kaplan, 2001).

One way for teachers to establish respectful rapport with parents is to adopt an open-door policy in their classrooms and to develop two-way communication between parents and themselves. For example, teachers and administrators use newsletters, email, and websites to notify parents about assignments, activities, or opportunities to volunteer for classroom or other school activities. In addition, parents are more apt to use the resources that are available to enhance the learning of their children if they are aware of their availability. The use of email is an effective tool of communication in schools because of its convenience. In most school districts email is used by teachers for classroom announcements and by administrators to send messages to parents. Email allows teachers and parents to communicate with one another even if they are unable to discuss concerns directly. The rapidity of email enables parents to communicate with teachers to voice their concerns or merely to check on the progress of their children (Parkay & Stanford, 2004).

To keep the lines of communication open, teachers need to reiterate to parents throughout the school year that they are welcome to ask questions about learning activities for their children. Parents are more inclined to ask questions and to participate in activities if teachers invite them to do so. In addition, it is important for teachers to contact parents about positive aspects of their children's education. Parents need to hear about the successes of their children in addition to teachers' concerns, and teachers who emphasize the positive qualities of students are more inclined to establish strong rapport with parents than are those teachers who concentrate only on problems (Gestwicki, 1996).

CONFERENCES WITH PARENTS

Clear communication also is the key to effective parent–teacher conferences. Most school districts have set times throughout the year when schoolwide parent conferences are held (McNergney & McNergney, 2004). For example, school districts typically hold **parent–teacher conferences** during the first month of the academic school year. These conferences provide parents and teachers with opportunities to meet one another. Parents profit from these visits because they are able to ask teachers questions, and teachers are able to clarify their expectations about academics and behavior. Also, teachers who are respectful of parents are more apt to gain their trust than are teachers who rush through conferences and do not allow parents to voice their concerns (Finders & Lewis, 1994). Equally important, parent–teacher conferences are helpful to teachers because they are opportunities for teachers to become more knowledgeable about students' home cultures and environments.

To ensure that parents are aware of conferences, teachers ought to contact parents by letter, phone, or email (Gestwicki, 1996). Maintaining contact with parents keeps the avenues of two-way communication open and provides parents with the opportunity to reschedule their conferences if necessary. Also, teachers should determine if they need translators for parents who request them. By using adult translators, teachers show parents that they want to establish open communication with them. Equally important, misunderstandings that are caused by language barriers are eliminated.

Another key aspect of preparing for parent conferences involves the preparation of pertinent information. For example, if the conference takes place at the beginning of the school year, teachers may use handouts to delineate their classroom rules/procedures and their requirements for academic work. Conferences that address academic difficulties require teachers to present parents with student work samples, so that parents are able to understand teachers' concerns. Likewise, when teachers discuss behavior problems with parents, they ought to show parents documentation about when, where, and how their children misbehaved. Providing parents with objective examples is critical in conferences about problems so that emotionalism and vague generalizations about the students are eliminated. As previously noted, it is important for teachers to highlight positive aspects of students' abilities and to show their receptivity of parents' questions and concerns.

Also, it is prudent to summarize the main topics of the conversation and to take notes for future reference. Recommendations that are made by teachers or parents should be delineated in the conference notes, which should be available to all parties. Later, teachers ought to contact parents to apprise them of their children's progress. Follow-up calls show a teacher's concern for students and their willingness to involve parents in a student's education (Parkay & Stanford, 2004).

Specifics on Conferencing with Parents or Guardians

When conferencing with parents, start on a positive note and share with them your vision of wanting to work together in the best interest of the child to help him be successful. Maintain an attitude of the teacher and parents being a team to benefit the child. Listen more than you talk. Learn what the child is interested in, how he spends his spare time, and what motivates him. Discover what his favorite subjects in school are, where he excels and what he wants to aspire to be when he is an adult. Most parents know and are eager to share information about their child that could give the teacher useful ideas and insights to benefit the student's well being.

© baldyrgan, 2014, Used under license of Shutterstock, Inc.

TIPS FOR FAMILY INVOLVEMENT

1. Parent conferences:
   a. Build rapport and express your desire for a partnership.
   b. Start and end on a good note.
   c. Be a good listener.
   d. Express desire to get ideas from parent.
   e. Don't give parenting advice.
   f. Don't talk only in punitive measures (rather than how can we help).
   g. Don't become the family's counselor.
   h. Don't convey that a certain behavior is indicative of serious problems (i.e., psychiatrist).

IDEAS FOR PARENTS AND CHILDREN TO POSITIVELY INTERACT

bake cookies	dance	go play at the park
	discuss living by principles	go skating
build a sand castle	draw pictures	go swimming
build a snowman	exercise	go to a play
build tents out of blankets and TV trays/chairs	explain driving laws as you drive	go to church
call grandparents	fly a kite	go to the library
camp in the backyard	go bowling	have a hug contest
chaperone a school dance	go camping	have a picnic in your own living room
chaperone a school field trip	go fishing	have a tickle fight
coach their team	go for a bike ride	have an end-of-school party
collect rocks or leaves	go for a walk	have the child teach the parent a computer/technology skill
color	go for ice cream	help with their homework
create a home recycling system	go on a picnic	
create fun, yummy snacks	go out for breakfast	invite a new student over to play
keep a family journal	play a board game	take treats to an elderly neighbor
learn about their family history	play cards	talk about drugs and alcohol use
learn simple first-aid skills	play in the mud	talk about values
listen with eye contact	play in the rain	teach the dog a trick
make a puppet	play in the sprinklers	visit a museum
make donuts	play together	visit an art gallery
paint their room	rake the leaves	volunteer at school
paint your daughter's toenails	read together	walk the dog
pay for the fast-food order for the car behind you	set goals	watch a movie
pick up litter	sing	watch the sunset
plan a formal dinner party	splash in puddles	watch their sports/performances
plan a vacation	take art lessons	water the plants
plant a garden	take flowers to a grave	write a letter
plant a tree	take them with you to vote	write thank-you notes

2. When necessary discretely provide parents with information on family services.

3. When conferencing with a parent, share information on how to best help the student be successful.

4. If the student is demonstrating minor but frequent problems, seek parents' ideas of how to make it better for everyone.

5. If the parent cannot come to a conference, set up an appointment for a phone conversation.

6. When necessary request an interpreter during a parent–teacher conference if the parents are limited English speakers.

7. Home–school communications should include written home notes/memos.

8. Don't bring children to a conference.

9. Don't tell a parent how "important it is for them to do it your way"

10. Don't counsel how to run their family.

PARENT INVOLVEMENT

1. When having students and parents work on school projects at home together, explain your expectations and workload for the student and for the parent. *Be aware that some students may have limited parent support at home and make home projects reasonable or do not require them.*

2. Involve parents in their child's education whenever it is reasonable and possible (e.g., school assignments and school activities). *Be aware that some children and schools may have very little parental support.*

Parent–Teacher Organization (PTO)

When many people consider parental involvement in the public schools, they usually think of parent–teacher conferences or meetings of the **Parent–Teacher Organization (PTO),** which are prevalent throughout Texas. PTO meetings help to open the avenues of communication between parents and school officials, and these meetings provide parents a forum to voice their concerns and to become involved in the school community. Parents who actively participate in the PTO have opportunities to participate in volunteer services or to discuss their concerns about academics, grading policies, or school-improvement activities. It is important for teachers to participate in these organizations to support the efforts of parents and to provide their input on key issues (Sadker & Sadker, 1997).

HELPING PARENTS TO HELP THEIR CHILDREN ACADEMICALLY

In addition to fostering conditions that encourage parents to become more involved in schools through the PTO, teachers increase parental support by involving parents in their children's homework. For example, Clark (1995) has designed learning activities in mathematics for home involvement. These learning activities are extensions of what students are learning in school, and parents have a repertoire of activities to enhance their children's learning. These mathematics exercises not only increased students' learning and academic achievement but also

© iofoto, 2014, Used under license of Shutterstock, Inc.

improved their relationships with their parents as a result of the additional time that they spent together working on homework.

Likewise, educators have involved parents in training programs to teach parents reading strategies to improve the reading levels of their children. Comer and his colleagues (Comer, 1988; Comer, Haynes, Joyner, & Ben-Avie, 1996), for example, have provided training sessions in literacy for parents whose children were attending traditionally low-achieving schools. Comer found that parents were receptive to these programs and that their children and sometimes even the parents themselves improved their reading skills as a result of the training. Teachers who are willing to provide instructional strategies for parents to employ at home increase the likelihood that parents will work with their children (Banks, 2001), and as parents become more aware of what is being taught and why these concepts are important, they usually take a more active role in their children's learning. These programs are especially important for parents from lower-income groups because they may not have the financial resources for educational materials or tutoring for their children (Anyon, 1997).

Parents' Home Cultures and Expertise

Another way to strengthen parental involvement is to use students' home cultures and the cultural resources of their communities. As previously discussed, teachers who tap into the **funds of knowledge** of their students enrich learning activities and foster community involvement. Learning experiences which build on students' background knowledge and show students that the expertise of their parents is valued by school personnel are significant methods to bolster parental involvement. Conversely, parents are shown how they are valuable resources and are able to contribute substantial knowledge for school assignments.

Similarly, teachers can involve parents in other areas of their children's learning such as language acquisition. Klassen-Endrizzi (2000), for example, used parent–teacher journals to study how parents' views of reading influenced those of their children. The teacher in Klassen-Endrizzi's study found that many parents did not enjoy reading and viewed reading as primarily decoding in contrast to understanding meaning. This background knowledge about students' home cultures and their parents' perceptions of reading was valuable for the teacher because the children typically viewed reading as their parents did, and the teacher adjusted her reading lessons to benefit the children. Learning about students' home cultures enables teachers to involve parents in the learning activities of their children, but it also provides teachers with valuable information that may improve their instruction.

In addition to learning about students' home cultures to improve parental involvement, educators can involve parents in schools by providing opportunities for them to volunteer in classrooms and other school-related activities. For example, some parents may want to assist teachers in tutoring students during class or after school. Such assistance enables teachers to help a wider range of students. Other parents may have lived through important historical events such as the Civil Rights Movement or the Gulf War, and they may want to share their experiences during social studies lessons. In addition, many parents are knowledgeable about common school curriculum (eg. Math, science, English Language Arts) and may even employ these in their workplace.

Community Involvement and Service Learning

Another way that school personnel keep the avenues of communication open is to involve communities in schools (Sadker & Sadker, 1997). Organizations such as Girl Scouts, Boy Scouts, or the Lion's Club are often willing to become involved in school functions and to help with various activities if school officials elicit their help. Likewise, senior citizens groups are another valuable source of expertise and talents. For example, senior citizens may work in after-school literacy programs for students or evening adult literacy programs for parents. In addition, some seniors may want to help with recreation programs for students.

Equally important, many school districts have formed partnerships with local businesses to enhance community-school relationships. Some corporations, for example, donate funds for technology such as computers and software to schools. Furthermore, some businesses have worked with school personnel in dropout prevention programs. In such cases it is not uncommon for corporations to allow their employees to work with selected students, eat lunch with them, and even make home visits to encourage them to continue their education (Parkway & Stanford, 2004).

Similarly, many schools design **service learning** projects in their curricula as a way to involve parents and communities in the education of students and conversely to involve students in their communities (Wade & Saxe, 1996). Some service learning projects concentrate on students tutoring peers or younger students, while other projects concern working with local government agencies to repair public facilities or parks. Students also may volunteer at local charities or at hospitals or nursing homes. Other projects have involved students planting gardens and then giving the fruits and vegetables to charities or homeless shelters.

In addition, service learning projects often have academic purposes as well. For instance, teachers in science programs may design service learning projects for students in which they work with local farmers or ranchers, and students may help conduct tests on soil quality. Similarly, science students in an urban area may develop a recycling program, or a social studies project may involve increasing voter turnout in a designated area. In these cases, students learn about citizenship and their future responsibilities, and parents and community members have additional opportunities to interact with students (Yates & Youniss, 1996).

District Parental Involvement Plans

Parental involvement also is improved if school districts implement district wide parental involvement plans. Teachers benefit these plans because they provide teachers with insights and support about ways to increase parental involvement. One example of a large-scale parental involvement plan is that of James Comer (1995), whose success in improving the academic achievement of various schools has become so influential that his methods of incorporating parents in school decision making has been called the "Comer Process." In Texas many independent school districts have implemented innovative programs to enhance parental involvement and to improve the quality of education.

The following examples of school improvement plans have increased parental involvement and academic achievement. The successes of the parental involvement plans provide food for thought for the classroom teacher, and they also emphasize the professional responsibilities of teachers to provide their support and expertise to ensure the effective implementation of such plans. All parties—teachers, parents, administrators, support staff, and members of the community—are necessary for substantial school improvement. An equally important theme of this section is that each school context is different and has its own set of problems; consequently, teachers, administrators, other school personnel, and parents of each district must develop there own plan of action of increasing parental involvement and, of course, academic achievement.

THE COMER PROCESS

Some districts have extended parental involvement to include parents more directly in decision-making processes about curriculum, the adoption of textbooks, or other changes in school policies. The research of James Comer et al. (1996) is especially helpful in showing how parents can become more involved in the decision-making processes of schools and how parents, students, and school personnel benefit from increased parental involvement.

One way that Comer and his colleagues (Comer, 1988; Comer et al., 1996) provided parents with opportunities for strong roles in the decision-making process of the school was to create the School Planning and Management Team (SPMT), which was comprised of administrators, teachers, parents, and support staff. The members of this group typically discussed important issues about school policy. They came to a consensus before making their decisions, and everyone had a voice in this process. An important innovation of Comer's methods of collaboration was his emphasis on what he termed a "no fault" policy, which established parameters of discussion that prevented parties (e.g., parents, teachers, administrators, and other school personnel) from blaming one another for problems in the school.

Instead, the SPMT focused on the identification of problems and on positive ways to solve them. Comer and his colleagues (Comer, 1988; Comer et al., 1996) found that the SPMT became a cohesive team, which was able to create a comprehensive plan for school improvement, to clarify fragmented policies, to improve the curriculum, and to develop in-service programs for teachers. In addition, the SPMT elicited input and participation from other committees in that the decisions of the SPMT were forwarded to other committees for their suggestions before being sent to the school board for approval.

Another innovation that increased parental involvement was the creation of the Student Staff Services Team (SSST), which was comprised of teachers, guidance counselors, psychologists, administrators, and support staff. However, parents, as well as teachers who were not part of the initial SSST, were encouraged to join this group and to voice their concerns and ideas. The primary function of the SSST was for the identification of inappropriate behavior in the school context, where both curative and preventative interventions are taken to help students and to maintain a positive school climate. In this respect, improving both academics and the behavior of students were the primary emphases of their plans for school improvement.

Perhaps the most important contribution of Comer's work is that his theory of educational reform stresses building an educational community through collaborative methods that include all stakeholders, especially parents. He has shown that increasing parental involvement is far more complex than creating a list of do's and don'ts of effective parental involvement strategies. Instead, his plan of school improvement and parental involvement are drawn from an ecological perspective in that he has shown how all aspects of the school environment affect one another. Because Comer found that effective communication between parents and school personnel was the key to substantial school improvement, he elicited the input of all stakeholders in the decision-making processes of school policies. Comer's collaborative efforts resulted in substantial improvement of parental involvement and academic achievement of schools, which was traditionally low.

IMPROVING PARENTAL INVOLVEMENT AT THE ELEMENTARY LEVEL

Like James Comer, Hueco Elementary School in the Socorro Independent School District has shown how parental and academic success can be substantially improved in areas with histories of low academic achievement. Hueco Elementary School employed the "Success for all Program," which was developed at Johns Hopkins University by Slavin, Karweit, and Wasik (1992). About 56% of the students enter Hueco Elementary School with limited proficiency in English, and the primary goal of this program is to ensure that by the third grade students have reading skills that enable them to succeed academically (Family Involvement in Children's Education, 1997a).

One way that school personnel have involved parents is to offer them workshops on effective reading strategies so that parents are more comfortable helping their children with reading. One program, Super Readers, encourages children to read to a parent each evening and motivates students to read more often by rewarding them for the books that they have read. Such rewards include t-shirts, books, pizza parties, and other prizes. Similarly, parents are trained in how to work with their children more effectively on mathematics, and teachers and parents have organized "math nights" during which parents work with their children on thematic-related problems.

In addition to offering parents workshops in reading and mathematics instruction, workshops have been developed on other topics. For instance, workshops have been offered on nurturing skills and positive discipline, child development and the development of children's self-esteem, drug prevention, health education and proper nutrition, citizenship, English as a second language, and computer skills. School personnel have found that parents are receptive to these classes, and more parents become involved in other school activities as a result of their positive experiences with these programs. Through these programs school officials are reaching out to parents to involve them in school activities and to address their concerns about how to meet the needs of their children.

In other efforts to improve parent–school relationships, school personnel have expanded the opportunities for parents to impact the quality of classroom instruction and enrich their own lives in the process. Parents, for example, have important roles in school policy through the Parent Communication Council and are able to voice their concerns and provide fresh ideas about how to implement programs more effectively. Furthermore, parents work more closely with teachers in classrooms and have provided valuable assistance. These innovative ways to involve parents have helped to increase academic achievement, and the commitments of both parents and school personnel have increased as a result of the improvements of parent–school relationships.

IMPROVING PARENTAL INVOLVEMENT AT THE HIGH SCHOOL LEVEL

In addition to schools in the Socorro Independent School District, there are other examples of Texas schools taking proactive measures to increase parental involvement and academic achievement. For instance, Roosevelt High School in Dallas is part of the Alliance School Initiatives. The "initiative is a partnership between the Texas Interfaith Education Fund (TIEF), whose separate chapters statewide include the Dallas Area Interfaith (DAI), the Texas Industrial Areas Foundation (TIAF) Network, and the Texas Education Agency (TEA). Many Alliance schools enroll large proportions of students from minority families living in low-income communities" (Family Involvement in Children's Education, 1997b, p. 1).

Parental involvement has increased significantly through the support of the Alliance and through the ongoing efforts of Roosevelt's administration, faculty, staff, parents, and other community members. In addition, the levels of achievement of Roosevelt High School increased significantly within 4 years of the initial implementation of this program. For instance, Roosevelt improved writing (from the 58th to the 80th percentile), reading (from the 40th to the 80th percentile), and mathematics (from the 16th to the 70th percentile) on standardized achievement tests.

One of the primary ways that Roosevelt High School increased levels of academic achievement was by improving parental involvement. Previously, parents—even those who attended PTO meetings—were not actively involved in the decision-making processes of schools nor were they asked to be, and most of the parents who attended PTO meetings were the parents of high academic achievers.

Consequently, the administration attempted to improve communication with all parents but especially with those parents whose children were failing one or more classes. To make sure that parents were aware of their children's academic performance, a core group of parents, teachers, and the principal delivered directly to parents the report cards of students who had one or more failing grades. In addition, teachers were later required to document that they notified parents whose children were failing a class, and this measure was required to be completed by teachers before a student was placed on academic probation.

Other ways that communication was enhanced between parents and the administration/faculty of Roosevelt High School was by giving parents opportunities to provide their input through information attained during meetings and through questionnaires and surveys. Many parents began to understand that their views and concerns did matter, and they felt welcomed to become an important part of the school's reform/improvement plan. In addition, a compact or official statement, which all parents, students, and teachers signed, was developed to improve communication between the school and parents. Components of the pact include requirements for homework assignments and communication between parents, teachers, and students.

Other measures also were taken to support parental involvement. For example, the school district provided workshops/classes on such topics as how to help their children with homework, how to improve students' reading or math scores on standardized tests, or how to develop effective study skills. Other classes focused on topics such as improving adult literacy and parenting skills. Also, Roosevelt High School hired a parent liaison, whose primary purpose is to inform parents about academic or disciplinary issues in addition to information about school-related meetings and activities. These innovative methods significantly improved parental involvement and the academic achievement of a formerly low achieving school.

CONCLUSION

Parental involvement is a critical component of any classroom and school improvement plan. Positive effects such as higher grades and standardized test scores, better attendance, decreases in discipline problems, higher levels of job satisfaction among teachers, and more positive relationships are common is parental involvement plans are effective and implemented well. When teachers and administrators work collaboratively with parents to improve parental involvement at the classroom, school, district, and community levels, parents tend to become more involved in school activities and their children's learning. Equally important, the input of parents in the decision-making processes of schools is essential because parents provide school personnel with valuable knowledge about their children. Educators need the support of parents just as parents need supportive educators for their children. Schools can no longer exclude parents from the processes of school improvement because they are a bridge between home and school cultures. As our society becomes more diverse, parental involvement will become an even more important component of effective teaching and school improvement.

CLASS ACTIVITY

View the DVD "The Early Career Teacher's Guide to Success in the Classroom Your Partners at Home: Working with Your Students' Parents" (Clear Channel The Master Teacher, Leadership Lane, P.O. Box 1207, Manhattan, Kansas 66505 www.masterteacher.com, 2006, ISBN: 1-58992-250-6).

Have the students follow along using the outline of the DVD (below) and write their own notes on a separate sheet of paper.

Introduction

Chances are good that you understand how important parental involvement is to student success. A parent's interest in and support of the school and teacher send a clear message to the student that education is a top priority in the family. You will find yourself dealing with parents in many different situations and circumstances so you need to be prepared to deal with anger, resistance, or a simple lack of understanding about how important parents can be in their child's academic success.

DVD Outline-Four Topics

CREATING OPPORTUNITIES FOR POSITIVE CONTACT WITH PARENTS

- Parents will be curious about the credentials and background of a new teacher. In particular, they will be looking for the ways you demonstrate your commitment to their child's academic achievement and well-being.

- Use every chance to communicate with parents about yourself and the benefits their child will receive from being in your class. Back-to-school night should be just the beginning of your efforts.

- Write letters to parents early in the school year explaining a little about yourself and follow up with weekly newsletters, if possible. Keep parents abreast of what's going on in your classroom so they can support your efforts at home.

- Give parents contact information including your phone number and email address. Explain to them how they can best contact you during the school day. Return all calls and emails promptly!

- Make phone calls to at least one household a week, if possible. Have at least one, sincere compliment to make about the student and give parents a chance to talk about their child, air any concerns they may have, and share anything special about the child you should know.

TURNING ANGRY PARENTS INTO ALLIES

- When dealing with parents who are angry, try to focus on the child's behavior or performance. Don't label the child but instead describe the problem that must be solved. Parents will be less defensive and more open to your suggestions if you take this tack.

- Ask a lot of questions and restate the answers so you can be sure you are understanding the parents' true concerns. Never forget that this is their child you're talking about! Take parents seriously and be sensitive to their issues.

- Be prepared with concrete suggestions for how everybody can contribute to a solution but be open to ideas from the parents as well. Give the parents regular feedback and keep them posted on progress or lack of it. Many problems take a good deal of time and effort to solve.

- Sometimes it's best to involve someone such as an administrator in a difficult situation. Another person's perspective can often be helpful. And remember that any time you feel physically threatened, you must remove yourself from the encounter and get help.

BUILDING YOUR CREDIBILITY AS A PROFESSIONAL

- To demonstrate your regard for a student's well-being, ask a lot of questions when you get a chance to chat with parents. Some questions you should ask might include: What information do you believe I need in order to reach and teach your child? What is your child good at? What does your child struggle with? May I call or email you when I have questions or concerns?

- Be ready to discuss what you have planned for the year with parents. Parents want to know what their child will be learning that year and some of them will want information about state academic standards and how your lessons address them.

- Parents will also want to know what your discipline philosophy is and how you handle classroom management. How do you maintain order? What steps will you follow when a serious incident occurs? How will you involve parents in discipline matters?

- Parents also want to know how they can help their child succeed in school so be ready with concrete suggestions about how much children should read each day or how valuable a quiet place to study is.

WORKING TOGETHER TO SOLVE PROBLEMS CONSTRUCTIVELY

- Sometimes parents have barriers to working productively with school personnel. If parents had negative experiences themselves as students, or if they have language or economic issues that make communicating or even getting to the school difficult, school may not seem like a welcoming or cooperative place.

- Work to establish a climate of equality and mutual dependence. Reinforce to the parents continually that you are all on the same side and all want good things for the student. Emphasize that your concern is the child's welfare.

- Don't overload parents with more than one concern at a time. Keep the scope of the problem small and then, when that problem is solved, you can move on to other goals, building on your success. And always do what you've promised to do.

Homework Assignment

Directions: You are going to synthesize all the information from your resources and the DVD into a faculty newsletter.

DISCUSSION ACTIVITIES

1. Interview at least two teachers and discuss how they involve parents in their children's learning and in school activities. Write a short report to summarize their methods to involve parents. Also, discuss how you will include parents in their children's learning.

2. Read several articles about the effects of parental involvement on academic achievement. Write an essay about how parental involvement enhances students' academic achievement and how you will include parents in the learning of their children.

Sample Test Questions

1. In May, a second-grade teacher feels the need to prepare the parents of her students for the following school year. With the increased emphasis on reading success for third graders, she wants to make sure the parents are aware of how they can build a partnership with the third-grade teachers and positively impact their students' success in the next grade.

   a. She holds a meeting for parents to explain the typical developmental growth for third graders.

   b. She holds a meeting for parents and reminds them of the ways they provided the students a home environment that fostered school success and asks them to continue this in the third grade.

   c. She arranges a visit to the third-grade classrooms to give the teachers an opportunity to meet the parents and the children and to share their expectations of themselves, the students, and the parents.

   d. She invites the parents to meet with her so she can share the credentials of the third-grade teachers and their test scores to date in order to reassure the parents that their students are going to be taught by capable teachers.

2. Parents of a middle school student named Carlos contact the eighth-grade team leader to express their concerns for their son's grades. They ask for an appointment to discuss appropriate ways to assist Carlos in his schoolwork.

   a. The eighth-grade team leader meets with the parents and explains that she has spoken with the other teachers on the team to get suggestions for the parents. They suggest providing a regular quiet place for Carlos to study at home with the expectation for assistance from the parents at home as needed.

   b. The eighth-grade team leader meets with the parents and shares some perspectives of the eighth-grade team. They suggest that the parents provide Carlos with a quiet place to study and sit with him to help him with the schoolwork.

   c. The eighth-grade team leader meets with the parents and discusses a plan she has devised. She wants the parents to communicate on a weekly basis in writing about Carlos's study habits.

   d. The eighth-grade team leader meets with the parents and outlines a plan of action. This includes the teachers communicating at the end of each week so that the parents will know if Carlos has earned a preplanned reward or punishment.

3. The parents of a tenth grader call the school to request a conference with the tenth-grade science teacher. When they arrive the parents express their dissatisfaction with the heavy load of homework and high expectations of their ninth grader. How can the teacher ensure that this meeting with the parents will yield positive results?

   a. The teacher can ask what the parents want him to do.

   b. The teacher can listen to the parents as they share their concerns and then tell them that no other parents have called with this concern.

   c. The teacher can listen to the parents' concern and then explain the rationale for the amount of work for the course.

   d. The teacher can explain that she has decreased the amount of work this year in comparison to other years and give examples of other teachers who assign even more homework.

Answers

1. A is not correct. It is a good idea, but it is too focused and narrow in scope. Parents need that and more.

    B is not correct. It is another good idea for parents, but the suggestion might be considered condescending to some parents. She can thank them for their support for the current year, but it is up to the next level of teachers to ask this of the parents.

    C is the correct answer. If her goal is to communicate with parents about the following school year and to inform them about the grade level expectations and pressures from assessments, this will adequately prepare parents for the change.

    D is not correct. It is not appropriate for the teacher to do this for the next grade-level teacher. The teachers at the next level can do this more effectively for themselves.

2. **A is the correct answer.** The team leader has spoken with the other teachers, and they suggest a plan of action that is not too prescriptive for the parents. The parents must make the final decision on how much assistance to provide for Carlos.

    B is not correct. This selection is similar to the first answer with the stipulation that the parents sit with Carlos as he works. The teachers don't need to make this suggestion to the parents. This is too prescriptive and the parents need to make that call.

    C is not correct. The team leader is telling the parents what to do without input from the other team members.

    D is not correct. It could be part of a solution, however, there is no mention of specific suggestions for improving work.

3. A is not correct. It implies the parents will make homework decisions for the student when the teacher is responsible for that type of decision.

    B is not correct. It does nothing to explain the situation to the parents. Instead, this solution compares these parents to others, which they do not want to hear. It is not an explanation for their concern.

    C is the correct answer. The teacher is not on the defensive and can explain the reasoning behind the homework and high expectations.

    D is not correct. It does not address the reasoning for the work or high expectations. The parents will not care what happened in previous years or with other teachers. It is unprofessional for the teacher to make comparisons with her expectations and those of others in this way.

REFERENCES

Anyon, J. (1997). *Ghetto schooling: A political economy of urban school reform.* New York: Teachers College Press.

Banks, J. A. (2001). *Cultural diversity and education: Foundations, curriculum, and teaching* (4th ed.). Boston: Allyn & Bacon

Banks, J. A. (2002). *An introduction to multicultural education* (3rd ed.). Boston: Allyn & Bacon.

Bianchi, S., & Robinson, J. (1997). What did you do today?: Children's use of time, family composition, and the acquisition of social capital. *Journal of Marriage and Family, 59,* 332–344.

Clark, C. S. (1995). Parents and schools. *CQ-Researcher, 5*(3), 51–69.

Clark, R. M. (1983). *Family life and school achievement: Why poor black children succeed or fail.* Chicago: University of Chicago Press.

Coleman, J. S., Campbell, E. Q., Hobson, C. J., McPartland, J., & York, R. L. (1966). *Equality of educational opportunity.* Washinsgton, DC: U. S. Government Printing Office.

Comer, J. P. (1988). Educating poor minority children. *Scientific American, 259,* 47–58.

Comer, J. (1995). School power: *Implications for an intervention project.* New York: Free Press.

Comer, J. P., Haynes, N. M., Joyner, E. T., & Ben-Avie, M. (1996). *Rallying the whole village: The Comer process for reforming education.* New York: Teachers College Press.

Cushner, K., McClelland, A., & Safford, P. (2003). *Human diversity in education: An integrative approach* (4th ed.). New York: McGraw-Hill.

Family Involvement in Children's Education. (1997a, October). *Hueco Elementary School: Promoting cultural understanding and communication in a rural school.* Available at http://www.ed.gov/pubs/FamInvolve/rhs.html.

Family Involvement in Children's Education. (1997b, October). *Roosevelt High School (The Alliance Schools Initiative): An inner-city high school joins a statewide effort.* Available at http://www.ed.gov/pubs/FamInvolve/rhs.html.

Finders, M., & Lewis, C. (1994). Why some parents don't come to school. *Educational Leadership, 51*(8), 50–54.

Gestwicki, C. (1996). *Home, school, and community relations* (3rd ed.). Albany, NY: Delmar.

Henderson, A., & Berla, N. (1994). *A new generation of evidence: The family is critical to school improvement.* Washington, DC: National Committee for Citizens in Education, Center for Law and Education.

Kaplan, D., Liu, X., & Kaplan, H. (2001). Influence of parents' self-feelings and expectations on children's academic performance. *Journal of Educational Research, 95*(6), 360–365.

Klassen-Endrizzi, C. (2000). Exploring our literacy beliefs with families. *Language Arts, 78*(1), 62–70.

Mansbach, S. C. (1993). We must put family literacy on the national agenda. *Reading Today, 37,* 37–42.

McNergney, R. F., & McNergney, J. M. (2004). *Foundations of education: The challenge of professional practice* (4th ed.). New York: Pearson Education.

Sadker, P. S., & Sadker, D. M. (1997). *Teachers, schools, and society* (4th ed.). New York: McGraw-Hill.

Slavin, R.E.,Karweit, N.L., & Wasik, B.A. (1992). Preventing Early School Failure: What Works? *Educational Leadership, 50(4).* 10–18.

Wade, R. C., & Saxe, D. W. (1996). Community service-learning in the social studies: Historical roots, empirical evidence, and critical issues. *Theory and Research in Social Education, 24*(4), 331–359.

Yates, M., & Youniss, J. (1996). Community service and political-moral identity in adolescents. *Journal of Research on Adolescence, 6*(3), 271–284.

Websites

http://www.tea.state.tx.us/nclb/QandA2002/policyguide.htm
Texas Education Agency site for Titles I–VII, including parent involvement in the Title I program.

http://www.tea.state.tx.us/comm/page2.html

TEA site with *Texas Education Today*, the state's official education communication for the public. Various editions of the publication are accessible with Adobe Reader.

http://www.tea.state.tx.us/comm/page1.html

TEA site with current press releases listed by topic and archives available back to 1999.

http://www.sbec.state.tx.us/SBECOnline/default.asp

TEA State Board of Education and Certification site devoted to information about becoming a teacher in Texas.

http://www.responsiveclassroom.org/

Website devoted to the responsive classroom with a free newsletter.

http://cte.udel.edu/TAbook/climate.html

Website focused on a positive classroom climate.

http://www.education-world.com/a_curr/curr155.shtml

Excellent website devoted to a plethora of educational issues including classroom climate.

online.fsu.edu/learningresources/handbook/instructionatfsu/PDF-Chptr5

Adobe PDF document of a textbook chapter addressing classroom management and climate.

Competency 12 _ _ _ _ _ _ _ _ _ _ _ _ _ _ _ _ _

Reflective Practice and Professional Responsibilities

Teri Bingham, EdD
West Texas A&M University

Angela Spaulding, EdD
West Texas A&M University

> **Competency 12:** The teacher enhances professional knowledge and skills by effectively interacting with other members of the educational community and participating in various types of professional activities.

The beginning teacher:

A. Interacts appropriately with other professionals in the school community (e.g., vertical teaming, horizontal teaming, team teaching, mentoring).

B. Maintains supportive, cooperative relationships with professional colleagues and collaborates to support students' learning and to achieve campus and district goals.

C. Knows the roles and responsibilities of specialists and other professionals at the building and district levels (e.g., department chairperson, principal, board of trustees, curriculum coordinator, technology coordinator, special education professional).

D. Understands the value of participating in school activities and contributes to school and district (e.g., decision making and problem solving, sharing ideas and expertise, serving on committees, volunteering to participate in events and projects).

E. Uses resources and support systems effectively (e.g., mentors, service centers, state initiatives, universities) to address professional development needs.

F. Recognizes characteristics, goals, and procedures associated with teacher appraisal and uses appraisal results to improve teaching skills.

G. Works productively with supervisors, mentors, and other colleagues to address issues and to enhance professional knowledge and skills.

H. Understands and uses professional development resources (e.g., mentors and other support systems, conferences, online resources, workshops, journals, professional associations, coursework) to enhance knowledge, pedagogical skills, and technological expertise.

I. Engages in reflection and self-assessment to identify strengths, challenges, and potential problems; improves teaching performance; and achieves professional goals.

KEY TERMS

apprenticeship of observation
collaboration
domains of knowledge
ERIC
field experiences
horizontal teaming
knowledge base
PDAS

peer coaching
portfolios
principals
prior knowledge
professional journals
Professional Learning Communities
reflection
reflective practitioner

regional support center
school boards
site-based management
stages of concern
superintendents
teacher as researcher
vertical teaming

THE REFLECTIVE TEACHER

Mindful reflecting on our life, and life in general, is so critical to our personal growth that philosophers and teachers throughout the centuries advocated self-reflection as an avenue of personal growth. For instance, over 2,400 years ago Socrates said, "The unexamined life is not worth living." Socrates believed life is too important not to live deliberately and mindfully.

Without constant professional growth a person is not able to perform at his or her highest levels of effectiveness. As the knowledge base of every profession continues to increase rapidly each year, professionals apply new conceptual knowledge to the constantly changing contexts of their work environments and must evaluate and understand the consequences of their actions to make prudent decisions that affect the lives of those they serve. For instance, physicians who stay current with the latest medical research and who carefully and reflectively examine their patients are more apt to diagnose a patient's malady correctly than are those physicians who do not study the latest medical research.

Like physicians, educators must make numerous professional decisions that affect the lives of others. Because teaching is a complex, higher cognitive activity, educators also must reflect on the consequences of their instructional decisions to maximize student learning and to foster a positive classroom climate (Richardson & Placier, 2001). In fact, deliberate reflection is so critical to the development of expertise in teaching that the State of Texas has devoted Competency 12 to the development of reflective practice and professional responsibilities.

Cognitive Learning Theory and Preservice Teachers' Background Knowledge

Researchers have found that one's **prior knowledge** is a critical factor in learning new concepts (Collins, Brown, & Holum, 1991; Glaser, 1984; Resnick & Klopfer, 1989). In other words, if one is able to link one's background knowledge to new concepts, then one typically will learn more easily and effectively. The influential role of preservice teachers' background knowledge in learning to teach is no exception. Although most students in teacher education programs have not taught in accredited schools as full-time teachers and have not planned and taught lessons on a daily basis, preservice teachers know much more about teaching than they realize because they have observed many teachers during their K–12 experiences. As noted by Lortie (1975) in his classic and frequently cited study, most individuals who become teachers have observed their own teachers from between 14,000 to 16,000 hours during what he calls their "**apprenticeship of observation**"; consequently, preservice teachers have extensive prior knowledge about teaching and schools before they take their first educations course.

In his interviews with 94 teachers, Lortie (1975) found that the apprenticeship of observation is very significant because this is the time in which a future teacher's conception of teaching and learning is formed. Consider, for example, how much most people would understand about law, lawyers, judges, and courtroom procedures if they had the opportunity to observe courtroom events on a daily basis for several years. They would understand many aspects of criminal and civil law even if one had not formally studied the law. Teaching is no exception in this respect, and many of the teachers whom Lortie interviewed noted that their decisions to teach and the ways that they did teach lessons were strongly influenced by their own teachers, whom they observed on a daily basis.

Their apprenticeship of observation is one of the most robust determinants of how one will teach and is their schemata of how classrooms are run and how lessons are taught.

Since most teachers are profoundly influenced by their apprenticeship of observation, it is important that preservice teachers are cognizant of ways that their teachers and school experiences have influenced their own conceptions of both teaching itself and the type of teachers that they hope to become (Feiman-Nemser & Remillard, 1996). Nevertheless, there are problems with relying on the models of one's former teachers, and although these models are valuable, they may not reflect current research and best practices. Beginning teachers must learn as much as possible about current research to foster student learning (Richardson & Placier, 2001). Equally problematic, the knowledge base of teaching is extensive—perhaps much more so than most people assume from their experiences during their apprenticeships of observation.

The Knowledge Base of Teaching

As noted by Shulman (1987), effective teachers must acquire knowledge and expertise in the following areas:

1. *Content knowledge*—knowledge of the particular subjects to be taught such as mathematics, English, or history.
2. *Pedagogical content knowledge*—the special amalgam of content and pedagogy that is uniquely the province of teachers, their own special form of professional understanding.
3. *Knowledge of learners and their characteristics*—understanding the diverse and complex needs of each student.
4. *General pedagogical knowledge*—with special reference to those broad principles and strategies of classroom management that appear to transcend subject matter.
5. *Knowledge of educational contexts*—ranging from the workings of the group or classroom, to the governance and financing of school districts, to the character of communities and cultures.
6. *Curriculum knowledge*—with a particular grasp of the materials and programs that serve as tools of the trade for teachers.
7. *Knowledge of educational ends, purposes, and values*—understanding the philosophical and historical grounds of each of these. (pp. 2–3)

The implications of Shulman's knowledge base of teaching are that the acquisition of expertise in several areas is necessary for effective teaching and that developing such expertise takes considerable time and effort. A preservice teacher's apprenticeship of observation and pedagogical training, which includes coursework, student teaching, and other education-related activities and studies, are a good beginning of the development of his or her professional knowledge. But, learning to teach and the acquisition of expertise in teaching take many hours of hard work, patience, and mindful reflection on one's practice.

Reflective Practice and Learning to Teach

Since the 1980s, teacher education programs throughout the United States have stressed reflective practice as a key component in learning to teach (Grimmett & Erickson, 1988). However, even in the early 1900s, John Dewey (1904, 1993) emphasized the importance of **reflection** in learning processes, and he stressed that people learn through their experiences if they understand the consequences and implications of events and ideas. Conversely, if people do not reflect meaningfully on and understand the significance of important concepts and events, then little learning occurs. During their reflecting is a time for teachers to recognize cause-and-effect behaviors, triggers and patterns. Imagine, for instance, that students are completing a laboratory in a high school biology class. The students carefully follow and reflect upon the laboratory procedures as they collect, record, and analyze their data. From this process, they write a report of their findings. Students who reflected on their data and understand how it applies to scientific concepts will learn much more from this instructional experience than students who did not make these conceptual connections. Mindful reflection on the significance of one's experiences is a key component for learning, whether one is a first-grade student or a veteran teacher.

Dewey advised teachers to consider carefully and deliberately the consequences of their actions and instructional plans so that they are able both to understand the implications of lessons and to improve their instructional practices. The reflective cycle of setting goals, planning instruction, reflectively evaluating one's progress, and trying to find more efficacious ways to accomplish one's instructional goals is pivotal for effective teaching, as exemplified in the teaching of Sylvia Ashton-Warner (1963), who developed her own theories about reading instruction from her experiences teaching Maori children in New Zealand.

Ashton-Warner (1963) found that traditional theories of teaching reading were effective for students of British heritage but not for Maori children, who did not have the background knowledge to prepare them for the traditional types of readers. Consequently, she designed her own materials, which used the background knowledge and interests of the Maori children as a beginning and pivotal point of her instruction. By constantly reflecting on and evaluating the consequences of her pedagogy, she created her own theory and methods of instruction for successfully teaching Maori children.

In other words, her theory guided her practice, and her reflections on her practice enabled her to refine her theory of teaching Maori children. Like Dewey (1916), Ashton-Warner believed that theory and practice are interwoven and are like two different sides of the same coin. No matter whether we see the "heads side" or the "tails side" of a quarter, we still have a quarter. In this respect, both sides of a quarter are important just as both theory and practice complement each other. Without sound theories to guide their practice, teachers may not use appropriate methods to guide their lesson planning. In addition, reflective teachers use their practical knowledge of learning, lessons, and students to revise their theoretical understanding of teaching and learning. During his long career as an educator, Dewey (1904) frequently tested his theories of teaching and learning in the classroom context, as did Ashton-Warner (1963).

More recently, Schon (1987) added an important aspect of reflection for professional educators. He concurred with Dewey that teachers must reflect on their actions before and after teaching a lesson, but, in addition, he believed that teachers must reflect on their teaching during their interactive lessons. Schon refers to the ability to reflect while one teaches as reflection-in-action. Teachers who use reflection-in-action efficaciously are able to *monitor and adjust* their instructional decisions during lessons to enhance student learning. In other words, teachers may determine from student feedback that they need to alter the course of their lesson to enhance student learning. Developing the expertise to reflect meaningfully on one's practice is a key aspect of learning to teach because it enables one to make sense of the fast-moving and often unpredictable aspects of the classroom environment (Munby, Russell, & Martin, 2001).

RESEARCH ON TEACHER DEVELOPMENT

To become experts in their profession, teachers typically progress through developmental stages during their acquisition of expertise. Fuller (1969) was one of the first researchers to develop a theory of developmental stages for teachers, and she conceptualized learning to teach with the following **stages of concern**: (1) survival concerns; (2) teaching situation concerns; and (3) pupil concerns. In stage one, Fuller stressed that most beginning teachers are concerned primarily about their own ability to survive their first year of teaching and about the adequacy of their teaching. Teachers in this stage usually are more worried about whether or not their peers and students will like them and value their work than whether or not their students are learning to their optimal capacities. This is not to suggest that teachers in this stage do not plan and implement effective lessons, but that they typically are worried about other aspects of teaching such as classroom management and maintaining control. For beginning teachers in this stage, classroom management is their primary concern. This, of course, makes sense because teachers will have difficulty implementing even brilliantly planned lessons if their classroom management skills are ineffective.

© altafulla, 2014, Used under license of shutterstock, inc.

Fuller's second stage of teacher development is called teaching situations concerns. In this stage, teachers have resolved most of their problems with classroom management and have gained confidence in their teaching. At this point, they are effective teachers and are concentrating on improving their lessons and adding new methods to their repertoire of instructional strategies. However, most teachers do not become expert teachers until the third development stage, the pupil concerns stage.

In the pupil concerns stage, teachers are comfortable with their curriculum and pedagogical methods without becoming complacent in their teaching contexts. At this point, a teacher's primary focus is on student learning. In other words, a teacher's classroom management is very effective and classroom routines unfold smoothly. The teacher has developed a wider range of efficacious instructional strategies that are appropriately matched to assignments and learner needs. In addition, teachers at this stage are concerned about the affective aspects of their classroom environments, especially in terms of how a positive classroom environment enhances student learning. The teacher zero's in an student success and asks himself, "are my students learning?"

More recently, Berliner (1994) developed another version of teacher development, which is based to some extent on the extensive research of the differences in cognitive processes of experts and novices. As indicative of the body of research on expert-novice studies on teaching (Borko, Bellamy, & Sanders, 1992; Kagan & Tippins, 1992; Peterson & Comeaux, 1987), there are significant differences in the ways that experts and novices process information about curriculum, instruction, and classroom events. Experts, for example, are more likely to interpret various aspects of teaching through the lens of their rich knowledge base of teaching and learning and, therefore, are more apt to give classroom events a more conceptualized interpretation than novice teachers usually are able to do (Bereiter & Scardamalia, 1993; McIntyre & Hagger, 1993).

In contrast, novice teachers often focus on the surface level of key events without understanding their complete significance. However, this does not imply that novice teachers are not making a positive impact on student learning; instead, the implication is that as novice teachers' schemata of instructional activities becomes more and more developed, the quality of their pedagogical decisions improves (Carter, 1990). Novice teachers just need opportunities to teach and to reflect on the consequences of their instructional decisions in terms of how they were played out as curriculum events during their interactive teaching sessions.

Like Fuller, Berliner (1994) posits that teachers progress through various stages of development: novice, advanced beginner, competent, proficient, and expert. However, Berliner does not believe that all teachers reach the proficient and expert levels despite many years of experience. Some teachers may reach and stay at the competent stage, never progressing to the expert level. Although one has the opportunity to learn from one's teaching experiences, not all teachers habitually reflect mindfully on their experiences to ensure continuous growth throughout their teaching careers. Teaching is a complex cognitive activity; consequently, it is not surprising that learning to teach—in terms of beginning at the novice stage and reaching the expert stage—requires constant reflectivity, professional development activities, and time. Beginning teachers should not expect to reach the expert stage in a couple of years because expert teachers did not develop their understanding of the complexities of teaching quickly.

PROFESSIONAL DEVELOPMENT AND COLLABORATION

Most teacher education programs require various **field experiences** for their preservice teachers. Field experiences provide preservice teachers valuable opportunities to observe and work with classroom teachers, and these experiences are especially productive if the interconnections of theory and practice are addressed (Dewey, 1916; Winitzky & Kauchauk, 1997). For example, preservice teachers may take extended field notes of an observed lesson, and then may analyze the data in terms of one or more specific themes (e.g., classroom management or questioning strategies). Such analyses enable preservice teachers (1) to examine the ways that activities unfold during interactive lessons, and (2) to apply educational research to their interpretations of the observed classroom events (Posner, 2000). When pre-service teachers work in collaboration with a mentor teacher in the classroom it provides an opportunity for the neophyte to learn in a real-world environment. Field experiences can bridge higher education to the realities of the classroom.

Similarly, many teacher education programs have expanded their field experiences with professional development schools. Another way to enhance the professional growth of teachers is through school-university partnerships that are established through professional development schools. Professional development schools (PDS) are elementary, middle, or high schools that have formed a partnership with a college or university for the purpose of reciprocal professional development. Such partnerships enable teacher education faculties to work closely with teachers to train preservice teachers within a school context. This allows preservice teachers to practice newly learned teaching strategies in a real-life classroom. Reciprocally, classroom teachers are afforded opportunities to restructure and reaffirm their own teaching practices as they learn about new research. In the PDS format, university and public school faculties often develop field experiences for preservice teachers, collaborate on research on best practices, and provide professional development. In short, professional development schools are advantageous opportunities for both university and public school faculties to create opportunities for reflective collaboration and opportunities for constructive feedback on their interactive lessons or curriculum (Darling-Hammond, 1999). Equally important, professional development schools provide preservice teachers with opportunities to learn how to collaborate with other teachers because working in various types of collaborative and/or team settings are part of a teacher's professional responsibilities.

Mentoring Programs

For example, some districts have formal **peer coaching** programs that encourage collaborative reflection that empower teachers to improve their practice. Peer coaching programs usually consist of dyads of experienced and novice teachers or dyads of teachers at different stages of concern, according to the aforementioned stages of Fuller (1969). In these programs, teachers guide one another's practice and provide feedback about how to improve their practice and how to evaluate their teaching in more productive ways (McIntyre & Hagger, 1993). In the cases of the beginning and experienced teacher dyads, experienced teachers often serve as models for beginning teachers. However, this is not to imply that experienced teachers do not learn from these coaching

© Lightspring, 2014, Used under license of shutterstock, Inc.

sessions as well. Beginning teachers, for example, may provide experienced teachers with fresh insights about teaching. Another benefit of peer coaching is that teachers are able to collaborate in an emotionally safe environment, which fosters peer-to-peer support and encouragement (Reed & Bergemann, 1992).

Teaming and Other Collaborative Activities

Another professional responsibility that fosters collaborative and reflective practice is teaming. Most school districts have developed faculty teams to enable teachers to work together to improve the curriculum and instructional practices for a given grade level, content area, or schoolwide area of focus. Teachers, for example, must become increasingly knowledgeable of the Texas Essential Knowledge and Skills (TEKS), which are delineated for grade levels and content areas. The TEKS are a content or curriculum guide for teachers as they prepare their students for the State of Texas Assessments of Academic Readiness (STAAR), which are criterion-referenced tests. The STAAR assesses students' knowledge and competencies in mathematics, science, social studies, reading, and writing. Because the STAAR tests are aligned with the TEKS, it is critical that teachers collaborate with colleagues at both the building and district levels to ensure that all teachers are supported in their instructional efforts of efficacious curriculum alignment.

Most districts use both vertical and horizontal teaming. **Vertical teaming** typically requires teachers to work with teachers who are one grade or level above them and one below. For example, a third-grade teacher may work with both a second- and a fourth-grade teacher to ensure that the curriculum from second through fourth grade is sequenced logically to maximize learning and to ensure students will have the prerequisite skills from one level to the next. Conversely, **horizontal teaming** provides teachers with opportunities to work with teachers from their own grade level or content area. For instance, all third-grade teachers may collaborate to improve their mathematics curriculum. Both vertical and horizontal teaming are effective ways to improve a school's curriculum and instructional practices, and each of these teams complements the other.

Collaborative activities, whether they take the form of teams, committees, or discussions about one's formal teaching evaluations, are integral components of a teachers' professional growth. These activities provide ways for teachers to enhance both their abilities to reflect on their instructional practice and their opportunities to collaborate with their peers. Most teachers will serve on a wide variety of committees or teams during their careers. For instance, teachers often serve on textbook adoption teams with other teachers, administrators, and parents, or they work on calendar committees that plan yearly school events. Sometimes teachers work in teams to improve their adaptations of their instructional methods and activities to enhance the learning of students with special needs. It is important that teachers serve on schoolwide committees even if the content of the committee does not directly involve their classroom duties so that they understand their own school culture more fully (Darling-Hammond, 1999).

Professional Responsibilities and Teacher Reflection

As previously noted, collaborative activities are important professional responsibilities and opportunities for reflective practice. However, teachers also must engage in individual activities to enhance their professional growth. One way to foster reflective practice is through conducting research on one's own teaching. For example, Hollingsworth (1995) emphasized the importance of the **teacher as researcher** model to improve one's practice. This model emphasizes the importance of teachers conducting research on various aspects of their teaching. This assists teachers in improving all aspects of their teaching. Such research is especially effective if teachers collaborate with their peers and exchange their perspectives and pedagogical expertise.

Regional Educational Support Centers

Another way to enhance the professional growth of teachers is through the educational opportunities offered by regional **educational support centers**. The purpose of the regional educational support centers is to deliver services and training to enhance student learning and professional development for teachers, administrators, and other school personnel. In addition, regional educational support centers disseminate important information from the Texas Education Agency to the local school districts, so that statewide initiatives can be implemented. Because the school population in Texas is quite diversified, the training and other professional development opportunities that the support centers offer educators is becoming increasing critical.

Staff Development

Like the regional support centers, staff development programs offer teachers the opportunities to build on their professional knowledge. For instance, it is not uncommon for districts to conduct workshops and other training sessions to assist teachers with various aspects of teaching such as classroom management, teaching techniques, multicultural education, or effective assessment practices. In a sense, staff development is a continuation of a teacher's formal training and has the potential to improve instruction, especially if the school or district provides teachers with opportunities to practice the methods taught and to receive feedback about their performance (Smylie, Bay, & Tozer, 1999). Another way to enhance the efficacy of staff development programs is for teachers to serve on committees that plan and implement these programs. Participating on committees provides teachers the opportunity for reflection, creativity, and meaningful collaboration with other educators.

© My Life Graphic, 2014, Used under license of Shutterstock, Inc.

PDAS and Professional Growth

Providing ample feedback to teachers about their practice is an important aspect of instructional improvement and deliberate reflection. In Texas, the teaching performance of educators is formally assessed and teachers are provided feedback about their teaching. Most school districts in Texas use the Professional Assessment and Development System (**PDAS**) to evaluate teachers, although school districts are allowed to develop and use their own evaluation system. The PDAS, however, is the evaluation system that is recommended by the commissioner of education. Each teacher is evaluated annually by a supervisor or a designated appraiser, who was approved by the district's board of trustees. The PDAS concentrates primarily on assessing a teacher's performance in fostering student learning, implementing a management and discipline plan, and participating in professional development.

If a teacher is evaluated as unsatisfactory in any PDAS domain, then both the teacher and his or her evaluator will design an improvement plan, which specifically addresses the deficiency. Professional development activities usually are recommended in addition to a designated time frame for improvement. One of the strengths of the PDAS is that each teacher is required to assess his or her performance with the completion of the Teacher Self-Report Form, which is an important part of a teacher's annual evaluation process. Completing the Teacher Self-Report Form provides teachers with opportunities for self-reflection.

Professional Organizations and Educational Literature

In addition, it is important that professional educators belong to at least one professional organization. Membership has many benefits for the professional development of educators. The greatest benefit for teachers to join a professional organization is for the opportunity to network with others. For instance, Phi Delta Kappa and Kappa Delta Pi are national professional organizations, which have members throughout Texas and the entire nation. Both of these organizations publish well-respected **professional journals** 10 times annually. Another national organization is the Association for Supervision and Curriculum Development (ASCD), which has members from all education-related fields. ASCD provides free information related to educational research and also publishes a journal. Furthermore, some teachers prefer to belong to professional organizations that concentrate on teaching and learning in specific content areas. The National Council of Teachers of English or the National Council of Teachers of Mathematics are two well-known examples of content-related organizations. These organizations usually publish their own journals as well (Parkay & Sanford, 2004).

Another valuable resource is the Education Resources Information Center (ERIC). **ERIC** is a group of clearinghouses that enables one to search for specific topic areas or journal articles that are identified by the criteria of the ERIC selection that one selects by given descriptors. If teachers want to find journal articles that discuss discovery learning, for example, then descriptors can be used to identify pertinent resources that will help in their research.

THE PRINCIPALSHIP, SUPERINTENDENCY, AND SCHOOL BOARDS

In addition to reading professional journals and joining professional organizations, it is important for reflective teachers to become knowledgeable of the responsibilities of school administrators and school boards. Like superintendents, principals are the administrators who directly supervise and evaluate faculty and staff. Also, they schedule classes, manage school budgets and supplies, hold parent-teacher conferences, and administer discipline whenever necessary. **Principals** work at the building level and must have strong leadership skills to be effective. They must create and maintain a positive learning environment and gain the support of parents, students, and teachers. In short, an effective principal is a strong instructional leader who is able to articulate and implement an efficacious mission statement (Schlechty, 1990). Many school districts have implemented the policy of **site-based management,** which provides principals the freedom to make more decisions that directly affect their schools. Site-based management policies also enable principals to involve teachers and other professionals in the decision-making processes of school improvement.

Nevertheless, principals do not have total autonomy because they answer to their **superintendent**, who is the executive officer of a district. The school board expects the superintendent to implement its policies. A superintendent has many responsibilities such as maintaining facilities and funds as well as recruiting, selecting, or promoting personnel. Policies and changes about curriculum and instruction of the organization of the schools may originate with the superintendent, although the school board must approve such policies before they are implemented. In addition, a superintendent has the responsibility to create and maintain positive relations with the local community. Other school administrators answer to the superintendent, and large districts typically have several assistant superintendents to assist the superintendent in running a school district. For instance, it is common for large districts to have assistant superintendents of personnel, curriculum and instruction, business, and research and development.

As previously noted, superintendents are ultimately responsible to their local school board. **School boards** have considerable responsibilities to run a school district. For instance, they approve school budgets, directly hire and evaluate superintendents, and indirectly hire all employees—including principals and teachers (Reed & Bergemann, 1995). School boards in Texas must follow the Texas Open Meeting Law, which requires school boards to conduct open meetings unless the topics in question are allowed by law to be discussed in closed sessions. The agenda for each school board session must be posted in a public place for at least 72 hours before the meeting is designated to begin. The three to nine members of the school board vote on policies.

Teacher Licensure

Teachers are required to reapply for licensure every *5* years. To qualify the State Board for Educator Certification (SBEC) requires teachers to complete at least *150 hours* of continuing professional development.

CONCLUSION

Because teaching is a higher cognitive activity and because the knowledge base of teaching is extensive, meaningful reflection is essential in acquiring the expertise to progress from Fuller's (1969) survival concern stage to the pupil concerns stage. Socrates offered posterity a valuable insight about human nature and life itself when he stressed the importance of self-reflection and the need to avoid the pitfalls of the unexamined life. For teachers the unexamined practice is devoid of collaborative activities and professional development and sometimes leads to complacent ineffectiveness. On the other hand, **reflective practitioners** who mindfully examine the consequences of and improve their practice will find that teaching is a rewarding profession with many opportunities for professional growth and development.

© baldyrgan, 2014, Used under license of Shutterstock, Inc.

TIPS FOR COMPETENCY 12: REFLECTIVE PRACTICE AND PROFESSIONAL RESPONSIBILITIES

1. The purpose of a mentor is to observe and give feedback to the teacher regarding the teacher's perceived area of need. They should discuss this in advance and the mentor should focus on that area in order to give appropriate and desired feedback to the teacher.

2. Mentoring may include having a teacher observe other effective teachers.

3. The main purpose for joining professional organizations is for networking.

4. One way to stay current on trends in education is to subscribe to a professional journal.

5. Know the best use of aides is for one-on-one tutoring of a student, small-group work, and grading objective assignments.

6. Know the function of the campus decision-making committee (site-based management, decision making) is to get input from representatives from all parties and get input and ownership regarding goals, school mission, and focus. It provides an opportunity to share expertise. Members include teachers, administrators, counselors, librarians, and other staff (secretaries, custodians, lunch workers).

7. Gangs related or other extreme discipline problems go directly to the Principal, not the student's parents or faculty meeting.

Professional Learning Communities

1. When teaming, build on each other's skills as they apply to students. Try to avoid working in isolation. Don't duplicate efforts or repeat work, but use strengths.

2. PLCs:

   a. work together to increase student success.

   b. spend time planning together, doing lesson studies, and book studies, reviewing assessments, revising lessons, reviewing data from standardized assessments, and problem solving.

   c. experienced teachers mentor new faculty.

3. In some large schools students can be divided into smaller learning communities (pods, teams) to maintain quality of teacher instruction and increase awareness of students.

DISCUSSION ACTIVITIES AND OUTLINES

Interconnection between Theory and Practice

1. Theory influences practice and practice informs theory. Sometimes classroom practices lead to new theories.

Reflective Practitioner

1. For students to learn from/by their experiences they must mindfully reflect on the event and understand its significance.
2. As a reflective practitioner teachers reflect and modify their instruction before, during, and after.

Teacher as Collaborator

1. The ability and willingness to collaborate well with others is an important skill.
2. The greatest benefit of teacher collaboration, as it relates to students, is improving student learning opportunities and creating a more positive school climate.

Teaming

1. Vertical teaming
2. Horizontal teaming
3. PLCs

Stages of Teacher Development
Fuller's Stages of Concern:

   a. Survival concerns

   b. Teaching situation concerns

   c. Pupil concerns

Activities

1. It is important that preservice teachers elicit their tacit knowledge about teaching because, as previously noted, this is the beginning of a preservice teacher's knowledge base of teaching. Write a short essay about your apprenticeship of observation. Consider those teachers who had a significant impact on you. What aspects of their teaching would you like to imitate or not imitate? What are the dispositions and characteristics of effective teachers in general? Try to conceptualize your views of effective teaching and teachers so that you can articulate the type of teacher that you hope to become.

2. Observe a teacher's lesson and take extended field notes during your observation. Make charts or diagrams of the major classroom events. Select one theme and analyze the data through the lens of this selected theme. Then write a short report of what occurred during this interactive lesson. Use current research on best teaching practices to guide your interpretations of the classroom events.

Sample Test Questions

1. Mrs. Bransky, a new second-grade teacher, has prepared a science project for her students. She, however, is not sure her students will be able to complete her activity. Mrs. Bransky should:

   a. consult with other second-grade teachers.

   b. ask the district's science curriculum specialist for any suggestions or supplemental materials.

   c. ask the librarian for information about relevant science materials.

   d. All of the above

2. Ms. Williams, a fifth-grade teacher, notes that each year some of her incoming students lack an understanding of how to work cooperatively in groups. She realizes that all of them have had the same fourth-grade teacher. What is the best course of action for Ms. Williams?

   a. Share her observations with the building principal and teach cooperative skills early in the school year.

   b. Work with her horizontal and vertical teams to improve students' academic and social skills without mentioning or ridiculing any teacher.

   c. Omit group work at this time.

   d. Mention to the fourth-grade teacher that she has had to spend valuable instructional time on teaching social skills to the fifth graders because most of them do not know how to work effectively in groups.

3. Ms. Johnson, a ninth-grade teacher, notices that a new student who enters her class midyear cannot read the textbook for his freshman history class. The most appropriate first step for Ms. Johnson is to:

   a. Provide the student with audiotapes of the text.

   b. Ask the special education teacher to come to the history classroom to observe the new student because the student may have a reading disability and, therefore, may need to be tested provided that his parents concur.

   c. Arrange for the student to come after school for tutoring.

   d. Ask the principal to place the student in a resource room so that he may have assistance reading the history textbook.

Answers

1. A is not correct. It is prudent to collaborate with other teachers.

   B is not correct. Curriculum specialists are very helpful to classroom teachers.

   C is not correct. Librarians are very helpful for classroom teachers in that they are aware of many resources available for classroom teachers.

   D is the correct answer. Collaboration with other teachers, curriculum specialists, and librarians fosters reflective practice and opportunities for professional growth.

2. A is not correct. Although it is wise to teach students how to perform in cooperative learning groups, it is imprudent to criticize a peer.

B is the correct answer. Working in vertical and horizontal teams helps to ensure that all teachers teach similar concepts and skills.

C is not correct. The only way students will learn how to work well in groups is to be taught how to do so; therefore, if the teacher eliminates group work, they will not learn the necessary social skills to be capable of doing so.

D is not correct. Addressing a peer in a critical way does little good and, of course, there is the possibility that the teacher was able to improve students' social skills last year.

3. A is not correct, although providing the audio tapes probably will benefit the student.

B is the correct answer. The first step in getting help for a student who has special needs is to consult the building special education teacher. While the classroom teacher waits for the official diagnosis to proceed, she can help the student based on her own observations and on suggestions from the special education teacher.

C is not correct, even though tutoring is very helpful.

D is not correct. A principal does not have the authority to place a student in a special education classroom.

REFERENCES

Ashton-Warner, S. (1963). Teacher. New York: Touchstone.

Bereiter, C., & Scardamalia, M. (1993). *Surpassing ourselves: An inquiry into the nature and implications of expertise.* La Salle, IL: Open Court.

Borko, H., Bellamy, M. L., & Sanders, L. (1992). A cognitive analysis of patterns in science instruction by expert and novice teachers. In T. Russell & H. Munby (Eds.), *Teachers and teaching: From classroom to reflection.* London: Falmer Press.

Carter, K. (1990). Teachers' knowledge and learning to teach. In W. R. Houston (Ed.), *Handbook of research on teacher education* (pp. 291–310). New York: Macmillan.

Collins, A., Brown, J., & Holum, A. (1991). Cognitive apprenticeship: Making things visible. *American Educator*, 15, 38–46.

Darling-Hammond, L. (1999). Educating teachers for the next century: Rethinking practice and policy. In G. A. Griffin (Ed.), *The education of teachers* (pp. 221–256). Chicago: University of Chicago Press.

Dewey, J. (1904). The relation of theory to practice in education. In C. A. McMurry (Ed.), *The relation of theory to practice in the education of teachers* (Third Yearbook of the National Society for the Scientific Study of Education, Part I) (pp. 9–30). Chicago: University of Chicago Press.

Dewey, J. (1916). *Democracy and education: An introduction to the philosophy of education.* New York: The Free Press.

Dewey, J. (1993). *How we think: A restatement of the relation of reflective thinking to the educative process.* Chicago: Henry Regnery.

Feiman-Nemser, S., & Remillard, J. (1996). Perspectives on learning to teach. In F. B. Murray (Ed.), *The teacher educator's handbook: Building a knowledge base for the preparation of teachers* (pp. 63–91). San Francisco: Jossey-Bass.

Fuller, F. (1969). Concerns of teachers: A developmental conceptualization. *American Educational Research Journal, 6*, 207–226.

Glaser, R. (1984). Education and thinking: The role of knowledge. *American Psychologist, 39*, 93–104.

Grimmett, P. P., & Erickson, G. L. (Eds.). (1988). *Reflection in teacher education.* New York: Teachers College Press.

Holingsworth, S. (1995). Teachers as researchers. In L. W. Anderson (Ed.), *International encyclopedia of teaching and teacher education* (2nd ed., pp. 16-19). Oxford, UK: Pergamon Press.

Kagan, D. M., & Tippins, D. J. (1992). How US teachers "read" classroom performances. *Journal of Education for Teaching, 18*, 149–158.

Lortie, D. C. (1975). *Schoolteacher: A sociological study.* Chicago: University of Chicago Press.

McIntyre, D., & Hagger, H. (1993). Teachers' expertise and models of mentoring. In H. H. D. McIntyre & M. Wilkin (Eds.), *Mentoring: Perspectives on school-based teacher education* (pp. 86–102). London: Kogan Page.

Munby, M., Russell, T., & Martin, A.K. (2001). Teachers' knowledge and how it develops. In V. Richardson (Ed.), *Handbook of research on teaching* (4th ed., pp. 877–904). Washington, DC: American Educational Research Association.

Parkay, F. W., & Stanford, B. H. (2004). *Becoming a teacher* (6th ed.). New York: Allyn & Bacon.

Peterson, P., & Comeaux, M. (1987). Teachers' schemata for classroom events: The mental scaffolding of teacher thinking during classroom instruction. Teaching and Teacher Education, 3, 319–331.

Posner, G. J. (2000). *Field experience: A guide to reflective teaching* (5th ed.). New York: Allyn & Bacon.

Reed, A. J. S., & Bergemann, V. E. (1995). *In the classroom: An introduction to education.* Guilford, CT: Dushkin.

Reed, A. J. S., & Bergemann, V. E. (1992). *A guide to observation and participation in the classroom.* Guilford, CT: Dushkin.

Resnick, L. B., & Klopfer, L. E. (1989). Toward the thinking curriculum: An overview. In L. B. Resnick & L. E. Klopfer (Eds.), *Toward the thinking curriculum: Current cognitive research* (pp. 1–18). Alexandria: VA: Association for Supervision and Curriculum Development.

Richardson, V., & Placier, P. (2001). Teacher change. In V. Richardson (Ed.), *Handbook of Research on Teaching* (4th ed., pp. 905–947). Washington, DC: American Educational Research Association.

Schlechty, P. C. (1990). *Schools for the 21st century: Leadership imperatives for educational reform.* San Francisco: Jossey-Bass.

Schon, D. (1987). *Educating the reflective practitioner.* San Francisco: Josey-Bass.

Schunk, D. (2000). *Learning theories* (3rd ed.). Upper Saddle River, NJ: Merrill/Prentice Hall.

Shulman, L. S. (1987). Knowledge and teaching: Foundations of a new reform. *Harvard Education Review, 57,* 1–22.

Smylie, M. A., Bay, M., & Tozer, S. E. (1999). Preparing teachers as agents of change. In G. A. Griffin (Ed.). *The education of teachers* (pp. 18–62). Chicago: University of Chicago Press.

Winitsky, N., & Kauchauk, D. (1997). Constructivism in teacher education: Applying cognitive theory to teacher learning. In V. Richardson (Ed.), *Constructivist teacher education: Building new understandings* (pp. 59–83). London: Palmer Press.

Websites

http://teacherpathfinder.org/ProfDev/professional.htm

Teacher/Pathfinder Professional Development: A source for information about professional development for inservices, preservices, continuing education, professional organizations, training of trainers, tutorials, and technology training.

http://db.educationworld.com/perl/browse?cat_id=1844

Over 1000 ERIC resources for teachers about professional development from Education World.

http://www.middleweb.com/ContntsTchDev.html

A site that explores middle school reform and provides links to professional development resources.

Competency 13

Legal and Ethical Requirements for Educators

E. W. Henderson, EdD, JD
West Texas A&M University

> **Competency 13:** The teacher understands and adheres to legal and ethical requirements for educators and is knowledgeable of the structure of education in Texas.

The beginning teacher:

A. Knows legal requirements for educators (e.g., those related to special education, students' and families' rights, student discipline, equity, child abuse) and adheres to legal guidelines in education-related situations.

B. Knows and adheres to legal and ethical requirements regarding the use of educational resources and technologies (e.g., copyright, fair use, data security, privacy, acceptable use policies).

C. Applies knowledge of ethical guidelines for educators in Texas (e.g., those related to confidentiality, interactions with students and others in the school community), including policies and procedures described in the Code of Ethics and Standard Practices for Texas Educators.

D. Follows procedures and requirements for maintaining accurate student records.

E. Understands the importance of and adheres to required procedures for administering state- and district-mandated assessments.

F. Uses knowledge of the structure of the state education system, including relationships among campus, local, and state components, to seek information and assistance.

G. Advocates for students and for the profession in various situations.

KEY ACRONYMS

AEP—Alternative Education Program

ARD Committee—Admission, Review and Dismissal Committee

IDEA—Individuals with Disabilities Education Act

IDEA 2004—Individuals with Disabilities Education Improvement Act of 2004

IEP—Individualized Education Program

FAPE—Free Appropriate Education

FERPA—Family Educational Rights and Privacy Act

STARR—State of Texas Assessments of Academic Readiness

TEA—Texas Education Agency

TEKS—Texas Essential Knowledge and Skills

TPIA—Texas Public Information Act

Educators fulfill their professional responsibilities in an environment governed by law. Legislatures at the federal and state level together with their respective agencies enact laws and regulations that directly and indirectly impact public education. Federal and state courts provide the official interpretation of these statutes and regulations and resolve conflicts between schools, teachers, parents, and students. School boards issue rules and regulations. Within this complex network of laws, educators are empowered and constrained in the performance of their professional duties. The effective professional educator must possess an understanding of the legal framework supporting education and the responsibilities of the school district and teacher within that framework.

Competency 13 is broadly defined to include many of the ethical and legal requirements that relate to public school education. The Competency is defined further in a series of statements that establish the legal knowledge that the beginning teacher must possess. The following review is organized to address these requirements. The review is not intended to serve as an exhaustive discussion of each topic, such depth being beyond the scope of this chapter. However, the following discussion provides an overview of legal and ethical requirements identified within the Competency.

SPECIAL EDUCATION

The beginning teacher knows legal requirements for educators related to special education and adheres to legal guidelines in education-related situations.

© Jaren Jai Wicklund, 2014, Used under license of Shutterstock, Inc.

In most respects, "special education" is simply effective education: assessment of individual strengths and weaknesses; individualized educational programming; instruction utilizing methods and materials designed to support learning; collaborative and coordinated delivery of education and related services; and planning for nonacademic as well as academic achievement. However, in other important respects "special education" is unique. Special education as delivered in public schools in the United States is a creation of federal legislation. The interpretation of this controlling and sweeping legislation remains the obligation of the judiciary. As a result, the mandates of the federal law and the interpretation of these laws by the courts dictate to a significant degree the roles and responsibilities of the public school educator.

The current legal foundation for the delivery of special education in America is federal legislation, namely Section 504 of the Rehabilitation Act of 1973 (Section 504) and the Individuals with Disabilities Education Act (IDEA). Together these statutes provide a comprehensive recognition of the legal rights of children with disabilities and detailed procedures for safeguarding these rights.

Section 504 of the Rehabilitation Act of 1973

Section 504 of the Rehabilitation Act of 1973 was enacted to protect children with disabilities from discrimination and to fully integrate disabled individuals into American life including public education. Although subsequent legislation, specifically IDEA, tends to eclipse the significance of Section 504, educators must be aware of its potential application in the classroom and their responsibilities under the law.

Major Principles of Section 504

- Who is protected?
  - ∗ Section 504 protects any person who:
    - has a physical or mental impairment that substantially limits one or more of such person's major life activities including learning and behavior,

- has a record of such an impairment, or

- is regarded as having such an impairment [Section 504, 29 U.S.C. Section 706(7)(B)]. The first eligibility category is frequently applied in public education settings; the second and third qualifications are generally applied in vocational or postsecondary education. In addition to satisfying one or more of the above-stated criterion, individuals must establish that they are "otherwise qualified."

For purposes of elementary and secondary education, students are "otherwise qualified" if they are a handicapped person:

- of an age during which nonhandicapped persons are provided such services,

- of any age during which it is mandatory under state law to provide such services to handicapped persons, or

- to whom a state is required to provide a free appropriate public education [under IDEA] [Section 504 Regulations, 34 C.F.R., Section 104.3 (k)(2)].

It has generally been concluded that although a student may not qualify for special education under IDEA, the student may qualify for protection under Section 504. Recently, this conclusion was challenged in the case of *N.L. v. Knox County Schools* (2003; hereafter "*Knox*"). In Knox, the United States Court of Appeals for the Sixth Circuit held that a student who is ineligible for services under IDEA is ineligible for services under Section 504. This issue will continue to be a source of controversy.

- Identification
  - ∗ Section 504 mandates that school districts annually attempt to identify children with disabilities who are not receiving an appropriate education. Acceptable efforts include publicizing parental and student rights under Section 504.

- Evaluation and Placement
  - ∗ Section 504 mandates assessment of students prior to placement. School districts are required to ensure that:
    - Tests and other evaluation materials have been validated for the specific purpose for which they are used and are administered by trained personnel in conformance with the instructions provided by the test producer;
    - Tests and other evaluation materials include those tailored to assess specific areas of educational need and not merely those that are designed to provide a single general intelligence quotient; and
    - Tests are selected and administered so as best to ensure that, when a test is administered to a student with impaired sensory, manual, or speaking skills, the test results accurately reflect the student's aptitude or achievement level or whatever other factor the test purports to measure, rather than reflecting the student's impaired sensory, manual, or speaking skills (except where those skills are the factors that the test purports to measure) [Section 504 Regulations, 34 C.F.R. Section 104.35(b)].

    Additionally, students who initially qualify for placement under Section 504 must be periodically reevaluated to determine qualification for continued placement.

- **Protection from Discrimination**
  - ∗ Section 504 guarantees that all students with disabilities are protected from discrimination in elementary, secondary, and postsecondary schools. Students with disabilities must be allowed an equal opportunity to benefit from educational services and programs.

- Free Appropriate Education
  - ∗ Section 504 requires that public elementary or secondary schools provide a free appropriate public education (FAPE) to qualified students regardless of the severity of their disabilities. Such appropriate education requires individualization and delivery of related services, if appropriate. Educational programming is the responsibility of a multidisciplinary team with knowledge of the student.

- Least Restrictive Environment
  * Section 504 requires that students with disabilities be educated to the maximum extent appropriate with students who are not disabled. Delivery of services in other than the regular classroom requires that the school demonstrate that an appropriate education with supplementary aids and services cannot be satisfactorily achieved in the regular setting and that the needs of the student would be better served by placement in a more restrictive setting.

- Procedural Safeguards
  * Section 504 mandates that schools must satisfy due process procedures including parental notice prior to assessment or placement of a child and the right to a due process hearing in the event there is a disagreement concerning evaluation or placement. Violations of Section 504 are enforced through the federal Office of Civil Rights and may result in the termination of federal funding to the offending agency.

- Reasonable Accommodation
  * Ensuring equal opportunity may require the school to make reasonable accommodations to educational programs and services. Regulations enacted pursuant to Section 504 specifically identify the following potentially necessary accommodations:
    - Academic adjustments including changes in the length of time permitted for the completion of degree requirements, substitution of specific courses required for the completion of degree requirements, and adaptation of the manner in which specific courses are conducted. Additionally, schools are prohibited from imposing other rules, such as the prohibition of tape recorders in classrooms or of dog guides in campus buildings, which have the effect of limiting the participation of handicapped students in the education program or activity.
    - Modification of examinations so that methods for evaluating the achievement of students who have a handicap that impairs sensory, manual, or speaking skills will best ensure that the results of the evaluation represent the student's achievement in the course, rather than reflecting the student's impaired sensory, manual, or speaking skills (except where such skills are the factors that the test purports to measure).
    - Utilization of auxiliary aids as are necessary to ensure that no handicapped student is denied the benefits of, excluded from participation in, or otherwise subjected to discrimination because of the absence of educational auxiliary aids for students with impaired sensory, manual, or speaking skills. Auxiliary aids may include taped texts, interpreters, or other effective methods of making orally delivered materials available to students with hearing impairments, readers in libraries for students with visual impairments, classroom equipment adapted for use by students with manual impairments, and other similar services and actions [Section 504 Regulations, 34 C.F.R. 104.44].

According to Yell (2006), the following are examples of reasonable accommodations in the classroom as contemplated by Section 504:

- Adjust placement of student (e.g., preferential seating)
- Alter physical setup of classroom
- Reduce distractions (e.g., study carrel)
- Provide increased lighting
- Schedule classes in accessible areas
- Allow more time to complete assignments
- Adjust length of assignments
- Modify pace of instruction
- Use peer tutors
- Provide outline of lectures
- Use visual aids

- Use advance organizers
- Highlight texts and worksheets
- Tape lectures
- Adjust reading level of materials
- Use specialized curricular materials
- Give tests orally or on tape
- Allow more time to complete tests
- Allow students to dictate answers
- Alter test format
- Use enlarged type
- Reduce reading level of test
- Provide interpreters
- Provided assistive technology devices and services

Individuals with Disabilities Education Act

In 1975, the federal Congress found that many children with disabilities were not receiving an education. Furthermore, Congress concluded that many children with disabilities were receiving services inadequate to meet their educational needs. To secure the right of all children to a free appropriate public education, Congress enacted Public Law 94-142: the Education of All Handicapped Children Act of 1975. The Act represented the most direct and significant involvement of the federal government in special education to that time. The Act was intended to ensure that all handicapped children have available to them a free appropriate public education that emphasizes special education and related services designed to meet their individual needs. Furthermore, the Act mandated procedural safeguards to protect the rights of children with disabilities and their parents or guardians.

Subsequently, Congress expanded and further defined the requirements of the Act. In 1990, the Act was amended and renamed the Individuals with Disabilities Education Act (IDEA). In 1997, the Act was reauthorized and restructured by Congress. Substantive changes were made that were intended to improve the quality of public education for children with disabilities. In 2004, Congress made significant changes to IDEA through the enactment of the Individuals with Disabilities Education Improvement Act (IDEA 2004). The 2004 Act brought changes in the IEP, discipline, assessment, attorney's fees, "highly qualified" teachers, scientifically based funding, and funding. Regulations implementing the Act remain pending.

Who Is Protected?

The Individuals with Disabilities Education Act requires that students with disabilities who are determined to be eligible under the provisions of the Act must be provided special education and related services designed to meet their individual needs. A student's eligibility for special education is determined by a multidisciplinary team on a case-by-case basis. Any determination of eligibility must be made in compliance with the procedural safeguards established by the Act. An eligible student is between the ages of 3 and 21 years and presents one or more of the disabilities delineated in the Act. Additionally, the child's education must be adversely impacted by the child's disability. A child with a disability whose education is not adversely impacted by the disability is not protected by the Act.

Categories of disabilities protected by IDEA include:

- Mental retardation
- Hearing impairment
- Deafness

- Speech or language impairment
- Visual impairment
- Blindness
- Emotional disturbance
- Orthopedic impairment
- Autism
- Traumatic brain injury
- Health impairment
- Specific learning disability
- Multiple disabilities

FUNDAMENTAL PRINCIPLES OF IDEA

In order to achieve its goal of ensuring that all handicapped children have available to them a free appropriate public education that emphasizes special education and related services designed to meet their needs, IDEA demands adherence to the following principles:

- Zero reject
- Nondiscriminatory identification and assessment
- Free appropriate public education
- Individualized educational programming
- Placement in the least restrictive environment
- Delivery of related services
- Procedural safeguards

In order to receive federal funding, states must submit special education plans that reflect the fundamental principles of IDEA.

Zero Reject

IDEA mandates that all children with disabilities who are eligible for services are entitled to free appropriate public education regardless of the severity of their disability, without exception. This principle is at the heart of IDEA and is reflected in all its requirements. It evidences a belief that all children have the ability to benefit from education and eliminates from consideration the exclusion of any child with a disability from public education.

Nondiscriminatory Identification and Assessment

Recall that Congress enacted the Education of All Handicapped Children Act of 1975 when it discovered that many children with disabilities were not receiving an education and that many more children with disabilities were receiving services inadequate to meet their educational needs. In response to these findings, the effective identification and accurate evaluation of children with disabilities became significant components of the new law. To satisfy this obligation, IDEA requires that prior to special education placement a comprehensive and individualized assessment of the child's needs must be conducted by a multidisciplinary team that includes at least one teacher in the area of the child's suspected disability. It is only through appropriate identification and assessment that effective educational planning and placement can be achieved. The individualization of special education and related services demands thorough and accurate assessment.

IDEA requires that assessment materials be administered in the child's native language or mode of communication, be validated for the specific purpose for which they are used, and be administered by trained personnel in conformity with the publisher's instructions. The evaluation must be designed to assess specific areas of educational need, and no single procedure may be used to determine eligibility. Assessment may be conducted at various points during the child's education including initial assessment (usually informal) prior to a referral of the child for special education; formal assessment to determine eligibility for special education and related services; ongoing assessment for the purposes of evaluating student progress and defining goals and objectives; and reevaluation to determine continued eligibility for special education.

IDEA provides procedural due process safeguards to ensure that children are appropriately identified. The protections related to assessment of students include the following:

- Parental notification of referral and intention to test or decision not to evaluate;
- Parental consent to testing;
- Rights to a hearing in disputes involving testing or decision not to test;
- Requirements concerning the qualification of evaluators;
- Requirements concerning the evaluation procedures and materials (with emphasis on nondiscrimination); and
- Requirements regarding the interpretation of test data.

Free Appropriate Public Education

IDEA guarantees that all children with disabilities have available to them a free appropriate public education. As defined by the law, the term "free appropriate public education" means special education and related services that:

A. have been provided at public expense, under public supervision and direction, and without charge;

B. meet the standards of the State educational agency;

C. include an appropriate preschool, elementary, or secondary school education in the State involved; and

D. are provided in conformity with the individualized education program required under IDEA [IDEA, 20 U.S.C. Section 1401(a)(18)].

Under the requirements of the law, the costs of the child's education and related services are irrelevant to the obligation of the school district to fully deliver appropriate special education and related services. Cost may be considered in designing the child's special education, but only to the extent of selecting between appropriate alternatives. In other words, the multidisciplinary team that designs the child's educational program may permissibly select the lowest cost services that have been determined to be appropriate, but cannot use cost as a factor in determining what is appropriate for the child.

IDEA does not dictate the special education and related services to be delivered in satisfaction of the Act's guarantee of an appropriate education. The appropriateness of a child's special education and related services must be determined by a multidisciplinary team after careful and nondiscriminatory assessment of the individual child's strengths and weaknesses. Due to the lack of statutory clarity regarding the definition of "appropriate," disagreements between parents and school districts have frequently arisen.

The United States Supreme Court has held that the Act requires the school to provide specialized instruction with sufficient support services to enable the child with a disability to benefit educationally from that instruction (*Hendrick Hudson District Board of Education v. Rowley*, 1982). So long as the school complies with the procedures required by the Act and delivers an individualized education program calculated to enable the child to receive educational benefits, the school has satisfied its obligations under the Act. The Court reasoned that while Congress intended to open the door to public education for children with disabilities, it did not impose a duty on schools to maximize the potential of each student with a disability.

Individualized Education Program

The Individualized Education Program (IEP) mandated by the Act is the principle vehicle by which an appropriate education is delivered to an individual child. All aspects of the child's special education are directed by the IEP. Not only does the IEP have significant pedagogical importance for the child, the IEP has significant legal implications. Accordingly, when disputes arise between the parents of a child with a disability and the school district, the IEP serves as the primary legal "evidence" of the appropriateness (or inappropriateness) of the education and related services proposed.

The term "individualized education program" is defined by IDEA as a written statement for each child that shall include:

- a statement of the child's present levels of academic achievement and functional performance;
- a statement of measurable annual goals including academic and functional goals;
- a statement of how the child's progress toward meeting the annual goals will be measured and when periodic reports on the student's progress toward meeting the goals will be provided to the parents;
- a statement of the special education and related services and supplementary aids and services, based on peer-reviewed research to the extent practicable, to be provided to the child to advance appropriately toward attaining the annual goals; to be involved and progress in the general education curriculum; to participate in extracurricular and other nonacademic activities; and to be educated and participate with other children with disabilities and nondisabled children in academic and nonacademic activities;
- an explanation of the extent, if any, to which the child will not participate with nondisabled children;
- a statement of any individual modifications in the administration of state- or districtwide assessments of student achievement that are needed in order for the child to participate in such assessment or a statement of why a student cannot participate in the regular assessment and how the alternative assessment was selected;
- the projected date for initiation of the services and modifications and the anticipated frequency, location, and duration of such services; and
- a statement of appropriate measurable postsecondary goals based on age-appropriate transition assessments related to training, education, employment, and independent living skills and the transition services needed to assist the student in reaching those goals. [IDEA 10 U.S.C. Section 1401 (a)(20)].

IDEA requires that the IEP be developed by a multidisciplinary team composed of the following members:

- the parent(s) or guardian(s) of a child with a disability;
- at least one special education teacher of the child;
- at least one regular education teacher of the child who must assist in the determination of positive behavioral interventions, and of supplementary aids, program modifications, and supports for school personnel that will be provided for the child;
- a representative of the local educational agency;
- an individual who can interpret the instructional implications of evaluation results;
- other individuals who have knowledge or special expertise regarding the child, including related services personnel as appropriate; and
- whenever appropriate, the child with a disability [IDEA Regulations, 34 C.F.R. Section 300.344].

The child's IEP must be in effect at the beginning of each school year and must be accessible to each regular education teacher, special education teacher, and related service provider who is responsible for implementing the IEP. Additionally, the IDEA regulations require that each regular education teacher, special education teacher, and related service provider must be informed of his or her specific responsibilities related to implementing the child's IEP, and the specific accommodations, modifications, and supports that must be provided for the child in accordance with the IEP [IDEA Regulations Section 300.341(a)].

The appropriateness of a child's special education is measured by whether the child's IEP is reasonably calculated to provide a meaningful educational benefit to the child. The United States Court of Appeals for the Fifth Circuit has held that a child's IEP is reasonably calculated to enable the child to receive educational benefits if it establishes the following:

WELCOME TO SCHOOL EVERYONE!

© Batshevs, 2014, Used under license of Shutterstock, Inc.

1. the educational program is individualized on the basis of the student's assessment and performance;

2. the program is administered in the least restrictive environment;

3. services are provided in a coordinated and collaborative manner by the key stakeholders; and

4. positive academic and nonacademic benefits are demonstrated (*Houston Independent School District v. Caius R.*, 2000).

If it is shown that the IEP fails to establish one of these requirements, the special education and related service to be delivered pursuant to the IEP will be deemed "inappropriate" and therefore in violation of the free appropriate public education mandate of IDEA.

Placement in the Least Restrictive Environment

The intention of the Congress in enacting IDEA was to open the door of education to the disabled. In other words, to fully include children with disabilities in the mainstream of American education. Congress formalized this intention in the IDEA mandate that:

To the maximum extent appropriate, children with disabilities are educated with children who are not disabled, and special classes, separate schooling, or other removal of children with disabilities from the regular educational environment occurs only when the nature or severity of the disability of a child is such that education in regular classes with the use of supplementary aids and services cannot be achieved satisfactorily. [IDEA, 20 U.S.C. Section 1412]

As with other decisions affecting the disabled child's education, the IEP team is charged with making appropriate placement decisions from a continuum of settings designed to meet the special education and related services needs of children with disabilities. This continuum of services must include instruction in regular classes, special classes, special schools, home instruction, and instruction in hospitals and institutions. Additionally, the school must provide supplementary services such as resource room or itinerant instruction delivered in conjunction with the regular classroom.

The continuum of services mandated by IDEA may be described as follows:

- Regular Classroom
  * Includes students who receive a majority of their education in a general education classroom with consultative services provided to the classroom teacher or instruction delivered in the regular classroom by a specialist.
- Resource Room
  * Includes students who received special education and related services in resource rooms with part-time instruction in the regular classroom.
- Separate Class
  * Includes students who receive special education and related services in self-contained special classrooms with part-time instruction in regular class or placed in self-contained classrooms full time on a regular school campus.

- Separate School
  - * Includes students who receive special education and related services in separate day schools.
- Residential Facility
  - * Includes students who receive education in a public or private residential facility at public expense.
- Homebound or Hospital Placement
  - * Includes students who receive education in hospital or homebound programs.

Once the IEP team determines that a child is eligible for services under IDEA, the team determines what special education and related services are appropriate for the child. Such a determination is based on the nondiscriminatory assessment of the child. Next, the IEP team determines whether the appropriate special education and related services can be satisfactorily delivered in the regular classroom with or without supplementary aids and services. Only if it is determined that services cannot be satisfactorily delivered in the regular classroom with supplementary aids and services does the IEP team consider more restrictive placements. In the event that the IEP team determines that a more restrictive placement is appropriate, the team must consider any additional opportunities for including the child in less restrictive settings. A national trend continues toward greater inclusion of disabled students in the regular school environment.

Determinations of least restrictive environment for placement purposes are frequently the subject of disputes between schools and parents of children with disabilities and have resulted in significant litigation. The United States Court of Appeals for the Fifth Circuit established a two-part test for determining whether the school has satisfied the least restrictive environment mandate of IDEA (*Daniel R.R. v. State Board of Education*, 1989):

> *First, has the school taken steps to accommodate the student with disabilities in the regular education classroom including the use of supplementary aids and services and modify the regular education program to facilitate the child's success in the regular classroom?*

> *Second, if the student is placed in a more restrictive setting, has the school provided the child with as much exposure to students without disabilities as possible (e.g., nonacademic classes, lunch, recess, etc.)?*

Related Services

IDEA mandates that all children with disabilities have available to them a free appropriate public education that emphasizes special education and related services designed to meet their unique needs and prepare them for employment and independent living. IDEA Regulations define the term "related services" as transportation and such developmental, corrective, and other supporting services as are required to assist a child with a disability in benefitting from special education.

The following services are included within IDEA's definition of related services:

- Speech-language pathology services
- Audiology services
- Counseling, including rehabilitation counseling
- Psychological services
- Physical and occupational therapy
- Recreation, including therapeutic recreation
- Orientation and mobility services
- Social work services in schools
- School health services
- Parent counseling and training

- Transportation
- Medical services for diagnostic or evaluation purposes
- Assistive technology

Based on the individual evaluation and assessment of a child, the IEP team determines which related services (if any) are necessary for the child to benefit from special education. Additionally, the IEP team determines how often a related service will be provided and where and by whom.

IDEA requires that schools adhere to fundamental principles embedded in the Act that are designed to guarantee the educational rights of children with disabilities. These principles demand nondiscriminatory identification and assessment and prohibit the exclusion of children due to the severity of their disabilities. The Act requires that children with disabilities receive special education and related services determined to be appropriate by a multidisciplinary team and documented in an individualized education program. Furthermore, that this individualized program be delivered to the maximum extent appropriate in the regular school environment. Supporting these fundamental principles are due process procedures intended to safeguard the rights of the child with a disability to a free appropriate public education.

STUDENT DISCIPLINE

The beginning teacher knows legal requirements for educators related to student discipline and adheres to legal guidelines in education-related situations.

Chapter 37 of the Texas Education Code governs discipline of students in the public school. The provisions of Chapter 37 are summarized in the following discussion.

Teacher-Initiated Removal

Chapter 37 requires each school district to adopt a student code of conduct that specifies standards for student conduct and outlines behavior for which a student may be disciplined including the circumstances under which a student may be removed from a classroom. A teacher *may* remove a student from the classroom to maintain effective discipline. A teacher may remove a student whom the teacher has documented as interfering repeatedly with the instruction or learning of other students in the class or whose unruly, disruptive, or abusive behavior seriously interferes with the instruction or learning of other students in the class. The principal may not return a removed student to the removing teacher's classroom without the teacher's permission unless a committee comprised of two teachers elected by the campus faculty and one professional staff member chosen by the principal determine that the teacher's classroom is the best or only alternative available [Texas Education Code, Section 37.002].

A teacher *must* remove a student from class who engages in conduct for which a student must be removed to an Alternative Education Program (AEP), suspended, or expelled.

Removal to an AEP

A student who is at least 6 years of age *must* be removed from class and placed in an AEP if the student:

- engages in conduct involving a public school that contains the elements of the offense of false alarm or report, or terroristic threat;
- commits the following on or within 300 feet of school property, or while attending a school-sponsored or school-related activity on or off of school property:
  - ✳ engages in conduct punishable as a felony;
  - ✳ engages in conduct that contains the elements of the offense of assault;

* sells, gives, or delivers to another person or possesses or uses or is under the influence of marijuana, a controlled substance, or a dangerous drug;

* sells, gives, or delivers to another person an alcoholic beverage, commits a serious act or offense while under the influence of alcohol, or possesses, uses, or is under the influence of an alcoholic beverage;

• engages in conduct that contains the elements of an offense relating to an abusable volatile chemical or engages in conduct that contains the elements of the offense of public lewdness or indecent exposure;

• engages in conduct on or off of school property that contains the elements of the offense of retaliation against any school employee;

• engages in conduct occurring off campus and while the student is not in attendance at a school-sponsored or school-related activity if:

* the student receives deferred prosecution for conduct defined as a felony under Title 5 of the Texas Penal Code (e.g., murder, kidnapping, public lewdness, indecent exposure, assault, and terroristic threat);

* a court or jury finds that the student has engaged in delinquent conduct or conduct defined as a felony under Title 5 of the Texas Penal Code; or

* the superintendent or the superintendent's designee has a reasonable belief that the student has engaged in a conduct defined as a felony offense under Title 5 of the Texas Penal Code [Texas Education Code, Section 37.006].

A student *may* be removed from class and placed in an AEP if the student engages in the following:

• conduct occurring off campus and while the student is not in attendance at a school-sponsored or school-related activity if:

* the superintendent or the superintendent's designee has a reasonable belief that the student has engaged in conduct defined as a felony offense other than those defined in Title 5, Penal Code; and

* the continued presence of the student in the regular classroom threatens the safety of other students or teachers or will be detrimental to the educational process [Texas Education Code, Section 37.006];

• becomes a member of, pledges to become a member of, or solicits another person to become a member of any public school fraternity, sorority, secret society, or gang [Texas Education Code, Section 37.121].

During mandatory placement in an AEP, the student is prohibited from attending or participating in a school-sponsored or school-related activity. A student who is removed following a teacher-initiated removal may be prohibited from attending or participating in a school-sponsored or school-related activity. Not later than the third day after a student is removed from class, a conference must be conducted between the principal/designee, the student's parent, the teacher removing the student, and the student. At the conference, the student is entitled to written or oral notice of the reasons for the removal, an explanation of the basis for the removal, and an opportunity to respond to the reasons for the removal.

The duration of any removal to an AEP may not extend beyond the end of the school year unless the school board determines that the student's presence in the regular classroom presents a danger to the student or others or the student has engaged in serious or persistent misbehavior in violation of the student code of conduct. The board must review the status, including the academic status, of each student in AEP at least every 120 days.

A principal may order the immediate removal of a student to an AEP if the principal reasonably believes that the student's behavior is so unruly, disruptive, or abusive that it seriously interferes with the instruction of the other students in the class or the operation of the school or a school-sponsored activity.

Suspension

Chapter 37 of the Texas Education Code provides that a student <u>may</u> be suspended for engaging in any conduct identified in the student code of conduct as behavior for which a student may be suspended. Before the suspension, the student must be provided an informal hearing at which the student is informed of the offense that the student is alleged to have committed and the basis of the accusation. Additionally, the student must be given an opportunity to explain his or her side of the story. A suspension may not exceed three school days.

Expulsion

A student *must* be expelled if the student, while on school property, or while attending a school-sponsored or school-related activity on or off school property:

- uses, exhibits, or possesses a firearm, an illegal knife, a club, or other prohibited weapon;
- engages in conduct that contains the elements of the offense of:
  * aggravated assault, sexual assault, or aggravated sexual assault;
  * arson;
  * murder, capital murder, criminal attempt to commit murder or capital murder, manslaughter or criminally negligent homicide;
  * indecency with a child;
  * aggravated kidnapping or robbery;
- commits one of the drug- or alcohol-related offenses that permit removal to an AEP if the student's conduct is punishable as a felony; or
- commits an expellable offense in retaliation against a school employee or volunteer [Texas Education Code, Section 37.007].

A student *may* be expelled if the student, while on school property, or while attending a school-sponsored or school-related activity on or off school property:

- sells, gives, or delivers to another person or possesses, uses, or is under the influence of any amount of marijuana or a controlled substance, a dangerous drug, or an alcoholic beverage;
- engages in conduct that contains the elements of an offense relating to abusable glue or aerosol paint, or relating to volatile chemicals; or
- engages in serious or persistent misbehavior while placed in an AEP for disciplinary reasons.

A student *may* be expelled if the student on or off school property:

- engages in conduct involving a public school that contains the elements of the offense of false alarm or report or terroristic threat;
- engages in an assault against a school district employee or a volunteer; or
- engages in criminal mischief or aggravated robbery against another student [Texas Education Code, Section 37.007].

Before a student may be expelled, the school board or its designee must conduct a due process hearing where the student is given prior written notice of the charges and proposed sanctions and is afforded a reasonable opportunity for preparation; is entitled to be represented by a parent or other adult; and is given an opportunity to testify and present evidence and witnesses and cross-examine the school district's evidence and witnesses. Although the district's policies may impose a time limit, there is no statutory limit on the duration of an expulsion. Students who bring a firearm to campus must be expelled for at least 1 year [Gun Free Schools Act, Title 20, United State Code, Section 8921].

A principal may order the immediate expulsion of a student if the principal reasonably believes that the action is necessary to protect persons or property from imminent harm. At the time of the emergency expulsion, the student must be given oral notice of the reason for the emergency action. Within a reasonable time after the expulsion, the student must be given a due process expulsion hearing as described above.

Other Forms of Discipline

USE OF CORPORAL PUNISHMENT

The Texas Education Code defines "corporal punishment" as "the deliberate infliction of physical pain by hitting, paddling, spanking, slapping, or any other physical force used as a means of discipline [Texas Education Code, Section 37.0011]. The Code authorizes the use of corporal punishment by an educator when a district's board of trustees has adopted a policy that permits corporal punishment as a method of student discipline. However, a child's parent or guardian may prohibit the use of corporal punishment by providing an annual written statement to that effect [Texas Education Code, Section 37.0011(b), (c)].

Similarly, corporal punishment has been sanctioned by the federal courts. The courts have held that no notice and hearing prior to the imposition of corporal punishment are required. A school employee who violates a district's corporal punishment policy may be subjected to a reprimand, suspension, termination, or contract nonrenewal depending on the seriousness of the employee's misconduct. In situations where a student suffers harm as a result of excessive force or as a consequence of the discipline (e.g., running laps), the governmental immunity that protects teachers from civil liability may not apply [Texas Education Code, Section 22.0511]. Likewise, the teacher could face criminal liability.

Discipline of Students with Disabilities

Texas law protects a student with a disability who receives special education services from confinement in a locked box, closet, or specially designed space [Texas Education Code, Section 37.0021]. However, the law recognizes "time-out" as an acceptable behavior management technique designed to provide a student with an opportunity to regain self-control. Separation from other students must be for a limited period in a setting that is not locked and from which exit is not physically blocked.

Two fundamental principles of IDEA must be considered when disciplinary action is imposed on a disabled student: appropriate education and least restrictive environment. Any disciplinary action regarding a student with a disability who receives special education services that would constitute a change in the child's place- ment may be taken only after the student's Admission, Review and Dismissal (ARD) Committee conducts a "manifestation determination" review to evaluate whether the behavior of the student was "caused by" or has a "direct and substantial relationship to" the student's disability. If the ARD Committee determines that the behavior of the student was not a manifestation of the student's disability, the student may be disciplined in the same manner as students without a disability. Generally, a child with a disability may be removed from his or her regular educational placement for disciplinary purposes to an AEP or suspended for not more than 10 school days in a single school year. If the district contemplates removal of the child for more than 10 days, IDEA requires that the district comply with certain procedural safeguards [Texas Education Code, Section 37.004]. Additionally, when a child with disabilities is suspended in excess of 10 school days or expelled, the school must continue to provide special education to the child.

CHILD ABUSE

The beginning teacher knows legal requirements for educators related to child abuse and adheres to legal guidelines in education-related situations.

The Texas Family Code requires anyone having cause to believe that a child's physical or mental health or welfare has been adversely affected by abuse or neglect shall immediately make a report to any local or state law enforcement agency, the Department of Protective and Regulatory Services, or other appropriate agency [Texas Family Code Section 261.101 *et seq.*]. A professional (including a teacher) must report suspected abuse or neglect or a belief that a child may be abused or neglected within 48 hours after the professional first sus- pects that the child has been or may be abused or neglected. A school district may not require that reports of suspected abuse or neglect be channeled through the school administration.

"Abuse" of a child includes the following acts or omissions:

- mental or emotional injury to a child that results in an observable and material impairment in the child's growth, development, or psychological functioning;
- causing or permitting the child to be in a situation in which the child sustains a mental or emotional injury that results in an observable and material impairment in the child's growth, development, or psychological functioning;

- physical injury that results in substantial harm to the child, or the genuine threat of substantial harm from physical injury to the child;

- failure to make a reasonable effort to prevent an action by another person that results in physical injury that results in substantial harm to the child;

- sexual conduct harmful to a child's mental, emotional, or physical welfare;

- failure to make a reasonable effort to prevent sexual conduct harmful to a child;

- compelling or encouraging the child to engage in sexual conduct;

- causing, permitting, encouraging, engaging in, or allowing the photographing, filming, or depicting of the child if the person knew or should have known that the resulting photograph, film, or depiction of the child is obscene or pornographic;

- the current use by a person of a controlled substance in a manner or to the extent that the use results in physical, mental, or emotional injury to a child;

- causing, expressly permitting, or encouraging a child to use a controlled substance; or

- causing, permitting, encouraging, engaging in, or allowing sexual performance by a child [Texas Family Code, Section 261.001].

"Neglect" of a child includes the following acts of omissions:

- the leaving of a child in a situation where the child would be exposed to a substantial risk of physical or mental harm, without arranging for necessary care for the child, and the demonstration of an intent not to return by a parent or guardian of the child;

- placing a child in or failing to remove a child from a situation that a reasonable person would realize requires judgment or actions beyond the child's level of maturity, physical condition, or mental abilities and that results in bodily injury or a substantial risk of immediate harm to the child;

- failing to seek, obtain, or follow through with medical care for a child, with the failure resulting in or presenting a substantial risk of death, disfigurement, or bodily injury or with the failure resulting in an observable and material impairment to the growth, development, or functioning of the child;

- the failure to provide a child with food, clothing, or shelter necessary to sustain the life or health of the child, excluding failure caused primarily by financial inability unless relief services had been offered and refused; or

- placing a child in or failing to remove the child from a situation in which the child would be exposed to a substantial risk of sexual conduct harmful to the child; or

- the failure by the person responsible for a child's care, custody, or welfare to permit the child to return to the child's home without arranging for the necessary care for the child after the child has been absent from the home for any reason, including having been in residential placement or having run away [Texas Family Code, Section 261.001].

The Texas Family Code makes failure to report suspected child abuse or neglect a Class B misdemeanor. Additionally, failure to report may constitute grounds for disciplinary action against a teacher or his or her certificate by the Texas State Board for Educator Certification. The law expressly protects those who do report in good faith from civil and criminal liability.

EDUCATIONAL RESOURCES AND TECHNOLOGIES

The beginning teacher knows and adheres to legal and ethical requirements regarding the use of educational resources and technologies (e.g., copyright, fair use, data security, privacy, acceptable use policies).

The federal copyright law protects the rights of the copyright owner to many uses of a protected work, notably rights to reproduce, distribute, make derivative works, and publicly display or perform the work [Copyright Act, Title 17, United States Code, Sections 101 *et seq.*]. But the Copyright Act permits several important exceptions to those rights. Specific exceptions are permitted for concerns such as distance learning, backup copies of software, and some reproductions made by libraries. The most significant exception to a copyright owner's rights is "fair use."

The Fair-Use Exception

The Copyright Act permits the reproduction of a copyrighted work for purposes such as criticism, comment, news reporting, *teaching* (including multiple copies for classroom use), scholarship, or research. In determining whether the use made of a work in any particular case is a "fair use," the factors to be considered include:

- the purpose and character of the use, including whether such use is of a commercial nature or is for nonprofit educational purposes;
- the nature of the copyrighted work;
- the amount and substantiality of the portion used in relation to the copyrighted work as a whole; and
- the effect of the use upon the potential market for or value of the copyrighted work.

While fair use is intended to permit copying for the purposes of teaching, research, and other such activities, a crucial point is that an educational purpose alone does not make a use fair. The purpose of the use is only one of four factors that users must analyze in order to conclude whether or not an activity is lawful. For example, some copyright analysts have concluded that if a work being used is a commercial product, the "nature" factor weighs against fair use. By that measure, no clip from a feature film or copy from a trade book could survive that fair use. Each situation must be evaluated in light of the specific facts presented. The intent of the law is to allow "fair use" but not to authorize the copying of entire works as a substitute for purchase.

Generally, it is permissible for teachers to make a single copy of a work for scholarly use for class preparation or multiple copies for classroom use of the following:

- 250 words or less from poems;
- complete prose works if less that 2,500 words;
- excerpts from prose works if not more that 1,000 words or 10% of the work;
- one chart, graph, diagram, or illustration from a book or periodical; or
- backup copies of purchased software.

Copies made pursuant to the "fair use" exception must include a notice of the copyright as it appears in the original work. Teachers may not copy the following:

- consumables such as workbooks;
- items used semester to semester; nor
- copy more than one poem, article, or essay by the same author, not more than two excerpts from a collection.

If the teacher wishes to copy items not permitted under the "fair use" exception or intends to use the copied material from semester to semester, the teacher should seek permission from the publisher or copyright owner.

ETHICAL GUIDELINES FOR EDUCATORS

The beginning teacher applies knowledge of ethical guidelines for educators in Texas (e.g., those related to confidentiality, interactions with students and others in the school community), including policies and procedures described in the Code of Ethics and Standard Practices for Texas Educators.

The Texas Administrative Code establishes the following professional standards for Texas educators:

The Texas educator shall comply with standard practices and ethical conduct toward students, professional colleagues, school officials, parents, and members of the community and shall safeguard academic freedom. The Texas educator, in maintaining the dignity of the profession, shall respect and obey the law, demonstrate personal integrity, and exemplify honesty. The Texas educator, in exemplifying ethical relations with colleagues, shall extend just and equitable treatment to all members of the profession. The Texas educator, in accepting a position of public trust, shall measure success by the progress of each student toward realization of his or her potential as an effective citizen. The Texas educator, in fulfilling responsibilities in the community, shall cooperate with parents and others to improve the public schools of the community [Texas Administrative Code, Title 19, Chapter 247, Rule 247.2].

In furtherance of these objectives, the Texas Administrative Code establishes a *Code of Ethics and Standard Practices for Texas Educators* that delineates enforceable standards for professional conduct, practices, and performance. These standards include the following:

Standard 1.1. The educator shall not knowingly engage in deceptive practices regarding official policies of the school district, educational institution, educator preparation program, the Texas Education Agency, or the State Board for Educator Certification (SBEC) and its certification process.

Standard 1.2. The educator shall not knowingly misappropriate, divert, or use monies, personnel, property, or equipment committed to his or her charge for personal gain or advantage.

Standard 1.3. The educator shall not submit fraudulent requests for reimbursement, expenses, or pay.

Standard 1.4. The educator shall not use institutional or professional privileges for personal or partisan advantage.

Standard 1.5. The educator shall neither accept nor offer gratuities, gifts, or favors that impair professional judgment or to obtain special advantage. This standard does not restrict the acceptance of gifts or tokens offered and accepted openly from students, parents, or others or organization in recognition or appreciation of service.

Standard 1.6. The educator shall not falsify records, or direct or coerce others to do so.

Standard 1.7. The educator shall comply with state regulations, written local school board policies, and other applicable state and federal laws.

Standard 1.8. The educator shall apply for, accept, offer, or assign a position or a responsibility on the basis of professional qualifications.

Standard 1.9. The educator shall not make threats of violence against school district employees, school board members, students, or parents of students.

Standard 1.10. The educator shall be of good moral character and be worthy to instruct or supervise the youth of this state.

Standard 1.11. The educator shall not intentionally or knowingly misrepresent his or her employment history, criminal history, and/or disciplinary record when applying for subsequent employment.

Standard 1.12. The educator shall refrain from the illegal use or distribution of controlled substances and/or abuse of prescription drugs and toxic inhalants.

Standard 1.13. The educator shall not consume alcoholic beverages on school property or during school activities when students are present.

Additionally, the Texas Administrative Code establishes enforceable standards governing the conduct of a Texas Educator toward professional colleagues. These standards include the following:

Standard 2.1. The educator shall not reveal confidential health or personnel information concerning colleagues unless disclosure serves lawful professional purposes or is required by law.

Standard 2.2. The educator shall not harm others by knowingly making false statements about a colleague or the school system.

Standard 2.3. The educator shall adhere to written local school board policies and state and federal laws regarding the hiring, evaluation, and dismissal of personnel.

Standard 2.4. The educator shall not interfere with a colleague's exercise of political, professional, or citizenship rights and responsibilities.

Standard 2.5. The educator shall not discriminate against or coerce a colleague on the basis of race, color, religion, national origin, age, sex, disability, or family status.

Standard 2.6. The educator shall not use coercive means or promise of special treatment in order to influence professional decisions or colleagues.

Standard 2.7. The educator shall not retaliate against any individual who has filed a complaint with the SBEC or who provides information for a disciplinary investigation or proceeding.

Additionally, the Texas Administrative Code establishes enforceable standards governing the conduct of a Texas educator toward students. These standards include the following:

Standard 3.1. The educator shall not reveal confidential information concerning students unless disclosure serves lawful professional purposes or is required by law.

Standard 3.2. The educator shall not intentionally, knowingly, or recklessly treat a student or minor in a manner that adversely affects the student's learning, physical health, mental health, or safety.

Standard 3.3. The educator shall not intentionally, knowingly, or recklessly misrepresent facts regarding a student or minor.

Standard 3.4. The educator shall not exclude a student from participation in a program, deny benefits to a student, or grant an advantage to a student on the basis of race, color, sex, disability, national origin, religion, family status, or sexual orientation.

Standard 3.5. The educator shall not intentionally, knowingly, or recklessly engage in physical mistreatment, neglect, or abuse of a student or minor.

Standard 3.6. The educator shall not solicit or engage in sexual conduct or a romantic relationship with a student or minor.

Standard 3.7. The educator shall not furnish alcohol or illegal/unauthorized drugs to any person under 21 years of age unless the educator is a parent or guardian of that child or knowingly allow any person under 21 years of age unless the educator is a parent or guardian of that child to consume alcohol or illegal/unauthorized drugs in the presence of the educator.

Standard 3.8. The educator shall maintain appropriate professional educator–student relationships and boundaries based on a reasonably prudent educator standard.

Standard 3.9. The educator shall refrain from inappropriate communication with a student or minor, including, but not limited to, electronic communication such as cell phone, text messaging, email, instant messaging, blogging, or other social network communication. Factors that may be considered in assessing whether the communication is inappropriate include, but are not limited to:

© Burlingham, 2014, Used under license of Shutterstock, Inc.

i. the nature, purpose, timing, and amount of the communication;

ii. the subject matter of the communication;

iii. whether the communication was made openly or the educator attempted to conceal the communication;

iv. whether the communication could be reasonably interpreted as soliciting sexual contact or a romantic relationship;

v. whether the communication was sexually explicit; and

vi. whether the communication involved discussion(s) of the physical or sexual attractiveness or the sexual history, activities, preferences, or fantasies of either the educator or the student.

The State Board for Educator Certification is empowered by the Legislature to enforce the *Code of Ethics and Standard Practices for Texas Educators*. This power includes conducting investigations concerning improper conduct by an educator and taking disciplinary action where warranted. Sanctions for violations of the *Code of Ethics* include placing restrictions on a teaching certificate, suspending or revoking a certificate, or imposing any additional conditions or restrictions the board deems necessary.

STUDENT RECORDS

The beginning teacher follows procedures and requirements for maintaining accurate student records.

The *Code of Ethics and Standard Practices for Texas Educators* emphasizes the importance of maintaining accurate and complete student records and protecting the confidentiality of student information [Code of Ethics, Standards 1.6, 3.1, & 3.3].

A child's educational records are protected by the federal Family Educational Rights and Privacy Act (FERPA) and the corresponding Texas Public Information Act (TPIA). Parents are granted the right to access their child's education records until the child reaches the age of 18 years or as long as the student is their dependent for federal income tax purposes. Unless a court has ordered otherwise, a parent retains the right to access their child's educational records even if the parent does not have legal custody of the child. Parents must be notified annually of their rights under FERPA and have the right to challenge educational records they believe to be inaccurate or misleading. These rights highlight the importance of maintaining accurate and complete educational records.

FERPA and TPIA prohibit the release of student information to third parties without parental consent. Significant penalties may be imposed for violations of these acts. School employees who have a "legitimate educational interest" are permitted access to student records without parental consent. "Educational records" are broadly defined to include "records, files, documents, and other materials that contain information directly related to the student." The Texas Education Code specifically defines student records to include the following:

- attendance records;
- test scores;
- grades;
- disciplinary records;
- counseling records;
- psychological records;
- applications for admission;
- health and immunization information;
- teacher and counselor evaluations; and
- reports of behavioral patterns [Texas Education Code, Section 26.004].

Certain practices by teachers have the potential to infringe the protections of FERPA and TPIA. For example, while it is a common practice to post student grades or to list them in other ways, caution must be exercised to eliminate any possibility that grades could be identified by individual. Likewise, although peer grading has been sanctioned by the United States Supreme Court, privacy must be safeguarded regarding grades that have been collected and recorded in the teacher's grade book [*Owasso Independent School District No I-011 v. Falvo*, 2002].

MANDATED ASSESSMENTS

The beginning teacher understands the importance of and adheres to required procedures for administering state- and district-mandated assessments.

In 1984, the Texas Legislature directed the State Board of Education to establish a statewide student knowledge- and skill-based assessment program. The State of Texas Assessments of Academic Readiness (STAAR) is the current program designed to reflect good instructional practice and accurately measure student learning. The program is intended to reflect a strong connection to the state-mandated curriculum (Texas Essential Knowledge and Skills "TEKS") and classroom teaching.

Educators participating in the statewide assessment program receive training in proper test administration. By following the testing procedures mandated by the program, the district can ensure the security and confidential integrity of the STAAR testing program and the uniform evaluation of all examinees throughout the state. Complete information regarding STARR administration, test security, and related resources are available from the Texas Education Agency.

STRUCTURE OF EDUCATION SYSTEM

The beginning teacher uses knowledge of the structure of the state education system, including relationships among campus, local, and state components, to seek information and assistance.

The Texas Legislature is empowered by the state constitution to establish and operate a system of free public schools in the state. The legislature enacts laws in furtherance of its obligation including the establishment of the State Board of Education and the Texas Education Agency ("TEA"). The State Board of Education is empowered by the legislature to establish a state curriculum and graduation requirements, determine the standards for satisfactory student performance on assessment instruments, adopt and purchase state textbooks, adopt rules governing extracurricular activities, and adopt rules for accreditation of school districts. The Texas Education Agency is empowered by the legislature to fulfill a variety of responsibilities including monitoring district compliance with federal and state programs, conducting research to improve teaching and learning, and maintaining an electronic information system.

The Texas Education Agency incorporates the office of the Texas Commissioner of Education who is appointed by the governor with the advice and consent of the Texas Senate. The commissioner serves a 4-year term. The legislature has delegated to the commissioner a number of duties including reviewing school district audit reports and imposing sanctions on low-performing school districts. The commissioner oversees the operation of 20 regional education service centers located throughout the state. The service centers assist school districts in improving student achievement and increasing the efficiency of school operations.

The governance of a school is delegated to the local school board of trustees, which is invested with broad power. Most districts elect their board members in at-large elections; trustees serve a term of 3 or 4 years. The board enacts rules and regulations governing the operation of the school. Among its many responsibilities, the board has authority to make employment decisions including the hiring of a superintendent. The superintendent is the chief operating officer of the school district and is responsible for implementing the policies of the board.

The school principal serves under the direction of the superintendent as the primary administrator of a campus. The principal is responsible for administering the day-to-day operations of the school. Principals assign and evaluate campus personnel, as well as make recommendations to the superintendent regarding suspension, nonrenewal, and termination of personnel.

CONCLUSION

Competency 13 broadly defines the ethical and legal knowledge that a beginning teacher must possess. The effective educator must demonstrate an understanding of the legal framework supporting education and the responsibilities of the school district and teacher within that framework. The information presented above highlights key legal requirements in special education, student discipline, reporting child abuse, maintaining student records, the structure of the state education system, and copyright protection. Additionally, the ethical requirements for Texas educators are outlined. Knowing and adhering to these legal requirements will foster effective education and protect the best interests of students, parents, and the teacher.

Discussion Questions

1. Why is IDEA's mandate of a "free appropriate public education" a subject of continuing litigation between schools and parents of children with disabilities?

© YuryImaging, 2014, Used under license of Shutterstock, Inc.

2. To what extent do you think students with disabilities should be included in the regular classroom? Should students with disabilities be fully included in regular classrooms for the entire school day or should a student's placement be individually determined using a continuum of placement options? How can teachers shape the attitudes of the students who are not disabled toward students with disabilities?

3. Discuss to what extent and under what circumstances students with disabilities should be disciplined in the same way as their peers who are not disabled. Should it matter that the student's misconduct is directly related to his or her disability? Or is it always possible to establish some tie between misconduct and disability?

4. Chapter 37 of the Texas Education Code attempts to bring a greater degree of safety to public schools and return student disciplinary decisions to local control. Compare and contrast the provisions of the chapter that make certain disciplinary action mandatory and provisions where the district has a greater degree of latitude. Discuss whether the statute achieves its purpose.

5. Review the *Code of Ethics and Standard Practices for Texas Educators*, which delineates enforceable standards for professional conduct, practices, and performance. Do these standards address the majority of situations with which a teacher may be confronted? Are there standards that should be included or omitted from the Code?

Sample Test Questions

1. Marcus is a third-grade student who resides with his mother. Marcus's mother as managing conservator has custody of him. Marcus's father has court-ordered visitation with his son on the first and third weekends of each month. Marcus's father has asked for copies of the child's educational records. The teacher should:

   a. Refuse the request, as a noncustodial parent is not entitled access to educational records.

   b. Seek permission from Marcus' mother prior to granting access.

   c. Grant the request as a noncustodial parent has the same right to access as the managing conservator.

   d. Require the father to provide a court order specifically granting the request.

2. Melinda is a student with disabilities who receives special education and related services in the regular classroom. Early in the school year, her teacher becomes concerned that the accommodations and modifications of the regular curriculum required by Melinda's IEP are not appropriate for the student. The annual meeting of the ARD Committee is not scheduled until the end of the school year. The teacher should:

   a. Exercise professional judgment and change the requirements of the IEP to more closely match the needs of the student.

   b. Continue to provide the accommodations and modifications required by the IEP and address her concerns at the year-end ARD Committee meeting.

   c. Continue to provide the accommodations and modification required by the IEP and request a meeting of the ARD Committee to reevaluate the child's educational plan.

   d. Advise the child's parents of Melinda's lack of progress.

3. Linda is an eleventh-grade student who is disruptive in the classroom. Despite efforts to modify Linda's behavior, the classroom teacher has been unsuccessful. The teacher wishes to remove Linda from his classroom. The teacher should:

   a. Document Linda's behavior that repeatedly interferes with the instruction or learning of other students in the class or unruly, disruptive, or abusive behavior.

   b. Do nothing, as it is not possible for a teacher to remove a student from class.

   c. Instruct the student to report to the library during his or her class period.

   d. Request that another teacher accept Linda into her classroom.

4. Robert is a fourth-grade student who is always appropriately dressed, well behaved and appears well cared for. From time to time, he is overheard making comments that lead the teacher to conclude that he has knowledge of intimate sexual conduct and may engage in sexual activity with adult family members. He has not exhibited any signs of physical abuse. The teacher should:

   a. Do nothing, as it would be inappropriate for him to intrude into the privacy of Robert's family.

   b. Refer him to the school nurse and thoroughly document the referral.

   c. Advise Robert's parents of his inappropriate comments.

   d. Immediately contact the local law enforcement agency to report suspected child abuse.

5. Ms. Smith teaches in a school with a high percentage of students whose families have limited financial resources. She recently identified a consumable workbook that she feels would be excellent for them. However, the cost of the workbook would be prohibitive for most of her students. The teacher should:

   a. Attempt to secure funding for the workbooks through administrative channels, and if unable to do so, document her efforts and duplicate the workbooks free of charge to students.

b. Request permission to duplicate the workbook from the copyright holder and, if permission is denied, identify alternative materials.

c. Duplicate the workbook but distribute the duplications to students one page at a time.

d. Duplicate the workbook as she deems appropriate as she purchased her copy of the workbook and, therefore, is free to do what she wishes.

Answers

1. A is not correct. It is directly contrary to the entitlement granted to the noncustodial parent in federal and state law.

   B is not correct. Neither the federal nor state law require permission from the custodial parent.

   C is the correct answer. Under FERPA and TPIA, a noncustodial parent has the same rights to his or her child's educational records as a custodial parent unless a court has ordered otherwise.

   D is not correct. The law does not require that the noncustodial parent have court-ordered authority. The statutes entitle the noncustodial parent access unless a court order restricts the access of the noncustodial parent.

2. A is not correct. Only the IEP team is empowered to modify the requirements of the IEP.

   B is not correct. The teacher should bring the inappropriate requirements to the attention of the IEP team so that more appropriate strategies may be employed in the classroom as soon as possible.

   C is the correct answer. Under IDEA, the teacher is legally obligated to continue to provide the modifications and accommodations required by the child's IEP. If in the teacher's professional opinion the requirements of the IEP are inappropriate, the teacher should request a meeting of the ARD Committee to review the appropriateness of the IEP.

   D is not correct. Advising the child's parents of her lack of progress does not address the inappropriateness of the IEP.

3. **A is the correct answer.** Under the Texas Education Code, in order to remove the student from class, the teacher must document that the student's behavior is so unruly, disruptive, or abusive or causes repeated interference with the teacher's ability to communicate effectively with the class or with the student's classmates' ability to learn.

   B is not correct. Texas law provides a method for removing a student from the classroom. C and D are not correct. The teacher is attempting to remove a student from class without complying with the requirements of the Texas statute.

4. A, B, and C are not correct. None of these actions by the teacher satisfy the requirement of Texas law that suspected abuse or neglect be reported to law enforcement authorities. The courses of action stated in choices A and C might subject the child to further abuse.

   D is the correct answer. Under the Texas Family Code, the teacher has a legal duty to report suspected abuse or neglect or a belief that a child may be abused or neglected within 48 hours after the professional first suspects that the child has been or may be abused or neglected. "Child abuse" includes sexual conduct harmful to a child's mental, emotional, or physical welfare; failure to make a reasonable effort to prevent sexual conduct harmful to a child; and compelling or encouraging the child to engage in sexual conduct.

5. **B is the correct answer.** Under federal copyright law, teachers may not duplicated workbooks without specific permission from the copyright holder.

   A, C, and D are not correct. They attempt to avoid the copyright protections of federal law. Inability to obtain a sufficient number of copyrighted materials or distribution of copyrighted materials in a piecemeal fashion does not avoid restrictions on the use of copyrighted materials. The purchase of a copyrighted work does not give the purchaser the right to duplicate and distribute the work unless specific permission has been granted by the copyright holder.

REFERENCES

Board of Education of Hendrick Hudson School District v. Rowley, 458 U.S. 176 (1982).

Copyright Act, Title 17, United States Code Section 101 *et seq.*

Daniel R.R. v. State Board of Education, 874 F.2d 1036 (5th Cir., 1989).

Education for All Handicapped Children Act of 1975, Title 20, United States Code, Section 1402 *et seq.*

Family Educational Rights and Privacy Act, Title 20, United States Code, Section 1232g.

Gun Free Schools Act, Title 20, United States Code, Section 8921.

Houston Independent School District v. Caius R., 200 F.3d 341 (5th Cir., 2000).

Individuals with Disabilities Education Act, Title 20, United States Code, Section 1400 *et seq.*

Individuals with Disabilities Education Act Regulations, 34 C.F.R. Section 300 *et seq.*

N.L. v. Knox County Schools, 315 F.3d 688 (6th Cir., 2003).

Owasso Independent School District No I-011 v. Falvo, 534 U.S. 426 (2002).

Rehabilitation Act of 1973, Title 29, United States Code, Section 794.

Texas State Board for Educator Certification, http://www.tea.state.tx.us.

Texas Education Agency, http://www.tea.state.tx.us

Texas Administrative Code, Title 19, Chapter 247, Rule 247.2.

Texas Education Code, Chapter 37.

Texas Family Code, Section 261.001 *et seq.*

Texas Public Information Act, Texas Government Code, Chapter 552.

Yell, M. (2006). *The law and special education* (2nd ed.). New Jersey: Prentice-Hall.

Websites

http://www.atpe.org/TeachersToolbag/studdisc.htm
Association of Texas Professional Educators

http://www.ed.gov/about/offices/list/osers/osep/index.html?src=mr
Federal Office of Special Education Programs

http://www.tea.state.tx.us
Texas Education Agency

http://www.dfps.state.tx.us/Child_Protection/About_Child_Protective_Services/reportChildAbuse.asp
Texas Department of Family and Protective Services

http://www.sbec.state.tx.us/SBECOnline/default.asp?width=1024&height=768
Texas State Board for Educator Certification

http://www.copyright.gov
United States Copyright Office

http://www.wrightslaw.com
Wright's Special Education Law and Advocacy